THE WORDS OF JESUS

THE WORDS OF JESUS

CONSIDERED IN THE LIGHT OF
POST-BIBLICAL JEWISH WRITINGS
AND THE ARAMAIC LANGUAGE

BY

GUSTAF DALMAN

PROFESSOR OF THEOLOGY IN THE UNIVERSITY OF LEIPZIG

AUTHORISED ENGLISH VERSION

BY

D. M. KAY, B.D., B.Sc.

PROFESSOR OF HEBREW AND ORIENTAL LANGUAGES IN THE UNIVERSITY OF ST. ANDREWS

I. INTRODUCTION AND FUNDAMENTAL IDEAS

Wipf and Stock Publishers
150 West Broadway • Eugene OR 97401

The Words of Jesus
by Gustaf Dalman

ISBN: 1-57910-072-4

Reprinted by *Wipf and Stock Publishers* 1997
150 West Broadway • Eugene OR 97401

AUTHOR'S PREFACE TO THE
ENGLISH EDITION.

——+——

THE work here introduced to English readers is the result of studies which have been pursued during a long series of years. The aim of these studies has been to ascertain the meaning of the words of our Lord as they must have presented themselves to the ear and mind of His Jewish hearers. The author is well aware that the last word has not been said on not a few important and difficult questions treated in this volume; but his wishes will be fulfilled if his work serves to strengthen the conviction that labour in this direction is not fruitless, and must be done by many co-workers, if Christian Theology is to be brought into more precise relations with its historical basis.

As to the relation of the English translation to the German original, I have only to add that the English version practically forms a second edition of the work. A number of small errors have been corrected by the author throughout the whole book, and the introductory part has been partly rewritten and rendered more complete. The "Messianic Texts," which form an Appendix to the German volume, have not been included in the English edition. As they may be had separately from the publisher of the German edition (J. C. Hinrichs, Leipzig), it seemed superfluous to reprint them here.

GUSTAF H. DALMAN.

LEIPZIG, 1st *April* 1902.

▼

NOTE BY THE TRANSLATOR.

THE Translator has endeavoured to furnish a faithful version of the German original, but is not responsible for the various positions maintained by the author. If the Gospel was first announced in the Aramaic language, it is obvious that the Greek versions of the Synoptists cannot be finally interpreted without taking due account of the Aramaic prototype. This factor is introduced by Dr. Dalman's line of research, and will be seen to contribute elements of great value in the minuter exegesis of the Gospels.

The Translator has to thank the Rev. Professor A. R. S. Kennedy, of Edinburgh, for the helpful interest he has taken in the process of translation, and for correcting the second proofs. In rendering into English the idea of the *malkuth Yahveh* (*Gottesherrschaft*, usually called "the Kingdom of God"), he hopes no inconvenience will be caused by the occasional use of "theocracy" as a shorter synonym for "Sovereignty of God." In citing the Talmud, b. before the name of the Tractate stands for Babylonian, j. for Jerusalem; a Baraitha is a tradition of the elders which did not happen to be incorporated in the authoritative collection of R. Yehuda ha-Nasi.

D. M. KAY.

CONTENTS.

ix

EDITIONS OF TEXTS USED.

A. APOCRYPHA.

H. B. Swete, The Old Testament in Greek, i.-iii., 1887–94.
O. F. Fritzsche, Libri apocryphi Veteris Testamenti Græce, 1871.
De Lagarde, Libri Veteris Testamenti apocryphi Syriace, 1861.
Sirach: Hebrew Text, 39$^{15\text{-}49}$, 11 ; edition of *A. E. Cowley* and *A. Neubauer,*
    1897 ; ed. of *R. Smend,* 1897.
    49$^{12\text{-}50}$, 22, ed. of *S. Schechter,* Jew. Quart. Rev. x. (1898) 197–206.
Tobit: Aram. Hebr. and Latin Texts, ed. of *A. Neubauer,* 1878.
    Hebrew Texts, ed. of *M. Gaster,* 1897.
Supplements to Daniel: Aram. Text, ed. of *M. Gaster,* 1895.

B. PSEUDEPIGRAPHA.

Psalms of Solomon: ed. of *H. E. Ryle* and *M. R. James,* 1891 ; ed. of *O. v.*
    Gebhardt, 1895.
Book of Jubilees: translation by *R. H. Charles,* Jew. Quart. Rev. vi. (1894)
    184 ff., 710 ff. ; vii. (1895) 297 ff.
Book of Enoch: translation by *G. H. Schodde,* 1882 ; by *R. H. Charles,* 1893.
    Greek text, *A. Lods,* 1892.
Assumptio Mosis: ed. of *R. H. Charles,* 1897.
Apocalypse of Baruch: Syriac text of *A. M. Ceriani,* 1871 ; translation by *R.*
    H. Charles, 1896.
2 *Esdras:* Syriac text of *A. M. Ceriani,* 1868.
    Latin text, ed. of *R. L. Bensly* and *M. R. James,* 1895.
Testaments of the Twelve Patriarchs: Greek text of *R. Sinker,* 1868, 1879.
    Hebrew version (Naphtali), ed. of *M. Gaster,* 1894.
Sibylline Oracles: ed. of *A. Rzach,* 1891.
Testament of Abraham: ed. of *M. R. James* and *W. E. Barnes,* 1892.
Slavonic Book of Enoch: ed. of *W. R. Morfill* and *R. H. Charles,* 1896.

C. TARGUMS.

Onkelos : Sabbioneta, 1557 (in the original).
Jerusalem Targums to the Pentateuch : Venice, 1591.
Targums to the Prophets and Hagiographa : Rabbinical Bible, Venice, 1517 ;
    Venice, 1525 ; Venice, 1548 ; Basle, 1618.
Targum sheni on Esther : ed. of *L. Munk,* 1876 ; ed. of *M. David,* 1898.

D. LITERATURE ON THE LAW.

Mishna: ed. Riva di Trento, 1559; Mantua, 1561; Cambridge(*W. H. Lowe*), 1883.
Tosephta: ed. Sabbioneta, 1555; Pasewalk (*M. S. Zuckermandel*), 1881.
Jerusalem Talmud: ed. Venice, 1524; Tractate Berachoth, ed. Mainz (*M. Lehmann*), 1875.
Babylonian Talmud: Tractate Taanith, ed. Pesaro (*c.* 1511); Sanhedrin, Sota, Nidda, Erubhin, Zebhachim, Menachoth, Bekhoroth, Meïla, Kinnim, Middoth, Tamidh, Teharoth, ed. Venice, 1520-23.
Tractates Shebhuoth, Eduyyoth, Abhoth, Horayoth, Moed Katon, Yebhamoth, Erakhin, Temura, Kerithuth, Nedarim, Nazir, Teharoth, ed. Venice, 1526-29.
For the whole Talmud: ed. Vienna, 1840-47; Variæ Lectiones, *R. Rabbinovicz. H. Ehrentreu*, 1867-97.
Abhoth of Rabbi Nathan: ed. Vienna (*S. Schechter*), 1887.

E. COMMENTARIES (Midrashim).

Mechilta: ed. Constantinople, 1515; Vienna (*J. Weiss*), 1865; Vienna (*M. Friedmann*), 1870.
Siphra: ed. Venice, 1545; Vienna (*J. Weiss*), 1862.
Siphre: ed. Venice, 1545; Vienna (*M. Friedmann*), 1864.
Midrash Rabba on the Pentateuch: ed. Constantinople, 1512; Venice, 1545; Salonica, 1593.
Midrash Chamesh Megilloth: ed. Pesaro, 1519; Venice, 1545; Salonica, 1593.
Midrash on Canticles: ed. *S. Schechter*, Jew. Quart. Rev. vi. (1894) 672 ff.; vii. (1895) 145 ff., 729 ff.; viii. (1896) 289 ff.
Midrash Tanchuma: ed. Venice, 1545; Mantua, 1563; Wilna (*S. Buber*), 1885.
Midrash on Psalms: ed. Constantinople-Salonica, 1512-15; Venice, 1546; Wilna (*S. Buber*), 1891.
Midrash on Samuel: ed. Constantinople, 1517; Venice, 1546; Krakau (*S. Buber*), 1893.
Midrash on Proverbs: ed. Venice, 1546; Wilna (*S. Buber*), 1893.
Pesikta: ed. Lyck (*S. Buber*), 1868.
Pesikta Rabbati: ed. Vienna (*M. Friedmann*), 1880.
Pirke Rabbi Eliezer: ed. Venice, 1544.
Tanna de-be Eliyyahu: ed. Venice, 1598.
Yalkut Shimoni: ed. Salonica, 1521-26.
Yalkut Makiri: Yeshaya, ed. Berlin (*J. Spira*), 1894.

F. LITURGICAL WORKS.

Siddur: Seder Rab Amram, ed. Warsaw, 1865; Maimonides in Mishne Tora, ed. Venice, 1524; Siddur Hegyon Leb, by *L. Landshuth*, Königsberg, 1845; Seder Abodath Yisrael, by *S. Baer*, Rödelheim, 1868.
Machzor, German rite: ed. Cremona, 1560; Venice, 1568; Venice, 1714-19.
Polish rite: ed. Sulzbach, 1699; Amsterdam, 1736.
French rite: Machzor Vitry, ed. Berlin, 1893-97.
Sephardic rite: ed. Livorno, 1845-46.
Roman rite: ed. Bologna, 1541.
Romanian rite: ed. Constantinople, 1520.
Yemen rite: two manuscripts in possession of Dr. Chamizer, Leipzig, No. 1 of the year 1659, No. 2, 16-17 century.

THE WORDS OF JESUS.

——+——

INTRODUCTION.

I. Aramaic as the Language of the Jews.

As the proof has been offered with comparative frequency of late [1] showing that the "Hebraists," [2] that is, the "Hebrew"-speaking Jews of Palestine, who formed a class distinct from the "Hellenists," did not in reality speak Hebrew but Aramaic, it seems superfluous to raise a fresh discussion on all the details of this question. Yet, while reference is made to my "Grammatik des jüd.-pal. Aramäisch" for information on all the Aramaic expressions that occur in the New Testament and Josephus, the most important sources of evidence now involved must here be shortly summarised.

1. *The custom, represented in the second century after Christ as very ancient, of translating into Aramaic the text of the Hebrew Pentateuch in the synagogues of the Hebraists of Palestine.*

M. Friedmann, Onkelos und Akylas (1896), 58 ff., 81 f., still holds fast to the traditional opinion that even Ezra had an Aramaic version of the Tora. In this he is mistaken. Yet the high antiquity of the Targum custom of interpreting is incontestable. About the year 200 A.D. the practice is so

---

[1] Most recently by *G. Meyer,* Jesu Muttersprache (1896), and *Th. Zahn,* Einleitung in das Neue Testament, i. (1897) 1-24.

[2] Acts 6¹ Ἑβραῖοι.

I

firmly established that the Mishna does not make it a matter
for prescription, but concerns itself only with the more
precise determination of details (Meg. iv. 5, 7, 11). In the
third century it was recommended—by Joshua ben Levi to his
sons—that one should not even in private read the text of the
Law without the traditional translation.[1] It was not practical
necessity that was the determining factor in this case, but
the inviolable custom according to which Bible text and
Targum were inseparable. There must, however, have been
a time during which a pressing necessity created this custom,
tending to depreciate the significance of the Bible text,—
a time, that is, when the Hebrew text was not understood by
those who frequented the synagogues. That even written
Targums existed in the time of Christ may perhaps be
concluded from the story[2] which represents Gamaliel I. as
having caused a Targum of Job to be built into the temple
while it was building, provided this Targum were written in
Aramaic and not in Greek. Gamaliel II. also would appear
to have seen a copy of the same Targum.[3] Of course it does
not follow that such Targums were widely distributed, least
of all that every one should have had them at home; only it
is clear that in public worship the Holy Scripture was not
read without the translation into Aramaic. This rendering,
according to Meg. iv. 4, was required to follow each single
verse in the Pentateuch, and every three verses in the
Prophets.

2. *The Aramaic titles for classes of the people and for
feasts attested by Josephus and the New Testament.*

Of these there may be named—

Φαρισαῖοι[4] = פְּרִישַׁיָּא (Hebrew would be פְּרוּשִׁים), " Phari-

---

[1] Ber. 8ᵃ; cf. *W. Bacher*, Agada der pälast. Amoräer, i. 141. That the
Targum should therefore be also "read," thus implying the possession of written
Targums, is, however, not to be inferred from the expression.

[2] Sabb. 115ᵃ; j. Sabb. 15ᶜ; Tos. Sabb. xiii. 2 ; Sophr. v. 15.

[3] See same passages except j. Sabb. 15ᶜ.

[4] *Zahn*, Einl. in d. N. Test. i. 23, maintains that the plural פְּרִישַׁיָּא lies at

sees"; Xaavaίaι (*Jos.* Ant. III. vii. 1) = כְּהֻנְיָא (Heb. כֹּהֲנִים),
"Priests"; ἀραβάρχης,[1] ἀραβάχης (ibid.) = רַבָּא כָּהֲנָא (Heb.
הַגָּדוֹל הַכֹּהֵן), "High Priest"; πάσχα = פַּסְחָא (Heb. פֶּסַח),
"Passover"; ἀσαρθά (Ant. III. x. 6) = עֲצַרְתָּא (Heb. עֲצֶרֶת),
"Pentecost"; Φρουραία,[2] Φρουραί = פּוּרַיָּא (Heb. פּוּרִים),
"Purim"; σάββατα = שַׁבְּתָא (Heb. שַׁבָּת), "Sabbath."

3. *The use of the Aramaic language in the Temple.*—
In support of this is the old tradition that John Hyrcanus
heard in the sanctuary a divine voice speaking in the
Aramaic language, j. Sot. 24[b]; cf. Ant. XIII. x. 3.[3] In the
temple, according to Shek. v. 3, vi. 5, the legends on the tokens
for the drink-offerings and on the chests in which the con-
tributions of the faithful were deposited were in Aramaic.
As now given in the Mishna text, some, however, of the names
are Hebrew. But the use of Aramaic in the other cases is so
striking in matters of the temple service, that one must regard
it as the sole language originally used in this connection.

4. *Old official documents in the Aramaic language.*—
These are, first, the "Roll concerning Fasts," a catalogue of
days on which fasting was forbidden, first compiled in the
time of the rising against the Romans, 66–70 A.D.; secondly,
the Epistles of Gamaliel II. (about 110 A.D.) to the Jews of
South Judæa, Galilee, and Babylon. Both of these were
destined for the Jewish people, and primarily, indeed, for those
of Palestine. For the "Roll concerning Fasts," see my

the basis of the Greek form Φαρισαῖοι, because the ending αῖοι represents a
Semitic final sound in i or ay; and that from פְּרִישַׁא there would have been
formed Φαρισᾶς. This is not convincing; for Φαρισᾶς would have been unsuitable as the name of a party, and the Greek language forms with equal ease
Λαρισσαῖος from Λάρισσα, and Ἀθηναῖος from Ἀθῆναι. But, of course, it is
probable that the formation of the Greek Φαρισαῖοι depended on the frequently
heard plural definite פְּרִישַׁיָּא. Besides, the analogy of Σαδδουκαῖοι must have co-
operated, and that goes back to צָדוֹק, definite צָדוּקָה, plur. def. צְדוּקַיָּא.

[1] *Wellhausen,* Isr. und Jüd. Gesch. 161, holds that χαναράβης was the
original reading; but it is possible that we have here one of the intentional
Græcisms of Josephus. ἀραβάχης was meant to suggest ἀραβάρχης.

[2] Φρουραί is due to a reminiscence of the Greek word φρουρά, plur. φρουραί.

[3] Cf. *Dérenbourg,* Essai sur l'histoire de la Palestine, 74; *Büchler,* Die
Priester und der Cultus (1895), 62 f.

treatise "Aramäische Dialektproben," 1–3, 32–34; cf. Jüd. Monatschr. xli. 326, and Gramm. d. jüd.-pal. Aram. 7 f. The Epistles of Gamaliel given in Aram. Dialektproben are attributed by the Palestinian Talmud Sanh. 18^d, and thereafter by Graetz,[1] Dérenbourg,[2] Neubauer,[3] and Büchler,[4] to the first Gamaliel; but this must be an error, as the four groups of Jews alluded to (Upper and Lower Galilee, Darom (South-west Judæa), and Babylon) point to a date after the destruction of Jerusalem.

5. *The language of the public documents* relating to purchase, lease-tenure, debt, conditional betrothal, refusal of marriage, marriage contract, divorce, renunciation of Levirate marriage. The Mishna gives the decisive formulæ of these documents, which were important for securing legal validity, for the most part in Aramaic, thus implying that this was the language commonly in use. References are given in Gramm. d. jüd.-pal. Aram. 12.[5] As there is no rule prescribing the language in which such documents must be drawn up, it is not surprising that the Mishna should also sometimes mention formulæ in Hebrew, as for divorce, Gitt. ix. 3, 5; and for emancipation, Keth. iv. 12; ix. 1, 5 for the marriage contract. How unimportant the choice of language was, appears from Keth. iv. 12, where an Aramaic form is given for dwellers in Jerusalem and Galilee, while one in Hebrew is given for dwellers in Judæa, with no intention, let us say, of emphasising the distinction of language, but by reason of the varying contents of the formulæ.—The previously mentioned Epistles of the Patriarch Gamaliel II. and the Roll concerning Fasts should properly be also reckoned among the public documents.

[1] *Graetz*, Geschichte der Juden, iii. 373.

[2] *Dérenbourg*, Essai sur l'histoire, 242.

[3] Studia Biblica (Oxford, 1885), 49.

[4] *Büchler*, Die Priester und der Cultus, 63.

[5] Only the formula for "conditional betrothals," סימפון (σύμφωνον), is not mentioned there; see, however, j. Kidd. 63^d, 64^a; j. Gitt. 49^a; j. Er. 21^b.

The language used in a certain family register (מְגִלַּת יֻחָסִין),
found at one time in Jerusalem, is open to question. According to the statement of Levi, one of the Palestinian
Amoraim (about 300 A.D.[1]), it was written in Aramaic; and
at any rate one sentence from it is reproduced in this
language. The contents, now distorted by additions, would,
however, refer it at the earliest to the end of the first
century. But in Yeb. iv. 13 Simeon ben Azzai (about
110 A.D.) says that he too had found a family register in
Jerusalem, in which there was used concerning some one
this formula in Hebrew — מַמְזֵר מֵאֵשֶׁת אִישׁ, "bastard
of a wedded wife."[2] Whether this register was the one
alluded to by Levi cannot indeed be affirmed with certainty;
but it is probably the same, and its language therefore
doubtful.

6. *The unquestioned adoption in the time of Jesus of the
Aramaic characters in place of the old Hebrew in copies of the
Bible Text.*

The change of character has the change of language as
its natural presupposition. The usual citation from Matt.
5[18], implying that ἰῶτα was the smallest letter, is certainly
inconclusive. Vav and yod were both represented at that
period by a long perpendicular stroke. The yod was distinguished by having a small hook at the top, and was thus
really larger than the vav. The original spoke, as in Luke
16[17], only of a single hook (μία κεραία), or perhaps of the
hook of the yod, as in Shem. R. 9 (whereas Vay. R. 19,
presupposing the later style of writing, mentions the yod
itself). The mention of the ἰῶτα in Matthew would be
intended for Greek readers. For them iota was actually

---

[1] See j. Taan. 68ᵃ; Ber. R. 98; cf. *Büchler*, Die Priester und der Cultus, 41 f.
[2] *H. Laible*, in *Dalman-Laible's* Jesus Christ in the Talmud, Midrash,
Zohar, and the Liturgy of the Synagogue, 30 f., incorrectly refers it to Jesus.
The discussion treats merely of the definition of the term "bastard." In
Yeb. 49ᵇ the discovered document is still further embellished with spurious
additions.

the smallest letter. Instead of on Matt. 5[18] stress must be laid much more on the fact that the Judaism of the second century possessed the Bible text only in "Assyrian," *i.e.* Aramaic handwriting,—a point of contrast with the Samaritans, and further on the fact that even the Alexandrian translation is already based upon Hebrew texts in this character.[1]

7. *The Syntax and the vocabulary of the Hebrew of the Mishna*, which prove themselves to be the creation of Jews who thought in Aramaic. *M. Friedmann* is right in saying in his Onkelos und Akylas, p. 88, that "the chief part of the Rabbinic vocabulary is in its forms of speech and its idioms Hebraised Aramaic."[2] In regard to the first point, it is specially noteworthy that the Imperfect with the Vav Consecutive has vanished from use, and that a tendency occurs to use the participle as a present tense.[3]

8. *The custom of calling the Aramaic "Hebrew."*— Josephus, indeed, showed himself (Ant. x. i. 2, xii. ii. 1) quite capable of distinguishing the language and written character of the "Syrians" from those of the "Hebrews." And yet between Hebrew and Aramaic words he makes no difference. According to Ant. I. i. 1, 2, σάββατα and ʼAδάμ belong to the Hebrew tongue, but ἀσαρθά as well (Ant. iii. x. 6) is a term of the "Hebrews." The "Hebrew" in which Josephus addresses the people of Jerusalem (Bell. Jud. vi. ii. 1) is even called by him (Bell. Jud. v. ix. 2) ἡ πάτριος γλῶσσα, though in the circumstances nothing but Aramaic can be looked for. Again, in the Johannine Gospel the Aramaic terms Βηθεσδά, Γαββαθᾶ, Γολγοθᾶ, ʽΡαββουνί are called "Hebrew," 5[2] 19[13. 17] 20[16]. Aramaic, too, must be meant by the "Hebrew tongue" in which Paul spoke

---

[1] See for this, *e.g.*, *S. R. Driver*, Notes on the Hebrew Text of the Books of Samuel (1890), lxv ff.

[2] See also *A. Geiger*, Lehr- und Lesebuch zur Sprache der Mischnah (1845), i. 3 ; *J. H. Weiss*, Mischpat lĕschōn ha-Mischnā (1867), 2 f.

[3] *A. Geiger*, loc. cit. i. 40.

to the people of Jerusalem (Acts 21⁴⁰ 22²), and in which
Jesus spoke to Paul (Acts 26¹⁴). Ἑλληνισταί and
Ἑβραῖοι were the names, according to Acts 6¹, of the two
parts of the Jewish people as divided by language, although
Συρισταί would have been the more precise counterpart
of Ἑλληνισταί. But if it was possible to characterise
Aramaic as "Hebrew," it is clear that Aramaic was the
everyday speech of the Jewish people at this period, in so
far, at least, as it was not Greek.

All the facts adduced do not justify us in making a
distinction between Judæa and Galilee, as if Hebrew was
at least partially a spoken language in the former. In an
essay which much requires revision, "The dialects of Palestine in the time of Christ,"[1] A. Neubauer has advanced
the following assertion : "In Jerusalem, and perhaps also in
the greater part of Judæa, the modernised Hebrew and a
purer Aramaic dialect were in use among the majority of
the Jews ; the Galileans and the Jewish immigrants from
the neighbouring districts understood their own dialect only
(of course closely related to Aramaic), together with a few
current Hebrew expressions such as proverbs and prayers."
Adequate proof for all three parts of this assertion is
awanting. Neither the dialect of the Galileans, which was
merely related to the Aramaic, nor the purer Aramaic of
the Judæans, nor their modernised Hebrew, can really be
demonstrated. That Aramaic had at least a distinct pre-
dominance in *Judæa* may be inferred with certainty from
the place-names in Jerusalem and its environs : Ἀκελδαμάχ
(חֲקֵל דְּמָא) ; Βηθεσδά (בֵּית חֶסְדָּא) ; Βηθζαθά, Βηζεθά (בֵּית זַיְתָא) ;
Γαββαθᾶ (גַּבְּתָא) ; Γολγοθᾶ (גֻּלְגָּלְתָּא) ; Ὁπλα, Ὀφλᾶς (עֹפְלָא) ;
Σαφείν (צְפִין) ; Χαφεναθά (כַּפְנָתָא).[2]

---

[1] *Studia Biblica*, Oxford, 1885, 39–74.

[2] The discussion of these words will be found in my Grammatik des jüd.-pal.
Aram. It may here be added that Γαββαθᾶ (Gram. p. 108) is incorrectly explained. גַּבְחְתָא, which properly means the baldness of the forepart of the head,
was a fitting name for the open space in front of the Antonia Castle which

In the same category comes also a Hebrew term, similar
to the foregoing, which was applied to the piece of ground
on the Mount of Olives where Jesus tarried on the night of
the betrayal. Whether one adopts the reading Γεθσημανεί
(= שְׁמָנִי נַּת for שְׁמָנִים נַּת), as I have done Gram. 152, or starting from the readings γεσσημανεί, γησαμανεί concludes for
שְׁמָנִי גֵּיא (= שְׁמָנִים גֵּיא, Isa. 28¹), the term is all the same
Hebrew and not Aramaic. But it does not therefore follow
that Hebrew was a language in everyday use. The fact that
Rabbinic literature beginning with the Mishna represents men
of the pre-Christian and Christian periods as often speaking
Hebrew and not Aramaic, proves nothing as to the language
actually spoken by these men. One might as well by the
same kind of "proofs" produce a demonstration that the
colloquial language of the Jews in Galilee had always been
Hebrew. From the strongly expressed antipathy to Aramaic [1]
on the part of Juda the first, the redactor of the Mishna, one
must at once conclude that this language was extruded so far
as possible from the old traditions. The more significant
on that account are all the Aramaic testimonies from earlier
times that remain despite this opposition. The Hebrew
form of any tradition thus proves nothing at all in favour
of the oral use of Hebrew at an earlier date. Büchler [2] may
be quite right in holding that Aramaic was the language
used in the temple and in the sacrificial service. But
when he feels obliged to infer, because the priests speak
Hebrew in the descriptions of the temple service given by
the Mishna in the tractates Yoma, Sukka, Tamid, Middoth,

served as a place of execution. Χαφεναθά (1 Macc. 12³⁷) is not noticed in the
Grammar. With this term may perhaps be compared the biblical הַטְּבָחִים בֵּין
(2 Kings 25⁴) and Onkelos' כְּפֶלְאָ for כְּפֵלָה (Gen. 23¹⁷); while the interchange
of n and l is illustrated by the name 'Ρουβῆλος in Josephus for the biblical רְאוּבֵן,
and Ξένιος (Ant. xi. v. 4) for the name of the month כִּבֵּר.

[1] Sot. 49ᵇ: "Wherefore should I use the Sursi in Palestine? Either the
sacred tongue [Hebrew] or Greek!" On "Sursi" vid. Gram. d. jüd.-pal.
Aram. 2.
[2] A. Büchler, Die Priester und der Cultus, 64 ff.

that therefore the Aramaic had been expelled from the temple during the revolt, 63–70 A.D., there is no sufficient basis for his conclusion. At all events, there is no ground for the opinion expressed by A. Resch,[1] that Hebrew was the language of the mother of Jesus, inasmuch as she belonged to South Palestine.

In regard to Galilee, however, Hebrew does not come seriously into question. During the rising of the Maccabees the Jewish population in Galilee was so inconsiderable, that 3000 men under Simon, about 163 B.C., had no other means of protecting them from their ill-disposed neighbours than by transporting them to Judæa.[2] John Hyrcanus (135–105) appears later to have conquered Galilee and to have forced it into Judaism, so that Aristobulus I. was able to continue the same process in Ituræa.[3] Jewish families must thereafter have established themselves in these parts again in considerable numbers and intermingled freely with the Judaïsed inhabitants, so that by the time of Josephus the chief element of the population of Galilee as a whole appears as "Jewish." Under these circumstances the Hebrew language was not to be looked for; and this applies also to the little Nazareth to which there is wrongly attributed an isolation from intercourse with the outer world. It had on the one side Ṣippori (Sepphoris), the then capital of Galilee, and on the other, in close proximity, the cities of Yapha and Kesaloth, and it lay on the important highway of commerce that led from Sepphoris to the plain of Megiddo and onward to Cæsaræa. The actual discourses of Jesus in no way give the impression that He had grown up in rural solitude and seclusion. It is true only that He, like the Galileans generally in that region, would have little contact with literary erudition. This implies, moreover, that from

---

[1] A. Resch, Aussercanonische Paralleltexte, iv. 224, Das Kindheitsevangelium, 323.
[2] 1 Macc. 5[20-23].　　　　　　　　　　[3] Ant. XIII. xi. 3.

this side He did not come into contact with the Hebrew tongue. The Aramaic was the mother tongue of the Galileans as of the people of Gaulonitis, and natives of Syria, according to Josephus (Bell. Jud. IV. i. 5), were able to understand it.

The language of the prayers in private use and that of the benedictions which were woven into the routine of daily life, may possibly have been Hebrew. But the Kaddish prayer in Aramaic and the explicit avowal of the Mishna Sot. vii. 1, that, *inter alia*, the daily repetition of the Shema, the daily prayer, and the blessing (grace) at meals might be said in any language (לָשׁוֹן בְּכָל),[1] are weighty evidence against determining the usage as it really existed among the people in accordance with the linguistic form of the Rabbinic tradition. If, then, it was conceded that the Hebrew language was not to be insisted on even in reading the Shema, that is, in the symbolic fulfilment of the duty to occupy oneself with the Law which had to be performed daily by every Israelite, it is clear that a very pressing necessity must have existed for this concession. The Hellenists, who understood no Hebrew at all, may well have been the chief occasion for this. But as Hebrew could not be quite unintelligible to the "Hebraists," there was no hindrance, in their case at least, to the use of their mother tongue in prayer. That even in the third century in Palestine Aramaic was still much used in prayer, may be gathered from the deterrent urged against it by Johanan (died 279 A.D.), one of the Palestinian Amoraim. He put forth the statement that the angels did not understand this language, and were therefore unable to bring Aramaic prayers before God.[2] There is a discussion (Ber. 40ᵇ) concerning the Aramaic blessing which

---

[1] This is the expression of the Mishna in the common text and in the Babylonian Talmud ; in the Palestinian Talmud and in the Mishna (ed. Lowe) the reading is "in their language," בִּלְשׁוֹנָם ; the sense, however, is the same.

[2] Sabb. 12ᵇ ; cf. *Bacher*, Agada der pal. Amor. i. 243.

the shepherd Benjamin, in Babylon, used to say over his bread; not, however, owing to the language used, but because it did not contain the name of God. That synagogue discourses intended for the people should have been pronounced in Hebrew, is an impossible supposition for a period in which the Aramaic version of the Bible text was a necessity. Otherwise there must have been an interpreter side by side with the speaker. The more the scribes obtained unlimited control of the Jewish religious system, so much the more did divine worship adopt the form prescribed by the learned, and specially calculated only for themselves. During the progress of this transition the popular language was gradually extruded from public worship. In this connection, also, Jewish popular life before the year 70 A.D. must not be judged from the appearances created by the Rabbinic literature.

Not even in regard to the legal schools of the earlier times is it incontestably certain that their language throughout was Hebrew, and that, in particular, the legal decisions were always formulated in that language. We are told, at any rate (Eduyoth viii. 4), that a certain Yose, who indeed is incorrectly styled Yose ben Yoezer of Zereda,[1] pronounced his decisions as to clean and unclean in Aramaic. This Yose appears to have lived about 100 A.D. One might conclude that at least in his school Aramaic was the prevalent language.

From all these considerations must be drawn the conclusion that Jesus grew up speaking the Aramaic tongue, and that He would be obliged to speak Aramaic to His disciples and to the people in order to be understood. Of Him, least of all, who desired to preach the gospel to the poor, who stood aloof from the pædagogic methods of the

---

[1] The appellation is held to be genuine by *H. Klueger*, Genesis und Composition der Halacha-Sammlung Edujot (1895), 84. See, however, *A. Büchler*, Die Priester und der Cultus, 63, 84 ; *D. Hoffmann*, Mischnajoth, Eduj. viii. 4.

scribes, is it to be expected that He would have furnished His discourse with the superfluous, and to the hearers perplexing, embellishment of the Hebrew form.

II. The Literary Use of Hebrew.

The Jewish people has written in Hebrew in all periods. German, Spanish, Arabic may be the sole language of intercourse, while literary work is done as exclusively in Hebrew. So it *may* have been also in the period when Aramaic was dominant.

And we possess, in fact, some examples of Hebrew authorship from the centuries before and after the birth of Christ. A Hebrew original must be regarded as probable for the *Assumption of Moses*, the *Apocalypse of Baruch*,[1] 2 *Esdras*,[2] the *Book of Jubilees*,[3] and for the Jewish groundwork of the *Testaments of the Twelve Patriarchs*.[4] The same language may be assumed for the whole series of writings composed under the names of Enoch, Noah, Abraham, Moses, Elijah, Isaiah, Baruch, and Ezra, and for the Psalms of Solomon, in so far at least as such works were written in any Semitic language. Who could without

---

[1] That I have in some respects serious misgivings regarding the considerations urged by *R. H. Charles* as proving a Hebrew original, see my notice of his edition of the Apocalypse of Baruch, Theol. Litbl. xviii. (1897) No. 15. The same reservation applies to Charles' conclusions as to the Assumption of Moses. Especially must his attempts at retranslation be pronounced almost throughout a failure. But in the affirmation of a Hebrew original he is right.

[2] See esp. *Wellhausen*, Skizzen und Vorarbeiten, vi. (1899) 234 ff.

[3] See *E. Littmann* in Kautzsch's Apokryphen und Pseudepigraphen, ii. 35.

[4] *M. Gaster*, The Hebrew Text of one of the Testaments of the Twelve Patriarchs, Proc. Soc. Bibl. Arch., Dec. 1893, Feb. 1894, believed he had discovered the original of the Testament of Naphtali ; but the conjecture of *A. Neubauer*, Mediæval Jewish Chronicles, vol. i. p. xxi, that Jerachme'el is the translator of the apocryphal writings contained in the Bodleian MS. used by Gaster, holds good also for the Testament of Naphtali. From Neubauer's communications regarding Jerachme'el one does not expect from the latter Semitic originals that had disappeared, but selections from Western literature which was inaccessible to Jews. See also *F. Schnapp*, Apokryphen und Pseudepigraphen, ii. 458 f.

hesitation have represented Moses or Baruch as the writer of a book in Aramaic? To Hellenists such a book might be offered without scruple, because the Hebrew original could not have been read by them. Among "Hebraists" it would be startling if, in place of the presumed Hebrew original, a mere Aramaic translation had come to light.

The *Book of Daniel* forms here no real exception. Its groundwork, comprising the contents of chaps. 1–6, has presumably been an Aramaic narrative of the experiences of Daniel and his comrades at the court of Babylon. A writing, in which visions were interpreted to the Kings of Babylon, used aptly enough the language current in the whole East at the time. The second part of the book, chaps. 7–12, gave — not less appropriately in Hebrew — visions which Daniel himself had had, together with their interpretation through an angel. The redactor may first have ventured to translate chaps. 1¹–2⁴ into Hebrew, and chap. 7 into Aramaic, and by this means as well as by the corresponding contents of the prophecy he welded the separate halves into one whole. In chap. 2 the world-power is in decay when the Kingdom of God makes its appearance; in chap. 7 ff. it is in reality full of the greatest menace against the people of God (cf. 2⁴²ᶠ· with 7²ᶠᶠ·). In chap. 7 is also to be noted the peculiar use of the Hebrew עֶלְיוֹנִין, occurring only in this chapter. That the Aramaic part did not begin originally with 2⁴ is self-evident. Further additions to the Aramaic part would naturally be composed in Aramaic, so that in the Aramaic translation of the supplements to Daniel (Song of the Three Children, Daniel and the Dragon), which M. Gaster has published,[1] at least the choice of language is happily inspired; though it must not

[1] *M. Gaster*, The Unknown Aramaic Original of Theodotion's Additions to the Book of Daniel, Proc. Soc. Bibl. Arch. xvi. 280 ff., 312 ff., xvii. 75 ff. Gaster has extracted the pieces from the Chronicle of Jerachme'el, who himself declares at the outset that he had translated them from the Greek Bible.

be fancied that this really represents the original from which Theodotion translated.

In regard to the Book of Enoch, the question as to its original language is complicated owing to the different origin of its parts. A Semitic original is beyond question for chaps. 1–36. In this section the terms φουκα, 18⁸, Μανδο-βαρα, 28¹, Βαβδηρα, 29¹, speak in favour of Aramaic by reason of the ending in -a, though פּוּך is only known as a Hebrew word, and מדבר, "wilderness," can be equally good Hebrew. In 10¹⁷ τὰ σάββατα αὐτῶν stands where "their grey old age" was to be expected; but that is susceptible of explanation equally well through Heb. שְׂבָתם as Aram. שְׂבָתהוֹן or שְׂבָתהוֹן. In 10⁹ μαζηρέους (cf. מַמְזֵר) may also be Hebrew or Aramaic. Expressions clearly Hebrew are— καὶ ἐγένετο, 6¹ (from Gen. 6¹); πρὸ τούτων τῶν λόγων, 12¹; φωνὴ βοῶν (cf. קוֹל קֹרֵא), 9²; as well as ἀπὸ προσώπου, 9¹⁰ 22⁷; ἐκ δεξιῶν (= southwards), 13⁷; and εὐφρανθήσονται εὐφραινόμενοι (= יִשְׂמְחוּ שָׂמוֹחַ), 25⁶. An original in *Hebrew* must be assumed for chaps. 72–82 on account of the Hebrew names for the phases of the sun and moon, 78¹f., and for the points of the compass, 77¹. As for chaps. 37–71, I can merely point out the Hebraising phrases "and it came to pass," 57¹ 68⁴ 70¹ 71¹; "and it will come to pass," 39¹ 52⁷; "before his face," 62². ¹⁰ 63⁹ 65⁶ 66³ 69²⁰. In chaps. 83–90 the repeated use (thirty times) of the redundant "begin" is striking, and is at least not old Hebrew (vid. IV. 8 below, pp. 26 ff.). As for the remainder and the book as a whole, I do not venture to make a final pronouncement.

There can be no doubt that the First Book of Maccabees is derived from a Hebrew original. When Jerome in the Prologus galeatus speaks of having the book before him in Hebrew, one must indeed, in view of the prevailing ambiguity of his statements on such matters, be careful to see whether he has here, too, perhaps made no distinction between Hebrew and Aramaic. But the language of the book confirms his testimony. Its phraseology is that of historical narrative in the Bible, which the author has obviously imitated of set purpose. It will suffice to adduce—εὑρίσκειν χάριν ἐνάντιόν τινος, 10⁶⁰ 11²⁴; διδόναι κέρας, 2⁴⁸; φοβεῖν φόβον μέγαν, 10⁸; πατάσσειν πλήγην μεγάλην, 5³, cf. 5³⁴ 8⁴; κόπτειν κοπετὸν μέγαν, 2⁷⁰ 9²⁰ 13²⁶; ὀργίζειν ὀργὴν μεγάλην, 16³⁶; ἀνὴρ πρὸς τὸν πλησίον αὐτοῦ (= one another), 2⁴⁰; ἐγένετο ὅτε, 5¹ 7² 9²³ 10⁶⁴· ⁸⁸; the frequent use of εἰς συνάντη-σιν, εἰς ἀπάντησιν = לְקִרְאַת; σφόδρα = מְאֹד; λέγων λέγοντες = לֵאמֹר; κατὰ πρόσωπον = לִפְנֵי. All this is specifically Hebrew and not Aramaic.

The Aramaic *Book of the Hasmonœans*,[1] which is modelled after the biblical Aramaic, is in no way connected with the First Book of Maccabees, and is, together with its Hebrew version,[2] of much later origin. Of the Book of Tobit we now possess four distinct Hebrew recensions and one Aramaic;[3] but though M. Gaster believes he has what is nearly the original in one of the Hebrew texts published by him, it still remains possible that all these Semitic texts are only translations from the Greek, and that the hypothetical Semitic original is lost to us. When Jerome says that he had completed the Book of Tobit with the help of a Hebrew translation, which latter he himself had got made from a Chaldaic text, it is possible that this text too may have been a translation from the Greek, and may itself have been in Syriac. The same possibility will hold of the Chaldaic text of the Book of Judith which Jerome used;

[1] See especially the edition of *M. Gaster*, "The Scroll of the Hasmonæans," in Transactions of the Orient. Congress, Lond. 1891, ii.; and, further, *A. Neubauer* in Jew. Quart. Rev. vi. (1894) 570 ff., also Gram. d. jüd.-pal. Aram. 6.

[2] See, *e.g.*, *Baer's* Seder Abodath Yisrael, 441 ff.

[3] Two Hebrew recensions were printed in Constantinople 1516 and 1519; *M. Gaster* edited in 1897 two more in "Two unknown Hebrew versions of Tobit" (also in Proc. Soc. Bibl. Arch.); *A. Neubauer* published an Aramaic text (together with the Hebrew of 1516), "The Book of Tobit, a Chaldee Text" (1877), see also Gram. 27 ff., and *Schürer*, Geschichte d. jüd. Volkes,[3] iii. (1898) p. 180 f.

although in this case a Hebrew original is the most probable. Whoever wrote after the model of the biblical books would naturally—as we have said above—if a "Hebraist," have used the "Hebrew" language, but if a Hellenist, the Greek language. In no case, however, has the abridged Hebrew reproduction of the story of Judith, which we possess in a twofold form,[1] an immediate connection with the original of the book.

If we turn now to the question of the language of a primitive Semitic gospel, it must be said that some of the incentives favourable to composition in Hebrew at that time do not in this case come into action. Jesus had taught in Aramaic; and in that language the "Hebraists" must have been taught concerning Him in Christian public worship, if the address were to be intelligible to all. If, further, the substance of such an address were noted down for the Aramaic speaking "Hebraists," composition in Hebrew after the model of the biblical books was, of course, not inconceivable, especially as those Jews who could read were also able to understand Hebrew, yet the more probable course with material already formulated by oral delivery was to write it down in the language in which it was spoken, particularly if the record were designed to afford convenient and reliable material for further recital or public exposition. Even some centuries later, the gospel of the Jewish Christians, according to the express testimony of Jerome, was composed not in Hebrew but in Aramaic. Hence there is much to justify the view—unless decisive evidence to the contrary should be found in Church tradition or in the Gospels themselves—that a collection of the sayings of our Lord designed for "Hebraists," in other words, a primitive gospel (Urevangelium), was written in Aramaic.

---

[1] *Jellinek* edited one recension in Beth ha-Midrasch, i. 130 f., *Gaster* another in Proc. Soc. Bibl. Arch. xvi. 156 ff.

III. The Semitisms of the Synoptic Gospels.

Not a little has been written on the "Hebraisms" of the New Testament since the first important investigation of them by Kaspar Wyss[1] and Johann Vorst[2] in the seventeenth century. But from the outset it has not been grasped with sufficient clearness that the Greek of the Jewish Hellenists must have been affected by Semitic tongues in several distinct ways. In the first place, it must be assumed that the Greek spoken from Syria to Egypt was in many particulars influenced, in no small degree, by the Aramaic language of the country ; and, further, it holds true for that portion of the Jewish people that adopted Greek in place of its Semitic mother-tongue, that this mother-tongue had been Aramaic, and that the world of thought peculiar to the Jews, which had then to be apprehended in a Greek mould, had already been fashioned in Aramaic and no longer in Hebrew. The spiritual intercourse also which Jewish Hellenists continuously had with Hebraists in Palestine implied a constant interchange between Greek and Aramaic (but not Hebrew) modes of expression. Hebrew influence was active only indirectly : first, in so far as a Hebrew past underlay the Aramaic present of the Jewish people ; secondly and in particular, because the Greek translation of the Old Testament had necessarily a powerful influence on the religious dialect.

In the case of the Synoptic Gospels of the Christian Hellenists, there has further to be added to the previously specified relations with Jewish Aramaic, the highly important consideration that the groundwork of the material elaborated by them had been originally created in Aramaic. And this holds equally true whether their basis presented itself to the

---

[1] *Kaspar Wyss*, Dialectologia sacra, Zürich, 1650.

[2] *Johann Vorst*, Philologia sacra, ii., Leyden, 1658, i., Amsterdam, 1665, with general title : De Hebraismis Novi Testamenti Commentarius, Amsterdam, 1665.

2

authors directly in its Aramaic form or already through the medium of Greek tradition, oral or written.

In these circumstances there can be no doubt that the Semitisms of the Gospels ought first to be looked for in the sphere of the Jewish Aramaic, and that only where this does not suffice for explanation, need it be asked how far Hebrew is to be held responsible for Semitisms. In the latter case a special examination is then required into the different possibilities involved. The material of the Synoptic Gospels might have partly or wholly been shaped in a Hebrew mould in which it became mixed with Hebraisms, and in this condition have reached the evangelists. A Hebraising influence, on the other hand, might also come into play after the material had already been moulded in Greek. During this phase such an influence is the less improbable, because in the oral presentation of the " gospel " at gatherings of the Christian community, as well as in any literary treatment applied to it, the Greek Old Testament furnished the readiest model. This version being the most important book read by the Christians in public and in private, the desire to give to the gospel a corresponding dress must naturally have existed ; and the conception of the Canon among the Christian Hellenists was none so sharply defined as to cause scruples in assimilating the form of new devotional lectionaries to the older Scriptures.

It is a serious defect in previous studies of the Semitisms in the Gospels, that too little account is taken of these circumstances. P. W. Schmiedel complains in his new edition of " Winer's Grammatik des Neutestamentlichen Sprachidioms," § 2. 1c, that the Aramaic constituents of the New Testament diction have not been sufficiently regarded. But he himself does not succeed in reaching any really tenable separation of Aramaisms and Hebraisms. Still less satisfactory is it with F. Blass, who calls special attention in his "Grammatik des neutestamentlichen Griechisch" (1896),

p. 4, to the Hebrew-Aramaic influence on the idiom, but makes no attempt to distinguish Aramaisms from Hebraisms; and in the Preface to his edition of the Gospel of Luke [1] he characterises as Aramaisms idioms which in some cases are equally good Hebraisms, and in others are pure Hebraisms and not Aramaisms at all. And how is it possible that J. Böhmer should still exclusively consult the Old Testament in his tractate, otherwise instructive in many respects, "Das biblische 'im Namen'" (1898), in which he aims at explaining linguistically and historically the variations εἰς τὸ ὄνομα, ἐπὶ τῷ ὀνόματι in the baptismal formula? In this very instance the key to the explanation of the expression is to be found in the usage of language among the Jews. Böhmer should at least have said why he looked for no information from that quarter.

A further deficiency in the current grammatical studies of New Testament Greek consists in the inadequate attention directed to the "Græcisms" of the Gospels, i.e. to the linguistic phenomena which have no immediate Semitic equivalent, and for which, therefore, the Hellenistic writers must perforce be held responsible. Previous translators of the Gospels into Hebrew have come to grief over these Græcisms, either because, like Delitzsch and, in a minor degree, Salkinson, they have refused to abandon the principle of a verbally faithful reproduction of the sacred Greek original,[2] or because they have not properly recognised the specific Græcisms, as appears to be the case with Resch, who was surely indifferent to any such consideration as that just mentioned.

Whosoever would know what was the Aramaic primary form of any of the Master's sayings will have to separate these latter Græcisms not less distinctly than the former

---

[1] F. Blass, Evangelium sec. Lucam (1897), xxi f.

[2] This is not mentioned as a censure. In this principle, so far as it is applied to a translation for *practical* purposes, I fully agreed with *Franz Delitzsch*, and was therefore able to act as editor of the revised 11th edition of his Hebrew New Testament, which appeared in 1892.

Hellenistic Hebraisms. Thus may be reached a verbal form which is at least not unthinkable in the utterance of Jesus, and which is most closely identified with the original Aramaic tradition of the apostles.

Even such *Aramaic* Hebraisms as the Targums present in great number, are not to be regarded as specially probable in the mouth of Jesus. Whoever compares the words of Jesus Himself with the hymns and discourses of other persons in the Lucan writings, will find it a peculiar characteristic of the style of Jesus, that Holy Scripture is cited but rarely, and only when it has to be adduced owing to a definite call for it, and that references to the letter of Scripture are confined to a very limited compass. Moreover, it is all the less probable that He should have spoken the Hebraising Aramaic of the Targums, inasmuch as no such practical use of it is anywhere to be found among the Jews. Even to Aramaic transmitters of His words we cannot therefore impute any tendency to Hebraise them, unless we are to assume on their part a purposeless, yet intentional, imitation of a Targum. The words of Jesus, purged of special Hebraisms of every kind, will accordingly have the highest probability of being original.

IV. SOME HEBRAISMS AND ARAMAISMS.

In order to inaugurate an investigation of the Synoptic Semitisms which will better satisfy the demands that must be made upon it, a number of these will now be discussed. Such phrases will be selected as either substantially define or are sufficient to define the general style of one or more Synoptists. The discussion of further details must be reserved till the examination of the special passages.

1. ἐλθών, ἐρχόμενος.

The participles ἐλθών or ἐρχόμενος are redundantly coupled with a finite verb by the three Synoptists, *but not by the Johannine Gospel.*[1] Jesus says, Matt. 5²⁴ ἐλθὼν πρόσφερε, "go, offer"; Matt. 12⁴⁴ (Luke 11²⁵) ἐλθὸν εὑρίσκει, "it goes and finds"; Matt. 25²⁷ (cf. Luke 19²³) ἐλθὼν ἐκομισάμην, "I should have gone and received"; Luke 15²⁵ ἐρχόμενος ἤγγισεν, "he came and drew nigh." A kindred use is πορευθεὶς ἐκολλήθη, "he went and joined himself to," Luke 15¹⁵. The narrative also makes use of such expressions: Matt. 2²³ ἐλθὼν κατῴκησεν, "he went and dwelt"; Matt. 15²⁵ ἐλθοῦσα προσεκύνει (Mark 7²⁵ εἰσελθοῦσα προσέπεσεν), "she came and fell down." This idiom corresponds to the redundant הָלַךְ and בּוֹא of the Old Testament; see, *e.g.*, Judg. 19¹⁰ וַיֵּלֶךְ וַיָּבֹא, "he went and came"; Hos. 5¹⁵ אֵלֵךְ אָשׁוּבָה, "I will go (and) return"; 1 Sam. 20¹ וַיָּבֹא וַיֹּאמֶר, "he came and said." In the Book of Enoch (Greek text) may be compared especially the conjunction of πορεύεσθαι with εἰπεῖν, 12⁴ 13¹·³ 15²; see also πορεύου καὶ δήλωσον, 10¹¹; πορευθεὶς ἐκάθισα, 13⁷. In Jewish Aramaic this idiom is also common. Exx.: אָזֵיל וּמְתְעֲבֵד, "he goes and becomes," Vay. R. 25; יֵיזֵיל יְמוּת, "let him go and die," j. Ter. 45ᶜ; יֵיזֵיל וְיַשְׂהֵיר, "let him go and testify," j. R. h. S. 58ᵈ; אֵיזֵיל וּמְשֵׁיזֵיב, "I go and rescue," j. Ter. 46ᵇ; אָתָא מֵעֲבַד כֵּן, "he came so to do," j. Khall. 60ᵇ; אָתָא שְׁאַל, "he came and asked," j. Shebi. 39ᵃ; יֵיתֵי וְיִפַּב, "let him come and marry," Ber. R. 65; אֲזַלַת וְאִתְנְסֵבַת, "she went and married," Ber. R. 17.

2. ἀφείς, καταλιπών.

The juxtaposition of καταλιπών and ἀφείς with a term signifying departure, where the idea of "leaving" can in no way be emphasised, occurs in the narrative of Matthew and Mark, *but not in Luke and John.* Examples: Matt. 13³⁶ ἀφεὶς τοὺς ὄχλους ἦλθεν, "He left the people and went"; 22²² ἀφέντες αὐτὸν ἀπῆλθαν (this also in Mark 12¹²), "they left Him and went away"; Mark 8¹³ ἀφεὶς αὐτούς—ἀπῆλθεν (Matt. 16⁴ καταλιπὼν αὐτοὺς ἀπῆλθεν), "He left them and

---

[1] John 11¹⁷ ἐλθών is indispensable; the reading, however, is doubtful.

departed"; Matt. 21¹⁷ καταλιπὼν αὐτοὺς ἐξῆλθεν; see also
Mark 4³⁶. In the Old Testament this is not a usual mode of
diction. Salkinson renders ἀφιέναι by עָזַב, Delitzsch sometimes by הִנִּיחַ. But the former signifies in the Old Testament " to desert, leave in the lurch," the latter " to leave or
let alone," and neither the one nor the other is employed in
idioms like those above quoted. This is the case, however,
in Jewish Aramaic: j. Sabb. 8ᶜ שַׁבְקֵיהּ וַאֲזַל לֵיהּ, " he left him
and went on "; j. Taan. 66ᶜ שַׁבְקוּנֵיהּ וַאֲזָלוּ לוֹן, " they left him
and went away." From these instances it may also be seen
how in similar cases ἀπῆλθεν standing by itself, which cannot be rendered into Hebrew merely by וַיֵּלֶךְ, presupposes the
use of the popular *Dativus commodi* of Jewish Aramaic.[1]

3. καθίσας.

In certain actions of a sedentary kind the evangelists
usually make superfluous mention of the posture. Examples:
καθίσαντες συνέλεξαν, " they sat down and collected together," Matt. 13⁴⁸; καθίσας — ἐδίδαξεν, " He sat down and
taught," Luke 5³; καθίσας ψηφίζει, " he sits down and reckons,"
Luke 14²³; καθίσας—βουλεύσεται, " he will sit down and
consult," Luke 14³¹; καθίσας—γράψον, " sit down and write,"
Luke 16⁶. Of the same nature is the instance where it is
said of Levi that Jesus saw him " sitting " (καθήμενον) at the
receipt of custom, Matt. 9⁹ (Mark 2¹⁴, Luke 5²⁷). In quite
the same way it is said, Judg. 19⁶ וַיֵּשְׁבוּ וַיֹּאכְלוּ, " and they sat
down and ate," for to the narrator the " sitting " is an immaterial concomitant. Again, the " sitting and judging " or
" sitting and ruling," as to which Joel 4¹², Zech. 6¹³ are to be
compared with Matt. 19²⁸ (Luke 22³⁰), falls into the same class.
In the Jewish Aramaic we find יְתִיב מִשְׁתָּעֵי, " He sat and recounted," Est. R. 3⁴; הֲווֹן יָתְבִין פָּשְׁטִין, " they sat and studied,"
Ber. R. 17; הֲוָה יָתֵיב מַתְנֵי, " He sat and taught," j. Ber. 6ᵃ.

---

[1] See my Gramm. d. j.-pal. Ar. 178.

4. ἑστώς, σταθείς.

Standing is the posture during prayer. Thus it is said, Matt. 6⁵ ἑστῶτες προσεύχεσθαι, "to stand and pray"; Mark 11²⁵ ὅταν στήκετε προσευχόμενοι, "when ye stand and pray"; Luke 18¹¹ σταθείς—προσηύχετο, "he stood and prayed." In the Old Testament, 1 Kings 8²², Neh. 9⁴, it is also implied that standing was the usual attitude at prayer; it is not, however, a regular phrase to say, "he stood and prayed." On the other hand, contrast קָאֵים מִצְלֵּי, "he stood praying," j. R. h. S. 58ᵇ; קָאֵים לְצַלָּאָה, Est. R. 3⁴.

In the same way ἵστημι is quite without force in: εἰστήκεισαν κατηγοροῦντες, "they stood and accused," Luke 23¹⁰; εἰστήκει — θεωρῶν, "the people stood beholding," Luke 23³⁵; cf. ἑστὼς καὶ θερμαινόμενος, "standing and warming himself," John 18¹⁸·²⁵. Further, we have from the Old Testament: וְעָמְדוּ זָרִים וְרָעוּ, "and strangers shall stand and feed," Isa. 61⁵; and from the rabbinical literature, הֲוָה קָאֵים וְחָצֵר, "he stood and reaped," Vay. R. 22; עָמְדוּ וְאָמְרוּ, "they stand and say," Mechilt., ed. Friedm. 45ᵇ.

5. ἀναστάς, ἐγερθείς.

A redundant ἀναστάς is found in the narrative of the Synoptists, but not in John. It is found with ἀκολουθεῖν, Matt. 9⁹ (Mark 2¹⁴, Luke 5²⁸); ἀπέρχεσθαι, Mark 7²⁴; ἔρχεσθαι, Mark 10¹·⁵⁰ (ἀναπηδήσας), Luke 15²⁰; πορεύεσθαι, Luke 1³⁹; ἐκβάλλειν, Luke 4²⁹; εἰσέρχεσθαι, Luke 4³⁸; διακονεῖν, Luke 4³⁹; ἄγειν, Luke 23¹; τρέχειν, Luke 24¹²; ὑποστρέφειν, Luke 24³³. Here also is to be reckoned ἀνέστη ἐκπειράζων, Luke 10²⁵. The synonymous ἐγερθείς is seen in Matt. 2¹³·¹⁴ (with παραλαμβάνειν), and in Matt. 9¹⁹ (with ἀκολουθεῖν). In words spoken by Jesus it is found with πορεύεσθαι, Luke 15¹⁸·²⁰, 17¹⁹. A glance at the examples specified by Hebrew Concordances for the terms וַיָּקָם, וַתָּקָם, וַיָּקוּמוּ, shows that this is a well-established Old Testament idiom. See also 1 Macc.

9⁴⁴, Book of Enoch 54³, 89⁴⁷·⁴⁸. In view of this fact, it is
hard to see how Blass in the Preface to his "Evangelium
secundum Lucam" (1897), p. xxiii, can without more ado
class it as an Aramaism. Still it is true that the same
mode of speech is quite possible in Aramaic. Examples are:
קָמוּ—לְמִבְנֵא, "they stood up to build," Ezra 5¹; קָם לֵיהּ מְצַלֵּי,
"he stood up to pray," j. R. h. S. 58ᵇ; קָם וְאָכַל לֵיהּ, "he stood
up and devoured him," Vay. R. 22; קָם וְהַב לֵיהּ, "he stood up
and gave him," Ech. R. i. 4; קָמוּן—וְאָרוּן, "they stood up and
protested," j. Keth. 30ᵈ; קָמוּ—וּמְחוֹנֵיהּ, "they stood up and
beat him," j. Yeb. 15ᵃ. The Imperative קוּם is common for
the mere interjection "up!" e.g. קוּם רְכוֹב, "up! ride," Vay.
R. 28; קוּם אִתְהַלֵּךְ, "up! go," j. Bikk. 65ᵈ; קוּם עֲבוֹד עֲבוֹדָה זָרָה,
"up! worship idols," j. Ab. z. 39ᵇ.

6. ἀποκριθεὶς εἶπεν.[1]

It is a well-known peculiarity of Hebrew narrative style
that a speech is introduced not simply by וַיֹּאמֶר, "and he
said," or וַיִּקְרָא, "he called," but by prefixing to these וַיַּעַן, "and
he answered." The same mode of reporting prevails also in
1 Macc., Tobit, Book of Enoch,[2] Apocalypse of Baruch,
2 Esdras, Assumptio Mosis; it is conspicuously rare, however,
in the Book of Jubilees and in Judith, and occurs occasionally
in the Second Book of Maccabees. The Synoptists have the
same mode of expression, and John's Gospel is here no exception. In the words spoken by Jesus it is found in Matt.
21²⁹·³⁰ 25¹² (cf. ver. ⁹) ²⁶·³⁷·⁴⁰·⁴⁴·⁴⁵, Luke 11⁷ 13²⁵ 15²⁹. In
these instances ἀποκριθεὶς εἶπεν is the formula most used;
in Mark 7²⁸ occurs also ἀπεκρίθη καὶ λέγει, the two finite verbs
being set side by side, and this latter is the formula nearly
always used in the Johannine Gospel. ἀποκρίνεσθαι may
also be made the principal verb to which the participle

---

[1] *J. Vorstius*, De Hebraismis Novi Testamenti, ii. (1658) 173–176; *D.
Schilling*, De Hebraismis Nov. Test. (1886) 165.

[2] See especially Enoch 1² 6⁴ 15¹ 21⁹ 22⁷·⁹ 24⁶ 25¹·³ 27¹.

λέγων is attached, see Matt. 25[9. 37. 44. 45], Mark 3[33] 5[9] 9[38] 15[9], Luke 3[16] 4[4], John 1[26] 10[33] 12[23]. Moreover, the formula also occurs where no explicit question has preceded, see Matt. 11[25] 17[4] (Mark 9[5]) 26[63] 28[5], Mark 10[51] 11[14] 12[35], Luke 1[60] 13[14] 14[3], John 5[17. 19].

The Hebrew idiom is naturally copied both by the LXX and by the Targums; but even in biblical Aramaic עֲנֵה וְאָמַר, " he answered and said," is frequently employed. In the later Jewish Aramaic this formula is quite unknown. The Aramaic Scroll of the Hasmonæans, the style of which is modelled on the Book of Daniel, is singular in having it eleven times. Direct speech is introduced by the simple אָמַר. Even in conversations which are considerably prolonged, no further introduction is added. The word for "answer" in Galilean Aramaic אֲגִיב is rarely used. In Ech. R. i. 4; j. Erub. 18[d] it is conjoined with אָמַר, but not so as to constitute a persistent formula. אֲתִיב, the word for "answer" used by Onkelos, appears to be as yet a learned term for "making good an objection." Probability supports the view that the formula in question was unknown in genuine Aramaic. In that case the evangelists can have borrowed it only from the Hebrew either directly or through the medium of the Greek Bible.

7. ἐλάλησεν (εἶπεν)—λέγων.

The circumstantially precise Hebrew phrase וַיְדַבֵּר אֶל פּ' לֵאמֹר, " and he spoke to . . . and said," is likewise foreign both to the biblical Aramaic and to the later Jewish-Aramaic dialects. Aramaic, it is true, has the word מַלֵּל for "speak" alongside of אָמַר; but the use of מַלֵּל is essentially narrower than that of the Hebrew דִּבֶּר. It is applied, indeed, as the introduction to a direct discourse, Dan. 6[22] אֱדַיִן דָּנִיֵּאל עִם מַלְכָּא מַלִּל, "then spake Daniel to the king, saying." But no parallel to this is found in the later literature.[1] Similarly

---

[1] Book of Enoch 21[5] seems, however, to presuppose it : וַיֹּאמֶר אֵלַי וַיְדַבֵּר אֵלַי.

in the single instance Ezra 5¹¹ the Hebrew לֵאמֹר is imitated by לְמֵמַר, whereas elsewhere for similar cases there is used only a finite verb coupled by ו, or a participle. When the Targums habitually render דִּבֶּר by מַלֵּל, and לֵאמֹר by לְמֵימַר, this should be pronounced a Hebraism; nor can it be otherwise regarded when the evangelists sometimes have recourse to the corresponding Greek expression of the LXX.

ἐλάλησεν—λέγων is found Matt. 23¹ᶠ· 28¹⁸, Luke 24⁶ᶠ·, Acts 8²⁶; εἶπεν—λέγων (εἶπαν—λέγοντες), Mark 8²³ 12²⁶ (discourse of Jesus), Luke 14³. Other instances are susceptible of a different explanation, viz. Matt. 14²⁷ (Mark 6⁵⁰), because emphasis may be laid on the fact that Jesus, hitherto silent as He moved over the lake, then addressed His disciples, and Matt. 13³ 22¹ because λαλεῖν (λέγειν) ἐν παραβολαῖς forms one composite expression. The expression accordingly is not a common one; further, it is never attested by more than one of the Synoptists in the same connection. Its occurrence also in Acts 26³¹ and John 8¹² is a warning against hasty inferences.

Nevertheless λέγων must not in every case be referred without further examination to the Hebrew לֵאמֹר. The latter can be coupled with numerous verbs of calling, asking, reminding, teaching, charging, murmuring, etc. But Aramaic, too, has similar conjunctions: גָּזַר וַאֲמַר, " he decided and said," j. Ab. z. 44ᵈ; בָּרֵיךְ וַאֲמַר, " he blessed and said," j. Ber. 11ᵇ; הֲוָה מַכְרֵיז וַאֲמַר, " he announced and said," j. Yeb. 12ᵈ; אַסְהֵיד וַאֲמַר, " he testified and said," Vay. R. 34.

8. ἤρξατο, ἤρξαντο.

The use of ἤρξατο, ἤρξαντο with an infinitive following, when nothing at all is to be said of any further development of the action thus introduced, is one of the peculiarities that mark the narrative style of all three Synoptists, John having it only once (13⁵), where it is perhaps due to the influence of the kindred passage Luke 7³⁸. In Matthew it occurs twelve times, in Mark twenty-six times, and in Luke twenty-six times. In words spoken by Jesus it is found Matt. 18²⁴ 24⁴⁹ (Luke 12⁴⁵), Luke 13²⁵· ²⁶ 14⁹· ¹⁸· ²⁹ 15¹⁴· ²⁴ 21²⁸ 23³⁰. Further, this phrase occurs outside narrative passages in the forms ἄρξῃ, ἄρξησθε, ἄρξεσθε. The expression is obviously quite conventional. It is altogether foreign to the Old Testament, but in chaps. 85–90 of the Book of Enoch it is found with abnormal frequency. Salkinson has ignored it in Luke 3⁸ 13²⁵ 14⁹· ²⁹ 15²⁴, but elsewhere has used הֵחֵל as equivalent. Similarly Delitzsch substitutes other turns of expression in Luke 3⁸ 14⁹· ²⁹, while in the other cases he also has recourse to הֵחֵל. Resch[1] entirely abandons the region of what is linguistically admissible by inserting הוֹאִיל as equivalent even in the historical narrative, as if a volition or determination to do something were to be expressed. And the statement of the same writer, that this הוֹאִיל " belongs very specially to the epic style of narration in the Old Testament," is incomprehensible. But all conjecture is rendered needless in this case by the fact that the Palestinian-Jewish literature uses the meaningless " he began " in the same fashion. The corresponding Aramaic term is the common word for " to begin," שָׁרֵי, Pael of שְׁרָא, " to loosen "; in Hebrew הִתְחִיל, derived from תְּחִלָּה, " a beginning," is its substitute. For שָׁרֵי see, e.g., j. Ber. 2ᶜ, 14ᵇ; j. Shebi. 35ᵇ; and for הִתְחִיל, j. Ber. 7ᵈ, 12ᵇ, 13ᵇ; j. Pes. 33ᵃ; Koh. R. v. 10. No example is known to me which would correspond to the use of ἄρχομαι in direct speech. But if שָׁרֵי coupled with a participle had become practically meaningless, it is easy to see why we should have : " ye will begin to stand without, — to say " (Luke 13²⁵· ²⁶), and "begin not to say" (Luke 3⁸). This was, of course, very little different from the mere " ye will stand,—say," " say not." When we find in Matt. 3⁹ μὴ δόξητε λέγειν in place of μὴ ἄρξησθε λέγειν in Luke 3⁸, this is only a *constructio ad sensum* variant in better Greek, which could also, however,

---

[1] Aussercanon. Paralleltexte, iii. 9.

havé been expressed in Aramaic. Even in Luke 14[9], where
Cod. D has omitted ἄρξη, there is hardly any real difference
in the feeling of the writer between ἄρξη—κατέχειν, " thou
shalt begin to take," and the simple " thou shalt take." Still
it may here be recalled that strangely enough the Hebrew
הוֹאִיל is in most cases rendered in the Targums by שְׁרִי,—as
in the LXX by ἄρχομαι,—so that שְׁרִי may thus express the
idea of " acquiescing in, consenting to." See Onk. Deut. 1[5];
Trg. Josh. 7[7] 17[12], Judg. 1[27. 35] 19[6], 2 Sam. 7[29], 2 Kings 5[23]
6[3]. This sense is *possible* also in Luke 14[9].

9. εὐθέως εὐθύς, παραχρῆμα.

The adverb εὐθέως, εὐθύς—the latter being the undisputed
reading in a few passages only—is used by Mark forty-five
times, by Matthew eighteen times, by Luke [1] eight times, and
by John seven times. The synonymous παραχρῆμα is found
twice in Matthew and ten times in Luke, Matthew and Luke
thus having the adverb for " straightway " with about equal
frequency though only half as often as Mark. In words
spoken by Jesus, εὐθέως (εὐθύς) is found Mark 4[5] (Matt. 13[5])
4[15. 16.] (Matt. 13[20]) [17.] (Matt. 13[21]) [20] 11[2.] (Matt. 21[2]) [3] (Matt.
21[3]), Matt. 24[29] 25[15], Luke 12[54] 14[5] 17[7] 21[9]. Salkinson has
recourse here to terms for " suddenly, quickly," such as כְּרֶגַע,
בְּרֶגַע זֶה, פִּתְאֹם, מְהֵרָה עַד, or to the verb מִהַר. Delitzsch, too, has
sought by various Hebrew expressions to do justice to the
awkward εὐθέως. Resch has frequently expelled it from
the text, but has occasionally used פִּתְאֹם. The Old Testament has, in fact, nothing corresponding. It is true also
that the rabbinic literature does not exhibit any such usage
with the same frequency ; but there can be no doubt that its
common use of מִיַּד, יַד וּ מָן [2] represents the Aramaic prototype
presupposed by the evangelists; see j. Ned. 41[c]; j. R. h. S. 58[a];

---

[1] In *Vogel*, Zur Charakteristik des Lukas (23), it is incorrectly stated that
Luke has εὐθέως only once, elsewhere constantly παραχρῆμα.

[2] This appears more appropriate than כֵּיוָן, which, especially in conjunction
with אֲשֶׁר or דְּ, usually stands for "as soon as.'

Vay. R. 22; Jerus. I. Gen. 1³, Ex. 19¹⁷; Hebr. j. Pes. 33ᵃ (*bis*); Ab. z. iv. 4. This מִיָּד does not mean " suddenly," but " without delay, forthwith, immediately thereafter," agreeably with the sense of εὐθύς and παραχρῆμα in the Gospels. It can generally be substituted where these occur.[1] That Matthew and Luke restricted its use is conceivable enough. Its excessive frequency in Mark must depend on the particular predilection of the author, and is due probably to Greek rather than Jewish-Aramaic influence.

10. πρόσωπον,

κατὰ πρόσωπόν τινος, " in presence of any one," Luke 2³¹, Acts 3¹³, cf. LXX 1 Chron. 28⁸ (לְעֵינֵי). The phrase, however, is also proper to classical Greek, and is therefore no Hebraism. In Hebrew לְאַפֵּי might also be used, as in 1 Sam. 25²³; in Aramaic, עַל אַפֵּי or בְּאַפֵּי, Gram. d. j.-pal. Aram. 183.

πρὸ προσώπου τινός, " before any one," is found in an Old Testament citation Mark 1², Matt. 11¹⁰ (Luke 7²⁷), in allusion to an Old Testament phrase Luke 1⁷⁶, in narrative Luke 9⁵² 10¹. It corresponds to the Hebrew לִפְנֵי. Theodotion, however, uses this phrase to reproduce לָקֳבֵל, Dan. 2³¹ (LXX ἐναντίον). One must not therefore necessarily predicate a Hebrew derivation for πρὸ προσώπου (which Luke also employs in Acts 13²⁴), although the idiom is a Hebraism. קֳדָם would be the Aramaic equivalent in Luke 9⁵², Acts 13²⁴.

The same applies to ἀπὸ προσώπου, used by Luke, Acts 3¹⁹ 5⁴¹ 7⁴⁵. It is an obvious Hebraism modelled on מִלִּפְנֵי. But Paul also employs it 2 Thess. 1⁹ with no Hebrew prototype, and Theodotion has ἀπὸ προσώπου in Dan. 7⁸, and the kindred ἐκ προσώπου in Dan. 2¹⁵ 6²⁷, as rendering for מִן קֳדָם, which would be the term to fill the place of Luke's ἀπὸ προσώπου.

ἐπὶ πρόσωπον πάσης τῆς γῆς occurs in an utterance of

---

[1] Perhaps with exception of Luke 19¹¹ where παραχρῆμα used by the narrator himself must mean " suddenly, unexpectedly."

our Lord, reported by Luke (21³⁵) for " upon the whole earth " ;
cf. Acts 17²⁶ ἐπὶ παντὸς προσώπου τῆς γῆς. This corresponds to the Hebrew עַל פְּנֵי; cf. Jer. 25²⁶ עַל פְּנֵי הָאֲדָמָה, LXX
ἐπὶ προσώπου τῆς γῆς. The Targums usually render the
phrase literally by עַל אַפֵּי. But it may be questioned whether
this was idiomatic Aramaic ; עַל אַפֵּי מַיָּא does occur Vay. R. 24,
but this is intended to mean " upon the surface of the water."
A mere " upon " would scarcely have been expressed in this
way. Luke has therefore in this instance made use of a
Hebraism.

On the other hand, it is no mere Hebraism when Luke
(20²¹) employs λαμβάνειν πρόσωπόν τινος, for which Mark
(12¹⁴) and Matthew (22¹⁶) put βλέπειν εἰς πρόσωπόν τινος.
The Hebrew equivalent is נָשָׂא פְּנֵי פ', e.g. Lev. 19¹⁵. Onkelos
has נְסַב אַפֵּי, and this occurs also j. Sanh. 29ᵃ נְסַב לֹן אַפִּין.
Thus the expression is also Aramaic. Its complete absorption
into the Hellenistic idiom appears from the formation of the
substantives προσωπολημψία, Rom. 2¹¹, προσωπολήμπτης,
Acts 10³⁴. A substantially different meaning belongs to
אַסְבַּר אַפִּין, סְבַר אַפִּין, which Levy in both his dictionaries puts
alongside of πρόσωπον λαμβάνειν. The former is not the
term for " to be partial to," but means " to regard favourably,
to give heed to," see Targ. Jerus. I. Gen. 32²⁰; b. Taan. 23ᵃ;
and for the expression סְבַר אַפִּין, " a glance," Vay. R. 5.

στηρίζειν τὸ πρόσωπον with Infinitive is used by Luke
(9⁵¹) for " to set one's face towards." This is the LXX
expression for the Hebrew שִׂים פָּנִים, e.g. Jer. 21¹⁰. Onkelos
has rendered this phrase literally by שַׁוִּי אַפִּין in Gen. 31²¹,
in which passage the LXX has varied the rendering; but
this literal rendering is avoided by the Targum in Jer. 21¹⁰,
Ezek. 6². On the other hand, the synonymous נָתַן פָּנִים is
literally translated in the LXX by διδόναι τὸ πρόσωπον,
2 Chron. 20³, Dan. 10¹⁵. In view of יְהַב עֵינֵיהּ בְּ, " he turned
his eyes upon," b. Sabb. 34ᵃ, יְהַב אַפִּין בְּ cannot, of course,
be quite impossible. But in the metaphorical sense repre-

sented in Luke 9[51] such an expression cannot be authenticated. Luke makes an inexact application of a Hebraism known to him through the Greek Old Testament.

Very exceptional is Luke 9[53] τὸ πρόσωπον αὐτοῦ ἦν πορευόμενον εἰς Ἱερουσαλήμ. The ·sense is, " he was minded to repair to Jerusalem." Resch compares Ex. 33[15] and 2 Sam. 17[11], in which latter passage the LXX has the same phrase. But in that case the meaning of פָּנֶיךָ הֹלְכִים is, " (if) thou thyself goest (not)," a sense quite inapplicable in Luke. In 2 Sam. 17[11] the Targum has rendered פָּנֶיךָ by אַתְּ, " thou," and therefore had no exact equivalent at hand. Hence this phrase of Luke is, like the preceding, a Hebraism incorrectly used, and incapable of imitation in Hebrew. Luke 9[53] refers back to ver. 51. The phrase there used, τὸ πρόσωπον αὐτοῦ ἐστήρισεν τοῦ πορεύεσθαι εἰς Ἱερουσαλήμ, ought properly to have been repeated. The expression in ver. 53 is a faulty abridgment of the complete locution. It agrees with the habit of Luke, pointed out by Vogel,[1] to use some expression that slips from his pen a second time after a short interval, and then perhaps never again.

11. ἐνώπιον.[2]

ἐνώπιον, used by the Hellenists in imitation of such Hebrew expressions as לִפְנֵי, לְעֵינֵי, is absent from Matthew and Mark, occurs once in John, and in Luke's Gospel about twenty times. Its use in Luke, and likewise in Paul and in the Apocalypse, merely proves the predominant influence of the Greek dialect represented by the LXX, but is no testimony in favour of a Semitic primary gospel, still less in favour of a Hebrew or an Aramaic form of the latter. The inferences based on this point by Blass[3] are hasty. According to Deissmann, indeed, Neue Bibelstudien, 40 f. (= Bible Studies

[1] *Th. Vogel*, Zur Charakteristik des Lukas nach Sprache und Stil (1897), 27 f.

[2] *J. Vorstius*, op. cit. ii. 214 ; *D. Schilling*, op. cit. 129.

[3] *F. Blass*, Evangelium secundum Lukam, xxii.

[T. & T. Clark], p. 213), the word belongs to "profane" or non-ecclesiastical Greek.

12. καὶ ἐγένετο, ἐγένετο δέ.[1]

The expression καὶ ἐγένετο or ἐγένετο δέ is used to introduce an added definiteness to an action about to be reported. It is found six times in Matthew,—five of these being in the phrase καὶ ἐγένετο ὅτε ἐτέλεσεν (συνετέλεσεν),—four times in Mark, forty-two times in Luke, *but is entirely absent from John*. The formula corresponds to the Hebrew וַיְהִי,[2] and occurs also in 1 Macc., Bel and the Dragon (LXX and Theod.), Judith (not in Tobit), Apocalypse of Baruch, 2 Esdras, and rarely in the Books of Enoch and Jubilees; but it has decidedly *no Aramaic equivalent*.[3] Even in biblical Aramaic it is already unfamiliar, and in the post-biblical Jewish Aramaic it has entirely disappeared. The rendering of ויהי by וַהֲוָה, which the Targums adopt, is clearly not endorsed by the spoken Aramaic. The Aramaic Scroll of the Hasmonæans in its present form begins, indeed, with the words וַהֲוָה בְּיוֹמֵי אַנְטִיּוּכַס, "and it came to pass in the days of Antiochus." But when it proceeds with מֶלֶךְ רַב וְתַקִּיף הֲוָה, this cannot be translated "there was a great and mighty king," because Antiochus himself is the king in question. On the contrary, the words וַהֲוָה בְּיוֹמֵי, probably an imitation of Esth. 1[1], and not attested, moreover, by all the authorities for the text, must be deleted, so that this instance has also to be eliminated. Any one desiring to collect instances in favour of a Hebrew primitive gospel would have to name in the first rank this καὶ ἐγένετο. Moreover, it must be observed that it is plainly Luke who makes so frequent use of the phrase, and that, too, through-

---

[1] *J. Vorstius*, op. cit. ii. 168–172 ; *D. Schilling*, op. cit. 163 f. ; *Th. Vogel*, Zur Charakteristik des Lukas, 46.

[2] See *F. E. König*, Syntax der hebr. Sprache, §§ 341s, 370.

[3] καὶ ἐγένετο is found, indeed, Dan. 3[7] in Theod., but not in the Aramaic ; similarly 3[91] LXX in the transition from the interpolated Song of the Three Children to the Canonical Text.

out both his writings, not, as might be expected, exclusively or chiefly in his initial chapters, for which many postulate a Semitic original. Even the "We-sections," for which, hitherto at least, critics have not assumed a Semitic original, are not without it; see Acts 21¹·⁵ 27⁴⁴ 28⁸·¹⁷. It is further to be remarked that the discourses of Jesus, which might well have afforded occasion for the use of the phrase, hardly ever contain it. As these are reported in Matthew it is not found at all,—in Mark it occurs only in 4⁴, where, however, the parallel passages Matt. 13⁴, Luke 8⁵ omit it; in Luke only in 16²² and 19¹⁵, while Paul in an address uses it twice, Acts 22⁶·¹⁷. Facts like these forbid the assumption of a Hebrew original as the necessary source of the phrase.

13. ἐν τῷ with the Infinitive.[1]

The infinitive preceded by ἐν τῷ and followed by the subject of the clause is used by Matthew only once (13⁴), and likewise only once by Mark (4⁴) in the parallel passage. Luke, on the other hand, has it twenty-five times, sometimes with καὶ ἐγένετο, sometimes independently, and not confined to any one section of the Gospel; John never has it. Examples: ἐν τῷ σπείρειν αὐτόν, Matt. 13⁴ (Luke 8⁵, Mark 4⁴); ἐν τῷ ὑποστρέφειν τὸν Ἰησοῦν, Luke 8⁴⁰; ἐν τῷ γενέσθαι τὴν φωνήν, Luke 9³⁶. This construction, which Blass records as an Aramaism,[2] has been formed by the LXX, after the model of the Hebrew בְ with the infinitive; see, e.g., Gen. 38²⁸ בְּלִדְתָּהּ; LXX ἐν τῷ τίκτειν αὐτήν. The Targums similarly copy it (Gen. 38²⁸ Onk. בְּמֵילְדַהּ), but in the spoken Aramaic it is wanting. Once, however, the biblical dialect (Dan. 6²¹) has the kindred construction of the infinitive with בְ. The particle כְּדִ (כְּדִי) with finite verb or participle is the substitute employed on the whole most

---

[1] J. Vorstius, op. cit. ii. 163–166; D. Schilling, op. cit. 162; F. Blass, Gramm. d. neutestamentl. Griechisch, 232.

[2] Evang. sec. Lucam, xxii.

3

frequently; see Dan. 6[11, 15], and Gramm. d. j.-pal. Aram. 185. Onkelos puts this particle when the Hebrew text has the infinitive with בְּ; see Gen. 29[13] בְּשְׁמֹעַ לָבָן; Onk. כַּד יִשְׁמַע לָבָן.

The construction ἐν τῷ occurs in the discourses of Jesus as given in Matthew, Mark, and Luke only in the instance ἐν τῷ σπείρειν, which is common to all three, and elsewhere only in Luke 10[35] 19[15]. There is thus no ground for maintaining that it originally belonged to the language of Jesus Himself. Besides, where it does occur, it may easily be traced to the Aramaic construction with כַּד. Here, too, as a narrator, Luke shows himself partial to Hebraising formulæ.

14. *The emphasising of the Verb by means of its cognate Substantive.*[1]

It is a mere repetition of the text of the LXX which is written in the citations, Matt. 13[14] (cf. Mark 4[12]) ἀκοῇ ἀκούσετε, βλέποντες βλέπετε; Matt. 15[4] (Mark 7[10]) θανάτῳ τελευτάτω; Acts 7[34] ἰδὼν εἶδον. The only instance that occurs independently of the Old Testament text in the discourse of Jesus is ἐπιθυμίᾳ ἐπεθύμησα, Luke 22[15]; cf. Acts 4[17] E, ἀπειλῇ ἀπειλησώμεθα; 5[28] παραγγελίᾳ παρηγγείλαμεν; 23[14] ἀναθέματι ἀνεθεματίσαμεν; John 3[29] χαρᾷ χαίρει. An allied usage is ἐφοβήθησαν φόβον μέγαν, Mark 4[41], Luke 2[9]; ἐχάρησαν χαρὰν μεγάλην, Matt. 2[10].

The Hebrew mode of emphasising the finite verb by adding its infinitive or cognate substantive, though still frequent in 1 Maccabees (see above), is in the Palestinian Aramaic of the Jews—apart from the Targums—quite unknown. The solitary example of its use is the *terminus technicus* of the Rabbinic schools in the Palestinian Talmud, מְסָבּוֹר סְבַר, "he gave it as his opinion," j. Erub. 18°; j. Yom. 42°; j. Keth. 28[b]. Apart from this, it is never used.[2]

---

[1] *Joh. Vorstius*, op. cit. ii. 177–193; *D. Schilling*, op. cit. 165 ff.
[2] See my Gramm. d. j.-pal. Aram. 226.

Hence we must not assume that Jesus was in the habit of using it. In Luke 2²⁵ the allusion to the LXX rendering of נְכְסֹף נִכְסַפְתָּה, "thou hast greatly longed for," Gen. 31³⁰, will have originated with the narrator. As the Synoptists do not use it anywhere else, while John has it only once, it is clear that an original in classical Hebrew need not be postulated as its source. Nor is it at all necessary to assume any such antecedent in the case of φοβεῖν φόβον μέγαν and χαίρειν χαρὰν μεγάλην, since reference to the LXX expressions for יָרֵא יִרְאָה גְדוֹלָה, Jonah 1¹⁰, and שָׂמַח שִׂמְחָה גְדוֹלָה, Jonah 4⁶, fully suffices for elucidation.

15. εἶναι with the Participle.

It is an established principle in regard to the Hebrew of the Old Testament that the union of הָיָה with the participle is quite permissible, even where there is no question of the continuance of an action.[1] In post-biblical Hebrew this became a very common construction when the reference is to the past.[2] This result was brought about by the influence of the Aramaic, as may be seen from the usage prevalent so early as the biblical dialect of Aramaic.[3] One example[4] from j. Ber. 2ᵈ will demonstrate how extensively the Galilean dialect can make use of this form: רַבִּי שְׁמוּאֵל בַּר נַחְמָנִי כַּד הֲוָה נָחֵית לְעַבּוּרָא הֲוָה מִתְקַבֵּל בֵּי יַעֲקוֹב נָרוֹסָא וַהֲוָה רַבִּי זְעֵירָא מִטַּמַּר בֵּינֵי קֻפַּיָּא מִשְׁמַעְנֵיהּ הֵיךְ הֲוָה קָרֵי שְׁמַע וַהֲוָה קָרֵי וְחָזַר קָרֵי עַד דַּהֲוָה שָׁקַע גּוֹ שִׁנְתֵּיהּ—"When Rabbi Samuel bar Nachmani went down to settle the leap year, he found hospitality with Jacob the grain merchant; and Rabbi Ze'ēra hid himself among the hampers that he might hear how he read the Shema, and (he observed that) he kept repeating it over till he fell asleep."

[1] *König*, Syntax der hebr. Sprache, § 239b, c.
[2] *A. Geiger*, Lehr- und Lesebuch zur Sprache Mischnah, i. 39 f.; *J. H. Weiss*, Mischpaṭ lĕschōn ha-Mischnā, 88.
[3] *E. Kautzsch*, Gramm. des Bibl.-Aram. 141; *K. Marti*, Kurzgef. Gramm. der bibl.-aram. Sprache, 104 f.
[4] Text according to Lehmann's edition.

The Synoptists make use of this idiom exclusively in the narrative coupled with ἦν and ἦσαν, but do not report it among the words of Jesus, which contain only once ἔσονται with the participle, Luke 17³⁵. The Gospel of John has ἦν with the participle only once (3²³). There is consequently no ground for attaching, as Blass[1] does, special significance to the fact that in the Acts (22¹⁹· ²⁰) the construction occurs twice in a discourse of Paul which was delivered in *Aramaic*, while in the second half of the Acts the construction is notably rarer than in the first half. But it must be remarked, as a very striking circumstance, that the construction is absent from the discourses of Jesus, although the parables might well have furnished occasion for the use of it.

The frequent use of the present tense in narrative in the Gospel of Mark is regarded by W. C. Allen, "The Original Language of the Gospel acc. to St. Mark" (Expos., 6th ser., vi. 436 ff.), as an Aramaism, on the ground that it goes back to the Aramaic use of the participle instead of the finite verb. But the secular Greek also allows the use of a present in historical narrative, and that not only in more extended passages for the sake of vivid presentation, but also in detached instances throughout the context of the narrative. Mark's fondness for the present tense is an individual trait, like his constant use of εὐθέως.

It appears, then, from the foregoing that we must class as distinct Aramaisms the redundant ἀφείς (καταλιπών) and ἤρξατο, as well as the adverb εὐθύς (παραχρῆμα). The use of εἶναι with the participle to represent a historic tense is Aramaic rather than Hebrew. The redundant use of ἐλθών, καθίσας, ἑστώς, ἀναστάς (ἐγερθείς) belongs equally to Aramaic and Hebrew. The genuine Hebraisms are the phrases connected with πρόσωπον, the construction ἐν τῷ with the infinitive, the emphasising of the verb by its cognate sub-

---

[1] *Blass*, Evang. sec. Lucam, xxi.

stantive, and the formulæ καὶ ἐγένετο, ἐλάλησεν λέγων, ἀποκριθεὶς εἶπεν.

As regards the distribution of these, the distinct Aramaisms, except ἀφείς, which Luke avoids, are represented in all three Synoptists. Further, the idioms with ἐλθών, καθίσας, ἑστώς, ἀναστάς (ἐγερθείς), and εἶναι with the participle are common to them all without exception, and these idioms are *possible* Aramaisms. The genuine Hebraisms are almost exclusively peculiarities of Luke's Gospel. καὶ ἐγένετο also is used predominantly by Luke; it is only ἀποκριθεὶς, which is of uncertain origin, that is to be found in all the Synoptists, and is even employed by John, who almost entirely avoids the other Hebraisms and Aramaisms. The Acts of the Apostles agrees in linguistic peculiarities with the Gospel of Luke.

The idioms discussed above are marks principally of the narrative style of the evangelists, and in the discourses of Jesus are to be looked for only in so far as these contain narrative, as in the parables. They show at once the incorrectness of Schmiedel's contention,[1] that the narrative style of the Gospels and the Acts is the best witness of the Greek that was spoken among the Jews. The fact is that the narrative sections of the Synoptists have more Hebrew features than the discourses of Jesus communicated by them.

In the discourses of Jesus, then, it is the distinct Aramaisms, except ἀφείς—accidentally absent perhaps—that are found, and also the possible Aramaisms ἐλθών, καθίσας, ἑστώς, ἀναστάς. Only in Luke—and even there in isolated instances—are to be found εἶναι with the participle, the specifically Hebrew ἐπὶ προσώπου, and the emphasising of the verb by its cognate substantive; and similarly, almost confined to Luke, ἐν τῷ with the infinitive. Luke, too, is the reporter of the Hebraism καὶ ἐγένετο, which, apart from Mark 4[4], occurs in the words of Jesus only in Luke 16[22] 19[15]

---

[1] Winer's Grammatik der neutestamentlichen Sprachidiome, § 4. 1[b].

εἶπεν—λέγων stands only in Mark 12²⁶, in a saying of our Lord.

As for ἀποκριθείς, which should perhaps be regarded as a Hebraism, it is found in the parables of the Two Sons, Matt. 21²⁸ᶠᶠ·; the Ten Virgins, Matt. 25¹ᶠ·; the Intrusted Talents, Matt. 25¹⁴ᶠᶠ·; (but not in Luke 19¹¹ᶠᶠ·); the description of the Last Judgment, Matt. 25³¹ᶠᶠ·; in the parable of the Importunate Friend, Luke 11⁵ᶠᶠ·; in the answer after the door has been shut, Luke 13²⁵; and in the parable of the Prodigal Son, Luke 15¹¹ᶠᶠ· It is wanting, however, where it might have been expected, in the parables of the Tares in the Field, Matt. 13²⁴ᶠᶠ·; the Unjust Steward, Luke 16¹ᶠᶠ·; the Rich Man, Luke 16¹⁹ᶠᶠ·; and the Vineyard, Luke 20⁹ᶠᶠ·

Again in this connection it is seen that the Hebraisms proper are special characteristics of Luke. There is reason, therefore, for a closer scrutiny of the style of this evangelist with its wealth of Hebraisms. In the examples already adduced, the fact of their occurrence is not more remarkable than the fact that each individual Hebraism occurs so seldom. If Luke had worked in dependence upon a Hebrew original, then such idioms must have occurred much more frequently than they do, for he does not shrink from using those Hebraisms which are most foreign to the feeling of the Greek language. Can the few cases of the Hebraistic use of πρόσωπον have slipped from his pen by mere inadvertence, while in general he studiously avoided this Hebraism? Other data of a like import may be mentioned. Only once (9²⁸) does he use the quite un-Aramaic phrase μετὰ τοὺς λόγους τούτους, Hebr. אַחֲרֵי הַדְּבָרִים הָאֵלֶּה; once, too, (1⁷⁰) διὰ στόματος, Hebr. פִּי [1]—also peculiarly Hebrew. In addition there fall from his pen such pseudo-Hebraisms as τὸ πρόσωπον, 9⁵³, mentioned above; ἐπεσκέψατο ἡμᾶς ἀνατολὴ

---

[1] Luke's peculiarity in using certain phrases only once or twice is pointed out also by *Vogel*, Zur Charakteristik des Lukas, 27; and by *Blass*, Philology of the Gospels (1898), 113 f., 118.

ἐξ ὕψους, 1⁷⁸,[1] formed entirely after the Greek Bible and quite impossible to reproduce in Hebrew; and the phrase, equally elusive of the translator's art, ἐν τῷ συνπληροῦσθαι τὴν ἡμέραν τῆς πεντηκοστῆς, Acts 2¹. The frequency of the Hebraisms used by Luke, especially in the first chapters of the Gospel, has led de Lagarde[2] to the very just conclusion that these chapters have throughout a colouring distinctly Hebrew, not Aramaic and not Greek. At the same time, this writer has made no further statement as to the origin of these Hebraisms. Resch is of opinion that they have arisen because the chapters were translated from a Hebrew original, although he himself perceives that the "Hebraisms and Old Testament Parallels" to Matt. 1. 2, Luke 1. 2, collected by him in "Kindheits-evangelium," 30–56 (half of which by the way should be deleted), demonstrate primarily only the close relation that subsists between those chapters and the Greek Old Testament.[3] While Resch holds Luke himself to be the translator, Blass[4] is convinced that Luke was quite ignorant of Hebrew; he supposes that Luke had before him the alleged Hebrew source (which had originated with one of the priests) in a Greek translation done in the style of the LXX, and, further, that in those chapters he had given his own personal style greater scope as he proceeded. Vogel[5] also adopts a "special source" for the beginning of Luke's Gospel, but affirms that his investigation had not disclosed any sharp distinction in point of style between the beginning and the rest of the book. Hence the assumption of a Hebrew document as the source for Luke 1. 2 must at any rate be held as still unproved; and it might even be maintained that the strongly marked Hebrew style of those chapters is on the whole due not to the use of

---

[1] See Fundamental Ideas, VIII. 10. [2] Mitteilungen, iii. 345.

[3] The variations in the text of the Greek should remove the intrinsic proof for the Hebrew original.

[4] Evangelium sec. Lucam, xxiii ; cf. Philology of the Gospels, 195.

[5] Zur Charakteristik des Lukas, 32f.

any primary source, but to Luke himself. For here, as in the beginning of the Acts, in keeping with the marvellous contents of the narrative, Luke has written with greater consistency than usual in biblical style, intending so to do and further powerfully affected by the "liturgic frame of mind" of which Deissmann[1] speaks. The correctness of our view as to the Hebraisms of Luke is corroborated by the Græcisms which also flow from his pen. As a Græcism, e.g., must be characterised the form of address $\mathring{a}\nu\theta\rho\omega\pi\epsilon$, Luke 5^{20} 12^{14} $22^{58.\ 60}$. Delitzsch, Salkinson, and Resch avail themselves here of בֶּן־אָדָם, though such an address is rare and in the passages concerned quite unsuitable. The same holds good of the form of address $\mathring{a}\nu\delta\rho\epsilon\varsigma$ $\mathring{a}\delta\epsilon\lambda\phi o\iota$ which Luke likes to use in the Acts (2^{29} 7^2 13^{15} $15^{7.\ 13}$ 22^1 $23^{1.\ 6}$ 28^{17}). Any one familiar with Jewish literature knows that אֲנָשִׁים אַחִים may, indeed, stand for "people, who are brothers," Gen. 13^8, but cannot be used as a form of address. A Jew speaking to Jews regularly addresses them as אַחֵינוּ, "our brethren," j. Yom. 43^d; j. Taan. 65^{ab}; j. Kidd. 64^c; Taan. ii. 1, אָחֵינוּ; while David, 1 Chron. 28^2, says to the people אַחַי וְעַמִּי, "my brethren and my people"; and this is made a precedent for every Israelitish king, Tos. Sanh. iv. 4.

And, finally, let the following points be noticed. The betrayer, according to Blass, was called $\Sigma\kappa\alpha\rho\iota\acute{\omega}\theta$ by Luke (6^{16} 22^3), agreeing with Cod. D 6^{16}; Tischendorf, Tregelles, Westcott-Hort prefer ᾿$I\sigma\kappa\alpha\rho\iota\acute{\omega}\theta$, 6^{16}; ᾿$I\sigma\kappa\alpha\rho\iota\acute{\omega}\tau\eta\nu$, 22^3. In any case, Luke was ignorant of the form אִישׁ קְרִיּוֹת (see under No. V.). The result of the investigations into the Hosanna cry detailed later[2] tends to show that Luke failed to understand this also. It is again probably a misinterpretation when he assigns to $B\alpha\rho\nu\acute{a}\beta\alpha\varsigma$, Acts 4^{36}, the meaning $v\grave{\iota}o\varsigma$ $\pi\alpha\rho\alpha\kappa\lambda\acute{\eta}\sigma\epsilon\omega\varsigma$, — with the explanation of which I too have wrestled,[3] — while we seem to have to do with the

---

[1] Bibelstudien, 71 [Eng. tr., p. 76].　　[2] Fundamental Ideas, VIII. 9.
[3] Gramm. d. jüd.-pal. Aram. 142.

Palmyrenian name ברנבו, "son of Nebo" (cf. the Palmyrenian names נבובל ,נבוזבד ,נבוקוא), as Deissmann[1] has correctly recognised. In regard to Luke's tradition of the voice at the Baptism and at the Transfiguration, and for his use of παῖς, Acts 3[4], see Fundamental Ideas, IX. 3. If these observations be correct, it follows that an immediate use by Luke of Semitic sources must be pronounced highly improbable. If he were born a Greek, as must be admitted on other grounds,[2] such use, moreover, can hardly be imagined.

If, then, in the case of that Synoptist who is most guilty of Hebraisms, these are due, in most cases, at least, to the author himself,[3] and should properly be called "Septuagint - Græcisms," the probability is that the same should apply to the other Synoptists as well. Let it suffice merely to recall the phrase καὶ ἐγένετο ὅτι ἐτέλεσεν (συνετέλεσεν), used five times by Matthew, who, apart from this, has καὶ ἐγένετο only once (9[10]), in agreement with Mark 2[15]. The way in which this expression is used shows beyond question that it originated with the author of our first Gospel. This applies likewise to the circumstantial formula, ἵνα (ὅπως, τότε) πληρωθῇ τὸ ῥηθὲν διὰ—λέγοντος, peculiar to Matthew, and used ten times by him. It sounds very like Hebrew, and should be compared with the common formula in ancient Jewish exegesis: לְקַיֵּם מַה שֶּׁנֶּאֱמַר, "in order to establish what was said."[4] And yet its formation must be

---

[1] Bibelstudien (1895), 177 f.; Neue Bibelstudien (1897), 15 f. [Eng. tr., pp. 309 f.,187 f.].

[2] Th. Vogel, op. cit. 18.

[3] Of course it is Luke in his character as Christian annalist that is here meant. His manner of speaking and writing on general topics appears in the preface to the Gospel—a passage which should not be regarded as evidence of exceptional literary elaboration.

[4] S. Bacher, Die älteste Terminologie der Jüdischen Schriftauslegung (1899), 170. Similar also is the formula introductory to Targum exposition: אֲכִיר רָאָתְכַּר עַל יְדֵי—וּנְבִיאָה, Röm. Machzor (Bologna, 1540), Schebuoth, and the formula in the Kiddush after Seder Rab Amram, i. 10[b]: כַּדְּבָר הָאָמוּר בְּשִׁירֵי עֻזְּךָ מִפִּי דָוִד מְשִׁיחַ צִדְקֶךָ, "according to the word which is spoken in the songs of Thy might by the mouth of David Thy righteous anointed."

ascribed to the Greek-writing author, a position which even
Resch, Kindheits-evangelium, 19 ff., does not venture to gainsay. Thus these Hebraisms of Matthew are also in reality
due to the influence of the Greek Bible (Greek Biblicisms).
And what is to be thought of the Ἰσκαριώτης or Ἰσκαριώθ
in Matthew and Mark ? And of the υἱοὶ βροντῆς, Mark 3¹⁷,
which may indeed be connected in a way with the strange
term Βοανηργές,[1] but is in no sense an accurate translation
of it ? It seems quite a Hebrew trait when in Matt. 26¹⁷
(Mark 14¹²) the day on which the Passover lamb was slain
is called " the first day of unleavened bread " (Luke 22⁷
even has " the day of unleavened bread "); and yet no
" Hebraist " would have specified that day in this manner,
quite apart from the fact that the designation " Feast of
unleavened bread " was uniformly replaced among the Jews
in later times, at least, by the name " Passover."

It will suffice here to have shown meanwhile that the
Hebraisms of the Synoptists, though undeniably present,[2] do
not constitute the proof of a Hebrew original; that, on the
contrary, the thesis is justified that the fewer the Hebraisms,
the greater the originality ;[3] the more numerous the Hebraisms in any passage, the greater the interference of Hellenistic
redactors. It must be noted that the Jewish Aramaic
current among the people was considerably freer from Hebrew
influence than the Greek which the Synoptists *write*, and
also that in the rabbinical sphere the special religious terminology—even in the case of recurring Hebrew formulæ—
exhibits a striking independence of the Old Testament.[4]

---

[1] See Gramm. d. jüd.-pal. Aram. 112, and p. 49 in this volume.

[2] *Franz Delitzsch's* verdict, "The Shemitic woof of the N.T. Hellenism is
Hebrew, not Aramaic " (The Hebrew New Testament, 31), is not without foundation, but still is not the correct conclusion.

[3] Cf. above, p. 19 f.

[4] Our Lord's manner of speech, therefore, is not a final test of His literary
knowledge. *A. Meyer*, Jesu Muttersprache, 56, discusses this point with too
much hesitancy. If Jerome expressly testifies that all the Jews of his time
knew the Hebrew Old Testament, could Jesus have been less familiar with it ?

V. ALLEGED PROOFS OF A PRIMITIVE HEBREW GOSPEL (UREVANGELIUM).

As the most effectual means of ascertaining the limits, content, and language of alleged Semitic sources of the Gospel, Resch,[1] especially, has recently indicated and sought to apply the method of tracing back to one Semitic term the several variants of a word in the Gospel text, as these may occur throughout the entire tradition within and without the Gospels. Wherever in the Synoptists he found such a retracing of the variants to a Semitic expression practicable throughout, he was led consistently enough to adopt a Semitic primary source containing the entire synoptic material, and even something in addition to it. This source, in his opinion, was written in Hebrew, and may be divided into the two documents תּוֹלְדוֹת יֵשׁוּעַ, "The Gospel of the Childhood," and דִּבְרֵי יֵשׁוּעַ, "The Sayings of our Lord." Recently this all-embracing source of the Gospels has been published by him tentatively in Hebrew and Greek under the title "Die Logia Jesu" (1898).[2] The three Synoptists, according to this theory, have merely made a different selection and arrangement of the same Hebrew material to which all alike had access. They cannot rank as independent authors. This conclusion has nowhere met with approval, and rightly. Even the method by which it was reached was wrong.[3]

The fact that Greek synonyms *may* often be traced back

See *S. Krauss*, The Jews in the Works of the Church Fathers, Jew. Quart. Rev. vi. (1894) 231 f. If a Hellenistic-Jewish mother and grandmother initiated Timothy from his childhood into the knowledge of the Holy Scripture (2 Tim. 3[15], cf. 1[5]), despite the fact that his father was a heathen, it follows that at least as much should be expected in a "Hebraist" family in Palestine.

[1] *A. Resch*, Aussercanonische Paralleltexte zu den Evangelien, i.-v., Leipzig, 1893-97.

[2] Besides the large edition, with notes in support of its readings, a smaller has also appeared, containing the Hebrew narrative without comment.

[3] It seems almost superfluous to repeat the condemnation of this method, as it has already been often enough insisted on by Resch's reviewers with gratifying unanimity ; see especially *Ad. Jülicher*, Gött. Gel. Anz. 1896, i. 1-9.

to one Hebrew word, though sometimes several Hebrew
synonyms also may be discovered, in no way proves that
a Hebrew word really lies behind the Greek synonyms.
One might almost as well name an Aramaic or an Arabic
word, and then in the same way proceed to argue an
Aramaic or Arabic original. The numerous proofs offered
by Resch in favour of a Hebrew original—in so far as
they are purely of this character — are therefore quite
devoid of cogency. Only in the case of striking deviations
among the variants could a testimony in favour of a Semitic
original be inferred with *some* degree of certitude, provided
there was found a Semitic term which perchance so solved
the problem of the divergent readings, that the one appears,
with good reason, to be a misunderstanding easily possible,
the other the correct interpretation of the Semitic expression. Even then, however, it would remain questionable
whether the divergent readings had not arisen through other
causes, so that it is only by accident that a Semitic term
appears to account for the deviation. This must indeed
be always the most plausible supposition, when one reflects
that the direct use of Semitic written sources, even by the
authors of our Gospels, is doubtful, and at any rate not
yet proved; further, that at a later date such writings
could have been read by only a very few in the Church
—even a Palestinian like Justin understood no Hebrew;
that in regard to a later circulation of Greek versions of
a Semitic primitive gospel equal uncertainty prevails, for
the statement of Papias in regard to Matthew's translation
of the Logia must not be referred to written works of this
class; and that, finally, it is much more likely that extra-
canonical gospels, gospel harmonies, translations, and popular
expositions in common use influenced the form which the
text assumed in the course of its transmission, than that
such an influence was exerted by the after-effects of the
alleged Semitic original document. A fundamental error

in Resch, and also in other biblical critics of our time, appears to me to be a marked depreciation of the capacity of the authors of the historical books of the Bible, who are treated too much as mere redactors and mechanical copyists or translators of source documents, and a not less exaggerated estimate of the precision of subsequent copyists, translators, and quotations of such books, which has gone so far that sometimes the most extravagant excess of an unscrupulous transcriber is, just because of its extravagance, pronounced to be the original reading, or the later correction of the author himself.

It is not possible to discuss here all that is advanced by Resch in favour of a Hebrew primitive gospel, and yet the inadequacy of his proofs must be demonstrated at this point, so as to place it beyond doubt that we are well entitled in our investigations to leave the Hebrew out of consideration, even despite the fact that a written source in Hebrew might possibly have been the intermediary between the words of Jesus spoken in Aramaic and the Gospels written in Greek. I therefore adduce chiefly such instances as those of which Resch, in opposition to Arnold Meyer,[1] has asserted that "they supply evidence distinctly against Aramaic, and as distinctly in favour of Hebrew as the original language of the דִּבְרֵי יֵשׁוּעַ." It will then appear that the evidence of these passages, to say the least, is invariably susceptible of, and not infrequently demands, a very different interpretation.

In Luke 9²⁵ Resch commends Salkinson's rendering of τί ὠφελεῖται by מַה בֶּצַע, on the ground that the variants τί κέρδος, τί ὄφελος are thereby accounted for. Now, this phrase מַה בֶּצַע, borrowed by Salkinson from Gen. 37²⁶, is, in view of Ps. 30¹⁰, admissible in this passage. But the variants given above admit of explanation without the help of a Semitic original.

---

[1] Aussercanon. Paralleltexte, iv. 224.

In Luke 10[7] Resch finds it noteworthy that the labourer, according to Luke, is worthy of "his hire" ($\tau o \hat{v} \ \mu \iota \sigma \theta o \hat{v}$ $a \mathring{v} \tau o \hat{v}$); according to Matthew, however, of "his maintenance" ($\tau \hat{\eta} s \ \tau \rho o \phi \hat{\eta} s \ a \mathring{v} \tau o \hat{v}$). The former, he holds, originates from Hebrew מְחִיר, the latter from מִחְיָה, which was read by mistake for מְחִיר. But מְחִיר cannot possibly be the basis. The day labourer's "hire" is called in Hebrew invariably שָׂכָר, Aramaic אֲגַר; "maintenance" would indeed be, in biblical Hebrew, מִחְיָה, while the later Hebrew, like the Aramaic, would use פַּרְנָסָה. And thus any retracing of the two expressions to one term as their source is impossible. Besides, there is no occasion for such an attempt. The proverb made use of by Jesus spoke naturally enough of the "hire," because that properly pertains to the day labourer. In Matthew "maintenance" is substituted for "hire," because in the context it could not be a question of "hire" which the disciples of Jesus would think of claiming, but merely of their "maintenance."

In regard to Luke 10[37] R. makes the remark that $\mathring{o} \ \pi o \iota \acute{\eta} \sigma a s \ \tau \grave{o} \ \acute{e} \lambda \epsilon o s \ \mu \epsilon \tau' \ a \mathring{v} \tau o \hat{v}$, in view of 2 Sam. 2[6], is an "emphatic and pure Hebraism." His point is the use of $\mu \epsilon \tau \acute{a}$ in this phrase. But עַם would in this connection be possible also in Aramaic. According to b. Tam. 32[a], King Alexander gives the advice that he who desires to be loved among men "should show kindness to men" (יַעֲבֵד טִיבוּ עִם בְּנֵי אֲנָשָׁא). Similarly, the Targum has unhesitatingly rendered 2 Sam. 2[6] by יַעֲבֵד יְיָ עִמְּכוֹן טִיבוּ. The fact is that Luke may quite well have simply adapted the LXX expression in 2 Sam. 2[6].

In Luke 11[3] R. calls attention to the fact that a "standard Semitic, more precisely Aramaic, original" of the Lord's Prayer was not transmitted, and maintains that לֶחֶם חֻקֵּנוּ is presumably the prototype of $\mathring{o} \ \acute{a} \rho \tau o s \ \mathring{o} \ \grave{e} \pi \iota o \acute{v} \sigma \iota o s$. If R. has discovered the true sense of $\grave{e} \pi \iota o \acute{v} \sigma \iota o s$ here, it may still be asked why Aramaic equivalents, such as לְחֶם מִפְּתָחָא or לְחֶם חֲסַרְנָנָא, should not equally suffice. R. should rather have affirmed still more distinctly that both Luke and Matthew in this case clearly rely upon a *Greek* source.

In Luke 12¹⁹ the rich man speaks "to his soul." In this R. detects a Hebraism. But this is also an Aramaic idiom, see Gram. d. jüd.-pal. Aram. 84 f. ; and it might for that matter derive its origin equally well from the Greek Bible.[1] The same holds of τὰς ψυχὰς ὑμῶν, Luke 21¹⁹.

In Luke 13²⁶ R. would alter the "teaching in the streets" to a "showing of the streets," because he regards the former as a misinterpretation of the original וּבִרְחֹבֹתֵינוּ הוֹרֵיתָ. But these Hebrew words would have been correctly rendered by the meaning expressed in Luke 13²⁶, namely, "In our streets hast Thou taught." "Our streets or lanes hast Thou shown us" would have had to be quite differently expressed, and is, moreover, a strange way of expressing what R. takes to be the true meaning, "Thou Thyself hast charged us to come hither." The entire situation, besides, is misunderstood by R.

In Luke 13²⁹ Ephrem's reading, which treats θάλασσα as one of the four points of the compass, is adequately accounted for by its concord with Ps. 107³ and Isa. 49¹². There is therefore no need to assume for it a special Hebrew source.[2] Besides, the text as altered by R., following Ephrem, would be no improvement, for no one could say what יָם should signify in the passage, since the West is previously specified. But even supposing it to have been uttered by Jesus through suggestion of Ps. 107³, in that case יָם is equally no designation of the West, and the Aramaic יַמָּא would have been quite suitable.

For βιάζεται, Luke 16¹⁶, R. gives as antecedent נִפְרַץ, "to spread out"; and for βιασταί, Matt. 11¹², פָּרִצִים, "those that break through." In that case neither evangelist has properly understood the former expression. But setting aside this

---

[1] Cf. the passages cited by *C. A. Briggs*, The use of נפש in the Old Testament, Journ. Bibl. Lit. xvi. 22 f.

[2] Resch's proof rests on the consideration that only in Hebrew can יָם stand for one of the directions, the Aramaic for West being מַעֲרָב.

assumption, the passage can be fully explained with the help
of the Aramaic; see " Fundamental Ideas," I. end.

In Luke 22⁷ R. believes that the difference between the
Synoptic and Johannine dating of the day of the Passion
may be explained by tracing τῇ πρώτῃ (ἡμέρᾳ) τῶν ἀζύμων
in Matthew and Mark back to the Hebrew קֹדֶם חַג הַמַּצּוֹת.
This, according to R., should mean " before the Feast of unleavened bread," whereas it has been incorrectly understood
of the first day of the feast. Hebrew would thus give an
easier solution than Aramaic. But the mistake is conceivable
only on the part of an " Aramaist " who at the word קדם
thought of קְדְמָי, " first," and besides קְדָם might mean " before "
in Aramaic as well. So that the solution through Aramaic
would be more complete. Nevertheless (1) it is in itself
hazardous, and (2) it leads to no result, because the possibility
advanced by Resch of an anticipatory celebration of the
Passover by Jesus and His disciples is just as incredible
as the more extravagant hypotheses of Chwolson and
Lichtenstein.[1]

On Luke 22⁴² R. remarks that the Lucan conception
παρενέγκαι and the παρελθέτω of Matthew point back to
the Hebrew חעבר (= תֵּעָבֵר or תַּעֲבֹר). Aramaic, he holds, would
not admit this twofold interpretation, because כוסא (read
כָּסָא), which would be the subject in the second case, is in
that language masculine, not as in Hebrew feminine. But
in the Mishna[2] also כום is of the masculine gender, so that
biblical Hebrew would be the only source of the ambiguity.
The variants, however, need by no means be ascribed to a
difference in translation. That the same thought may be
expressed by different writers in different terms, is an observation so common that it must always be the most natural
supposition in any temperate treatment of textual questions.

In another place[3] Resch lays some stress on the con-

[1] J. Lichtenstein, Kommentar zum Neuen Testament (Hebr.), Matt. 26¹⁸.
[2] Pes. x. 2, 4, 7.　　　　[3] Aussercanon. Paralleltexte, iii. 819.

sideration that from the *names* of the disciples of Jesus it
may be concluded that there were three languages in use in
their circle. Now there is no doubt that much Greek was
spoken in Palestine.[1] But in a period when names of the
most varied origin were in use among the Jews, no conclusion can be drawn for any special case. In spite of the
names of Philip and Andrew, it is highly improbable that
there were any "Hellenists" among the Twelve. And even
though all the names of the apostles had been Hebrew
names, there would still be no ground for thinking of special
"Hebraists" as contrasted with "Aramaists." For Jews in
all ages have borne Hebrew names.

For *Βοανηργές*, Mark 3[17], I had pointed out[2] *Βανηρογές*
as *possibly* the original reading, without, however, suggesting
a Hebrew source, as forms like קֹדֶש, אֲרֶן are possible in Jewish
Aramaic. R. regards this reading as settled, and treats the
term as Hebrew. The wholly inapt linguistic comments
which he adds to the peculiar *oa* may here be passed over;
it is enough to assert that all depends on a conjectural
reading, which is equally capable of explanation through
Aramaic. Further, Jesus could quite well have given a
Hebrew surname to the sons of Zebedee, though He never
spoke in the Hebrew language. Surnames such as הַקְטָן in
Talmudic times, and מְאוֹר הַגּוֹלָה in the Middle Ages, prove
nothing whatever as to the vernacular of those who made
use of these appellations. From the Old Testament it is
apparent that *Ζεβεδαῖος* had been for a long period an
established name among the Jews. And yet it is presumably
either of Aramaic or of North-Palestinian origin. In

---

[1] On this point see *Th. Zahn*, Einleitung in d. N. Test. i. (1897) 24–51;
S. Krauss, Griech. u. latein. Lehnwörter im Talmud, Midrasch und Targum,
i. (1898) xiii–xxii.

[2] Gramm. d. jüd.-pal. Aram. 112. I should prefer now to assume that either
o or *a* is a gloss, which subsequently found its way into the text. *βονη* and *βανη*
are equally possible. If Mark desired to signify the Galilean indistinctness of
the *a*, then *o* would quite suffice; *oa* remains meaningless. If Mark really
wrote *oa*, his unfamiliarity with Aramaic was the cause.

4

Palmyra the name occurred in the forms זבדא, זבדי, זבדבול,
זבדלא, זברנבו, זברעתה; in Greek, Ζάββας, Ζαββίβηλος, Ζαββεάθης;
the Jews had זבד, זבור, זבדי, זבדיאל, זבדיה, זבדיהו, in which the
divine names יהו, יה, אל correspond to the Palmyrene בול,
נבו, עתה. Resch's affirmation[1] of a Hebrew origin of the
name must therefore be seriously restricted.

In regard to Βαρθολομαῖος, Resch makes the comment
that בַּר was "usual," even in Hebrew. That is quite
inaccurate. It occurs in the Old Testament only in Prov. 21[2]
and Ps. 2[12], and in the latter instance it is doubtless a wrong
reading. It is, on the other hand, significant that the New
Testament names which have בַּר in composition are not
accompanied by one single example with בֶּן.

Λεββαῖος, for which R. twice puts לְבִּי (!), should, in his
opinion, be connected with the Hebrew לֵב, " heart," since the
bearer of this name was also called Θαδδαῖος, Mark 3[18]. The
latter name R. would derive from the Aram. תַּד, " breast-
nipple," [2] which he thinks also denotes the male breast in
Aramaic. The latter contention is incorrect, and proof of
the currency of such names is wanting. In any case תַּדִּי is
to be taken with תּוודם (Θευδᾶς) and הודום, and is therefore
of Greek extraction, while Λεββαῖος corresponds to the
Nabatæan לבאי. Any other derivation would require to be
substantiated. The same individual was probably called in
Semitic לְבִּי, and in Greek Θευδᾶς, from which תַּדִּי had been
formed. To establish a more intimate connection between
the two names is unnecessary. The surname Καναναῖος
also points, according to R., to a Hebrew origin. But his
derivation from קַנְאָא is impossible, as קַנְאָן is the necessary
counterpart, and that would be an Aramaic nominal form.
If, however, the text be altered to Κανναῖος, as seems to
me commendable, then the Aramaic קַנָּי, " Zealot," is reached
at least as easily as the Hebrew קַנָּא.

---

[1] Loc. cit. 822.

[2] *Holtzmann* expresses a similar opinion in Commentary on the two names.

As for Ματθαῖος, the case is similar to that of the synonymous Ζεβεδαῖος. It is the name מתיה, מתתיהו, מתתיה, which did not appear among the Jews till a late period, and may be compared with the Palmyrene מתבול (Ματθαβώλ) and its abbreviation מתא (Ματθᾶς).

The names יוֹחָנָן, יַעֲקֹב, יְהוּדָה (יוּדָה), שִׁמְעוֹן (Greek form קִימוֹן,[1] but not שִׁימוֹן — so Resch), לֵוִי give no information as to the language spoken by those who were so called, so that Ἰσκαριώθ, Ἰσκαριώτης alone remains for consideration. There is every probability that Ἰσκαριώθ without the article was the original reading, from which arose through misunderstanding Ἰσκαριώτης as well as Σκαριώθ and Σκαριώτης. With Ἰσκαριώθ agrees ὁ ἀπὸ Καρυώτου found in Cod. Sin. John 6⁷¹; Cod. D John 12⁴ 13². ²⁶ 14²², inasmuch as the former points back to the Hebrew אִישׁ קְרִיּוֹת and the latter to the equivalent Aramaic דְּקְרִיּוֹת or דְּמִן קְרִיּוֹת. Both may be verified as Jewish usages. There is mentioned, j. Sabb. 14ᵈ, a Christian יַעֲקֹב אִישׁ כְּפַר סַמָּא, b. Sot. 43ᵇ a יְהוּדָה אִישׁ כְּפַר עַכּוֹ, Ab. iii. 7 an אֶלְעָזָר אִישׁ בַּרְתּוֹתָא, j. Bez. 61ᶜ a תּוֹדֹס אִישׁ רוֹמִי, and further with Aramaic designation j. Ab. z. 42ᵃ יְהוֹשֻׁעַ דְּסִכְנִין.[2] וַבִּי דַּאֲלֶכְסַנְדְּרִיאָה, Ech. R. Peth. The introduction of the name of the place by means of דְּמִן is less common, as אֲבְדִּימֵי דְּמִן חֵיפָה, Midr. Till. 31. 6 ; יוֹסֵי דְּמִן כְּסָרִי, b. Sanh. 108ᵃ, or by means of מִן, as מַתְּיָה מִן דבתרתה, j. Orl. 60ᵈ; יְהוּדָה מְפוֹרָא, b. Tam. 27ᵃ;[3] נתנוי דמן אורשלם, Corp. Inscr. Sem. ii. 1, 320. But such being the usage, and אִישׁ קְרִיּוֹת being a common enough form of surname, showing that one with this name was a "Kariothite," it thus becomes very sur-

---

[1] G. A. Deissmann, Bibelstudien, 184 [Eng. tr. p. 315], draws attention to the fact that this is the genuinely Greek name Σίμων. For Hellenists it was an easy step to substitute this name for Συμεών ; in the form קִימוֹן it then found its way into the language of the " Hebraists " also.

[2] The construction with דְּ appears to have been the one commonly used in Palestine.

[3] These periphrases are used by preference when a place-name does not readily lend itself to the formation of the corresponding Gentilic designation. Otherwise we should expect titles like Hebr. הַמִּוְצָעִי, Aram. צָפֹרְאָה.

prising that it should have been left untranslated. One
would have expected ὁ ἀπὸ Καριώθ, like ὁ ἀπὸ Καρυώτου
in Cod. D,[1] and like John 21[2] Ναθαναὴλ ὁ ἀπὸ Κανᾶ, just
as Josephus, Bell. Jud. IV. vi. 2, speaks of a certain Ἄνανος
ὁ ἀφαμμαοῦς, supposing they did not venture to write
ὁ Καριώθιος or something similar. It is a very plausible
conjecture that Ἰσκαριώθ was already unintelligible to the
evangelist. Some late writer thought of a place Ἰσκάρ
or Ἰσκάρια, and therefore formed Ἰσκαριώτης, while the
originator of the text of the Synoptists in Cod. D preferred
Σκαριώθ and Σκαριώτης, because he followed a Syrian
exemplar.[2]

Mistakes of this kind are inconceivable on the part of
one who had before him אִישׁ קְרִיּוֹת in a Hebrew source and
wished to translate it. They explain themselves, however,
if we suppose that יְהוּדָה אִישׁ קְרִיּוֹת was encountered by a
Hellenist in a Greek or Aramaic environment. Even the
latter is quite possible, because such surnames, whether they
were Hebrew or Aramaic in form, usually remained un-
altered without regard to the language being used at the
time; cf. e.g. שְׁמַלְיֹ הַדְּרוֹמִי, j. Ab. z. 41[d] in an Aramaic
narrative. As the Hebrew formation with אִישׁ occurs also
in still later periods, it is clear that Hebrew was not necessarily the spoken language where such a surname originated.[3]

---

[1] E. Nestle, Philologica sacra, 14 f., Expository Times, ix. (1897–98), 140, 240,
holds that Cod. D has preserved the original reading of the Johannine Gospel.
The peculiar ending, however, is already in itself an obstacle, as it suggests the
Greek καρυωτός. The suspicion that the Greek reading Ἰσκαριώτης lies at the
basis, is not improbable. See, further, F. H. Chase, The Syro-Latin Text of the
Gospels (1895), 102 ff., Expository Times, ix. (1897–98), 189, 285 f., who affirms
a Syriac origin for the reading.

[2] Syr. Sin. and Peshita have סכריוטא, Evangel. Hieros. זכריוטא, Syr. Cur.
אסכריוטא and אסקריוטא.

[3] The case is probably different with the later designation of the Jewish
Christians as Ἐβιωναῖοι. Undoubtedly the prevalent opinion is (see recently
G. Uhlhorn, Prot. Real.-Enc.[3] under "Ebioniten") that the Christians were
generally known as אֶבְיוֹנִים, "poor" among the Jews, or that they themselves
adopted this designation in Palestine. But since the Jews, any more than the
Jewish Christians, did not speak Hebrew, and since this name for the Jewish

Lastly must be mentioned the utterance of Jesus from the Cross, Mark 15³⁴ (Matt. 27⁴⁶), to which Resch[1] attributes decisive finality in regard to the language in which the primary Gospel was written. He is convinced that the Hebrew form of the utterance represented in Cod. D by ἠλεὶ ἠλεὶ λαμᾶ ζαφθανεί, that is, אֵלִי אֵלִי לָמָה עֲזַבְתָּנִי, was the original. Not till a later date, when Hebrew was no longer understood, did the Aramaic setting of our present texts come into being. Resch attaches importance to the fact that the Evangel. Hierosol. expressly explains אֵלִי by אֱלֹהִי. This last consideration means very little. The translator followed his Greek exemplar and could render ὁ Θεός μου only by אֱלֹהִי. At all events every Jew who spoke Aramaic was quite familiar with the word אֵל, which for that very reason is taken over into the Onkelos Targum without change from the Hebrew text. If Jesus uttered the words of the Psalm in the Aramaic language, then it was precisely אֵלִי that was most naturally to be expected. Thus the mistake of the people in supposing Elijah summoned, decides nothing as regards the original Hebrew form of the whole utterance. It is also impossible to see for what section of Greek - speaking Christians the Hebrew form should have been replaced by the Aramaic with a view to easier comprehension. Such Christians, indeed, understood equally little of both languages, and therefore required the immediate addition of the Greek equivalent. As the Gospel of Mark in other cases is peculiar in giving the words of Jesus as originally pronounced, it may be inferred that the saying in question was also from the first a constituent part of this Gospel; and since the sayings of our Lord communicated by Him in other cases (5⁴¹ 7³⁴) are given in Aramaic, then anything different should not be looked for in this

Christians is unfamiliar among the Jews, it is difficult to accept the opinion as correct. The old derivation from a proper name 'Εβιών is still the best, though we do not know any proper name of this form.

[1] Aussercanon. Paralleltexte, ii. 356.

case. Whether, then, Jesus uttered the Aramaic אֱלָהִי or the Hebraistic אֵלִי, is in itself of minor consequence. The latter appears to me to have the greater probability in its favour, as being the less natural in the Aramaic context. Supposing that this were so, it is then conceivable that to secure greater uniformity of language, one copyist corrected ἠλεί into ἐλωεί,[1] so that the whole clause should be Aramaic, while another changed λεμᾶ σεβαχθανεί into λαμᾶ [ἀ]ζαφ-θανεί,[2] so as to have the whole in Hebrew. From a statement of Epiphanius, cited by Resch, it is evident that the apparent bilingual character of the saying had, in fact, been remarked upon.

On principles similar to those of Resch,[3] though with the aid of a very different linguistic equipment, *E. Nestle* has also collected evidence in favour of a Semitic source for our Gospels. He has, however, expressly declared [4] that he has not extended the theory of a Hebrew original to the whole extent of the Lucan writings, nor even decided as to whether the sources used by Luke were in Hebrew or in Aramaic. A few remarks may now be made on such of Nestle's observations as fall within the domain of Hebrew (excepting, however, meantime his explanation of the reading οἱ λοιποί, Luke 11² Cod. D).

In Luke 12¹ Blass has adopted into the text the reading

---

[1] ἐλωεί, for which Eusebius, Demonstr. Ev. x. 8, even puts Ἐλωείμ instead of ἐλαεί, I have explained, Gram. d. j.-pal. Ar. 123, as an echo of the Hebrew אֱלֹהִים. It is more probable, however, that the duller sound of the ā is represented, although this cannot be supported by instances in Palestine during the earlier period.

[2] עֲזַבְתָּנִי, transliterated into Greek required ἀζαφθανεί, for θ changes a preceding β into φ; cf. the χ in σεβαχθανεί = שְׁבַקְתָּנִי, and Gram. d. j.-pal. Ar. 304. It is credible enough that those who understood Syriac only should have again transformed the Hebrew ἀζαφθανεί into Aramaic, read ζαφθανεί = עֲזַבְתָּנִי, and then translated ὠνείδισάς με with Cod. D Mark 15³⁴. See *Chase*, The Syro-Latin Text of the Gospels, 107.

[3] Of less consequence are the unmethodical investigations of *H. P. Chajes*, who, in his treatise "Markus-Studien" (1899), aims at showing that several *Hebrew* editions of the (assumed) Aramaic Logia were used by the Synoptists.

[4] Philologica sacra (1896), 55.

of Cod. D, πολλῶν δὲ ὄχλων συνπεριεχόντων κύκλῳ ὥστε ἀλλήλους συνπνίγειν, where the common text has, ἐπισυναχθεισῶν τῶν μυριάδων τοῦ ὄχλου ὥστε καταπατεῖν ἀλλήλους. According to Blass, the latter was the older text of Luke, the former being the Roman edition as revised by him. Now, Nestle is of opinion that Luke first of all misread in his text רבבות, "myriads," but afterwards recognised that רבות was the right word. But the critic should then have said what he supposes to represent ὄχλος in the alleged source. Can עַמִּים רַבִּים have been confused with רִבְבוֹת עַמִּים? The question, moreover, is concerned not merely with πολλῶν and μυριάδων, but with the complete change in the expression of the thought, which is to be explained in the context. It remains, after all, most reasonable to suppose an undesigning alteration of the tenour of the whole sentence at the instance of a scribe who was not in the habit of slavishly binding himself to his exemplar in non-essentials. N. himself mentions the possible dependence of the manuscript on some gospel harmony, Philolog. sacra, 88.

A like conclusion will commend itself in the case of the readings Luke 22¹⁶ πληρωθῇ of the common text, and καινὸν βρωθῇ found in D and accepted by Blass. In Nestle's opinion, אָכַל, "to eat," and כָּלָה, "to complete," have come into collision; and he notes that the LXX, 2 Chron. 30²², has συνετέλεσαν (ויכלו) in place of the ויאכלו of the Massoretic text.[1] In that passage, however, וַיְכַלּוּ may be the true reading, unless הַמּוֹעֵד, like חַג elsewhere, is to be understood of the offering at the feast. But what has this to do with Luke 22¹⁶, where the question is concerned not with "eating" and "completing," but with "eating anew" and "fulfilling"? What we here find in Cod. D is merely a variant intended to explain the awkward πληρωθῇ, and suggested by Matt. 26²⁹, Mark 14²⁵.

---

[1] According to Philol. sacra, 38, N. no longer lays stress on the derivation of the reading from a Hebrew text, though still regarding it possible.

We cannot accept N.'s observation on Matt. 27⁵¹, which makes καταπέτασμα depend on a misreading and mistranslation, and finds the true reading in the Gospel of the Hebrews, which, by the testimony of Jerome, made mention, not of the rending of the veil of the temple, but of the splitting of the lintel. בַּפְתֹּר, "lintel," he holds, has been read as פְּרֹכָה, "curtain." But בַּפְתֹּר is nowhere found as the name for the lintel; it cannot therefore have stood for it in the Gospel of the Hebrews, especially as the latter was written in Aramaic. Perhaps its account was affected by the later ignorance of the fact that in the last temple the entrance to the sanctuary was closed by a curtain of extreme costliness, see Bell. Jud. v. v. 4. The New Testament expositors also usually neglect this consideration, so that the question has arisen how it was possible to observe the rending of the curtain, *i.e.* the one in front of the Holy of Holies. τὸ καταπέτασμα τοῦ ναοῦ is, however, the curtain at the entrance to the temple building, not that before the Holy of Holies, which would have to be otherwise designated.

The existence of a primary gospel in the Hebrew language had to be considered antecedently improbable, because no occasion was discovered for the use of this language. And if we have now succeeded in showing that the special Hebraisms of the Synoptic Gospels are to all appearance of Greek origin, that the attempts hitherto made to infer a Hebrew original from the variants in the Gospel texts are unsuccessful, and that signs are not wanting to show that the authors of our Gospels, in their present form at least, were not conversant with the Hebrew language, then it will no longer seem hasty if the title of this section spoke of " *alleged* proofs of a primitive Hebrew gospel."

VI. TESTIMONIES IN FAVOUR OF A PRIMITIVE ARAMAIC GOSPEL.

Apart from the well-known testimonies in Eusebius, we have no certain traces of the existence of a primitive gospel in a Semitic language. It may now be considered an acknowledged fact that Jerome was mistaken, and that he himself latterly perceived his error in believing that the original of Matthew in Hebrew still existed in his day. The various forms of the texts of the Gospels in the Aramaic language, which are now known to us, are derived from Greek originals. Even the Aramaic Gospel of the Hebrews used by Jerome was to all appearance the reproduction of a Greek gospel. We learn incidentally from Eusebius [1] that the first Palestinian martyr, Procopius, had exercised in the service of the Christian community of Scythopolis the threefold office of Scripture-reading, Aramaic interpretation (ἑρμηνεία τῆς τῶν Σύρων φωνῆς), and exorcism. If the Reader of a Palestinian congregation was also Aramaic Interpreter, it follows that there could not have been in Palestine about 300 A.D. any Bible in the vernacular of the land. The reading of Holy Scripture in the Greek language was accompanied by an oral translation into Aramaic.

According to Eusebius, the Church in his time possessed a fourfold testimony in regard to a "Hebrew" original of Matthew, first in the form of a tradition to the effect that Pantænus had found such a work in India (Hist. eccl. v. 10), and next in the form of statements made by Papias, by Irenæus, and by Origen (Hist. eccl. iii. 39, v. 8, vi. 25). Eusebius believes that it is throughout the canonical Gospel of Matthew that is referred to, and could cite in his support the statements of Irenæus and Origen, who were of the same opinion. The declaration of Papias, however, is open to question, and would have had greater weight with us had

[1] *B. Violet*, Die paläst. Märtyrer des Eusebius von Cæsarea, 4, 7, 110.

we known in what connection it stood in his work. When he says of Matthew, τὰ λόγια συνεγράψατο (συνετάξατο), one must naturally suppose he meant only a collection of "sayings." Papias' own work, from which Origen made this quotation, bore indeed the title λογίων κυριακῶν ἐξη-γήσεις, and contained accordingly expositions of those "sayings" of our Lord of which Matthew had made a "Hebrew" collection. Only from the unknown context might it *possibly* become clear that the work of Matthew contained anything besides *dicta*. The translator into Syriac, who straightway put down אונגליון for τὰ λόγια,[1] has certainly not given the exact sense of Papias within the limits expressed by him. From the statement of Papias, Resch, it is true, has derived the assumed title of his comprehensive documentary source of our Gospels דִּבְרֵי יֵשׁוּעַ, on the supposition that Papias meant by τὰ λόγια to represent precisely the above Hebrew title, and that the latter is in the last resort equivalent to "History of Jesus," just as in the Books of the Kings דִּבְרֵי פ׳ often refers to the acts and experiences of a king. But Papias gives no hint that τὰ λόγια was the title of the work of Matthew in question; and even if he so considered it, he would still in any case have understood it to refer only to the "sayings," not to the "deeds" or "life history," of Jesus.[2] But if this work of Matthew were composed in Aramaic, then a title such as פִּתְגָמֵי יֵשׁוּעַ or מִלֵּי יֵשׁוּעַ for a narrative gospel would be highly improbable.[3]

It is really an *Aramaic*, not a Hebrew original of

---

[1] So *Eusebius*, Hist. eccl. syr., edited by *P. Bedjan*, Paris, 1897; by *W. Wright* and *N. McLean*, Cambridge, 1898, without giving variants.

[2] Cf. the anonymous treatise, "The Oracles ascribed to Matthew by Papias of Hierapolis," 1894, 48–91.

[3] Post-biblical Jewish literature recognises דִּבְרֵי פ׳ as a title of written works only in the sense that the contents are thereby referred to as the words of the person named in the superscription. A "History of Jesus" would have been called in Hebrew מַעֲשֵׂה יֵשׁוּעַ, in Aramaic עוֹבָדָא דְיֵשׁוּעַ, as written by Shemtob Ibn Shaprut in the unprinted Eben Bokhan (MS. of the Jewish theol. Sem. in Breslau, f. 180ᵇ).

Matthew that is attested by the ancient tradition. This holds incontestably so far as Eusebius [1] is concerned, for, according to him, the apostles had been reared "in the Syrian language." Eusebius also alludes to the fifth word of Jesus on the Cross in its Aramaic form, speaking of it as "Hebrew." [2] In saying that Matthew, whom he elsewhere calls a "Syrian," [3] first of all preached to the "Hebrews," and then on departing from them left behind with them his Gospel written πατρίῳ γλώττῃ, Eusebius means that Matthew had written down his Gospel in the mother-tongue common to himself and his kinsfolk, that is to say, according to Eusebius' own view of the linguistic situation of that period, in Aramaic. Eusebius, therefore, must have understood all the earlier statements communicated by him in regard to the language of the original Matthew as referring to Aramaic, and in this he was certainly not mistaken. In the case of Irenæus [4] we know for certain that he spoke of words which are Aramaic as being "Hebrew." But in all these notices the emphasis is not laid on the consideration that the work of Matthew had originally been written in Hebrew as opposed to "Syriac," but only on the fact that Matthew had composed his work in the language peculiar to the "Hebraists." Any one who, like Eusebius, is convinced that the mother-tongue of the "Hebraists" was Aramaic, can think of no other language in this connection. [5] It must be conceded that even if that work had for any reason whatever actually been composed in Hebrew, still the testimonies about it would scarcely have been expressed otherwise. But in virtue of this mere *possibility*, the testimonies do not become actual witnesses in favour of a primitive gospel in *Hebrew*. A treatise by Matthew in the Palestinian Jewish

[1] Demonstr. ev. iii. 7. 10.   [2] Ibid. x. 8.
[3] Quæst. ev. ad Steph. in Mai, p. 27.
[4] Adv. hær. i. 21. 3 ; cf. Epiph. Hæres. xxxiv. 20.
[5] An Aramaic original Matthew is postulated also by *Th. Zahn*, Einl. in das N. Test. ii. § 54.

vernacular[1] is attested, but not a Hebrew Matthew. The
conjecture that this treatise of Matthew was a collection of
the sayings presupposed by the canonical Gospels of Matthew
and Luke is an attractive one, but hitherto, at least, it has
not been established by linguistic evidence. Indeed, it must
be confessed that even if the sections common to Matthew
and Luke did actually originate from that source, still it was
at least not the Semitic original, but only a Greek translation,
that lay before the evangelists.

The early Church testimonies in regard to the origin of
Mark's Gospel would have considerable importance for our
aim, provided that Mark, in his capacity of interpreter of
Peter, were the same individual who was wont to translate
the Aramaic discourses of Peter into Greek. In that case
his Gospel, too, would go back to an Aramaic original, even
though it were only orally formulated. Irenæus,[2] Clement,[3]
and Eusebius[4] must, in fact, have so conceived the situation.
But the oldest testimony on this point, that of the Presbyter
in Papias,[5] is apparently intended to imply that Mark was
only the author of a gospel which was founded on the spoken
communications of Peter, Mark being thus in a sense his
interpreter, even though he had never actually filled such an
office in relation to Peter. In that case it would be most
likely that Mark should proceed upon the Greek expositions
of Peter, for Peter must have appeared (Acts 10[24]) from a
very early date as a preacher of the gospel in the Greek
language. And thus a primary form in Greek would have
to be assumed for the Mark document.[6] F. Blass,[7] who
understands the statement of Papias to signify that Mark
actually accompanied Peter as interpreter, holds indeed that

---

[1] This case is quite similar to that of the original of the ἱστορία Ἰουδαϊκοῦ
πολέμου πρὸς Ῥωμαίους of Josephus, which was composed according to the
preface in τῇ πατρίῳ (understand γλώσσῃ).

[2] Adv. hær. iii. 1. 3, x. 6. [3] *Eusebius*, Hist. eccl. ii. 15, 16.

[4] Hist. eccl. iii. 14. [5] Loc. cit. iii. 39.

[6] See also above, p. 42, and p. 49, footnote 2.

[7] *F. Blass*, Philology of the Gospels, 196, 210 ; cf. 194.

there existed an Aramaic original of Mark which was unknown to Papias, and of which traces may be recognised in
the various readings of our manuscripts. He holds that
Mark was also the author of the Aramaic source which he
postulates for Acts 1–12. But such conjectures entirely
abandon the region of what has been or can be proved.

Just as J. A. Bolten,[1] a century ago, had frequently
endeavoured in the exposition of Matthew to recover the
original Aramaic terms, so in recent times attempts have
been made for particular passages of the Gospels to go back
to an Aramaic original, in the first instance by J. T.
Marshall,[2] and subsequently by E. Nestle,[3] J. Wellhausen,[4]
A. Meyer,[5] and M. Schultze.[6] Wellhausen and A. Meyer aim
chiefly at reaching the Aramaic word uttered by Jesus ;
Marshall and Nestle strive to demonstrate the existence of
an Aramaic documentary source. Marshall has even believed
himself in a position to furnish provisionally, as the result of
his investigations, the content and limits of an Aramaic
primary gospel.[7] Th. Zahn,[8] who considers our entire
Gospel of Matthew to be a translation from the Aramaic,
seeks support for this position especially from the style in
which Semitic words are communicated.

In regard to Marshall and Meyer, it is here sufficient

[1] *J. A. Bolten*, Der Bericht des Matthäus von Jesu dem Messia, Altona,
1792 ; see *A. Meyer*, Jesu Muttersprache, 25, 105 ff.

[2] Expositor, Ser. 4, ii. 69 ff. ; iii. 1 ff., 109 ff., 205 ff., 275 ff., 375 ff., 452 ff. ;
iv. 208 ff., 373 ff., 435 ff. ; vi. 81 ff. ; viii. 176 ff.

[3] Philologica sacra, Berlin, 1896. A collection of observations published
in Christl. Welt, 1895 and 1896 ; Expositor, Stud. u. Krit., and other
periodicals.

[4] Nachr. Ges. Wiss. Gött., 1895 ; Phil. hist. Kl. 11 f. ; Gött. Gel. Anz.
1896, i. 265 ; Skizzen und Vorarbeiten, vi. 188–194.

[5] Jesu Muttersprache, Leipzig, 1896.

[6] Gram. der aram. Muttersprache Jesu (1899), 80–83, where Schultze aims
at translating the words of the Lord into biblical Aramaic without discussing
the question of the linguistic form of a primitive gospel.

[7] Expositor, Ser. 4, vi. 81 ff. See also *Resch*, Aussercanon. Paralleltexte,
i. 157 f. Here may also be mentioned *W. C. Allen's* Essay, "The Original
Language of the Gospel acc. to St. Mark," Expositor, Ser. 6, vi. 436–443.

[8] Einl. in das N. Test. ii. § 56.

to refer to the trenchant criticisms which their work has provoked.[1] Some of their points will claim attention at a later stage. Of far greater consequence are the pertinent observations of Wellhausen and Nestle, though even in their case we feel the absence of a careful separation of Hebrew and Aramaic possibilities. Wellhausen, indeed, considers that the Aramaic form of the primitive gospel has been established by general considerations, and does not require to be vindicated by fresh evidence.[2] He must, however, be reminded that the Jewish literature to this day is still mainly composed in Hebrew. For my own part I do not see more than a high probability for an Aramaic primary gospel, and dare not speak of a *certainty* resting on proofs. Further, the points urged by Zahn prove truly enough the existence of an Aramaic background to the Gospel accounts, but do not suffice to show convincingly the existence of a Gospel in the Aramaic language.

Genuine proofs of an Aramaic, as opposed to a Hebrew, written source of the Synoptists are the harder to produce, because the same idioms and the same construction of clauses as are found in Aramaic are possible even in biblical Hebrew, and still oftener in the style of the Mishna. A whole series of comments that could be made on the synoptic text would therefore apply equally to either language. But the previous attempts to adduce such proofs are defective on other grounds. To justify this view in detail, some observations by Wellhausen will first be examined, and then the remarks of Nestle, which are pertinent to the question.

Wellhausen claims that the striking variations δότε ἐλεημοσύνην and καθάρισον, Luke 11[41] and Matt. 23[26],

---

[1] See in opposition to Marshall, *W. C. Allen*, Expositor, Ser. 4, vii. 386–400, 454–470; *S. R. Driver*, ibid. viii. 388–400, 419–431 ; against Meyer, *J. Wellhausen*, Gött. Gel. Anz. 1896, i. 265–268 ; *G. Dalman*, Theol. Litzeitg. 1896, 477 ff., Lit. Centralbl. 1896, 1563 f. ; *A. Merx*, Deutsche Litzeitg. xix. (1898) 985–991.

[2] Skizzen u. Vorarbeiten, vi. p. v.

are derived from זכי, which means "to give alms" and "to cleanse." This instance seems an attractive proof expressly in favour of a written Aramaic source, as the Hebrew for "cleanse" would be טִהַר. W. in his discussion refers to my Gram. d. jüd.-pal. Aram., in which the meaning "to give alms" is authenticated for זכי. He further pleads the consideration that in the Arabic he has found the substantive "zakāt," which contains the root-form, while the corresponding form in Aramaic זכוּ seems to be wanting in the Jewish literature. But זְכוּתָא, like its Hebrew equivalent צְדָקָה, is quite common in this literature. It does not matter much that זְכוּתָא does not appear to occur in connection with alms, since even then it would not lose the sense of "practice of virtue," "meritorious action"; cf. מִצְוְתָא, "practice of the commandments" for "alms" (Vay. R. 34). The verb זכי can mean "to act meritoriously by giving alms," but also "to procure [for another] that merit by asking alms" (see j. Pes. 31ᵇ). But why should Luke not have arrived at his expression by starting from the Greek καθάρισον? The purifying of the cup filled with plunder could be brought about only by its being emptied, the contents being given away. It coincided with the intention of Jesus if His saying were applied to almsgiving. According to the reading τὸ δὲ ἔσωθεν ὑμῶν in Luke 11³⁹, the idea implied would indeed be that what was latent in the heart of the Pharisees should be distributed like alms. But as an idea so absurd cannot be attributed to the evangelist, we should, like Blass, read ὑμῖν.

In Luke 24³² Wellhausen is quite justified in retracing, as Mrs. A. S. Lewis does, the readings καιομένη and βεβαρημένη back to יקיד and יקיר. He has not, however, noted that the lucid βεβαρημένη adopted by Blass is disclosed to view solely through early versions. It would never have stood in the (primitive) Greek text. The interchange of יקיד and יקיר on the part of Syrians might very easily happen, because

in Syriac ר and ד are distinguished solely by the position of
a diacritic point. But this does not touch the question of
a primitive Aramaic gospel.

It is in itself an attractive conjecture that is made by
W. in suggesting that in Luke 4²⁶ the woman to whom
Elias was sent should be characterised not as " a widow,"
ארמלתא, but as " a heathen," ארמיתא corresponding to the
mention in ver. 27 of Naaman as ὁ Σύρος. Notwith-
standing, I am unable to assent to it. To " the many
widows in Israel " of ver. 25 there stands quite suitably
in contrast " the widow of Sidonian Sarepta " of ver. 26.
Besides, πρὸς γυναῖκα χήραν is just as much occasioned by
γυναικὶ χήρᾳ, 1 Kings 17⁹ LXX, as Ναϊμὰν ὁ Σύρος is by
the like expression in 2 Kings 5²⁰ LXX. So that there is
really no call for emendation of the text.

Another phrase, which W. regards as an Aramaism, is
ἀναστήσονται ἐν τῇ κρίσει μετὰ τῆς γενεᾶς ταύτης, Matt.
12⁴¹ (Luke 11³²). Its meaning must be, " they will measure
themselves in the Judgment with this generation." But this
form of expression is found in the Old Testament in Isa.
54¹⁷ תָּקוּם אִתָּךְ לַמִּשְׁפָּט, LXX ἀναστήσεται ἐπὶ σὲ εἰς κρίσιν,
Targum יְקוּם עִמָּךְ לְדִינָא; also in Ps. 94¹⁶ מִי יָקוּם לִי עִם מְרֵעִים,
LXX τίς ἀναστήσεταί μοι ἐπὶ πονηρευομένους. For the
Jewish Aramaic compare also j. Kidd. 64ᵃ חַד בַּר נָשׁ קָם עִם
חַבְרֵיהּ בְּשׁוּקָא, " some one began a litigation with [rose up
against] his neighbour on the street." Further, κατακρι-
νοῦσιν αὐτήν, " they will show it to be in the wrong, will
overcome it," need not be an Aramaism. W. connects it
rightly enough with the Aramaic חַיֵּב, but we have a corresponding expression also in Hebrew in הִרְשִׁיעַ; see Isa. 54¹⁷
תַּרְשִׁיעִי, LXX ἡττήσεις, Targum תְּחַיְּבִינֵהּ.

Just as little is it necessary to detect with W. an
Aramaism in ἀνθρώπῳ βασιλεῖ, Matt. 18²³, along with
which may be mentioned Matt. 22², where the same phrase
is repeated, also Matt. 13⁵², 20¹; cf. 21³³ with ἀνθρώπῳ

οἰκοδεσπότῃ, and Luke 24¹⁹ with ἀνὴρ προφήτης. The Old Testament says: בֹּהֵן אִישׁ, Lev. 21⁹ (LXX ἀνθρώπου ἱερέως); אִישׁ נָבִיא, Judg. 6⁸ (LXX ἄνδρα προφήτην); and in Jewish Aramaic literature the idiom is also found; see, e.g., גְּבַר סָב, j. Sanh. 25ᵈ, but I do not think it ever stands at the opening of a parable, as in Matthew. But ἀνὴρ βασιλεύς is, of course, good Greek, and ἄνθρωπος βασιλεύς also is not impossible.

In Mark 1⁴¹ Cod. D has the unmeaning ὀργισθείς for σπλαγχνισθείς of the common text. Like J. D. Michaelis[1] a century ago, Nestle holds that in this case אתרחם, " he was moved with compassion," has been interchanged with אתרעם, " he was angry." That might well be correct, yet it would apply only to the Syriac of Edessa. In this instance we perceive the impression of Syriac influence on Cod. D, and that all the more surely because Ephrem knew this reading; see *Chase*, The Syro-Latin Text of the Gospels, 88 f. This author, however, supposes that the confusion is between אתרחם and אתחמת.

The readings ἔξω τῆς χώρας, Mark 5¹⁰, and εἰς τὴν ἄβυσσον, Luke 8³¹, are by Nestle traced back to לתחומא and לתהומא, the former meaning " to the frontier," the latter " into the deep." As " to the frontier " did not suit the context, Mark, it is thought, changed it to " across the frontier." But without imputing an erroneous translation of this kind, the variation explains itself from the consideration that in Mark the idea was the removal of the demons to a distant land (cf. Tob. 8³), but in Luke their banishment to the place of chastisement for the reprobate. In Mark 5¹¹ (Luke 8³²) a herd of swine is mentioned as being " beside " or " upon the mountain "; in Matt. 8³⁰ as being " a good way off from them " (μακρὰν ἀπ' αὐτῶν). Nestle holds that מוּרָא, " mountain," and מְרַא, " distance," are here in confusion. But this מוּרָא is foreign to the Jewish Aramaic;

---

[1] Einleitung in die Schriften des Neuen Bundes, i. (1788) 585.

5

and the difference admits of another explanation. Mark and Luke represent the entire incident (Mark 5², Luke 8²⁷) as proceeding upon the seashore, the herd being in the immediate vicinity "upon the mountain." Matthew does not locate the episode on the seashore, but regards Jesus as being "in the country of the Gadarenes" on the way to Gadara (Matt. 8²⁸), which was situated some six miles inland. The herd of swine is supposed to be at some distance, because, as represented in ver. 32, it was necessarily near the seacoast.

In Matt. 5⁴⁸ τέλειοι, τέλειος correspond to οἰκτίρμονες, οἰκτίρμων in Luke 6³⁶. From the Concordance N. finds that the LXX in certain circumstances puts both ἵλεως and φίλος for the Hebrew שלם, and he notes that in de Lagarde's "Onomastica Sacra" Σολομών is explained as ἐλεήμων ἢ εἰρήνικος. Therefore N. infers οἰκτίρμων presupposes an original שלם. But despite all this שלם does not mean "merciful," and could be so rendered only by a very slipshod translator. The expression in Luke is occasioned by the fact that the divine nature has just before been characterised as χρηστός. Matthew uses τέλειος because the conduct of men in other relations is forthwith to be mentioned, and it was necessary to provide for the transition.

The peculiar phrase in Mark 8¹⁰ εἰς τὰ μέρη Δαλμανουθά,[1] has been derived by J. Rendel Harris[2] from the Aramaic למנותא דלמנותא on the supposition that the second למנותא was an inadvertent repetition, while the real name of the place has disappeared. Nestle[3] has, independently of Harris, hit upon the same idea. To this, however, the serious objection has to be urged that τὰ μέρη with the meaning of "district" is a pure Græcism, quite incapable of being literally reproduced in Aramaic. מְנָוָתָא in all the

---

[1] See thereon Gram. d. jüd.-pal. Aram. 133.   [2] Codex Bezæ, 178.
[3] Philologica sacra, 17.

Aramaic dialects means "portions" but not "district." The Syriac translators were therefore obliged to substitute other expressions : thus we find in place of it אתרא, "region," Mark 8¹⁰ Pesh., Matt. 2²² Cur. Sin. Pesh., Matt. 16¹³ Cur. Pesh. Hier.; תחומא, "district," Matt. 15²¹ Cur. Sin. Pesh. Hier., Matt. 16¹³ Sin.; ארעא, "land," Matt. 2²² Hier. Nor in Jewish Aramaic would expressions other than these be possible. Therefore Δαλμανουθά cannot be explained by means of למנותא.

In Mark 10³⁰ Jesus speaks of a "hundredfold" recompense for His disciples, whereas Matt. 19²⁹ (Luke 18³⁰) mention a "manifold" recompense. Now Cod. D has "hundredfold" in Matt. also, and in Luke "sevenfold." In Nestle's opinion "sevenfold" was the original, and this has been received into the text of Blass. This may *possibly* be correct, but there is no necessity for deriving the expression from a Semitic original. Seven stands as a number suggesting completeness without mathematical precision, cf. the seven years of Anna's wedded life, Luke 2³⁶; the seven evil spirits, Luke 8² 11²⁶; the seven brothers, Luke 20²⁹; the sevenfold daily trespass, Luke 17⁴. In this way "manifold" and even "hundredfold" can be used in place of "sevenfold."

At the first glance there is something plausible in N.'s remark on Luke 19¹⁷, that the mention of the "cities" as reward of the faithful servants in contrast with the "talents" of Matt. 25¹⁶ᶠᶠ. is to be explained by interchange of בְּכָּרִין, "talents" and כַּרְכִין, "cities." On closer inspection, however, it becomes evident that this is not correct. כַּרְכִין is not the common word for "cities" in a general sense, so that the confusion was not so natural as might appear. In Matt. 25²¹· ²³ it is not "talents" that are given to the servants, but their Lord will set them over "many things." When Luke defines the "many things" by "cities," the addition depends on the fact that in his representation the

situation treats of a king who enters upon his dominion —
an idea wholly absent from Matthew.

In Matt. 23²³ and Luke 11⁴² ἔλεος and ἀγάπη τοῦ θεοῦ
should in N.'s opinion be traced back to one form with רחם
as its root. His supposition is that רַחֲמִין, " compassion,"
and רַחְמְתָא, " love," were confounded, τοῦ θεοῦ being appended to the latter. But it is at least equally credible
that the Greek synonyms ἔλεος and ἀγάπη were interchanged, and that ἀγάπη was afterwards explained as " the
love of God."

In Mark 11⁴ ἐπὶ τοῦ ἀμφόδου is represented as being
properly the translation of Βηθφαγή, Luke 19²⁹. This
latter, it is said, in accordance with the Syriac בית פגעא,
might in fact have been rendered " at the parting of the
ways." But ἐπὶ τοῦ ἀμφόδου means only " on the street ";
פגעא is not the term for " a network of roads " or " cross-
roads," [1] either in the Syriac of Edessa or in the Palestinian
Aramaic ; and בֵּית is not used for בְּ in Palestinian Aramaic.
Besides, Βηθφαγή has the indeclinable ending ē, and is,
therefore, not of Greek origin. From the Talmud we
learn that בית פאגי was really the name of a place,[2] not of
a cross-roads merely. So that Mark, if he translated,
would have translated wrongly. If one is not content to
derive פאגי from פַּג, " unripe figs," as I have done,[3] then it
is preferable to pronounce the origin of the word obscure [4]
rather than to decide upon פגעא.

In Matt. 27³⁴ " vinegar mingled with gall " is put for
the " wine mingled with myrrh " of Mark 15²³, through the
confusion, as Nestle holds, of מרה, " gall," with מורה, " myrrh."

---

[1] The fact that the Syrians in one case attempt to assign the meaning
" cross-roads " to בית פגא would have significance only if פגעא could be adduced
with this meaning in other instances.

[2] But not of two places, as *Starck*, Palästina und Syrien, 35, represents.

[3] Gram. d. jüd.-pal. Aram. 152.

[4] Can πάγος, " village," perhaps be traced in the name ? According to the
Talmud, Bethphage was situated just beyond the city boundary of Jerusalem
proper.

But Matthew's representation is satisfactorily accounted for through intentional allusion to the drinking of gall in Ps. 68[22] LXX, and does not call for the assumption of a Semitic source.

In Acts 2[47] Cod. D has πρὸς ὅλον τὸν κόσμον for π. ὁ. τ. λάον of the *Textus Receptus.* N. traces these variants to the confusion of עֹלָם, "world," and עַם, "people," and adduces other instances where this mistake occurs. He does not expressly say, however, whether he means that Luke had subsequently recognised his original reading עם to be incorrect, and, accordingly, in the revised edition had substituted κόσμον for λάον, or whether a later writer was the first to bring Luke's document into accord with the alleged source. In the text of the Palestinian Talmud, Ber. 4[b] and Bab. mez. 8[d], we also find כולי עלמא wrongly put for כל עמא. For this, however, it is no mere misreading on the part of a copyist that is responsible, but the fact that both are quite equivalent periphrases for "every one," the former being the dominant Babylonian usage, the latter the Palestinian usage. Admitting, however, that כל עמא, "all the people," and כל עלמא, "the whole world," are merely different expressions for "every one," in the same sense as in Acts 2[47], the reading nevertheless allows of explanation without reversion to a Semitic original quite as satisfactorily through an interchange of the Greek terms, as is done by B. Weiss;[1] and there is no occasion to consider with Harris[2] a Latin, or with Chase[3] a Syriac text as responsible for the various reading.

The theory of a Semitic source is raised to "perfect certainty" in N.'s judgment by the various reading ἐβαρύνατε, "ye oppressed," supplied by Cod. D Acts 3[14], in place of ἠρνήσασθε, "ye denied," of the common text. Blass[4] appeals

---

[1] Der Codex D in der Apostelgeschichte (1897), 58.
[2] Codex Bezæ, 103 f.
[3] The Old Syriac Element in the Text of Codex Bezæ (1893), 28.
[4] Philology of the Gospels, 194.

to this "discovery" of Nestle as the most important proof of the Aramaic source used by Luke for Acts 1–12.[1] כפר, "to deny," and בבר, "to molest," are supposed to have been interchanged in this case.   Both by Nestle and Blass, therefore, ἐβαρύνατε will be reckoned a gross error.   In the first edition of the Acts, Luke himself had fallen into this mistake: only in the second edition had he rectified it, after he had made a fresh study of his source.   Now Blass, at least, according to whom Luke understood only a little Aramaic and no Hebrew at all, should hardly attribute to him any acquaintance with the Hebrew הִכְבִּיר, which occurs only in Job, and, moreover, is never used for "molest."[2]   If, however, Luke were well versed in Hebrew, this peculiar freak, impossible from the Aramaic side, would be unpardonable.   Long ago, however, Harvey,[3] and after him Chase,[4] had found a most satisfactory explanation of the reading of Cod. D, by referring it to the Edessene בבד, "to irritate," which could be interchanged with כפר, "to deny." Nestle[5] finds this also to be plausible, and, as it seems, would therefore consider it possible that Luke was familiar with the Syriac of Edessa, and thence arrived at his false reading.   But far more acceptable would still remain the theory of Harvey and Chase, that the reading of Cod. D originates not from Luke, but from a defectively written or falsely read Syriac gospel text.   And since "to be angry with" is in Edessene not כבד but אתכבד, Harris[6] will be right in saying that ἠτήσατε read as ἡττήσατε has been the source of the Latin reading aggravastis, which on its part again determined the Greek text of Cod. D.

[1] B. Weiss, Der Codex D in der Apostelgeschichte, 25, holds that ἐβαρύνατε may possibly have been an ancient reading, without giving any opinion on its genesis.

[2] The same would hold of the Edessene אכבר, "to make much ado."

[3] W. Wigan Harvey, Iren. adv. Hær. ii. (1857) 55.

[4] The Old Syriac Element in the Text of Codex Bezæ, 38.

[5] Philologica sacra, 40 f.

[6] J. Rendel Harris, Codex Bezæ (1891), 162 ff.

If our criticism of the proofs hitherto adduced in support of a primitive Aramaic gospel be sound, then clearly the account of the primitive Church in regard to an Aramaic original of Matthew must be pronounced as still lacking confirmation by convincing proofs.

Since, however, the proofs of a *Hebrew* written source proved equally inconclusive, one is obliged to resort to the considerations urged long ago by B. Weiss and others, to the effect that the occasional agreement of the Synoptists in Greek expressions implies that the documentary sources used by them were written in Greek. In this there is nothing improbable. The Christian Church, even while in Jerusalem, included in its numbers numerous Hellenists, *i.e.* Greek-speaking Jews, Acts 6[1] 9[29]. From the very beginning it thus used two languages, and in gatherings of the community the deeds and words of Jesus must have been recounted in Greek and in Aramaic. The "Hebraists" would mostly all have understood some Greek, but the Hellenists very often no Aramaic or Hebrew. A gospel-source in Greek need not, by reason of its language, have been any later in origin than one written in a Semitic dialect. It is thus *possible* that the oldest Christian writing may have been composed in Greek; and its Semitisms, so far as they are not Biblicisms, are in that case due to the Aramaic oral archetype (*Urgestalt*) of the Christian tradition.

VII. The Problem before us and the previous Studies in the same Field.

If this work, as planned by the writer, is not to be reared from the outset on an unstable foundation, it cannot proceed, as the foregoing considerations show, upon the definite theory of a Semitic written source elaborated in our Synoptic Gospels. What is firmly established is only the fact that Jesus spoke in Aramaic to the Jews, and that the original apostolic band at the beginning preached concerning Him—though not exclusively—in that language. For the words of Jesus only is an Aramaic original form incontestably secure; for them alone does the earliest Church tradition assert a written Semitic source. Hence arises for literary science the right and the duty of investigating *in what form the words of Jesus must have been uttered in their original language, and what meaning they had in this form for the Jewish hearers.* Of course absolute certainty in regard to minutiæ cannot possibly be expected concerning the precise form in which these words proceeded from the mouth of Jesus. But it will be recognised with greater certainty than heretofore how much there is in form and content that is specifically Greek, and what at least may be regarded as most nearly approaching to the original setting. The more one is convinced that the Gospels contain historically trust-worthy communications in regard to the teaching of Jesus, the more important must it appear to get even one step nearer to the original by a fresh apprehension of His message in the light of the primary language and the contemporary modes of thought.

As the *words* of our Lord must thus be the proper subject of our study, it has, of course, to be kept in view that they are presented to us in writings whose authors have so recounted them that their individual apprehension of them, their style and mode of expression, have not failed to exert a certain influence. It follows, therefore, that the investigation should not be limited entirely to the speeches reported by a Synoptist. Whatever their writings may afford towards elucidating the words of Jesus must be sought out and applied for the end in view. In regard to the Johannine Gospel, its exclusion from the scope of the inquiry seems to us justified, because the author's individuality impressed itself so strongly on the Greek he wrote, that a reconstruction in Aramaic would here have too little prospect of success.

But even those who may think differently will not gainsay that a separate treatment of the synoptic material, at least by way of introduction, is not only justifiable but requisite.

The remark which was made after the discovery of the Hebrew fragments of Ben Sira, that all the attempts to reconstruct the original had failed,[1] cannot be indiscriminately applied to every work of this kind. For the book of the son of Sirach was very obscure in the original language to begin with; and the extant early versions were defective in the highest degree. But in regard to the original of the words of Jesus and their rendering into Greek, no such assertion can be hazarded. Thought and expression in this case are clear and unmistakable, free from useless ornament and artificial elaboration. In this case, therefore, a retranslation will have better prospect of success. But even in the accounts of the evangelists themselves, emphasis must not be laid on the unessential details in the reported dicta, which each narrator in turn could represent with some variation, but only on the leading thoughts and pervading ideas. It were no small achievement to succeed in apprehending these, in the light of the Aramaic language and the contemporary circle of ideas, with increased precision and closer approach to the original sense. And such an aim must be pronounced quite attainable, provided it be pursued with the proper means.

It is obvious enough that a mere Aramaic translation of the words of our Lord, as given in the Synoptists, would have little scientific value. For it is precisely the untranslatable that has to be made intelligible. Where several renderings are possible, the reader must be made aware of this. When the choice falls upon a particular rendering, the reasons in its support must not be omitted. And the

[1] See specimens in *Cowley* and *Neubauer*, The original Hebrew of a portion of Ecclesiasticus (1897), xviii.

work would be but half completed, if at the same time an adequate insight were not given into the significance of the newly recovered text, and the form thence acquired by the problems of exegesis. Nothing but a running commentary, which takes account of the tentative translations, can therefore appear adequate to the end in view.

No definite hypothesis in regard to the origin and mutual relations of the Synoptic Gospels can be assumed as the basis of our inquiry, without thereby anticipating conclusions which may appear as a possible result of the investigation. Only the various contingencies involved must not be left out of view. Naturally all questions of exegesis and gospel criticism are not intended to receive final solution; here the aim is rather to offer materials and indicate points of view which suggest themselves in considering the Aramaic archetype, and in reviewing the contemporary ideas. To New Testament science remains the task of applying our results to the working out of its own problems, and of thus conducting the inquiry to its proper goal.

As a number of ideas of substantially the same import recur throughout the discourses of Jesus, it will be desirable to begin by submitting the most important of these to a special consideration. The discussion of the words of Jesus in relation to their collective import will subsequently afford an occasion in later volumes of this work to add, if necessary, more precise definitions, and also to treat other ideas according to the same method. Thus our researches will also be guarded against a false Judaising of the words of Jesus, such as easily arises and often has arisen, where isolated dicta, separated from their context, have been compared with rabbinic ideas and expressions. Further, the theory which has been advanced, e.g., by Schnedermann,[1] that Jesus at first began His work with Jewish ideas and then gradually charged these with a new content, cannot justify itself in presence of

[1] Die Vorstellung vom Reiche Gottes, i. (1896), ii. 1 (1893), 2 (1895).

the Gospel accounts.[1] For there the teaching of Jesus, extending only over a short period of time, appears, in regard to the fundamental conceptions, uniform and unvarying. Each single idea must be apprehended in its coherence with the whole. What we deem of real significance and worthy of our investigation, is not the superficial notion of a casual hearer of Jesus, but the intimate understanding of a constant disciple and follower.

It is regrettable that there are so few previous studies from which material directly contributory to our aim can be derived. Even after the dictionaries of Levy, Kohut, Jastrow have been supplemented by my own works, " Grammatik des jüdisch-palästinischen Aramäisch," and " Aramäisch-neuhebräisches Wörterbuch," there still remain large blanks in regard to the syntax, phraseology, and vocabulary of the separate dialects. Compilations begun by me, and to be rendered more complete by continuous reading, must serve to supply the deficiency.

The absence of preliminary studies in the region of *Jewish Theology* is no less marked. Even an adequate treatment of the ideas of the Apocrypha and Pseudepigrapha is not yet to be had. *M. Vernes*, Histoire des Idées Messianiques (1874); *J. Drummond*, The Jewish Messiah (1877); *V. H. Stanton*, The Jewish and the Christian Messiah (1886); *Oehler v. Orelli*, art. " Messias," Prot. Real-Encyklopädie,[2] ix. (1881), 641–672; *E. Schürer*, Geschichte des jüd. Volkes im Zeitalter Jesu Christi,[3] ii. (1898), Section on the Messianic Hope, 496–556 ; *M. Marti*, Geschichte der israelit. Religion[3] (1897), 270–310; *R. H. Charles*, Eschatology of the Apocryphal and Apocalyptic Liturature, in Dictionary of the Bible, i. (1898), 741–749, and Critical History of the doctrine of the Future Life (1899); *E. Hühn*, Die messianischen Weissagungen des israelitischjüdischen Volkes bis zu

---

[1] Against Schnedermann, see especially *E. Haupt*, Die eschatologischen Aussagen Jesu in den synopt. Evangelien (1895), 63 ff.

den Targumim, i. (1899)—after all these a good deal remains
to be done. The commentaries, however, of *Ryle* and *James*
on the Psalms of Solomon (1891), of *R. H. Charles* on the
Ethiopic Book of Enoch (1893), on the Apocalypse of Baruch
(1896), on the Assumption of Moses (1897), and especially
the translations and expositions of these books published in
1900 by *E. Kautsch,* " Die Apokryphen und Pseudepigraphen
des Alten Testaments," must be regarded as a gratifying
advance on their predecessors. Yet nearly all even of the
authors here mentioned are lacking in a first-hand acquaintance with the later Jewish literature—an indispensable requirement where the problem is to elucidate
Jewish writings whose Hebrew original has first to be
ascertained.

In regard to the special rabbinic literature, it would be
particularly desirable to know what it has to say as to the
religious ideas of the Jews at the beginning of the second
century of our era—the earliest period for which it affords
intimate and reliable information. *F. Weber's* " Jüdische
Theologie," even in the second edition (1897),[1] freed as it has
been by I. I. Kahan from not a few defects, here leaves one
quite in the dark through failing to supply the necessary
separation of the earlier from the more recent, of the Palestinian from the non-Palestinian, as well as through the lack
of a more thorough treatment of details. The " Real-
Encyclopädie für Bibel und Talmud," with its supplements
(1884–1900), by *J. Hamburger,* is altogether a mere accumu-
lation of unsifted material, the several items of which require
first to be verified. " Der Leidende und der sterbende
Messias der Synagoge im ersten nachchristl. Jahrtausend "—
a treatise published by myself (1888)—endeavours to give
reliable data on one important topic. Apart from the concise
and excellent monograph of *D. Castelli,* Il Messia secondo gli
Ebrei (1874), the only works that attain the level worthy

[1] See my review in Theol. Litbl. 1897, col. 382 f.

of the theme are the treatises [1] of *W. Bacher*, which are far too sparingly used by theologians—" Die Agada der Tann-aiten" i. (1884), ii. (1894); " Die Agada der palästinens-ischen Amoräer" i. (1892), ii. (1896), iii. (1899).[2] After their completion by the anonymous Haggada of Palestine, these works will form a valuable thesaurus of the dicta of the Palestinian Rabbis, and furnish the means of attaining a real " theology of the early Palestinian synagogue."

Specially useful help should have been obtainable from the collections of rabbinic parallels to New Testament pas-sages which have been prepared by Christians and Jews in early and in recent times. Among Christian works of this class may be named: *Joh. Lightfoot*, Horæ hebraicæ et talmudicæ in quatuor Evangelistas, published by J. B. Carpzov, Leipzig, 1684 ; *Christ. Schöttgen*, Horæ hebraicæ et talmudicæ in universum Novum Testamentum, Dresden-Leipzig, 1733 ; *Joh. Gerh. Meuschen*, Novum Testamentum ex Talmude et antiquitatibus Hebræorum illustratum, Leipzig, 1736 ; *J. Jak. Wettstein* (Wctstcnius), Novum Testamentum Græcum, Amsterdam, 1751, 1752; *F. Nork*, Rabbinische Quellen und Parallelen zu neutestamentlichen Schriftstellen, Leipzig, 1839 ; *Franz Delitzsch*, Horæ hebraicæ et talmu-dicæ in Luth. Zeitschrift, 1876–8 ; *Carl Siegfried*, Analecta Rabbinica, 1875, Rabbinische Analekten, Jahrb. f. prot. Theol. 1876 ; *A. Wünsche*, Neue Beiträge zur Erläuterung der Evangelien aus Talmud und Midrasch, Göttingen, 1878.

Of Jewish productions, which, chiefly with an apologetic aim, institute comparisons between rabbinic and New Testa-ment sayings, there may be cited : *M. Duschak*, Die Moral der

---

[1] In order to call increased attention to Bacher's writings, as well as to set a better example in citing rabbinic sayings than that now prevalent in the commentaries, I shall make frequent reference to these writings, although for my own work they were not, properly speaking, a source.

[2] "Tempus loquendi. Über die Agada der palästinischen Amoräer nach der neuesten Darstellung" (1897), by *M. Aschkenaze*, is intended to be a criticism of vol. ii. der Ag. d. pal. Am. The author, however, demonstrates only his own amazing ignorance.

Evangelien und des Talmud, Brünn, 1877 ; *E. Schreiber*, Die Principien des Judentums verglichen mit denen des Christentums, Leipzig, 1877 ; *E. Soloweyczyg*, Die Bibel, der Talmud und das Evangelium, the German by M. Grünwald, Leipzig, 1877 ; *E. Grünebaum*, Die Sittenlehre des Judenthums audern Bekenntnissen gegenüber, 2nd ed., Strassburg, 1878 ; *S. Blumenau*, Gott und der Mensch, in Aussprüchen der Bibel alten und neuen Testaments, des Talmud und des Koran, Bielefeld, 1885.

Nearly all these works, however, are found to contribute only occasional observations. The relation of any particular case to the whole data in the domain of Rabbinism is not systematically set forth. Moreover, agreement and divergence between New Testament and rabbinic statements are not determined with sufficient care. These comparisons have thus caused in many minds an impression, very unfavourable to scientific progress, that little of fundamental importance is to be learned from such parallels. Such a book as *Wünsche's* "Neue Beiträge," by reason of quite superficial and inaccurate assertions and faulty translations, must even be characterised as directly misleading and confusing. It is obvious enough, further, that Jewish handling of the material for polemic purposes is hardly calculated to demonstrate the real difference between the words of Jesus and the sayings of the Rabbis.

No other course is open but to supply the deficiency in this case also by independent work on the post-canonical literature of the Jews. Our discussion will consequently be encumbered by researches which might well have been conducted elsewhere; but I trust it will not appear a blemish if Jewish materials, which may ultimately render important service in various ways to Biblical Theology, should here be found collected and sifted.

VIII. The Selection of the Dialect.

A serious difficulty in the way of our investigations consists in deciding the dialect of Aramaic, which they shall
presuppose. There is no justification indeed for Th. Zahn's [1]
misgiving that the distinction, adopted in my Grammar, of a
" Judæan " and a " Galilean " dialect of Jewish Aramaic rests
upon uncertain grounds. The two dialects so designated are
so sharply defined in point of grammar and vocabulary, that
their separation did not call for the exercise of exceptional
penetration. But in applying these designations, nothing is
fixed in regard to the time when these dialects flourished,
and the extent over which they then prevailed. The
" Judæan " dialect is known to us from literary remains of
Judæan origin in the period from the first to the third
(Christian) century; the Galilean dialect from writings of
Galilean origin in the period from the fourth to the seventh
century. That the " Galilean " at the time of its dominance among the Jews of Galilee was accompanied in other
parts of Palestine by sister-dialects closely akin, is proved
by the Samaritan Aramaic, and the still more closely related
Christian Palestinian Aramaic. This latter had even extended its sway into Egypt, as is proved by the liturgy for
the Blessing of the Nile, brought to light by G. Margoliouth.[2]
Aramaic was not merely a Church language in that region,
for in commenting on Isa. 19[18], Jerome explicitly states
that there were still, as was well known, five cities in Egypt
in which " the language of Canaan, namely the Syriac," was
spoken.[3] On the other hand, the Palmyrene and Nabatæan
Aramaic about the time of Christ must be pronounced as
standing closer to the " Judæan " than to the " Galilean "

---

[1] Einleitung in das Neue Testament, i. (1897) 19.

[2] G. Margoliouth, The Liturgy of the Nile (1896).

[3] *S. Krauss*, Jew. Quart. Rev. vi. (1894), 249, strangely considers, despite
the unmistakable statement of Jerome, that the Coptic language is meant.
" Syriac " being the Semitic language of Canaan in his own day, Jerome finds

dialect. It has, however, to be taken into account that our knowledge of the Aramaic of Palmyra and Nabatæa is derived exclusively from inscriptions, while the " Galilean " is a popular dialect elevated to a literary language.

One will best do justice to the ascertainable situation in saying, that in the time of Christ there was prevalent over all Palestine, from the extreme north to the south, a single literary language in Aramaic, varying but slightly in the different parts of the country. In this literary Aramaic are written the Aramaic sections in Daniel and in Ezra, the Targum of Onkelos, and the other documents assigned to the Judæan dialect,[1] as well as the Palmyrene and Nabatæan inscriptions. Concurrently (with this literary dialect) there existed a whole series of popular dialects : a Middle Palestinian, which we can recognise in a later phase as Samaritan Aramaic, and a North Palestinian, which is known to us in a Jewish and a Christian form—both belonging to a subsequent period. It is highly probable that after the final overthrow of the Judæan centre of Jewish-Aramaic culture, which was the result of the Bar Kochba revolution, the North Palestinian popular dialect got the upper hand over nearly all Palestine.

According to Matt. 26[73] (Mark 14[70], Luke 22[59]), Peter was recognised in Jerusalem as a Galilean on the strength of a few words, and was consequently termed a companion of Jesus. It must therefore be inferred that Jesus was likewise recognisable by His language. We must not, through following the Galilean dialect as known to us, explain this incident from the consideration that the Galileans were accustomed at a later period to soften the gutturals. Peter's denial contained the expression οὐκ οἶδα, " I do not know,"

Isaiah's prophecy fulfilled in the "Syriac" speaking inhabitants of Egypt. His description of the "Canaanitic" as occupying a position between the Hebrew and the Egyptian, and as being closely akin to Hebrew, corresponds only with what he calls "Syriac," but not with the Coptic language.

[1] Enumerated in Gram. d. j.-pal. Aram. 5-12.

or "I do not understand," Matt. 26⁷⁰ (Mark 14⁶⁸, Luke 22⁵⁷). In Galilean this would be לִית אֲנָא חָכֵם or לֵינָה חָכֵם, but in Judæan לִית אֲנָא יָדַע. In their use of the Galilean dialect there was nothing in any way inviting disparagement towards Jesus or His disciples. The anecdotes told in Babylon centuries later, b. Erub. 53ᵇ,[1] about the speech of uneducated Galilean women, must be regarded as a caricature of the truth even in their own late period. The Galilean as it is known to us from written works bears as yet no trace of decay or of corruption from outside influence. It is true only that certain signs of more advanced development as compared with the Judæan dialect may be detected in it. It cannot, however, be regarded as a later phase of the latter dialect. It is, of course, not unlikely that the language of Galilee underwent some changes between the time of Jesus and the fourth century. The pronunciation, the formation and scope of words, were in the earlier period indeed nearer by some degrees to the Judæan. For our purposes the scope of terms is of principal importance; and in that respect there can be no doubt that the number of Greek loan-words had increased, while it is highly probable that new Aramaic words from the north-east had found their way in and obtained currency by extruding others. Moreover, the possibility must not be excluded that Jesus, when speaking publicly, sought to conform to the Judæan dialect. If the Galilean taxgatherer Matthew really recorded the words of Jesus in Aramaic, it is most probable that he should avail himself of the literary language of Judæa, and not of the Galilean popular dialect. To all appearance his book was least of all addressed to Galilean readers.

---

[1] Compare on this point Gram. d. j.-pal. Aram. 43 f., where I have shown that the defective pronunciation of the gutturals cannot have been developed so markedly in the earlier period even in Galilee. Among the Babylonian Jews the change had gone much further; see C. Levias, A Grammar of the Babyl. Talmud, Am. Journ. Sem. Lang. xiii. 29 f.

It might seem as if the linguistic basis presupposed in our work were indeed highly uncertain. To a certain extent this is true. Any investigator who will be conscientious and sure of his steps, must take into consideration the whole field of linguistic possibilities lying between the biblical and the Galilean dialects of Aramaic.[1] The Judæan term must be considered side by side with the Galilean. And yet it will appear that the area of language coming into question is comprised within very narrow limits, and that most of the competing options that arise are of little or no weight in determining the exegesis. On the whole, the uncertainty as to language in this case is less considerable than that which confronts the translator of the Gospels into Hebrew, who, finding the biblical Hebrew impracticable, tries to steer a middle course between the language of the son of Sirach and that of the Mishna.

It is to be regretted that the most extensive literary monument of the *Judæan* dialect is a *Targum*. Translations of sacred books attached themselves then even more closely than now to the verbal tenour of the original. The Greek translation of the LXX is already an illustration of this tendency, and it was afterwards surpassed in that direction by the translation of Aquila. The method of Aquila's translation was further repeated in the probably contemporary Targum of the Pentateuch, which, by a curious accident, was adorned in Babylon with the name of Aquila in the form of "Onkelos." Only there resulted in that case, owing to the kinship of Aramaic and Hebrew, a linguistic product which was not quite so peculiar as in the Greek work of Aquila. By comparison with the other literary remains of Jewish Aramaic, it may, however, be

[1] *M. Schultze,* in his "Grammatik der aram. Muttersprache Jesu" (1899), has dealt exclusively with the biblical Aramaic, but has furnished it with a vocalisation based upon the biblical transliteration of Semitic names, and representing, as the author intends, the Galilean pronunciation.

determined with sufficient certitude what should be regarded as Hebraisms in the Targum. Genuine Aramaic is,
of course, most clearly recognisable in cases where the
Targum, despite its aim of precisely copying the original,
finds itself constrained to adopt divergences in style.

The following may be specified as *Hebraisms* which
essentially determine the style of the Targum: (1) the
frequent use of the construct state, whereas an Aramaic
original would have employed more commonly the circum-
locution with דְּ; (2) the regular use of the separate יָת as
substitute for the Hebrew accusative particle, whereas
Aramaic consistently dispenses with such a particle; (3)
the reproduction peculiar to the Targum of the biblical
כִּי, in all its meanings, by אֲרֵי,[1] which latter is known in
the Hebrew of the Mishna in the form הֲרֵי, restricted to
the meaning " see," and which in the remaining Aramaic
literature is wholly wanting in this sense; (4) the emphasising of the verb by apposition of the infinitive; (5) the use
of the Aramaic וַהֲוָה for the Hebrew narrative formula וַיְהִי,
which is foreign to Aramaic; (6) the use of the verb מַלֵּל
for the Hebrew דִּבֶּר in all cases of its occurrence, and of
לְמֵימַר for the Hebrew לֵאמֹר; (7) the frequent employment
of the Perfect as historic narrative tense where the Aramaic
would have had recourse to the Participle, either by itself
or preceded by הֲוָה; (8) the common use of the Infinitive
with prepositions, where Aramaic would have formed a
subordinate clause with דְּ.

In regard to Nöldeke's[2] assumed disfigurement of the
Targum of Onkelos by the Babylonian dialect, I am still
unable to cite a single case in point except the occasional
use of infinitive forms in *ō-ē*.[3] One instance may show how
careful we should be in putting forward any such assumption.

[1] See Gramm. d. j.-pal. Aram. 186 f., 190 f.; *Nöldeke*, ZDMG xxii. (1868)
489.

[2] *Th. Nöldeke*, Die semit. Sprachen, 32.

[3] Gram. d. j.-pal. Aram. 225 ff.

The Palestinian Abbahu says, b. Sukk. 5[b], that the name given to a "boy" (יְנוֹקָא) in Babylon was רָבְיָא. Now the Onkelos Targum uses רָבְיָא for "boy," while the Galilean dialect does not employ this word. But since the Mishna attests the corresponding Hebr. רוֹבֶה and the Samaritan likewise knows רְבִי, it is clear enough that רָבְיָא was not unknown in Palestine. Thus, when it occurs in Onkelos, the word should not be styled as a Babylonian intrusion.

The regrettable defect of the Judæan Aramaic above referred to, is in some measure compensated by our having the *Galilean* dialect made known to us almost exclusively through the short stories interspersed in the Palestinian Talmud and Midrash; and these stories bear throughout the mark of their artless popular origin. In this case we are furnished with what is so much missed in regard to the Samaritan, the Christian-Palestinian, and the earlier Syriac of Edessa, namely the really living speech of the people. By comparing this vernacular with the biblical Aramaic and the idiom of the Judæan documents (apart from the Targums), we have the only possible means of learning what was the style and mode of expression of the Jewish Aramaic of Palestine.

If the view put forward by Nöldeke, Buhl, Cornill, Ginsburger,[1] and others were correct, that the so-called *Jerusalem Targums* of the Pentateuch include sections from a very ancient and possibly pre-Christian period, then these, after deduction of the Hebraisms, would, of course, represent the best model for our work. Regard for this possibility caused me to give a prominent place in the Gram. des jüd.-pal. Aramäisch to the grammatical material in these Targums. But from that scrutiny I became convinced that the most primitive elements in regard to linguistic development to be found in these Targums are exactly the parts taken from the

---

[1] *M. Ginsburger*, Zum Fragmententargum, Jüd. Monatsschr. xli. (1897) 289–296, 340–349.

Onkelos Targum.[1] The style of these Targums had not as yet been closely studied, and theories regarding their origin had been based chiefly on the nature of their contents. But even on that ground I could discover no sound proofs of a great antiquity. As one passage from the Jerusalem Targum I. has been relied upon as a decisive evidence of its pre-Christian elements, it requires to be mentioned. In Deut. 33[11] the words run thus: "Bless, O Lord, the possession of the Levites, who give the tithe of the tithe, and graciously accept the offering of Elijah the priest, which he presents upon Mount Carmel; break asunder the loins of Ahab his enemy, and the necks of the false prophets who withstand him, and let there not be to the foes of Yokhanan the high priest a foot to stand upon." Now as John Hyrcanus was less favourably remembered among the Jews at a later date, this statement, it is held, must have originated soon after his own time, and have been written by those who were among his partisans. By these, one would presume, are meant the Sadducees, a fact in itself suspicious. But one who is familiar with the nature of these Targums will think first of a Midrash which applied the words of Scripture to John [Yokhanan]. At the most, therefore, we should have before us traces of a very old Midrash. As to the age of the Targum passage, nothing could be concluded. But we are not unacquainted with the Haggada which is here alluded to. The Midrash on Ps. 67, in speaking of the verse in question, says the Greek domination was destined to fall by means of the tribe of Levi; and in the Midrash on Genesis (Bereshith Rabba 99) it is also said, with reference to this verse, that the Greek domination was destined to fall by means of the sons of Hasmonai, because they were of Levitic descent. Accordingly the enemies of Yokhanan in the Targum are the Greeks (Syrians), and any one who has read the Roll of the

---

[1] See Gram. d. j.-pal. Aram. 21–26; and *J. Bassfreund*, Das Fragmenten-Targum zum Pentateuch (1896), 65 ff., 98.

Hasmonæans is aware that for the Jews the high priest Yokhanan, *the son of Mattathias*, was the most conspicuous champion against the Greek oppressors, and the proper "Maccabean." None but he could be named if a personal representative of the Hasmonæan house in its struggle against Greece had to be cited.[1] Since, however, the representations given in the very late Roll of the Hasmonæans are wholly unhistorical, the passage in question becomes in reality an evidence for the late date of the Jerusalem Targum I. It is only in so far as they are evidence of an early form of the Onkelos Targum, and in so far as the Galilean dialect is traceable in them, that the Jerusalem Targums of the Pentateuch can yield us any assistance. The want of due precaution in the use made of them by J. T. Marshall is one of the things which were bound to render his efforts to reproduce the "Aramaic Gospel" a failure.

The Palestinian Lectionary of the Gospels, along with the other biblical lessons extant in the same language,[2] would, owing to the close relationship of its dialect with the Galilean, offer inestimable service towards the recovery of the Aramaic original of the words of Jesus, if it were not, like all the other ancient translations, merely a Targum, *i.e.* an imitation of the Greek original in the Aramaic dialect of the Christians of

[1] Rabbinic tradition, by the way, elsewhere distinguishes "the high priest Yokhanan" (Hyrcanus) from "King Yannai" (Alexander Jannæus). To the former a series of praiseworthy acts are ascribed, the only complaint being that he finally became a Sadducee ; the latter ranked as really impious. Raba b. Ber. 29ᵃ declares explicitly : "Yannai was an ungodly man from the beginning, but Yokhanan was a pious man from the beginning." It was Yokhanan who was informed by a divine voice in the temple of the victory of the "boys" in Antioch (j. Sot. 24ᵇ).

[2] The parts of the Scripture from the Old and the New Testaments, which had been published up to September 1897, are enumerated by E. Nestle in Studia Sinaitica vi., A Palestinian Syriac Lectionary, edited by *Agnes Smith Lewis*, xiv. ff. Since then has been added *G. Margoliouth*, The Palestinian Syriac Version of the Holy Scriptures, four recently discovered portions, London, 1897, and the excellent new edition of the Evangeliarium Hierosolymitanum by *Agnes Smith Lewis* and *Margaret Dunlop Gibson*, under the title "The Palestinian Syriac Lectionary of the Gospels," London, 1899.

Palestine. The slavish nature of the imitation is illustrated, *e.g.*, by the fact that the verb, with trifling exceptions, has no pronominal suffixes attached, because the Greek language only uses the personal pronouns independently.[1] For that very reason, however, this version, in parts where it does diverge from the tenour of the Greek, indicates all the more surely such Greek constructions as were repugnant to the Aramaic language. Besides, there is some suspicion that the Palestinian Gospel Lectionary has been influenced in its vocabulary by the Syriac version of Edessa. Unfortunately the "Idioticon des christlich - palästinischen Aramäisch" (1893), by *F. Schwally*, gives no light on this, as on other important points. Schwally has aimed at collecting the differences in the matter of vocabulary between the Christian Palestinian and the Edessene. But one does not learn what words are common to the two dialects, or which of such words in their turn are not found in the Palestinian Aramaic known from other sources.[2] It is not the ecclesiastical Aramaic of Palestine that can give any assistance, but only the idiom thence ascertained which was actually spoken by the Palestinians. A service similar to that of the Palestinian Lectionary is rendered also by the Edessene version in its various recensions now known to us (Cureton., Sinait., Peshita). But no assistance derived from any of these Aramaic versions can be used towards the attainment of a genuine Aramaic diction, unless the same mode of expression can be attested in the Jewish Aramaic. If we were to make the Jerusalem Lectionary the basis of our investigation, as proposed by Wellhausen,[3] it would first be necessary to prove that in it, and not in the Jewish Aramaic, was the language of Jesus and the earliest apostles preserved. But this supposition cannot be seriously entertained. The

[1] *Nöldeke*, ZDMG xxii. (1868) 505 f.
[2] See the incomplete suggestions of *Nöldeke*, ZDMG xxii. (1868) 517, 522.
[3] Gött. Gel. Anz. 1896, 265.

Christian Palestinian literature is a clear proof that there was practically no spiritual intercourse between the primitive Aramaic-speaking Jewish-Christian Church and the Jewish people. The Church of the Greek and Edessene languages is the spiritual mother of the Palestinian-Aramaic communities. Their language contained, indeed, a number of Hebrew words which occur also in Jewish Aramaic. But the presence of the terms merely proves the influence of the language which had been spoken by the very numerous Jews in Palestine at a prior period. A Jewish derivation, such as Nöldeke [1] supposes, cannot be inferred from this circumstance. Even if it should have taken place, the Jewish elements would have been obliterated long before. If, further, any grave doubts may justly be entertained as to whether the Jewish Galilean of the year 400 was altogether similar to the language of Jesus, then by abandoning the field of the Jewish Aramaic every valid foundation would be wholly lost.

We shall therefore have every reason to guard against giving too much weight to the Syriac versions of the Gospels. The Targum of Onkelos and the Palestinian Talmud and Midrash remain our most important criteria. As the idiom of the first of these, whose vocabulary can also be tested by the Hebrew of the Mishna, represents in any case a stage of the language nearer to the time of Jesus, we shall attach ourselves principally to it, not failing, however, to note the divergences of the Galilean dialect. The vocalisation will be guided by the tradition as to the pronunciation represented in the Targum manuscripts from Yemen, with the exceptions specified in my " Aramäische Dialektproben," iv. ff., especially as regards the Galilean. It should be explicitly affirmed, however, that in many an instance a different pronunciation prevailed in the time of Jesus ; cf. Gramm. d. jüd.-pal. Aramaic, 46, 48, 50 f., 59 ff., 64 ff.

[1] ZDMG xxii. 522 f., Die semitischen Sprachen (1887), 33.

FUNDAMENTAL IDEAS.

I. THE SOVEREIGNTY OF GOD.

A. Sovereignty of Heaven, Sovereignty of God, Sovereignty.

THE expression ἡ βασιλεία τῶν οὐρανῶν is altogether peculiar to the Gospel of Matthew, of which it is as characteristic as is the cognate appellation ὁ πατήρ (μου, ἡμῶν, ὑμῶν) ὁ ἐν οὐρανοῖς (ὁ οὐράνιος).[1] Mark and Luke have uniformly, Matthew has rarely, ἡ βασιλεία τοῦ θεοῦ.

The Jewish expression[2] corresponding to ἡ βασ. τ. οὐρανῶν is in Aramaic מַלְכוּתָא דִשְׁמַיָּא, in Hebrew מַלְכוּת שָׁמַיִם. In the latter it is worthy of notice that שָׁמַיִם is always without the article,[3] from which it appears that the Aramaic שְׁמַיָּא is in the definite form only because the indefinite form of this word does not occur in Jewish Aramaic. The Mishna says מַלְכוּת שָׁמַיִם, *e.g.* Ber. ii. 2; and similarly without the article, מוֹרָא שָׁמַיִם, "the fear of God," Ab. i. 3; שֵׁם שָׁמַיִם, "the name of God," Sanh. vi. 4; בִּידֵי שָׁמַיִם, "through, by God," Sanh. ix. 6; on the other hand, invariably מִן הַשָּׁמַיִם, "from heaven," Sanh. x. 1; Ned. x. 6.[4] The difference is to be attributed to the fact that in the last-mentioned phrase the locative sense of שָׁמַיִם was still consciously

---

[1] Fundamental Ideas, VI.

[2] According to *Stave*, "Über den Einfluss der Parsismus auf das Judenthum" (1898), 180 ff., the Persian idea of the "Supreme Sovereignty" exerted some influence when the term originated. This is possible, but not necessary.

[3] See *Franz Delitzsch*, Neue Beobachtungen über hebr. Spracheigentümlichkeiten, v., Theol. Litbl. 1887, No. 48.

[4] See also Fund. Ideas, VIII.; *E. Schürer*, Jahrb. f. prot. Theol. 1876, p. 171 ff.; *Ch. Taylor*, Sayings of the Jewish Fathers [2] (1897), 67.

present, whereas, in the other cases, שָׁמַיִם is purely a substitute for "God." Compare, further, b. Mo. Kat. 15a,
מְנֻדֶּה לְשָׁמַיִם, "one who is banished by God," and יְרַחֲמוּ עֲלֵיהֶם
מִן הַשָּׁמַיִם, "mercy is shown to them from heaven."

Although מַלְכוּתָא דִשְׁמַיָּא is thus tantamount to the
"sovereignty of God," it does not thence follow that all
trace of the thought, that in the phrase the dwelling-place
of God was being named instead of Him who was there
enthroned, must have been obliterated. Simeon ben Lakish,
about 260 A.D., contrasted the "sovereignty of earth (מַלְכוּת
הָאָרֶץ) with the "sovereignty of heaven" (מַלְכוּת שָׁמַיִם).[1] For
him, therefore, "heaven" is in this case the dwelling-place
of God. Similarly, the Babylonian saying,[2] מַלְכוּתָא דְאַרְעָא כְּעֵין
מַלְכוּתָא דִרְקִיעָא, "the earthly government resembles the heavenly
government," has regard to the seat of human kings, and of
God. Again, Yokhanan ben Zakkai, about 80 A.D., makes
mention of "the yoke of the heavenly sovereignty" (עֹל
מַלְכוּת שָׁמַיִם) alongside of "the yoke of flesh and blood" (עֹל
בָּשָׂר וָדָם),[3] thereby bringing "God" into contrast with "men."
The difference in the point of view is, however, of small
importance, because in every case the "heavenly sovereignty,"
in contradistinction to the "earthly," is nothing else than
the "sovereignty of God" as opposed to all human government. There is no ulterior idea present in regard to the
derivation or the nature of the divine sovereignty. It can
only be ascribed to unfamiliarity with Jewish phraseology,
that it is still commonly the custom to see in ἡ βασιλεία
τῶν οὐρανῶν a reference to the transcendental character
of the object so designated.[4] It is not the βασιλεία that

---

[1] Ber. R. 9. [2] b. Ber. 58a.

[3] j. Kidd. 59d; see *Bacher*, Agada der Tannaiten, i. 30 f. Cf. in the mouth
of Chanina (about 80 A.D.) the antithesis of עֹל הַקָּרוֹשׁ בָּרוּךְ הוּא and עֹל בָּשָׂר וָדָם,
Ab. d. R. Nathan, 30.

[4] See, e.g., *V. H. Stanton*, The Jewish and the Christian Messiah (1886), 209;
W. Baldensperger, Das Selbstbewusstsein Jesu² (1892), 197 f.; *L. Paul*, Die
Vorstellungen vom Messias und vom Gottesreich bei den Synoptikern (1895),
21 f.; *K. G. Grass*, Das von Jesus geforderte Verhalten zum Reiche Gottes,

is indicated as transcendent in this phrase, but the βασιλεύς. ἡ βασιλεία τῶν οὐρανῶν is the sovereignty of the transcendent God. Least of all has the plural שָׁמַיִם—for which no singular form exists—anything whatever to do with the heavens being seven in number. A Hellenist might *possibly*, indeed, attach some such notion to the Greek οἱ οὐρανοί, but that is not a sufficient reason for imputing the idea to Matthew, who makes no allusion of the kind.[1] Evidence of the meaning attached by Jesus to the words τῶν οὐρανῶν is afforded also by the substitute τοῦ θεοῦ, which is used exclusively in Mark and Luke. The evangelists have clearly considered the two phrases as synonymous; and as they thus coincide with the Jewish meaning of the expression מַלְכוּת שָׁמַיִם, it is safe to assume the same interpretation in the case of Jesus.

According to J. Weiss[2] and H. J. Holtzmann,[3] it was only Matthew who imputed the expression to Jesus, the original actually spoken being ἡ βασιλεία τοῦ θεοῦ. But modern misunderstandings of ἡ βασ. τῶν οὐρανῶν render it only too credible that Mark and Luke, out of regard to heathen readers, avoided the specifically Jewish expression, and followed the Greek Bible, which mentions no "sovereignty of heaven," but only "the sovereignty of God." See Ps. 103¹⁹ 148¹¹· ¹²· ¹³, Tob. 13¹, Wisd. 6⁵ 10¹⁰,[4] Ps. of Sol. 17¹⁴, Dan. 3⁵⁴ (Song of the Three Children). This is the usage also of the Targums, which put מַלְכוּתָא דַיְיָ where the Hebrew text speaks of Jehovah as being King (see below). Jesus will

---

Mitt. u. Nachr. f. d. ev. K. in Russl. 1895, p. 52 ; H. J. Holtzmann, Lehrb. d. neutestamentl. Theologie (1897), i. 189 f. ; A. Meyer, Die moderne Forschung über d. Gesch. des Urchristenthums (1898), 73.

[1] In opposition to Holtzmann, loc. cit. 191.

[2] J. Weiss, Die Predigt vom Reiche Gottes (1892), 9.

[3] Lehrb. d. neutest. Theologie, i. 191 f.

[4] E. Issel, Die Lehre vom Reiche Gottes im Neuen Testament (1895), 20, thinks that in this passage the "fulfilment of the Messianic promises" is implied by βασιλεία θεοῦ; it is, however, merely a glimpse given to Jacob into God's position as sovereign that is meant.

have preferred the popular expression because He also readily abstained from the use of the divine name.

No doubt can be entertained that both in the Old Testament and in Jewish literature מַלְכוּת, when applied to God, means always the " kingly rule," never the " kingdom," as if it were meant to suggest the territory governed by Him. For the Old Testament, see Ps. 103[19] 145[11. 12. 13], cf. Obad. [21], Ps. 22[29] (מְלוּכָה) ; for the Jewish literature, the instances to be cited later on.[1] To-day as in antiquity an Oriental " kingdom " is not a body politic in our sense, a people or land under some form of constitution, but merely a " sovereignty " which embraces a particular territory. We shall be justified, therefore, in starting from this signification of מַלְכוּת as employed by Jesus. Krop,[2] indeed, in his definition " un domaine à la tête duquel se trouve un roi," has regarded the locative as the primary sense of the expression. Bousset,[3] too, finds that only now and then does the sense " sovereignty of God " take the place of " kingdom of God," and he seeks for special reasons for this interchange. But it is more correct to regard, with B. Weiss,[4] as fundamental, the meaning, " the full realisation of the sovereignty of God," and then to adhere uniformly [5] to the term " sovereignty," so as never to lose sight of the starting - point. The German word " Herrschaft " (sovereignty) can also in a secondary sense denote a region, so that German is free from the embarrassment felt, e.g., by Candlish,[6] who tried to alternate the words " reign " and " kingdom."

In two cases there occurs the expression ἡ βασιλεία τοῦ

---

[1] See also Fund. Ideas, I. 8.—E. Schürer, Jahrb. f. prot. Theol. 1876, p. 183, defines מַלְכוּת שָׁמַיִם not quite accurately as the "kingdom in which heaven, i.e. the heavenly King, rules."

[2] F. Krop, La pensée de Jésus sur le royaume de Dieu (1897), 21 f.

[3] W. Bousset, Jesu Predigt in ihrem Gegensatz z. Judentum (1892), 97.

[4] B. Weiss, Lehrb. d. bibl. Theol. des N.T.[6] (1895) 46.

[5] This is advocated also by K. G. Grass, loc. cit. 50 f.

[6] Candlish, The Kingdom of God (1884), quoted by Stanton, The Jewish and the Christian Messiah, 217.

πατρός (αὐτῶν, μου), Matt. 13⁴³ and 26²⁹. For the latter passage the parallels Mark 14²⁵, Luke 22¹⁸ have τοῦ θεοῦ. It need cause no surprise that Jesus should occasionally avail Himself of this mode of expression, for He loved to characterise God as " Father."

In the same category should also be reckoned Matt. 6³³ (Luke 12³¹), where ἡ βασιλεία αὐτοῦ points back to ὁ πατὴρ ὑμῶν ὁ οὐράνιος, ver. 32 (cf. Luke 12³⁰ ὑμῶν ὁ πατήρ); and also Matt. 25³⁴, where ἡ βασιλεία is unprovided with a further qualification only because, in view of its being prepared for " the blessed of My Father," the addition appeared unnecessary.

The question becomes more delicate when ἡ βασιλεία, in some cases where the context is not so obvious, appears to be without any supplement. This happens only in Matthew, and almost exclusively in composite expressions. Here we find : οἱ υἱοὶ τῆς βασιλείας,¹ 8¹² 13³⁸; ὁ λόγος τῆς βασιλείας, 13¹⁹ (Luke 8¹¹ ὁ λ. τοῦ θεοῦ ; Mark 4¹⁴ ὁ λόγος only); and τὸ εὐαγγέλιον τῆς βασιλείας, 4²³ (wanting in Mark 1³⁹, Luke 4⁴⁴), 9³⁵ (wanting in Mark 6⁶, Luke 13²²), 24¹⁴ (Mark 13¹⁰ τὸ εὐαγγέλιον only, cf. Matt. 26¹³, Mark 14⁹). Of these passages, however, 4²³ and 9³⁵ are due to the narrator. A fuller designation is not in itself impossible, as appears from τὰ μυστήρια τῆς βασιλείας τῶν οὐρανῶν, Matt. 13¹¹ (Luke 8¹⁰ τὰ μ. τ. β. τοῦ θεοῦ, Mark 4¹¹ τὸ μυστήριον τ. β. τ. θ.).

When הַמַּלְכוּת is used in Jewish literature without further definition, what is meant is always the secular " government " for the time being, whether the ruler himself or merely the officials representing him be the object of attention. Compare, for example, the expression קָרוֹב לַמַּלְכוּת " connected with the (Roman) government," b. Sanh. 43ᵃ;² b. Bab. k. 83ᵃ; cf. b. Sot. 41ᵇ with Ab. iii. 8 (Nekhonya ben ha-Kanna about

---

¹ Cf. on the expression, Fund. Ideas, I. 4c.

² It is incorrect to make this passage apply to a relationship with the royal family of the Jews, and to turn it into a proof of the Davidic descent of Jesus.

70 A.D.) : " Every man, who takes upon himself the yoke of
the Law, is set free from the yoke of the (foreign) government (עוֹל מַלְכוּת), and from the yoke of providing a livelihood "
(עוֹל דֶּרֶךְ אֶרֶץ). See also Sot. ix. 17 ; j. Ber. 6ᵃ, 13ᶜ ; j. Ter.
46ᵇ. In this case מַלְכוּת by itself cannot be supposed to
represent the sovereignty of God. And as Jesus always
uses, except in the instances given, fuller expressions, it
should not be assumed that even for Him " the sovereignty "
had as yet become an equivalent term for " the sovereignty of
God." Within the Christian community, and specially the
Greek-speaking part of it, this identification is more credible.
And in it the terms used by Matthew will have been
formed.

B. THE JEWISH USE OF THE IDEA.

The first consideration in the Jewish view is that the
sovereignty of God is an eternal one. The Targum of
Onkelos in Ex. 15¹⁸ puts : " God . . . His kingly sovereignty endures for ever and ever " (יְיָ מַלְכוּתֵיהּ קָאִים לְעָלַם
וּלְעָלְמֵי עָלְמַיָּא), for the Hebrew יְהוָֹה יִמְלֹךְ לְעוֹלָם וָעֶד, thus substituting for the personal terms of the text an equivalent
of a more abstract character. This sovereignty began when
Abraham made God known upon earth. In Siphre Dt.
113 (Fr. 134ᵇ) it is said : " Before our father Abraham
came into the world, God was, as it were, only the king
of heaven ; but when Abraham came, he made Him to be
king over heaven and earth." Thereafter at the Red Sea
and at Sinai Israel gave allegiance to this sovereignty of
God.[1] Thenceforward it has its earthly presence in Israel.
It is to the sovereignty of God in this sense that Eleazar
ben Azaria (about 100 A.D.) refers in a saying, which also
shows the connection of the expressions " heavenly Father "
and " sovereignty of heaven " : " One should not say : I
have no inclination for garments of mixed stuffs, swine's

[1] Mechilta, ed. Friedm. 67ᵃ.

flesh, forbidden wedlock ; but one should say : I have
indeed inclination for such things, but what shall I do
when my heavenly Father has forbidden them to me ? (מַה
אֶעֱשֶׂה וְאָבִי שֶׁבַּשָׁמַיִם גָּזַר עָלַי כָּךְ) ; [for thus are we taught,[1] Lev.
20²⁶] : 'and I have separated you from the peoples, that
ye should be mine';—here we find him (i.e. man, according
to the Scripture text) separating himself from transgression
and thereby taking upon himself the sovereignty of God "
(נִמְצָא פּוֹרֵשׁ מִן הָעֲבֵרָה וּמְקַבֵּל עָלָיו מַלְכוּת שָׁמַיִם).[2]   According to
Simeon ben Lakish (c. 260 A.D.),[3] the proselyte who adopts
the law thereby " takes upon himself the sovereignty of
heaven." In the statement of Yokhanan ben Zakkai,[4] adduced on page 92, the Israelite who voluntarily becomes
a slave for life declares that he renounces the yoke of the
heavenly sovereignty (פָּרַק עוֹל מַלְכוּת שָׁמַיִם), and takes upon
himself the yoke of man (קִבֵּל עוֹל בָּשָׂר וָדָם).   Here the sovereignty of God is called a yoke, because God is able to
compel Israel, even against his will, to accept His service.
In Siphra 112ᵇ, He says to Israel : " In spite of you—do I
set up My sovereignty over you " (עַל כָּרְחֲכֶם—מַמְלִיךְ אֲנִי מַלְכוּתִי
עֲלֵיכֶם). How little of realistic mysticism is here asscociated
with the sovereignty of God becomes clear also from the
fact that the daily recitation of the " Shema," with the
reading of Deut. 6⁴⁻¹⁰ (where the One God requiring undivided love is acknowledged), is regarded as a continually
repeated " taking upon one's self of the yoke of the
sovereignty of God." In this sense Gamaliel II. (c. 110
A.D.) replied to those who maintained that as a bridegroom
he was free from the duty of the reading of the Shema on
the evening of his marriage : " I yield not to you in that—to
lay aside even for one hour the sovereignty of God "[5] (לִבְטֵל
מִמֶּנִּי מַלְכוּת שָׁמַיִם שָׁעָה אַחַת). Joshua ben Korkha (c. 150

---

[1] This is wanting in Siphra, Venice edition (1545), ed. princ.
[2] Siphra, ed. Weiss, 93ᵈ ; see Bacher, Ag. d. Tann. i. 228.
[3] Tanchuma, ed. Buber, לך לכה 6 ; cf. Bacher, Ag. d. p. Am. i. 374.
[4] j. Kidd. 59ᵇ.   [5] Ber. ii. 5.

A.D.) says that in the recitation of the Shema, Deut. 6[4-8] ought to precede Deut. 11[13-21], because the "yoke of the divine sovereignty" (עוֹל מַלְכוּת שָׁמַיִם) must be assumed prior to the "yoke of the commandments" (עוֹל מִצְוֹח).[1] And the expression קִבֵּל עוֹל מַלְכוּת שָׁמַיִם is found exactly as a designation for the recitation of the Shema, e.g. j. Ber. 4ᵃ, 7ᵇ.

Thus the sovereignty of God belongs, in the first instance, to the current age,[2] and is as yet fully acknowledged only in Israel. The future will, however, bring a fuller development. The present reveals in two directions an imperfect realisation of the idea. Israel is under foreign domination, and the peoples do not acknowledge the divine sovereignty. If the sovereignty of God is to appear in all its glory, Israel must be set free from the sway of the peoples, and the Gentile world be subjugated to God. The former is part of the common prayer for synagogues of the dispersion, being introduced in the eleventh petition of the "Eighteen Prayers": הָשִׁיבָה שׁוֹפְטֵינוּ כְּבָרִאשׁוֹנָה וְיוֹעֲצֵינוּ כְּבַתְּחִלָּה וְהָסֵר מִמֶּנּוּ יָגוֹן וַאֲנָחָה וּמְלוֹךְ עָלֵינוּ אַתָּה יְיָ לְבַדְּךָ בְּחֶסֶד וּבְרַחֲמִים [3] בְּצֶדֶק וּבְמִשְׁפָּט בָּרוּךְ אַתָּה יְיָ מֶלֶךְ אוֹהֵב צְדָקָה וּמִשְׁפָּט "restore our judges as of old and our counsellors as in the beginning; put away from us sorrow and sighing; and be Thou alone King over us, O Jehovah, in mercy and compassion, in grace[4] and justice! Blessed art Thou, O Jehovah, a King who lovest grace and righteousness." Another prayer,[5] speaking of the full realisation of God's sovereignty over Israel, says: יִשְׂמְחוּ בְּמַלְכוּתְךָ שׁוֹמְרֵי שַׁבָּת—כֻּלָּם יִשְׂבְּעוּ וְיִתְעַנְּגוּ מִטּוּבֶךָ, "they shall delight in Thy sovereignty—every one of those that keep the Sabbath day; they shall all be satisfied and refreshed in

---

[1] Ber. ii. 2.

[2] This is rightly affirmed by S. Schechter, Jew. Quart. Rev. vii. (1895) 195 ff.

[3] Thus in Seder Rab Amram, i. 8ᵃ; but Machzor Vitry, 67, has וְצַדְּקֵנוּ בַּמִּשְׁפָּט, "and pronounce us free in the judgment."

[4] On this translation of צֶדֶק and צְדָקָה see my treatise, "Die richterl. Gerechtigkeit im Alten Testament," 5 ff.

[5] Seder Rab Amram, i. 29ᵇ.

Thy goodness." To a later period belongs the divine word attached to Zech. 9⁹ in Pesikta Rabbati, 159ᵃ. Speaking as the future King of Zion, God there addresses the pious in Israel thus: "Ye pious ones of the world! although, strictly speaking, I owe you words of praise, since ye waited for My law although not for My sovereignty (שֶׁחִפִּיתֶם לְחוֹרָתִי וְלֹא חִפִּיתֶם לְמַלְכוּתִי),[1] yet I swear to you that I will bear witness for good to every one who waits for My sovereignty, as it is said: 'Wait patiently for Me, saith Jehovah, against that day when I rise up as witness-bearer'— in favour of the sorrowful ones who mourn with Me over My ruined house and My desolated palace."

In regard to the future recognition of God throughout the entire Gentile world, the Sibylline Oracles, iii. 47, has the following: βασιλεία μεγίστη ἀθανάτου βασιλῆος ἐπ' ἀνθρώποιει φανεῖται; and iii. 76: καὶ τότε δ' ἐξεγερεῖ βασιλήϊον εἰς αἰῶνας πάντας ἐπ' ἀνθρώποις. Joshua ben Khananya (c. 100 A.D.), speaking of the time when all service of other gods shall be abolished, says: "Then shall God alone be absolute in all the world, and His sovereignty will endure for ever and ever" (וִיהִי הַפָּקוֹם יְחִידִי בָעוֹלָם וּתְהִי מַלְכוּתוֹ לְעוֹלָם וּלְעוֹלְמֵי עוֹלָמִים).[2] The "Kaddish"[3] prayer in Aramaic, dating back to a great antiquity, concludes with the wish: וְיַמְלֵיךְ מַלְכוּתֵיהּ בְּחַיֵּיכוֹן וּבְיוֹמֵיכוֹן וּבְחַיֵּי דְכָל בֵּית יִשְׂרָאֵל בַּעֲגָלָא וּבִזְמַן קָרִיב, "and may He (God) set up His sovereignty in your lifetime, and in your days, and in the lifetime of the whole house of Israel, (yea) speedily, and in a time that is near."[4] What

---

[1] Cod. de Rossi, 1240, in Parma, has חיביחם both times; but the citation introduced at the end from Zeph. 3⁸ proves that חכיחם must be meant.

[2] Mechilta, edition by Friedmann, 56ᵃ; see Bacher, Ag. d. Tann. i. 147.

[3] On this see Zunz, Gottesdienstliche Vorträge,² 385; Landshuth, Seder bikkur cholim ma'bar jabbok we-sepher ha-chajjim (1867), lix.–lxviii.; Dalman, "Jüd. Seelenmesse und Totenanrufung," Saat auf Hoffnung, xxvii. (1890) 169 ff.

[4] So in Seder Rab Amram, i. 3ᵇ, and in Machzor Vitry, 64. Maimonides (in Mishne Torah) after מַלְכוּתֵיהּ inserts וְיַצְמַח פָּרְקָנֵיהּ וִיקָרֵב מְשִׁיחֵיהּ וְיִפְרוֹק עַמֵּיהּ, "and may He cause His redemption to spring up and His anointed to come near and ransom His people."

is then destined to happen is consistently detailed in the
prayer עָלֵינוּ,[1] which originated in Babylon *c.* 240 A.D.   In it
the hope is expressed that God will ultimately " bring the
world into order by means of His kingly sovereignty " (לְתַקֵּן
עוֹלָם בְּמַלְכוּת שַׁדַּי), so that then " all shall submit themselves to
the yoke of this sovereignty " (יְקַבְּלוּ כֻלָּם אֶת עוֹל מַלְכוּתֶךָ וְתִמְלוֹךְ
עֲלֵיהֶם).   The same sense appears in the ancient prayer : [2] מַלְכֵּנוּ
אֱלֹהֵינוּ יַחֵד שְׁמָךְ בְּעוֹלָמֶךָ יַחֵד מַלְכוּתֶךָ בְּעוֹלָמֶךָ וְיַחֵד זִכְרָךְ בְּעוֹלָמֶךָ, " our
King, our God, make Thy name one in Thy world, make Thy
sovereignty absolute (lit. ' one ') in Thy world, and make
absolute the remembrance of Thee in Thy world."   Present
and future are included in the doxology : [3] דְּיֵי הִיא מַלְכוּתָא
בְּעָלְמָא הָדֵין וּבְעָלְמָא דַעֲתִיד לְמֵיתֵי, " to Jehovah belongs the
sovereignty in this age and in that to come."   Similarly
it is said in the Psalter of Solomon, 17[3f.] : τὸ κράτος τοῦ
θεοῦ ἡμῶν εἰς τὸν αἰῶνα [4] μετ' ἐλέου, καὶ ἡ βασιλεία τοῦ θεοῦ
ἡμῶν εἰς τὸν αἰῶνα ἐπὶ τὰ ἔθνη ἐν κρίσει, " the might of our
God is (upon us) [4] for ever with mercy, and the sovereignty of
our God is upon the peoples for ever in judgment."

Since God is in reality Ruler even now,—a fact which
only requires to be openly recognised,—the establishment
with power of His sovereignty may after all be termed an
" appearing."   Thus the Assumptio Mosis (10[1]) already says :
" Parebit regnum illius (scil. Domini)."   The Midrash on
Cant. 2[12] represents the " sovereignty of God " as one day
taking the place of the " ungodly sovereignty " (מַלְכוּת הָרְשָׁעָה),[5]
and says of the former : הִגִּיעַ זְמָנָה שֶׁל מַלְכוּת שָׁמַיִם שֶׁתִּגָּלֶה, " the
time has arrived for the sovereignty of God to be re-
vealed."   The relation of God to Israel during this sovereignty
is the subject of the petition, Sopher. xiv. 12 : תִּגָּלֶה וְתֵרָאֶה

---

[1] *Zunz*, loc. cit. 386 ; and for the text of the prayer, Machzor Vitry, 75 ;
Baer's Seder Abodath Jisrael, 131.

[2] Seder Rab Amram, i. 9ª.

[3] Machzor Vitry, 343.

[4] ἐφ ἡμᾶς, "upon us," has obviously to be supplied.

[5] The Roman rule is here meant.

מַלְכוּתוֹ עֲלֵינוּ, "may His sovereignty over us be made open and manifest!"

This mode of expression is specially popular with the Targum writers, who wish to avoid the thought that God in person should appear on earth. In place of הִנֵּה אֱלֹהֵיכֶם, "behold your God," Isa. 40⁹, the Targum says: אִתְגְּלִיאַת מַלְכוּתָא דֶאֱלָהֲכוֹן, "the sovereignty of your God has become manifest"; and in place of יְהֹוָה מֶלֶךְ, "Jehovah shall reign," Mic. 4⁷ תִּתְגְּלֵי מַלְכוּתָא דַיָי, "the sovereignty of God will be manifest." Expressions of similar tenour occur in the Targum for the passages, Isa. 31⁴ 52⁷, Ezek. 7⁷·¹⁰ 11²⁴, Obad. ²¹, Zech. 14⁹.

It cannot be ascertained that any idea of a pre-existence of the divine rule in heaven was contemplated in this connection. That which exists from the first is God as Ruler or Sovereign. The new element, which the future brings, belongs to the sphere of the earthly realisation of His sovereignty. There is here no thought of pre-existent "realities" emerging into the course of the world.[1] But while for the Jews the מַלְכוּת of God invariably means the governance exercised by Him, it is quite compatible with this idea that different terms had to be used when the blessings promised to Israel in the Messianic age were to be indicated.[2]

C. THE APPLICATION OF THE IDEA OF THE DIVINE SOVEREIGNTY IN THE WORDS OF JESUS.

A preliminary analysis of the Jewish usage of the idea of the divine government had to be premised, in order that its specific application by Jesus might appear in the proper

---

[1] See also Fundamental Ideas, I. 6 f. ; *Holtzmann*, Lehrb. d. neutest. Theol. i. 189.

[2] *F. Krop*, La Pensée de Jésus sur le royaume de Dieu, 22, incorrectly holds that "the reaction against the Messianic hopes after the fall of Jerusalem" has contributed to this result. This reaction is just as little demonstrable as its alleged results. *Holtzmann*, loc. cit. i. 189, is also inaccurate in speaking of the "kingdom of heaven" as only another name for "the days of the Messiah."

light. This application may be studied to best advantage, in connection with the various composite expressions into which the idea in question enters, in the discourse of Jesus. We give them in six groups.

1. THE SOVEREIGNTY OF GOD IS THE SUBJECT OF AN ANNOUNCE-
MENT IN CONNECTION WITH THE VERBS εὐαγγελίζεσθαι,
κηρύσσειν, διαγγέλλειν.[1]

It cannot, however, be pronounced certain that Jesus ever directly coupled any one of these verbs with ἡ βασιλεία τοῦ θεοῦ (τῶν οὐρανῶν). Luke alone has on one occasion (4⁴³) ascribed to Jesus the words εὐαγγελίζεσθαι τὴν β. τ. θ. The parallel passage, Mark 1³⁸, has κηρύσσειν with no object. The passive ἡ β. τ. θ. εὐαγγελίζεται is likewise found only in Luke (16¹⁶) with no parallel in Matt. 11¹², and, moreover, raises difficulties to the Semitic translator, the passive of בַּשֵּׂר meaning always " to receive a message," but not " to be announced." [2] Even the substantive εὐαγγέλιον is only once, Matt. 24¹⁴, connected with ἡ βασιλεία. The parallel passage, Mark 13¹⁰, omits βασιλεία, just as it is also omitted, Matt. 26¹³, in connection with εὐαγγέλιον. In Mark 1¹⁵, but not in the parallel, Matt. 4¹⁷, Jesus speaks of " believing in the gospel," without further qualification. The formula ἕνεκεν ἐμοῦ καὶ (ἕνεκεν) τοῦ εὐαγγελίου is so expressed only in Mark 8³⁵ 10²⁹, whereas in Matt. 16²⁵ (Luke 9²⁴) and Matt. 19²⁹ (Luke 18²⁹) the gospel is not mentioned. It was within the Christian community that τὸ εὐαγγέλιον and εὐαγγελίζεσθαι, with or without ἡ β. τ. θ., first attained the position of a formula.

In the verb בַּשֵּׂר, which must be assumed to be the

---

[1] The association with ὁμοιοῦν and ὅμοιος εἶναι is not taken into consideration here, as being without weight for the idea of the β. τ. θ.

[2] In Matt. 11⁵ (Luke 7²²) πτωχοὶ εὐαγγελίζονται corresponds accurately with the Aramaic מִתְבַּשְׂרִין מִסְכְּנִין. Only בְּשׂוֹרָא טָבָא as complement can hardly be dispensed with.

THE SOVEREIGNTY OF GOD 103

original Aramaic expression, the idea of glad tidings is not so
inherent as in the Greek εὐαγγελίζεσθαι. Even in the Old
Testament, 1 Sam. 4[17], בִּשֵּׂר is used of mournful tidings. The
Aramaic בְּשׂוֹרְתָא is applied, Ber. R. 81, to the announcement
of a death;[1] and a glad message, Meg. Taan. xii., Ech.
R. i. 31, expressly adds the adjective בְּשׂוֹרְתָא טָבְתָא (cf.
Ber. ix. 1, Hebr. בְּשׂוֹרוֹת טוֹבוֹת). Consequently בִּשֵּׂר will have
to be translated by "announce"—even in such sentences as:
יְהֵא מְבַשֵּׂר [2] לְחַיֵּי הָעוֹלָם הַבָּא, "may he receive the announcement
promising the life of the age to come," j. Keth. 35[a]; יְהֵא מְבַשֵּׂר
שֶׁבֶּן הָעוֹלָם הַבָּא הוּא, "may he receive the announcement that he
is a son of the age to come," j. Shek. 47[c] (Meïr, c. 180 A.D.);
רוּחַ הַקֹּדֶשׁ מְבַשֶּׂרֶת וְאוֹמֶרֶת, "the Holy Spirit announces (in the
Scripture) and says," b. Sot. 11[a], 46[a].

Closely related also is the phrase: מֻבְטָח הוּא שֶׁהוּא בֶּן הָעוֹלָם
הַבָּא, "he is assured that he is a son of the age to come," b.
Keth. 111[a] (Yokhanan), or: הוּא מֻבְטָח לְחַיֵּי הָעוֹלָם הַבָּא, Siphre Deut.
305, edition Friedm. 129[b]; compare also: אַבְטַחְתַּנִי לְמִחְסַן עָלְמָא
דְאָתֵי, "thou hast assured me that I shall inherit the age to
come," Targ. Ruth 2[13]; אַבְטְחָךְ לָךְ וְלַאֲבוּךְ לְעָלְמָא דְאָתֵי, "he has
assured thee of the age to come for thyself and for thy
father," b. Sanh. 98[a]. The phraseology is important as the
New Testament conception of the "promise" (ἐπαγγελία,
ἐπαγγέλλεσθαι) is to be derived from it. Compare, further,
Jas. 2[5], where ἡ βασιλεία is the object of promise; 1 John
2[25], which makes ἡ ζωὴ ἡ αἰώνιος the content of the promise;
and 1 Tim. 4[8] ἐπαγγελία ζωῆς τῆς νῦν καὶ τῆς μελλούσης.
To the same class belongs the sentence, which occurs several
times, אֵין הַבְטָחָה לַצַּדִּיק בָּעוֹלָם הַזֶּה, Ber. R. 76, "for the pious
there is no assurance (promise) in this age"; and in the
Apoc. of Baruch 53[3] "the promise of life hereafter" (Syr.
מלכנא דחיי דמן בתר כן).

It thus appears that the sovereignty of God is the

[1] Targ. Lam. 1[1] puts the fuller form בְּשׂוֹרְתָא בִישָׁא, "bad news."
[2] j. Kil. 32[b] has the erroneous reading פַּתֵּי.

content of a "message" or "tidings," and not without further qualification of "a message of glad tidings." With this distinction agrees the fact that its proclamation, according to Matt. 4^{17} (Mark 1^{15}), cf. Luke 24^{47}, should above all things lead to repentance.

The germs of this development may be seen in the Old Testament in such passages as Isa. 40^9 41^{27} 52^7. The Apocalypse of Baruch mentions the message of salvation, 46^6, 77^{12}. Subsequently Elijah ranks as the herald of salvation according to Targum Jerus. I. on Num. 25^{12}; Pesikta Rabbati, chap. 35 end; Midrash Vayyosha;[1] cf. *Justin*, Dial. c. Trypho, c. 8. To the Messiah Himself the same function is assigned in Schir. R. 2^{13}; Pes. Rabb. chap. 36; Trg. Ech. 2^{22}, by Eleazar ben Kalir in "Az milliphne bereschith."[2]

In Luke 9^2 κηρύσσειν τ. β. τ. θ. is found as part of a mandate laid by Jesus upon His disciples. Mark 3^{14} has κηρύσσειν with no complement, while in Matt. 10^7 (cf. Luke 10^9) the charge is thus expressed: κηρύσσετε λέγοντες ὅτι ἤγγικεν ἡ βασιλεία τῶν οὐρανῶν. This last form of the charge commends itself as most natural on the lips of Jesus. Of this, κηρύσσειν τὸ εὐαγγέλιον, Matt. 24^{14} (Mark 13^{10}), 26^{13} (Mark 14^9) should be regarded as an abbreviation. The shorter form points back to בַּשֵּׂר בְּשׂוֹרְתָא, with which compare: בְּשׂוֹרְתָא טָבְתָא אִתְבַּשַּׂרְתְּ, "thou hast received good tidings," Ech. R. i. 31; and also in Samaritan הָדָא בְסָרְתְּה דְּאֲנָה מְכַסַּר לָךְ,[3] "this announcement which I declare to thee," Marka, Death of Moses, 26. Even where εὐαγγέλιον is not present, בַּשֵּׂר would not be inadmissible for κηρύσσειν. Of course there is also available the Aphel form אַבְרֵי,[4] which corresponds still more closely to the Greek term, and is a verbal form derived

---

[1] *A. Jellinek*, Beth ha-Midrasch, i. 54; *D. Castelli*, Il Messia secondo gli Ebrei, 196, 201, cites also b. Erub. 43^b; b. Pes. 13^a; Deb. R. 3; but in these passages the announcement of salvation is not attributed to Elijah.

[2] See my treatise, "Der leid. u. d. sterb. Messias der Synagoge," 73.

[3] The same passage contains an undefined form ביסרה (בְּכָרָה), which would lead us to expect בְּסָרְתָא as the defined form.

[4] The Peal also seems to occur Koh. R. 7^{11}; Marka, Death of Moses, 12.

from the noun כָּרוֹז = κήρυξ. It is already used in Dan. 5²⁹, and is applied, e.g. j. Ber. 7ᶜ, to an intimation which was to be proclaimed in the synagogue. קְרָא occurs, indeed, through the influence of the Hebrew, in the Targum in Lev. 25¹⁰, Isa. 61¹, meaning "to proclaim"; but elsewhere in the Jewish-Aramaic literature קְרָא seems to be used only for "to summon, to name, to read."

διαγγέλλειν τὴν β. τ. θ. occurs in Luke 9⁶⁰, but is wanting in the parallel passage Matt. 8²². Doubtless it is merely a Greek variant for κηρύσσειν, so that a special Aramaic term corresponding to it is not a matter of necessity. If such a term were wanted, אוֹדַע, "to make known," might be proposed, as it can be cited in the sense required from the Book of Daniel, the letters of Gamaliel,[1] and j. Ber. 7ᶜ; j. Ned. 40ᵃ; Vay. R. 25.

There still calls for notice λαλεῖν περὶ τῆς β. τ. θ., occurring in the narrative Luke 9¹¹, for which Mark 6³⁴ offers merely διδάσκειν πολλά. A phrase established by tradition is obviously not present in this instance. In Aramaic מַלֵּל בְּמַלְכוּתָא דִשְׁמַיָא would be unusual, all the more as מַלֵּל, so common in the Targums, is elsewhere surprisingly rare. The only instances known to me for מַלֵּל are Ber. R. 32⁴⁷; b. Sot. 35ᵃ; pass. אִתְמַלַּל, j. Schek. 50ᵃ.[2] In place of it אִשְׁתָּעֵי, properly "to relate," is used in Vay. R. 34; b. Yom. 9ᵇ; b. Sot. 35ᵃ. One might rather expect to find תַּנֵּי בְ, "to instruct in," which likewise occurs in Vay. R. 34;[3] cf. Hebr. שָׁנָה, for religious instruction of every kind (e.g. Ab. d. R. Nathan, 18).

Peculiar difficulty attaches to the phrase now to be mentioned : πᾶς γραμματεὺς μαθητευθεὶς (ἐν) τῇ βασιλείᾳ (or εἰς τὴν βασιλείαν) τῶν οὐρανῶν, Matt. 13⁵². A verb, to which μαθητεύειν in the sense here represented would correspond, does not exist in the Jewish Aramaic (or in

---

[1] See "Aram. Dialektproben," 3.

[2] Even here the sense of מיין רמחללין בעלמא is not properly intelligible.

[3] Vay. R. 34, קְנָא, to learn, is found beside פני, to teach. But פני also means "to relate," j. Maas. Sh. 55ᶜ.

Hebrew). One could only substitute: כָּל סָפְרָא דְּהוּא תַלְמִיד
לְ(בּ)מַלְכוּתָא דִשְׁמַיָּא, "every scribe who is a disciple of the
sovereignty of God." But probably the phrase is due to the
author writing in Greek. In that case no precise equivalent
in the words of Jesus need be sought for.

In regard to ὁ λόγος τῆς βασιλείας, see above, p. 95.
τὰ μυστήρια τ. β. τ. ο., Matt. 13¹¹ (cf. Mark 4¹¹, Luke 8¹⁰),
would be in Aramaic: רָזֵי מַלְכוּתָא דִשְׁמַיָּא; cf. Apoc. of Bar. 81⁴
"he made known to me the mystery of the times" (Syr.
אודעני רזא דזבנא). Subsequently the Greek word also came to
be used by the Jews of Galilee, מִלָּה דְמִסְטֵרִין, "mystery," Ber.
R. 74. It is significant that according to Pes. Rabb. 14ᵇ the
Mishna is the "secret counsel" (מִסְטֵירִין) of God proving the
Jews to be the sons of God, and has been entrusted for
guardianship to them and not to the Christians.

2. THE SOVEREIGNTY OF GOD IS REGARDED AS AN APPROACHING DISPENSATION, BEING THE SUBJECT OF THE VERBS ἐγγίζειν, ἐγγὺς εἶναι, φθάνειν, ἔρχεσθαι, ἀναφαίνεσθαι.

(a) *To be at hand, near* (ἐγγίζειν, ἐγγὺς εἶναι).

In addition to ἤγγικεν (ἤγγικε), Matt. 4¹⁷ (Mark 1¹⁵)
10⁷ (Luke 10⁹), Luke 10¹¹, there occurs also ἐγγύς ἐστιν,
Luke 21³¹, in which case, however, the parallels in Mark
13²⁰, Matt. 24³³, do not contain β. τ. θ. as subject. Both
are capable of reproduction in Aramaic. ἤγγικεν would
be קְרֵבָא, or קְרֵבַת with or without לְמֵיתֵי; cf. Targ. Ech. 4¹⁸
קְרֵב סוֹפַנָא, "our end is come near"; and Targ. Isa. 13²²
קָרִיב לְמֵיתֵי עִדָּן, "the time is at hand." For ἐγγύς ἐστιν
reference can be made to Onk. Deut. 32³⁵ קָרִיב יוֹם; Jerus. I.
קָרִיב הוּא יוֹמָא; Jerus. II. קָרִיב לְמֵיתֵי יוֹם; Targ. Isa. 56¹ קָרִיב פֻּרְקָנִי
לְמֵיתֵי, "my redemption is nigh"; and Apoc. of Bar. 23⁷
(Syriac version) קריב הו פורקני דנאתי. For the phrases under
consideration, therefore, we may perhaps assume the original
to have been קְרִיבָה מַלְכוּתָא דִשְׁמַיָּא לְמֵיתֵי. This form of expres-

sion is more probable than the Aramaic מְטָא, to arrive, to which also it would be possible to revert. The Targums usually put this word for the Hebr. בּוֹא, when the latter is meant to express that a set time has arrived, e.g. Targ. Ezek. 7[2. 6. 7. 12]; Amos 8[2]; Jonah 2[1], and Cant. 7[13] (in this מְטָא זְמַן פֻּרְקָנָא, "the time of redemption has come").

(b) To come (φθάνειν, ἔρχεσθαι).

To מְטָא, just mentioned under (a), one must revert for the original of ἔφθασεν ἐφ᾽ ὑμᾶς, Matt. 12[28] (Luke 11[20]). In Dan. 4[21] מְטָא עַל means "to come upon any one" in such a way that he cannot escape, Theod. ἔφθασεν ἐπί τινα. This, too, can be united with לְמֵיתֵי, Targ. Ezek. 7[2]: מְטָא פּוֹרְעָנוּת קִצָּא לְמֵיתֵי עַל, "the judgment of the end has arrived [that was] to come upon," etc.

ἔρχεσθαι is predicated of the divine "sovereignty" in the Lord's Prayer, Matt. 6[10] (Luke 11[2]); also Luke 17[20] 22[18] (the parallels, Matt. 26[29], Mark 14[25], are differently expressed), Mark 9[1] (differently Matt. 16[28], Luke 9[27]). With this may be compared Bar. Apoc. 44[12] "there cometh . . . the new age" (Syr. אתא . . . עלמא חדתא); Targ. Mic. 4[8], לָךְ עֲתִידָא מַלְכוּתָא לְמֵיתֵי, "to thee shall the kingly sovereignty come"; and Mark 11[10] εὐλογημένη ἡ ἐρχομένη βασιλεία τοῦ πατρὸς ἡμῶν Δαυείδ.

(c) To appear (ἀναφαίνεσθαι).

The term ἀναφαίνεσθαι, represented solely by Luke as narrator (Luke 19[11]), is the expression used by preference in connection with מַלְכוּתָא דַיְיָ throughout the Targums (see above, p. 100 f.). It also meets us in Assump. Mos. 10[1], and Apoc. of Baruch 39[7] (in this case applied to the sovereignty of the Messiah).[1] As a parallel to the sentence given on p. 100 from the Midrash on Canticles,

---

[1] Syr. תתגלא רישותה דמשיחי, "the sovereignty of mine anointed will be made manifest."

there may be cited the saying from the Hagada on Canticles vi. 10 : [1] "As the circuit of sun and moon is accomplished in view of all, so shall the sovereignty of the Messiah, when it appears, be revealed openly to the world (כְּשֶׁתִּגָּלֶה הַמָּשִׁיחַ מַלְכוּת תִּגָּלֶה בְּפַרְהֶסְיָא לְעוֹלָם). The rare occurrence of the expression on the lips of Jesus shows, at least, that it was not commonly used by Him.

On the term ἐντὸς ὑμῶν ἐστίν, Luke 17[21], see at the end of No. I.

3. THE SOVEREIGNTY OF GOD IS LIKEWISE REGARDED AS AN APPROACHING DISPENSATION, BEING THE OBJECT OF THE VERBS ἰδεῖν AND προσδέχεσθαι.

(a) To see (ἰδεῖν).

In Luke 9[27] Jesus speaks of a "seeing" of the sovereignty of God. In Mark 9[1] it is said that men should see the sovereignty of God coming with power. The former is not a mere synonym for the latter; for "to see the sovereignty of God" means "to survive to be a participator in it," just as רָאָה לֶעָתִיד לָבוֹא, j. Sanh. 29[c] (Baraitha), means "to live on into the age to come as a partaker in it." See also the phrase adduced below : רָאָה בַנֶּחָמָה, "to see the consolation." The meaning is not quite the same in Targ. Isa. 53[10] יֶחֱזוֹן בְּמַלְכוּת מְשִׁיחֲהוֹן, "they, the forgiven Israelites, will see the sovereignty of their Messiah"; nor in the sentence from an ancient Kedushah of the morning prayer on the Sabbath : [2] עֵינֵינוּ תִרְאֶינָה בְּמַלְכוּתֶךָ, "may our eyes see Thy (God's) royal sovereignty." In these cases, then, the thought is not of a special participation in the sovereignty that is to appear. Of a mere vision of the future mention is also made in Bar. Apoc. 51[8] "They will see the age which is now invisible to them, yea, see the

---

[1] Jew. Qu. Review, vii. (1895) 157.
[2] Seder Rab Amram, i. 10[b].

time which is now hidden from them " (Syr. חזין גר הו עלמא דלא מתחזא להון השא ונחזון לובנא דהשא כסא מנהון).

(b) To expect, look for (προσδέχεσθαι).

According to the Gospel narrative, Mark 15[43] (Luke 23[51]), the sovereignty of God is being " looked for " (προσ-δέχεσθαι), just as the consolation of Israel or the redemption of Jerusalem was " looked for," according to Luke 2[25. 38]. The Aramaic word for this is סַבַּר, Onk. Gen. 49[18]; Targ. Isa. 30[18] 64[3]; Hab. 2[3]; cf. the form שְׂבַּר, which has made its way into late parts of the Old Testament, LXX Dan. 7[25] προσδέξεται for Aramaic סבר, as also the substantive סִבְרָא, " expectation," Ber. R. 53. The Pael סַבִּי occurs both in the Jerus. Targums to the Pentateuch and in the Evang. Hieros. for " to look for, expect." [1] I cannot, however, verify either this or even סַבַּר in the Jewish-Galilean literature.[2]

Note.—The expression " to look for the consolation of Israel " has its parallels in Bar. Apoc. 44[7] " Ye will see the consolation of Zion " (Syr. תחזון בבויאה דצהין), and in the Targumic מְחַמְּדִין לִשְׁנֵי נֶחְמָתָא, " they who long for the years of the consolations," Targ. 2 Sam. 23[4], Jer. 31[6]. In these instances, according to Targ. 2 Sam. 23[1] יוֹמֵי נֶחְמָתָא, " the days of the consolations," are identical with סוֹף עָלְמָא, " the end of the age." A formula of asseveration put into the mouth of Simeon ben Shetach in b. Shebu. 34[a] as early as 100 B.C., which is also used by Eleazar ben Zadok,[3] j. Keth. 35[c] (c. 100 A.D.), is thus expressed : אֶרְאֶה בַנֶּחָמָה, " I shall see the consolation !" and a Baraitha b. Taan. 11[a] pronounces the following verdict against any one who in time of distress separates himself from the community : אַל יִרְאֶה בְנֶחָמַת הַצִּבּוּר, " let him not see the consolation of the com-

---

[1] Late Hebr. צָפָה, " to hope for," may be mentioned at the same time.

[2] סְכִי בִי, Vay. R. 34, does not mean ''hope in me," but from אִסְתַּכַּל בִּי in apposition—it is equal to "look upon me ! "

[3] See Bacher, Ag. d. Tann. i. 52.

munity!" See also the Targ. Isa. 4³ יֶחֱזֵי בְנֶחָמַת יְרוּשְׁלֵם "he shall see the consolation of Jerusalem"; and 33²⁰ עֵינֶיךָ יֶחֱזְיָן בְנֶחָמַת יְרוּשְׁלֵם, "thine eyes shall see the consolation of Jerusalem." " Consolation " is, throughout these instances, not the resurrection, but redemption in its full extent.

4. THE SOVEREIGNTY OF GOD IS AN ORDER OF THINGS UNDER WHICH MEN ARE PLACED.

(a) *To sit at table, to eat bread* (ἀνακλίνεσθαι, ἄρτον φαγεῖν).

The patriarchs and all the prophets can be "seen" as subjects of the sovereignty of God, Luke 13²⁸. The context of the passage, as well as the parallel, Matt. 8¹¹, shows, however, that we have not here to do with a current expression. Currency may rather be assumed of the "reclining at table" (ἀνακλίνεσθαι), in the sovereignty of God, Matt. 8¹¹ (Luke 13²⁹); cf. ἀνάκεισθαι in the parable of the Wedding Feast, Matt. 22¹⁰· ¹¹, and the eulogy of one that sat at meat with Jesus (Luke 14¹⁵): μακάριος ὅστις φάγεται ἄρτον ἐν τῇ β. τ. θ. As to drinking in the sovereignty of God, it is mentioned by Jesus, Matt. 26²⁹ (Mark 14²⁵, Luke 22¹⁸), in connection with the consummation of the passover there, Luke 22¹⁵· ¹⁶.

That there should be feasting in the Messianic age is implied rather than asserted by the ancient stories of Leviathan and Behemoth, which creatures were one day to serve as food for the pious. The first mention of this is in an ancient portion of the Apocalypse of Baruch (29⁴); afterwards it occurs in the Book of Enoch 60⁷⁻⁹· ²⁴, and in 2 Esd. 6⁴⁹⁻⁵². It is something quite different when, as in the case of Jesus, the time of salvation is merely *likened* to a feast. Dropping the figure, such a comparison only implies that the Messianic age brings joy and gratification. Thus the Slavonic Enoch (42⁵)[1] says that the angels will

[1] Edition by *Morfill* and *Charles*, Oxford, 1896.

bring in Adam and the patriarchs to Paradise, "as one invites those with whom one loves to celebrate the festivals," and that these will then "with joy await his feast, in pleasure and untold abundance in the rapture and bliss of the light and in the life that never ends." About 120 A.D. Akiba speaks of a "repast" (סְעוּדָה) with which the present age concludes, Ab. iii. 16 ; and Jacob likens the age to come to a banqueting-hall (טְרִקְלִין), into which one enters from the vestibule (פְּרוֹזְדוֹר) of the current age (Ab. iv. 16), a simile which is repeated in Tosephta Ber. vii. 21. Only from a later period do we find traces of an actual repast which God prepared for the pious—"the feast of Paradise" (הַסְּעוּדָה שֶׁל גַּן עֵדֶן).[1] Then the fable of Behemoth and Leviathan is also combined therewith. Detailed descriptions of this feast are given in *Jellinek's* Beth ha-Midrasch iii. 76, v. 45 f., vi. 150 ff. Noteworthy is the passage in the Book of Elijah (loc. cit. iii. 67) :[2] אֲנִי רוֹאֶה אַבְרָהָם יִצְחָק וְיַעֲקֹב וְכָל הַצַּדִּיקִים יוֹשְׁבִים, "I see Abraham, Isaac, and Jacob, and all the righteous sitting"; and Targ. Eccl. 9[7], where God says to each of the pious : אֲזֵל טְעוֹם בְּחֶדְוָא לַחְמָךְ וּשְׁתִי בְּלֵב טַב חַמְרָא דְּאִצְטְנַע לָךְ בְּגַן עֵדֶן, "come, eat thy bread with joy, and drink with a merry heart the wine which is reserved for thee in Paradise." See also Targ. Ruth 2[12], לְמֶהֱוֵי חֻלְקָךְ עִם שָׂרָה וְרִבְקָה וְרָחֵל וְלֵאָה, "that thy portion may be with Sarah and Rebekah, and Rachel and Leah."

From the Gospels it may be inferred that the conception of an actual repast for the pious was already an old-established idea. Even for Jesus this repast was no mere figure of speech. But He speaks of it in plain language only for the purpose of emphasising the fellowship which the righteous of all ages are destined to enjoy. Never did He refer to the repast merely as a repast. Even in the "satisfaction"

---

[1] Schem. R. 45 (*Assi*) ; see also *Hamburger*, Real-Encyc. f. Bibel u. Talm. ii. 1312 ff.

[2] See also *M. Buttenwieser*, Die hebr. Elias-Apokalypse (1897), 25, 66.

through the sovereignty of God spoken of in Matt. 5[6] (Luke 6[21]) there is no idea of a repast.   It is rather meant to express figuratively, like Isa. 65[13f.], the complete contentment of those who are for the present suffering want.

The determination of the Aramaic expressions to be used here is not without difficulty.   Late Hebrew has הֵסֵב [1] for to "recline at table."   To this corresponds in the Targums אַסְחַר; see, e.g., Onk. Gen. 37[25] וְאִסְחַרוּ לְמֵיכַל לַחְמָא, "and they lay down to eat bread."   Both verbs in themselves mean merely "to form a circle round a table."   In the Galilean dialect of the Palestinian Talmud (Ber. 12[b]; Taan. 66[a]), and in the Palestinian-Christian dialect, the usual word for this was, at a later date, רְבַע, "to lie down."

For "to eat," אֲכַל is a term common to all Aramaic dialects.   "To take food, take a meal," could be rendered by קְעַד, although the Gal. and the Pal.-Chr. dialects use נְגַס.   "To eat bread" for the simple "to eat" occurs in the Old Testament, and hence also in the Targums, pretty frequently, Gen. 37[25], Ex. 2[20], 2 Sam. 9[7]; in the Gospels, Matt. 15[2], Mark 3[20] 7[2, 5], Luke 14[1,2]   In the later Jewish literature I find but few examples.   In b. Ber. 42[b] a summons to eat is expressed: נֵיכוֹל לַחְמָא, "let us eat bread"; and b. Bab. mez. 86[b], the Palestinian Tankhum bar Khanilay, speaking of Moses, says that he did not "eat bread" on Sinai, while the angels, when visiting Abraham, "ate bread."   It is self-evident that the Babylonian popular expression כְּרַךְ רִיפְתָא (properly "to roll bread") for "to eat" is unsuitable.   In Ber. R. 82 a saying of Joshua [3] (c. 100 A.D.) is given to the effect that the righteous man will be satisfied "with the bread of the age to come" (מִלַּחְמוֹ שֶׁלְעוֹלָם הַבָּא).   But the mention of the bread is here due to Prov. 28[19], and does not therefore imply a prevalent idiom.   On the other hand

---

[1] Similarly, as early as Cant. 1[12] מֵסֵב, "dinner-party."

[2] Cf. *Joh. Vorstius*, De Hebraismis Novi Testamenti, ii. 255 ff.

[3] See *Bacher*, Ag. d. Tann. i. 190.

must be cited the ancient phrase לְחֶם עֲבַד, " to prepare a meal," Dan. 5¹, Hebr.: עָשָׂה לְחֶם, Eccles. 10¹⁹, which the later Rabbinical literature does not use, in the same sense at least. The benediction given to him who should " eat bread " in the theocracy would be thus rendered in Aramaic: טוּבוֹהִי דְּאָכִיל לַחְמָא בְּמַלְכוּתָא דִשְׁמַיָּא. It is striking in this case that the term " theocracy " should here be used by another in the sense regularly given to it by Jesus, although the discourse of Jesus did not furnish a direct occasion for this use. Some expression, more common among the Jews, perhaps בְּעָלְמָא דְאָתֵי, " in the age to come," might here be substituted.

(b) *To be greatest, least* (ὁ μικρότερος, ἐλάχιστος, μείζων, μέγας).

The righteous shine forth as the sun in the theocracy, Matt. 13⁴³ conformably with Dan. 12³. As, however, in Dan. 12³ the stars are also introduced into the comparison, the idea developed by Paul,[1] and by Yehuda i.,[2] is not excluded, that the lustre is of different kinds, and that, therefore, degrees of rank are to be found among the righteous. One may in the theocracy be ὁ μικρότερος, Matt. 11¹¹ (Luke 7²⁸), or ἐλάχιστος, Matt. 5¹⁹, *i.e.* " the least," but also " the greatest " (ὁ μείζων), Matt. 18¹ (where, however, the parallels, Mark 9³⁴, Luke 9⁴⁶, speak only of the greatest among the disciples of Jesus), or " great " (μέγας), Matt. 5¹⁹.

This gradation recalls the statement of Joshua ben Levy (c. 250), that there are men who are " esteemed " (יְקָרִים) in this present age, but who will be despised (קְפוּיִּים, properly, " floating on the surface ")[3] in the age to come ; and another of his son Joseph, who on his deathbed had a vision of a " world turned upside down " (עוֹלָם הָפוּךְ), in which the " highest found themselves lowest, and the lowest highest " (עֶלְיוֹנִים לְמַטָּה וְתַחְתּוֹנִים לְמַעֲלָה), which, however, was not to apply in the case of his own father.[4] Simeon ben Azzay (c. 110)

---

[1] 1 Cor. 15⁴¹.   [2] See farther on.   [3] b. Pes. 50ª.
[4] Loc. cit. and b. Bab. b. 10ᵇ ; see *Bacher*, Ag. d. pal. Amoräer, i. 187, ii. 105.

said:[1] "He who, for the sake of the Tora, renders himself
even a simpleton, will in the end be exalted." Yirmeya[2] also
taught on similar lines in a later period: "He who humbles
himself in this age for the sake of the word of the law, will
be made great in the future age." According to Yonathan
ben Eleazar (c. 240 A.D.),[3] all are aware that in the age to
come there will be great and small, only in the present age
it is not known who is in reality great, and who is small.
An Aramaic narrative[4] tells of a woman who is afraid
that the acceptance in this age of a heavenly gift prejudices
the status in the other world, and she therefore causes the
gift to be returned. The principle :[5] כָּל צַדִּיק וְצַדִּיק יֵשׁ לוֹ עוֹלָם
בִּפְנֵי עַצְמוֹ, "each righteous one (after death) has his own world
for himself," ranked as a truth generally recognised. With
this Yehuda i. (c. 200) is in accord when he explains (Siphre
to Deut. 11²¹, ed. Friedmann, 83ª), that the righteous will
in the future have different grades, envying one another no
more than the stars in spite of their different brilliance. A
specially elevated third class of the pious is the subject of
remark j. Chag. 77ª. The Palestinian Talmud (in the same
passage) holds that there will be seven such classes, an
opinion supported elsewhere.[6]

In a similar way Jesus entertained the idea of different
grades among those who had part in the theocracy. But
the principle on which these ranks are assigned is not that
of the Rabbis.

As Aramaic has no superlative, there is at our disposal
for "the least," "the greatest," only זְעֵירָא, רַבָּא. Between
ὁ μείζων, Matt. 18¹, and μέγας, Matt. 5¹⁹, the only difference
would be that in the former case רַבָּא, in the latter רַב, should

---

[1] Ber. R. 81 ; b. Ber. 63ᵇ ; see *Bacher*, Ag. d. Tann. i. 416.
[2] b. Bab. m. 85ᵇ.
[3] Pesikta Rabb., ed. Friedmann, 198ᵇ ; cf. *Bacher*, Ag. der pal. Am. i. 87.
[4] Ruth R. iii. 1 ; cf. Schem. R. 52.   [5] Vay. R. 18 ; cf. Ruth R. iii. 1.
[6] Siphre, ed. Friedm. 67ª ; Vay. R. 30 ; Midr. Ps. 16¹² ; cf. *Bacher*, Ag.
d. Tann. i. 19, 44.

be presupposed. With the expression may be compared:
רביתא, read רַבְּתָא, זְעֵירְתָּא, "a great thing," "a small thing,"
j. Keth. 29°, and רַבָּה דַּהֲוָה בֵינֵיהוֹן, "the greatest of them,"
Ber. R. 38.

(c) *The sons of the theocracy* (οἱ υἱοὶ τῆς βασιλείας).

The expression peculiar to Matthew: οἱ υἱοὶ τῆς βασιλείας,
Matt. 8¹² 13³⁸, still calls for mention here. On the omission
of τῶν οὐρανῶν see above, p. 95 f. The son as such is he
who belongs to the father's house by being born of his spouse.
But the idea that the son, in contrast to the slaves, is the
father's legitimate successor, in short, the heir, is so habitual
in antiquity that the thought of the son almost immediately
involves that of the heir, cf. Matt. 21³⁸ (Mark 12⁷, Luke 20¹⁴),
Rom. 8¹⁷, Gal. 4⁷. The "sons of the theocracy" are thus
those who belong to it in virtue of their birth, who thereby
have a natural right to the possession of it. This is the
sense in which the "sons of the theocracy" are spoken
of in Matt. 8¹², who are cast forth from its sphere.—
In Matt. 13³⁸, on the other hand, the υἱοὶ τῆς βασιλείας
are set side by side with the υἱοὶ τοῦ πονηροῦ. In this case
the "sons" are those who have in themselves the nature of
the father. The sons of the theocracy are thus the men of
a cognate disposition with it, the "righteous" (δίκαιοι); cf.
v.⁴³. Of the same character are the expressions: οἱ υἱοὶ
ὑμῶν (τῶν Φαρισαίων), Matt. 12²⁷ (Luke 11¹⁹); υἱοὶ τῶν
φονευσάντων τοὺς προφήτας, Matt. 23³¹; υἱὲ διαβόλου, Acts
13¹⁰; בֶּן הַמְרַצֵּחַ הַזֶּה, "this son of a murderer," 2 Kings 6³²;
קַנַּאי בַּר קַנַּאי, "zealot, son of a zealot," Vay. R. 33; בַּר פַּחִין,
"son of obscure parents," j. Sanh. 30°. The first-named
idiom is recalled by the comparatively frequent expression:
בַּר עָלְמָא דְאָתֵי, "a son of the age to come," b. Taan. 22ᵃ; in
Hebr. בֶּן הָעוֹלָם הַבָּא, b. Pes. 8ᵃ; b. Bab. b. 10ᵇ; j. Shek. 47°;
בְּנֵי הָעוֹלָם הַבָּא, j. Ber. 13ᵈ; בְּנֵי הָעֶלְיָה, "the sons of the upper
room" (the heavenly world), b. Sukk. 45ᵇ. Such is the

designation of one who has an assured claim to the future age.—On the other hand, the בְּנֵי מַלְכוּתָא, Targ. Eccl. 5³, are the citizens of a realm already in existence; בְּנֵי קַרְתָּא, j. Taan. 66ᶜ, the inhabitants of a city; בְּנֵי הַחֻפָּה, j. Sukk. 53ᵃ, the guests at a wedding; cf. οἱ υἱοὶ τοῦ νυμφῶνος, Matt. 9¹⁵; οἱ υἱοὶ τοῦ αἰῶνος τούτου, Luke 16⁸.

5. THE THEOCRACY IS AN ORDER OF THINGS TO WHICH MEN ATTAIN, FROM WHICH ALSO IT IS POSSIBLE TO BE EXCLUDED.

(a) *To attain to, enter into* (εἰσέρχεσθαι, εἰσπορεύεσθαι).

One can "attain to" (εἰσέρχεσθαι εἰς) the theocracy according to Matt. 5²⁰ 7²¹ 18³ 19²³ᶠ· (Mark 10²³ᶠᶠ·, Luke 18²⁴ εἰσπορεύεσθαι, ²⁵), 23¹³; cf. Luke 11⁵², Mark 9⁴⁷ 10¹⁵ (Luke 18¹⁷). It is the same meaning that appears in the attaining "unto life" (εἰς τὴν ζωήν), Matt. 18⁸ (Mark 9⁴³· ⁴⁵) ⁹ 19¹⁷, and in the parable "unto the joy of the Lord" (εἰς τὴν χαρὰν τοῦ κυρίου), Matt. 25²¹· ²³, and also "through the narrow gate" (διὰ τῆς στενῆς πύλης), Matt. 7¹³ (Luke 13²⁴). The "attaining to His glory," which Jesus, Luke 24²⁶, announces in regard to Himself, is cognate. One can also be "not far" (οὐ μακράν) from the theocracy, Mark 12³⁴. The phrase: βιάζεσθαι εἰς τὴν β. τ. θ., Luke 16⁶, will receive separate consideration below.

εἰσέρχεσθαι εἰς τὴν β. τ. θ. has its Jewish parallel in אָתָא לְעָלְמָא דְאָתֵי, "to attain to the age to come," b. Chag. 15ᵇ; b. Sanh. 98ᵃ, 105ᵃ; Hebr. בּוֹא לְעוֹלָם הַבָּא, b. Sanh. 110ᵇ (Baraitha); Tos. Sanh. xiii. 1 (Joshua ben Khananya, *c.* 120); בּוֹא לֶעָתִיד לָבוֹא, j. Sanh. 29ᶜ; cf. the causative אַיְתִי לְעָלְמָא דְאָתֵי, "to bring into the age to come," b. Taan. 29ᵃ; Hebr. הֵבִיא לְעוֹלָם הַבָּא (Eleazar ben Azarya, *c.* 110 A.D.), Siphre, ed. Friedm. 73ᵇ.[1] Quite unusual is the phrase: עַל לְחַיֵּי עָלְמָא, "to enter

[1] See *Bacher*, Ag. d. Tann. i. 221. Bab. mez. ii. 11 has לְחַיֵּי הָעוֹלָם הַבָּא.

into the life eternal," Targ. Ps. 40⁸.¹ Hence the rendering "to attain to" corresponds more closely to the original (Aramaic) than "to enter into."

There is one instance to which this does not apply: εἰσέλθατε διὰ τῆς στενῆς πύλης, Matt. 7¹³ (cf. Luke 13²⁴). For this, recourse must be had to עַל, "to enter into." The appeal therefore runs: עֲלוּ ² בְּתַרְעָא עֲקָא, with which compare עָלִין בְּחַד תְּרַע, "entering in through one door," j. Sabb. 17ᵇ; and עָאל בְּהָדָא נְקְבָּא, "he slipped through that hole," Koh. R. 5¹⁴.

The idea that one attains to the life to come through sufferings and self-sacrifice is not unfamiliar to the Jews. The Second Book of Esdras speaks (7¹³ff.) of the difficulty of attaining to the future life, and compares it (in v.⁷) to the narrow road leading, between fire and water, to a city stored with good things. According to Vay. R. 30 (cf. Pes. 179ᵇ), King David addresses to God these words: "Show to me what gate may be wide open into the life of the age to come" (אֵיזֶה פִּילוֹן מְפֻלָּשׁ לְחַיֵּי הָעוֹלָם הַבָּא). The divine reply, according to Azarya, is: "If thou art in need of life thou art in need of afflictions" (אִם חַיִּים אַתָּה צָרִיךְ יִסּוּרִין אַתָּה צָרִיךְ). On "attaining to life," see also No. III.

As for attaining to "the joy of the Lord" (εἰς τὴν χαρὰν τοῦ κυρίου), Matt. 25²¹·²³, it has to be observed that the Hebrew שִׂמְחָה, "joy," is also used specially for "the joy connected with a festival." This sense is already present in late books of the Old Testament, 2 Chron. 30²³, Neh. 12²⁷. In Sukk. v.¹ שִׂמְחַת בֵּית הַשּׁוֹאֵבָה is the title of a special festivity during the feast of Tabernacles. "To come to the wedding-feast" is expressed in Tob. 9² HL³ by בּוֹא בְשִׂמְחָה. It is prescribed, j. Mo. k. 80ᵈ, that one should not intermix

---

¹ "To come into," moreover, is also generally expressed by עַל לְ, s. j. Pea 21ᵃ; Vay. R. 37; less frequently עַל בְּ, j. Sanh. 21ᵇ; and עַל בּ, j. Taan. 66ᶜ. Even "to fall into" is נְפַל לְ, j. Maaser. 52ᵃ.

² Galil. עִלּוֹן.

³ By these letters (HL) M. Gaster designates the Hebrew recension of the Book of Tobit, published by him; see *M. Gaster*, Two unknown Hebrew versions of Tobit, London, 1897.

one שִׂמְחָה with another שִׂמְחָה, and therefore no marriage
should be appointed to take place on a feast day. In Deb.
R. 9 a father says: "I will lift up wine in honour of my
son's wedding" (לְשִׂמְחָתוֹ שֶׁל בְּנִי). The Aramaic reproduction
of the same statement, Koh. R. 3², has instead לְמִשְׁתִּיתֵיהּ, "for
his banquet." This use of מִשְׁתִּיתָא for "wedding-banquet"
illustrates how it happens that in Matt. 22² Jesus can speak
of a "wedding-feast" (γάμοι), while Luke 14¹⁶ recognises
only a "great supper" (δεῖπνον μέγα). Still in Luke 12³⁶
14⁸ the word γάμοι implies any form of entertainment. In
any case it was not from his own wedding-feast that the
Master came home (Luke 12³⁶), but from that of another
person. שִׂמְחָתָךְ is in Vay. R. 28, "thy wedding," and just
in the same way the corresponding Aramaic word הֶדְוָתָא is
used for "wedding," b. Gitt. 68ᵇ. See also Pesikt. 193ᵃ:
מֶלֶךְ שֶׁבָּאַת לוֹ שִׂמְחָה, "a king to whom there came a festival."
Whence it appears that עוֹל לְחֶדְוַת מָרָךְ would certainly have
been understood by the hearers to signify, "enter thou into
the festival of thy Lord."

(b) To invite (καλεῖν).

Not without "being bidden" does one enter to the
banquet in the theocracy. In 1 Thess. 2¹² Paul has the
expression: τοῦ θεοῦ τοῦ καλοῦντος ἡμᾶς εἰς τὴν ἑαυτοῦ
βασιλείαν καὶ δόξαν, which shows affinity with the "invitation" in the parable of the Supper, Matt. 22³ᶠ· ⁸ᶠ· ¹⁴ (Luke
14¹⁶ᶠ· ²⁴). Jewish literature affords similar examples. The
Galilean Amora Yokhanan (c. 260 A.D.) affirms, b. Bab. b. 75ᵇ,
that only "those who are invited" (מְזֻמָּנִים) go up to the
"Jerusalem of the age to come" (יְרוּשָׁלַיִם שֶׁלְעוֹלָם הַבָּא). Simeon
ben Lakish (c. 260 A.D.) declares, Midr. Tehill. 14⁷, that
Jacob rejoices above all the patriarchs in the coming of
the period of "joy" for Israel, "because he is called to the
banquet" (לְפִי שֶׁהוּא מְזֻמָּן לַסְּעוּדָה), conformably with Isa. 48¹²
(יִשְׂרָאֵל מְקֹרָאִי). The same expression is somewhat differently

applied, b. Ab. zar. 17ᵃ, where a heavenly voice says of the penitent Eleazar ben Durdaya that he is "destined for the life of the age to come," מְזֻמָּן לְחַיֵּי הָעוֹלָם הַבָּא. This expression is also attributed to a voice from heaven in regard to another person, b. Taan. 29ᵃ. This use agrees, however, with Acts 13⁴⁸ τεταγμένοι εἰς ζωὴν αἰώνιον.

For "to invite" the Targum of Onkelos, influenced by the Hebrew, has always קְרָא; see Gen. 31⁵⁴, Ex. 34¹⁵, Num. 25² ; the Targum on the prophets, e.g. 1 Sam. 9²⁴, has וַיְמֵן (זְמַן), just as in late Hebrew (see above, and Sabb. 153ᵃ). The invited person is זְמִינָא, Targ. 1 Sam. 9¹³, 1 Kings 1⁴¹. Still the Hebr. קְרָא does occur Koh. R. 7⁸ ; and צְיַח, which is the equivalent of the Hebr. קְרָא, in the Galilean dialect, is found Vay. R. 28, while the Jerus. gospel uses only קְרָא. Hence Matt. 22¹⁴ πολλοὶ γάρ εἰσιν κλητοί, ὀλίγοι δὲ ἐκλεκτοί, could be expressed in Aramaic by סַגִּיאִין זְמִינִין זְעֵירִין בְּחִירִין.

(c) To be fitted for, to be worthy of (εὔθετος εἶναι, καταξιωθῆναι).

One must, moreover, be *worthy* of entrance into the theocracy. In Luke 9⁶² Jesus uses the words : "he who is not fit for the theocracy" (εὔθετός ἐστιν τῇ β. τ. θ., or εἰς τὴν β. τ. θ. ; cf. Luke 14³⁵ εἰς κοπρίαν εὔθετον). In Luke alone (20³⁵) is also found the expression : καταξιωθῆναι τοῦ αἰῶνος ἐκείνου τυχεῖν ; cf. Acts 13⁴⁶ ἀξίους τῆς αἰωνίου ζωῆς, and 2 Thess. 1⁵ καταξιωθῆναι τῆς β. τ. θ. "To be worthy of the age to come" is a common expression with the Rabbis; see Aram. זְכָא לְעָלְמָא דְאָתֵי, b. Erub. 54ᵇ ; b. Gitt. 68ᵇ ; זְכָא וּשְׂבַע כֵּן—לְעָלְמָא דְאָתֵי, "to be worthy of being satisfied with—in the age to come," j. Taan. 66ᵉ ; Hebr. זָכָה לְעוֹלָם הַבָּא, b. Bab. b. 10ᵇ ; זָכָה וְנָחַל שְׁנֵי עוֹלָמִים, "to be worthy of inheriting two worlds," b. Ber. 51ᵃ ; זוֹכֶה לִירֵשׁ הָעוֹלָם הַזֶּה וְהָעוֹלָם הַבָּא, "he is worthy of possessing this age, and that which is to come," j. Ber. 11ᶜ ; זָכָה לַמַּלְכוּת, "he was worthy to become king," j. Ber. 4ᶜ. This זְכָא corresponds without doubt

to καταξιωθῆναι, including within itself also the idea of
τυχεῖν. For εὔθετος recourse may be had to כָּשֵׁר;[1] cf. Onk.
Ex. 4¹³ מַן דְּכָשַׁר לְמִשְׁלַח, "he who is fit to be sent"; Ber.
R. 9: כָּל מִי שֶׁהוּא מִתְכַּשֵּׁר בִּמְלֶאכֶת הַפַּרְדֵּס יִכָּנֵס לָאוֹצָר, "every
(worker) who proves himself fit in the work of the garden
has access to the storehouse"; also Targ. Lam. 1⁶. כָּשֵׁר
is preferable to חֲזֵי (Galil. חֲמֵי) as used in Targs. Jerus. I.
and II. Ex. 4¹³ מַן דְּחָמֵי לְמִשְׁתַּלָּחָה; for this חֲזֵי, like its late-
Hebrew parallel רָאוּי, is meant to be a passive participle,
and should be pronounced[2] accordingly, though earlier it
does have the sense "worthy." The phrase: בֵּן רָאוּי לְמַלְכוּת,
Bem. R. 9²⁴, means "a son who is worthy to be king."
See also Onk. Gen. 49³ לָךְ הֲוָה חֲזֵי לְמִסַּב, "thou wast
worthy (it beseemed thee) to take"; cf. Jerus. I. Gen. 22¹,
and j. Bab. b. 16ᵈ לֵית חֲמֵי לֵיהּ מַפְּקָה, "it did not beseem
him to drive out." חֲזֵי (חֲמֵי) might, indeed, be expressed in
Greek by ἄξιος, and thus be preferably used in repro-
ducing ἄξιοι τῆς αἰωνίου ζωῆς, Acts 13⁴⁶, though here also
זְכָא could be proposed; see Deb. R. 1: זוֹכֶה לְחַיִּים, "he has a
claim upon the life (to come)." The Christian Palestinian
uses for ἄξιος שׁוֹי, which means literally "similar to," "corresponding." The same root is already used in biblical
Hebrew for "deserving," e.g. Esth. 7⁴; also in Neo-Hebraic,
and, further, in Aramaic, Onk. Gen. 23¹⁵; Vay. R. 9;
Targ. Esth. ii. 2. 1. But the sense of "equal," "equivalent,"
is too conspicuous to permit its being substituted in every
case where ἄξιος may occur; see the dictum of Yannai
(c. 230 A.D.):[3] דְּשַׁיֵּים אָרְחֵיהּ שַׂגִּי שָׁוֵי, "he who appraises his way
is of great worth."

---

[1] In the Galilean dialect I can verify כָּשֵׁר only in the sense "honest," j. Ab.
z. 39ᵇ, where כָּשֵׁר is the contrary of לֵיצָן, "scoffer"; and j. Taan. 65ᵇ, where
כַּשִּׁירָא is found by the side of חַצְּפָא, "insolent."

[2] The superlinear pointing has frequently, by mistake, חֲזֵי, חֲמֵי; see my
"Aram.-Neuhebr. Wörterbuch" under חֲמָא, חֲמָא.

[3] Vay. R. 9; cf. Bacher, Ag. d. p. Am. i. 38.

(d) *To close against, to cast forth from, to go out* (κλείειν, ἐκβάλλειν, ἐξέρχεσθαι).

Jesus speaks of the Pharisees "closing" (κλείειν) the theocracy against men, Matt. 23[13]; of the "keys" (κλεῖδες) thereof, Matt. 16[19]; of "closing the door of the marriage chamber," Matt. 25[10] (Luke 13[25]); of "casting forth" (ἐκβάλλειν) from this chamber, Matt. 22[13]; Luke 13[28]; cf. Matt. 13[42. 50] 25[30]; of "being expelled" (ἐξέρχεσθαι) from the theocracy, Matt. 8[12].

Similar ideas are reported from Eleazar ben Zadok (c. 100 A.D.). He declares that the life of him who has misused the law will be eradicated from the present and the future world (נֶעְקְרוּ חַיָּיו מִן הָעוֹלָם הַזֶּה וּמִן הָעוֹלָם הַבָּא);[1] and with regard to the godless, he teaches that in the present world God accumulates good fortune upon them, "in order afterwards to cast them forth, and to compel them to take the lowest position" (לְטָרְדָן וּלְהוֹרִישָׁן לַמַּדְרֵיגָה הַתַּחְתּוֹנָה).[2] See also the expressions: טְרַד מִן הָעוֹלָם הַבָּא, "to reject from the future world," b. Bab. b. 15[b]; אִתְּרִיד מֵהַהוּא עָלְמָא, "to be rejected from the other world," b. Chag. 15[a]. "To close against" in the Aramaic of the Book of Daniel, and of the Targ. of Onkelos, would be אֲחַד; in the dialect of the Targ. to the prophets אֲגִיף (this also in the Hebrew of Nehemiah, and in the Mishna), in Galilean טְרַד. For "casting forth," טְרַד alone comes into question; "to be expelled from" is נְפַק.

On "the keys" of the theocracy, see No. VIII. 6.

6. THE THEOCRACY IS A GOOD WHICH ADMITS OF BEING STRIVEN FOR, OF BEING BESTOWED, OF BEING POSSESSED, AND OF BEING ACCEPTED.

(a) *To strive for, seek, ask* (ζητεῖν, αἰτεῖν).

Instead of being anxious about food and raiment, one ought "to seek earnestly after the theocracy" (ζητεῖν τὴν

---

[1] Siphre, ed. Friedm. 84[b]; cf. *Bacher, Ag. d. Tann.* i. 52.   [2] b. Kidd. 40[b].

βασιλείαν αὐτοῦ, scil. τοῦ πατρός), Luke 12³¹ (Matt. 6³³, where καὶ τὴν δικαιοσύνην is added). In the same category are also the injunction " to seek " (ζητεῖν) that one may " find," Matt. 7⁷ᶠ· (Luke 11⁹ᶠ·), and the parable of the Merchant " seeking " goodly Pearls, and " finding " one of great price (Matt. 13⁴⁵ᶠ·).

For ζητεῖν in the two meanings, to " strive for " (something desirable) and to " search for " (something that is hidden), the corresponding Aramaic word is בְּעָא. This means to " strive for, covet eagerly," Dan. 6⁵; Onk. Num. 16¹⁰ (where the office of high priest is the object of the desire), and also " to seek," Onk. Gen. 37¹⁶; Targ. 1 Sam. 10²; Koh. R. 7¹¹ (where the passive אִתְבְּעֵי means " to be sought for ").

The same verb (בְּעָא) is also in use for " to ask "; see Dan. 6⁸; Onk. Deut. 4²⁹; Vay. R. 32; j. Taan. 66ᵈ. But in Matt. 7⁷ᶠ· (Luke 11⁹ᶠ·), where αἰτεῖν stands alongside of ζητεῖν, some other word must be found for the former. The only term that admits of being proposed is שְׁאַל; see Vay. R. 5, which describes what constitutes judicious and injudicious " asking."

Among the means used to win entrance to the theocracy, there is found, according to Matt. 19¹², self-mutilation, διὰ τὴν β. τ. οὐρ. That this is meant figuratively appears most obviously from the consideration that, if it were meant literally, Jesus would here be putting Himself into such an avowed opposition to the Mosaic law as He gives no pre-cedent for elsewhere. Even Josephus [1] affirms that, accord-ing to the law, those who emasculated themselves should be excommunicated, and that it was forbidden to castrate men or animals. The application to animals, unexpressed in the law, has been subsequently deduced by the Rabbis, b. Sabb. 110ᵇ,[2] from Lev. 22²⁴. A metaphorical use of סָרֵס גַּרְמֵיהּ,

---

[1] Antt. IV. viii. 40.

[2] See also Onk. and Jerus. I. on Lev. 22²⁴.

" to castrate one's self," to denote voluntary celibacy, I cannot find in the Rabbinic literature. The saying ascribed to Jesus though not recorded in the Gospels (Agraphon):[1] ὁ κατὰ πρόθεσιν εὐνουχίας ὁμολογήσας μὴ γῆμαι ἄγαμος διαμενέτω, succeeds probably in giving the sense of the saying of our Lord, but agrees nevertheless as little with the tendency of Rabbinism as the other. Simeon ben Azzay (c. 110 A.D.), who lived unmarried so as not to be impeded in the study of the law, had to bear reproach for his celibacy, and he ranked ever after as a notable exception.[2] A vow of abstinence from conjugal relations would necessarily entail the obligation to dissolve the marriage.

The word that commends itself most to replace διά, " for the sake of," is לְשׁוּם. It would also be the most suitable in regard to the leaving of one's family and property " for the sake of " (εἵνεκεν) the theocracy, Luke 18²⁹ (Matt. 19²⁹ ἕνεκα τοῦ ἐμοῦ ὀνόματος, Mark 10²⁹ ἕνεκεν ἐμοῦ καὶ ἕνεκεν τοῦ εὐαγγελίου). Similarly, Gamaliel III. (c. 210 A.D.) says, Ab. ii. 2 : " all those who exert themselves on behalf of the community should do this ' for the sake of God,' לְשֵׁם שָׁמַיִם " ; and Jose ha-Kohen (c. 100 A.D.):[3] " may all thy works be performed ' for the sake of God,' לְשֵׁם שָׁמַיִם."

(b) To give (διδόναι).

To him that asketh " it will be given " (δοθήσεται), Matt. 7⁷ (Luke 11⁹), and " it is your Father's good pleasure to give you the kingdom " (δοῦναι ὑμῖν τὴν βασιλείαν), Luke 12³². There can be no doubt that Luke, in placing the latter sentence in sequence to the invitation to seek the kingdom of the Father (v.³¹), has intended " kingdom " to bear the same sense in both cases. Since, however, v.³² in virtue of the emphasis and content must originally have stood in

---

[1] Clem. Alex. Strom. iii. 15. 97 ; cf. *Nestle*, Nov. Test. Græc. Supplem. 86.
[2] *Bacher*, Ag. d. Tann. i. 410.
[3] Ab. ii. 12 ; cf. *Bacher*, Ag. d. Tann. i. 72.

a *different* connection, the "kingdom" in the words of Jesus is here meant of a special authority destined to devolve upon His disciples, who were for the time being quite powerless. The statement thus belongs to a different series of our Lord's sayings, to which we shall return at the close of this discussion. On the other hand, Matt. 21⁴³ belongs to this category, in saying that the theocracy will be "given" to a nation bringing forth the fruits thereof.

For "to give" Aramaic puts at our disposal יְהַב, with imperfect and infinitive formed from the stem נְתַן. But in Galilean these borrowed forms also are occasionally supplied from יְהַב.[1] *Aἰτεῖτε καὶ δοθήσεται ὑμῖν· ζητεῖτε καὶ εὑρήσετε* is, therefore, to be thus restored: שְׁאִילוּ[2] וְיִהֲבִין לְכוֹן בְּעוֹ וְאַתּוּן[3] מַשְׁכְּחִין. Bar. Apoc. 44¹⁵ may be compared: "to these is given the life to come," Syr. להלין מתיהב עלמא דאתי.

(c) To accept, to receive, to take (δέχεσθαι, λαμβάνειν).

One has to "accept" (δέχεσθαι) the theocracy, when it is offered, as a little child, Mark 10¹⁵ (Luke 18¹⁷). To this passage Dan. 7¹⁸ (cf. 6¹) יְקַבְּלוּן מַלְכוּתָא, "they will receive the sovereignty," is not available as a parallel, for it means "they shall become rulers." We might with better reason adduce the phrase: קַבֵּל עָלָיו מַלְכוּת שָׁמַיִם, "to take upon oneself the sovereignty of God," or: קַבֵּל עוֹל מַלְכוּת שָׁמַיִם, "to take upon one's self the yoke of the sovereignty of God" (see above, p. 98); for in this case the idea of voluntary submission to the divine authority is present, if not also the idea of appropriating a gift. The same verb (קַבֵּל) is found in Dan. 2⁶, j. Ber. 6ª, for the "acceptance" of presents, and is in use, with the same meaning, in the Targ. of Onkelos. In the sense of "accepting" it is applicable in this connection.

"To be received" (Syr. קבל) is predicated of the promised future age, Bar. Apoc. 14¹³ 51³. In the Targ. Cant. 7¹⁴

---

[1] See Gram. d. j.-pal. Aram. 253.　　[2] Galil. שְׁאֵלוּן.　　[3] Galil. בְּעוֹן·

it is proclaimed by God to the Messiah, קוּם קַבֵּל מַלְכוּתָא דְּנְמִית לָךְ, "up! receive the sovereignty which I have kept for thee."

From "accept" (actively) is to be distinguished the "taking" (λαμβάνειν) of what is bestowed; see Matt. 7[8] (Luke 11[10]) 21[22] (Mark 11[24]); cf. Bar. Apoc. 51[3] "that they may take and receive the immortal life" (Syr. דנסבון ונקבלת עלמא דלא מאת). This "taking" is in Aramaic נְסַב.

(d) To take possession of (κληρονομεῖν).

Those who have the right thereto acquire the theocracy as a possession (κληρονομεῖν), Matt. 25[34], cf. 1 Cor. 6[9f.] 15[50] Gal. 5[21], just as David according to 1 Macc. 2[57] "received as a possession" the throne of an eternal sovereignty (ἐκληρονόμησεν, Syr. Vers. ירת). "To possess one's self of the future age" is a very popular Jewish expression, whose use from the end of the first century onwards can be demonstrated. Bar. Apoc. 44[13], cf. 2 Esd. 6[17], speaks of "taking possession of the promised age" (Syr. ירת זבנא דאמיר). Eleazar ben Zadok (c. 100 A.D.) has יָרֵשׁ הָעוֹלָם הַבָּא, b. Kidd. 40[b]. נָחַל חַיֵּי הָעוֹלָם הַבָּא is found b. Sot. 7[b] in a Baraitha; יָרֵשׁ חַיֵּי הָעוֹלָם הַבָּא, j. Pes. 33[a]. See, further, j. Ber. 11[a]; יָרֵשׁ הָעוֹלָם הַזֶּה וְהָעוֹלָם הַבָּא; b. Ber. 51[a] נָחַל שְׁנֵי עוֹלָמִים; but also יָרֵשׁ גַּן עֶדֶן, "to take possession of Paradise," j. Ber. 7[d]; Aram. יָרַת גַּן עֶדֶן, j. Pea 15[c]. Besides, we may compare Dan. 7[18] יַחְסְנוּן מַלְכוּתָא, "they shall possess the sovereignty"; cf. Onk. Gen. 49[24] אַחְסֵין מַלְכוּתָא, "he took possession of the sovereignty"; Targ. Cant. 1[3] בְּדִיל דְּיַחְסְנוּן עָלְמָא הָדֵין וְעָלְמָא דְאָתֵי, "that they may possess themselves of this age and that which is to come"; Targ. Ruth 2[13] לְמֵחְסַן עָלְמָא דְאָתֵי; Targ. Jerus. on the Ten Words (Machz. Vitry, 341): יַחְסְנוּן בְּנֵי יִשְׂרָאֵל עָלְמָא דְאָתֵי, "the children of Israel will possess themselves of the world to come."

Even in the Old Testament יָרֵשׁ and נָחַל can hardly be distinguished in meaning; the Targ. of Onk. replaces יָרֵשׁ by

יָרַת and אַחְסֵן, and for נָחַל it has usually אַחְסֵן, without, however, following any recognised principle in this mode of
translating. This much, however, is assured, that neither of
these words originally means to take possession of a paternal
estate, and therefore the rendering by "inherit" is inaccurate. The context must determine whether inheritance is
really meant, or whether it is the acquisition of any object
to which there previously existed a title, or to which the
title was contemporaneous with its acquisition. In Matt.
25³⁴ it is the occupation of a possession, antecedently destined
for the recipients, that is in view. Of course the idea of
the legal title of the heir may also be included, as is the
case in Jas. 2⁵, where the κληρόνομοι τῆς βασιλείας are
spoken of; and also in Eph. 5⁵, in the expression: ἔχειν
κληρονομίαν ἐν τῇ βασιλείᾳ Χριστοῦ καὶ θεοῦ.

The "taking possession of the theocracy" has a synonym
in "taking possession of the earth" (κληρονομεῖν τὴν γῆν) on
the part of the meek, Matt. 5⁴. This phrase has its origin
in Ps. 37¹¹, where the meek similarly possess the land
(וַעֲנָוִים יִירְשׁוּ אָרֶץ, LXX οἱ δὲ πραεῖς κληρονομήσουσιν (τὴν) γῆν).
That the expression is metaphorical in Matt. 5, there can be
no doubt. In the Book of Enoch also 4⁶ᶠᶠ· κληρονομήσουσιν
τὴν γῆν appears to be a name for the collective blessings of
salvation received by the "elect." This is expressly stated
Sanh. x. 1, where the phrase in Isa. 60²¹ "to possess the
land," is explained as referring to participation in the future
age.[1] Reference to the same idea may further be seen in
Kidd. i. 10 : "Every one who fulfils one commandment has
the favour of God, and God gives him long life, and he in-
herits the earth" (וְנִחַל אֶת־הָאָרֶץ). On the other hand, the
Book of Jubilees (32¹⁹), as well as the Targ. of Onk., understands the promise of possessing the land expressed to Jacob,
Gen. 28¹⁴, as applying to the possession of the whole earth—

[1] The statement is absent from the Mishna of the Palest. Talmud and from
the edition of Lowe.

a view with which Paul agrees when he calls Abraham (Rom. 4¹³) κληρόνομος τοῦ κόσμου. Cf. Vay. R. 36. "in time to come they (the Israelites) will take possession of the world from one end to the other" (עֲתִידִין לִירַשׁ מִפּוֹף הָעוֹלָם וְעַד סוֹפוֹ).

Only once does Jesus use the expression "to take possession of" in this connection,—apart from the case just mentioned of Matt. 5⁴, which is based upon a text in the Psalms,—and this single instance is also found in Matthew. Consequently the phrase, though not uncommon in Jewish literature and employed also by Paul, cannot have been a usual one with Jesus.

Any real parallel to the common Jewish formula: "to have part in the age to come," is entirely wanting in the words of Jesus. See Hebr. יֵשׁ לְ—חֵלֶק לְעוֹלָם הַבָּא, Tos. Sanh. xiii. 2 (Eliezer ben Hyrkanos, c. 100 A.D.); with a negative, אֵין לְ—חֵלֶק לְעוֹלָם הַבָּא, Tos. Sanh. xiii. 1 (Gamliel II. c. 110); אֵין לְ—חֵלֶק לֶעָתִיד לָבוֹא, j. Sanh. 28ᵇ (Joshua ben Levi, c. 230); j. Shebi. 35ᶜ (Khamma bar Khanina, c. 270); Aram. צַדִּיקַיָּא אִית לְהוֹן חֻלְקָא בְּעָלְמָא הָדֵין וּלְעָלְמָא דְאָתֵי, "the pious have part in this world and in that to come" (cf. 1 Tim. 4⁸), Targ. Esth. ii. 2. 7; חֻלָק טָב לֵית לְהוֹן עוֹד עִם צַדִּיקַיָּא לְעָלְמָא דְאָתֵי, "there remains no more for them a good portion with the pious in the world to come," Targ. Eccl. 9⁶; cf. Targ. Ruth 2¹³.—In the New Testament, see ὁ ἔχων μέρος ἐν τῇ ἀναστάσει τῇ πρώτῃ, Rev. 20⁶; and among the words of Jesus, only τὸ μέρος αὐτοῦ μετὰ τῶν ὑποκριτῶν θήσει, Matt. 24⁵¹.

(e) To belong to.

That which was received, whether it be an actual possession or merely the title thereto, becomes thereafter the peculiar property of the receivers. The theocracy is referred to as such a property in the phrases: αὐτῶν ἐστίν, Matt. 5³ (Luke 6²⁰ ὑμετέρα ἐστίν), and τῶν τοιούτων ἐστίν, Matt. 19¹⁴ (Mark 10¹⁴, Luke 18¹⁶). Aramaic would express the former merely by הִיא (דִּילְכוֹן) דִּילְהוֹן, the latter by לְמָן דְּבָוָתְהוֹן הִיא.

With the former may be compared Bar. Apoc 44[13] "theirs is the earth in the age that is promised" (Syr. דילהון דמליך דובנא ירחותא הי); and Pesikt. 59[b] (Meïr) הָעוֹלָם הַזֶּה שֶׁלָּנוּ וְהָעוֹלָם הַבָּא שֶׁלָּכֶם, "to us (the heathen) is this age, to you (the Jews) is the age to come." For דְּבָוָתְהוֹן may be cited תְּנֵי עִם דְּבָוָתָךְ, "learn thou with thy fellow," Vay. R. 34; אַף חַד דִּבְוָתֵיהּ, "yea even one such," Ech. R. 1[5]; מוֹלִידִין דְּלֵית בָּוָתְהוֹן, "they beget children who are not such as they are," Shir. R. 1[6]; לֵית דִּבְוָתָךְ, "there is none such as thou," Onk. Deut. 33[29]; cf. Targ. Eccl. 7[22]. A fuller expression would be לְמָן דְּדָמֵי לְהוֹן, "of one who resembles them"; cf. Palmyr. Customs Tariff, ii. b. 10 : כָּל מָדִי דְּמָא לְהוֹן, "everything of that kind."

(f) To be made ready, prepared (ἐτοιμάζεσθαι).

For the righteous the theocracy has been "prepared" (ἡτοιμασμένη), Matt. 25[34], just as eternal fire has been for the wicked, v.[41]. Of the same nature is Matt. 20[23] (Mark 10[40]), which says that to sit at the right hand of the Messianic King is destined for those "for whom it has been prepared—by God" (οἷς ἡτοίμασται—Matt. ὑπὸ τοῦ πατρός μου). The parable of the Great Supper also treats of a "preparation" (ἐτοιμάζειν), and a "being ready" (ἔτοιμος εἶναι) of the supper, Matt. 22[4. 8] (Luke 14[17]). From Matt. 20[23] it further follows with certainty that the preparation does not necessarily imply the pre-existence of what is prepared, but is synonymous rather with its being "allocated." In the same way Matt. 25[34], according to which the "theocracy" has been "prepared" (Aram. מְעַתַּד or מִתְעַתַּד) for the righteous since the creation of the world, need not be interpreted as signifying its pre-existence.

Similarly in 2 Esd. 8[52] it is said: "prepared is the age to come" (Syr. אתעתד עלמא דעתיד); and in Assump. Moses 1[14] Moses says of himself: "excogitavit et invenit me qui ab initio orbis terrarum præparatus sum ut sim arbiter testamenti illius "—from which R. H. Charles wrongly infers the personal pre-existence of Moses.[1]

On the other hand, we must not adduce in comparison with the above the Jewish utterances in regard to the pre-existence, or the latent existence for the time being, of things or persons.

Siphre, Deut. 37, ed. Friedm. 76[b], speaking of the law, the temple, and Palestine, declares that these were created before all other things.[2] A certain Baraitha, according to Midr. Tanchuma, ed. Buber, Bem. 17[b], named seven things as having priority to the world: the throne of God, the law, the temple, the patriarchs, Israel, the name of Messiah, and repentance. It is added in the passage that other authorities name also paradise and hell (Gehinnom). The two latter are again adduced b. Ned. 39[b] instead of the patriarchs and Israel. According to Ber. R. 1, which contains the first-named enumeration with Israel omitted, it was, however, only the first couple that were really created before the world, the others being merely designed; and Midr. Psalms (Ps. 93) with a variant list affirms no more than the planning of all the seven items. The tradition was in this case clearly not fixed.

The "light" of Gen. 1[3] has been preserved on behalf of the pious ever since the Creation, Ber. R. 3.[3] Fruits "were made ready for the righteous in Paradise" (אִתְעַתַּדוּ לְצַדִּיקַיָּא בְּגִנְּתָא דְעֵדֶן), Targ. Cant. 8[2]; Perek Gan Khayyim (Jellinek, Beth ha-Midrash, v. 47). Wine is kept in its own grape-clusters since the six days of creation (יַיִן הַמְשָׁמָּר בַּעֲנָבָיו מִשֵּׁשֶׁת יְמֵי בְרֵאשִׁית), b. Sanh. 99[a] (Joshua ben Levy); cf. Targ. Cant. 9[7] (חַמְרָא דְּאִצְטְנַע לָהּ בְּנֵי עֵדֶן); Pirke Mashiakh (Jellinek, Beth-ha-Midrash, iii. 76); Se'ūdath Livyathan, loc. cit. vi. 151;

---

[1] R. H. Charles, The Assumption of Moses (1897), 6. See also my treatise, "Der leid. u. d. sterb. Messias," 72.

[2] The idea is somewhat different in Ass. Mos. 1[17], which says that from the beginning Zion was destined to the temple mount.

[3] Cf. "Der leid. u. d. sterb. Messias," 58.

Jerus. I. Gen. 27[25]. As to the fabulous animals, Leviathan and Behemoth, which are destined to supply the "feast of Paradise," see above, p. 110 f. All the above are created things which merely for a time were withdrawn from use.

A pre-existent *Jerusalem*,[1] which in the end descends upon the earth, is the subject of remark in Bar. Apoc. 4[3ff.] though only in an interpolation, in 2 Esd. 13[36], and in the Book of Elijah (*Jellinek*, Beth ha-Midrash, iii. 67). In the Testament of Dan. ἡ νέα Ἱερουσαλήμ is referred to as existing at the end, but nothing is said of pre-existence. Meïr [2] (*c.* 160 A.D.), b. Chag. 12[b], speaks of there being in the fourth of the seven heavens, Jerusalem, the temple, and an altar on which Michael offers sacrifice; but he does not state that these things are ever destined to be removed to the earth. Yokhanan (*c.* 260) represents God as affirming [3] by an oath: "I shall not enter into the Jerusalem on high until I be come into the Jerusalem on earth." That the earthly Jerusalem should at some future day be replaced by the heavenly, follows neither from this statement nor from the kindred paraphrase of Ps. 122[3] in the Targum. Midrash Tanchuma, Par. Pikkude (near beginning, ed. Venice, 1545, 50[a] f., not in ed. Buber), correctly apprehends the passages cited in saying that God through His great love for Jerusalem on earth had fashioned for Himself a heavenly counterpart of it into which His glory (Shekina) was not to enter until the desolate Jerusalem on earth should again be built up. Thus the belief in a celestial pre-existence of the Jerusalem to come is restricted within very narrow limits in the Jewish literature. And in the New Testament, what is said of Jerusalem "that is above," or the "heavenly Jerusalem,"

---

[1] *Chr. Schoettgen's* treatise, De Hierosolyma cœlesti in his Hor. hebr. et talm. 1205–1248, chiefly on account of including misunderstood Cabbalistic material, is more perplexing than instructive.

[2] Meïr, according to *Bacher*, Ag. d. Tann. ii. 65. The text of the Talmud names Simeon ben Lakish (*c.* 260 A.D.).

[3] b. Taan. 5[a]; Midr. Psalms 122[3].

Gal. 4²⁶, Heb. 12²², must not be combined with the statements concerning Jerusalem coming down from heaven, Rev. 3¹² 21². ¹⁰.

The name of the Messiah is premundane according to the Book of Enoch 48³ (Similitudes), and the Baraitha given above on the things that were prior to the world, also according to Targ. Mich. 5¹, Zech. 4⁷. A personal existence of the Messiah, celestial though not premundane, is taught Enoch 39⁶ᶠ· 46¹ 62⁷ (Similitudes), — Enoch 48⁶, with its contention that the Messiah is prior to the world, is an interpolation,—2 Esd. 12³² 13²⁶· ⁵² 14⁹, and after that not again till Pesikt. Rabb. chap. 33 (ed. Friedm. 152ᵇ).¹ This differs somewhat from the occult existence of the Messiah before His open manifestation upon the earth or in Paradise, if in the latter case He is temporarily transferred thither from the earth.² The statements as to pre-existence in the Similitudes of Enoch, of 2 Esdras, and in Pesikta Rabbati, moreover do not presuppose any human birth of Messiah. He is to make His appearance upon earth as a fully developed personality. And this is quite distinct from the later Jewish doctrine of the pre-existence of the souls of all men. Judaism has never known anything of a pre-existence peculiar to the Messiah *antecedent to His birth as a human being.* Baldensperger,³ nevertheless, holds that from the date of the Similitudes of Enoch, "the heavenly pre-existence of the Messiah" attained the position of a "dogma in apocalyptic circles." But we have seen that after the Similitudes of Enoch the only representatives of the idea independent of Enoch are 2 Esdras in the first Christian century, and the Appendix to Pesikta Rabbati, independently of both these sources, in the seventh or eighth century. The dominance

¹ Cf. "Der leid. u. d. sterb. Messias," 58.
² Loc. cit. 39, 77 f.
³ *W. Baldensperger,* Das Selbstbewusstsein Jesu im Lichte der messian-ischen Hoffnungen seiner Zeit² (1892), 85. In other points, too, the statements of this book on Jewish matters require careful revision.

of the idea in any Jewish circle whatever cannot seriously be upheld.

With what is advanced on p. 128 f., as well as under VIII. 3,—based on admittedly meagre data,—may be compared the words of *E. Schürer*, Gesch. d. jüd. Volkes [2] ii. 423 [[3] ii. 503], Eng. Tr. Div. II. vol. ii. p. 133 f., which have caused various mischief in the New Testament theology of the last decade,[1] " All the blessings of the future world come down from above, from heaven, where they have previously existed from all eternity. There they are treasured up for the pious as an 'inheritance' which will one day be apportioned to them. In particular, there already exists there the all-glorious new Jerusalem, which in the time of the consummation will descend to the earth to replace the former city. There, too, already exists in the fellowship of God the *Messiah*, who has been chosen by God from all eternity as the perfect king of Israel. Every good and perfect thing, indeed, can come down only from above, while every earthly thing in its present condition is the direct contradiction of the divine. Ultimately, therefore, the hope for the future generally supersedes the limits of this earthly existence. Not even in the Kingdom of Glory upon the *renovated* earth is the final salvation to be found, but in a state of absolute transfiguration in heaven."

Of all this the beginning and end are quite inaccurate; as for the rest, it is true that such ideas have occasionally presented themselves in sporadic fashion in Judaism. But a picture of "the Messianic hope" among the Jews in the time of Christ ought never to have been given in these terms. The conception of God and his control of the world was in that age more transcendental and supernatural than at an earlier period. That the future salvation should for that reason have been apprehended more and more as

---

[1] See, *e.g.*, *H. H. Wendt*, Die Lehre Jesu, ii. (1890) 297 ; *A. Titius*, Die neutest. Lehre von der Seligkeit, i. (1895) 6.

"purely transcendental," is an idea that is justifiable only to a very limited extent.

(g) To take away (αἴρειν).

What has been given may be "taken away" again. The theocracy will "be taken away" (ἀρθήσεται), Matt. 21⁴³, from the Jews, as from those who have the first claim to its possession. The whole verse recalls 1 Sam. 15¹⁸, where, however, in place of "to take away" the verb used is "to rend away from" (Hebr. קָרַע, Targ. אֲעַדִּי). "To take away" is in Aramaic נְטַל or נְסַב. For the former, which appears to correspond to an older usage,[1] see Targ. Eccl. 2¹⁵ אִתְנְטַלַת מִנֵּיהּ מַלְכוּתָא, "the sovereignty was taken from him"; Midr. Abba Gorion 1¹ אִתְנְטִלָא יְקָרָא דִּבְנֵי אֱנָשָׁא, "the lordship of men was taken away." For the latter, which answers to the Galilean usage, see אִתְנְסִיב הוֹדָא מִן בְּרִיתָא, "the excellency was taken away from men," Est. R. 1¹.

7. THE SOVEREIGNTY OF MESSIAH.

Lastly, there fall to be enumerated the passages in which the sovereignty of the Messiah is spoken of. Here we encounter the expression ἐν τῇ βασιλείᾳ αὐτοῦ, Matt. 16²⁸ (Mark 9¹, and Luke 9²⁷ τὴν βασιλείαν τοῦ θεοῦ); ἐν τῇ βασιλείᾳ σου, Matt. 20²¹ (Mark 10³⁷ ἐν τῇ δόξῃ σου), Luke 23⁴²; ἐν τῇ βασιλείᾳ μου, Luke 22³⁰. Just as in Dan. 6²⁹ בְּמַלְכוּת דָּרְיָוֶשׁ must be translated "during the reign of Darius," so is it with ἐν τῇ βασ. μου, σου, αὐτοῦ in this case; and the equivalent Aramaic בְּמַלְכוּתִי, בְּמַלְכוּתָךְ, בְּמַלְכוּתֵיהּ, would have to be rendered "when I am king," etc., and Luke 23⁴² merely "as king."

"Out of His sovereignty" (ἐκ τῆς βασιλείας αὐτοῦ), the angels of the Son of Man "gather together"[2] all causes

---

[1] See the Neo-Hebraic נָטַל, "to take away," Sabb. i. 1.

[2] The metaphor is borrowed from the harvest-field.

of offence and evil-doers, Matt. 13[41]. According to Luke 22[20] the Messiah "gives in charge" ($\delta\iota\alpha\tau\iota\theta\epsilon\sigma\theta\alpha\iota$, Aram. מְסַר) to His own, who thereby themselves obtain the rank of rulers, that sovereignty which was committed by God to Himself; and from Luke 12[32] the "giving" ($\delta\iota\delta\acute{o}\nu\alpha\iota$, Aram. יְהַב)[1] of the sovereignty to the little flock appears to have been so destined from the first (see above, p. 124). This $\beta\alpha\sigma\iota\lambda\epsilon\acute{\iota}\alpha$, which is allotted by God through the Messiah to His disciples, is sharply distinguished from that which is elsewhere called $\acute{\eta}$ $\beta\alpha\sigma\iota\lambda\epsilon\acute{\iota}\alpha$ $\tau o\hat{v}$ $\theta\epsilon o\hat{v}$. In this case it is merely a ruler's prerogative that is bestowed, whereas $\acute{\eta}$ $\beta.$ $\tau.$ $\theta.$, as being a gift to men, never contains, and, from its associations, is incapable of containing, such a significance. Two distinct series of ideas are presented. The one connects itself with Dan. 7[14. 27], where the "sovereignty," מַלְכוּתָא, is assigned first to the Son of Man, and then to the saints of the Most High. The other series of ideas is founded probably upon Dan. 2[44], which says that the "God of heaven" will at the end set up an imperishable "sovereignty" (יְקִים אֱלָהּ שְׁמַיָּא מַלְכוּ דִּי לְעָלְמִין לָא תִתְחַבַּל), which will annihilate all other sovereignties. Here too, however, it must be emphasised, that Jesus has given to the thought in the Book of Daniel a new application originally foreign to it, which excludes the idea of an "establishment" of the theocracy, although, indeed, in Acts 1[6] the term in question[2] is used to denote the royal sovereignty of Israel.

8. CONCLUDING DISCUSSION.

The use of מַלְכוּתָא in certain cases to denote the *sphere* of the sovereignty of God is rarely found in the mouth of Jesus. The use of מַלְכוּת for "realm," in the secular sense,

---

[1] Cf. Dan. 7[27] יְהִיבַת — מַלְכוּתָא.

[2] $\dot{\alpha}\pi o\kappa\alpha\theta\iota\sigma\tau\acute{\alpha}\nu\epsilon\iota\nu$, in the Christian-Palestinian version אקים; *A. Lewis*, A Palestinian Syrian Lectionary, 132.

is found, indeed, in the late books of the Old Testament, *e.g.*
2 Chron. 20³⁰ 36²², Esth. 3⁶ 5¹· ³ 7², Dan. 9¹ 11⁹, and Aram.
Ezra 7¹³, Dan. 4¹⁵ 5¹¹. But even this application of the
word to earthly "kingdoms" is rare in the subsequent
Jewish literature.[1] In this literature מַלְכוּת שָׁמַיִם is never
once used to specify the locus of the divine sovereign
power. It denotes always this power itself in its present
and future manifestation,[2] without implying that the idea
was or tended to become distinctively eschatological. The
notion of any transference of the divine sovereignty to
another is accordingly never entertained in the Jewish
literature. And Jesus, likewise, never says that God should
hand over *His own* sovereignty to the Messiah. To the
Messiah, according to Luke 22²⁹, God grants the royal
dignity, *i.e.* that which is peculiar to the Messiah, and He
on His part, again, imparts it to His own disciples. Still
less can any unmediated transference of the divine lordship
to men be contemplated. The parallels adduced above from
the Jewish literature have proved that the true affinity of
the idea of the sovereignty of God, as taught by Jesus, is
to be found, not so much in the Jewish conception of מַלְכוּת
שָׁמַיִם as in the idea of the "future age" (הָעוֹלָם הַבָּא), or that
of the "life of the future age" (חַיֵּי הָעוֹלָם הַבָּא). This conception is among the Jews, in a similar way, a comprehensive
term for the blessings of salvation, just as the "sovereignty of
God" is with Jesus; and, further, the "sovereignty of God"
is for Jesus invariably an eschatological entity, of which a
present can be predicted only because "the end" is already
approaching. It is not unlikely that in the time of Jesus
the idea of "the future age," being the product of the schools
of the scribes, was not yet familiar to those He addressed;
see under No. II. It cannot therefore be said that He
rejected it, and intentionally substituted another term in
place of it. Independently of the schools and of the apoca-

---

[1] See above, p. 95 f.   [2] Cf. p. 96 ff.

lyptic literature of His time, He created His own terminology. We may assume that He borrowed the term "sovereignty of God" as an eschatological designation from the Book of Daniel, and that He used it by preference for the reason that regard for the honour of God took precedence in His view of all else, and also because He considered it certain that the chief end of mankind was to find their salvation in the most intimate relation to God, and in full obedience to His will.   He was further convinced that the purpose of God was directed principally to the bestowal of blessing on men, and not to the mere exaltation of the divine majesty over the world.   Hence, in His view, the completed establishment of God as sovereign implied, for those who experienced it, absolute happiness.

This thought was not entirely new.   That Jahve's kingship, especially in so far as Israel is concerned, but also in its extension over all peoples, has for aim and result the happiness of men, is clearly stated, among other passages, in Ps. 96–99.[1]   Translated into the style of the earlier Targums, Ps. 97[1] would run:[2] "the royal sovereignty of the Lord has become manifest; let the earth rejoice; let all the isles be glad."   The king, of course, is there regarded principally as the judge of his people, and the judge is ranked first and foremost as the vindicator and deliverer.[3] At the same time it must be noticed that in the Old Testament period from the time of Chronicles the tendency arises to speak less of the king Yahve, and of His "being" or

---

[1] On this point see *J. Boehmer*, Das Reich Gottes in den Psalmen, Neue kirchl. Zeitschr. 1897, pp. 620–651, 746–763, 819–840 ; also *H. Roy*, Die Volksgemeinde und die Gemeinde der Frommen im Psalter (J. B. des theol. Sem. d. Brgem. 1896, 1897), 32.

[2] The extant Jewish Targum to the Psalms was composed at a late date, and is of little use for our purpose.

[3] See my treatise, "Die richterliche Gerechtigkeit im A. T.," 1897, 10 f. ; and *T. K. Cheyne*, The Origin and religious Contents of the Psalter (1891), 344 : "The essential part of deity as well as of royalty—was ability to help or save."

"becoming" king, and more of His "kingly sovereignty" (מַלְכוּת),—a tendency which in the Targums has led to the regular insertion of the abstract מַלְכוּתָא wherever God is represented in the Old Testament as personally ruling like a king. This change is the result of an advance in the idea of God, which went beyond the more childlike conceptions of earlier times, and also an advance in the general mode of thought because the formation of abstract terms became more and more a necessity. Thus, then, the "kingly-sovereignty" of God appears as the decisive element in the salvation of the community of revelation with reference to its present and to its future.

There was already in existence, prior to the time of Jesus, a tendency which laid little stress on the Jewish national element in the hope for the future.[1] This aspect of the future hope Jesus thrust still further into the background, placing the purely religious element decisively in the foreground, and He thereby extended the conception of the "sovereignty of God" so as to include within it the blessings mediated by this sovereignty. For Him the sovereignty of God meant the divine power which, from the present onwards with continuous progress, effectuates the renovation of the world, but also the renovated world into whose domain mankind will one day enter, which is even now being offered, and therefore can be appropriated and received as a blessing.

It must not, moreover, be forgotten that the preaching of Jesus in regard to the sovereignty of God was directed to a people among whom large sections not only fixed their aspirations on the restoration of the "sovereignty," i.e. the political independence of Israel, but were themselves eager to take active measures in setting up this sovereignty. According to the statement of Josephus,[2] Judah[3] of Gaulonitis, from

---

[1] This is the subject of remark in O. Holtzmann, Neutest. Zeitgeschichte (1895), 243 f.

[2] Antt. XVIII. i. 1, 6 ; Bell. Jud. II. viii. 1. [3] Cf. Acts 5³⁷.

the city of Gamala, in the time of Jesus called the movement of the " zealots " into active life. Their principle was to recognise God alone and no man as the " leader and Lord " over Israel (ἡγημόνα καὶ δεσπότην). The sons of this man, Jacob, Simon, and Menahem, and another of his kindred, Eleazar, continued this agitation of Judah till after the destruction of Jerusalem.[1] This party also included Judah, son of Hezekiah, who just after the death of Herod made himself master of Zeppori, the chief city of Galilee in the neighbourhood of Nazareth, and who is represented as having aimed at usurping the sovereign power.[2] This movement, to which one of His own disciples had once adhered, must have been well known to Jesus. From the account of the Temptation it appears that the tempter had sought to suggest similar ideas in his own inner consciousnesss. Moreover, it is indubitable that He developed His own ideas in regard to the sovereignty of God in conscious opposition to the Zealot movement. His verdict as to the tribute-money, Matt. 22[21] (Mark 12[17], Luke 20[25]), shows that He did not consider the political dominance of the Romans to be any infringement of the sovereignty of God. It is not the rule of foreigners over the nation, but the rule of all ungodly powers in the inner life of men, that the sovereignty of God aims at removing ; and it is no human agency, not even the Messiah, that by earthly means establishes this sovereignty, but God Himself ; for this He does for the present through the mere word of preaching and through miracle ; in the future, however, through the complete advent of supramundane power into this present world. Lütgert[3] rightly lays stress on the fact that the kingdom of

---

[1] Antt. xx. v. 2 ; Bell. Jud. ii. xvii. 8, vii. viii. 1.

[2] Antt. xvii. x. 5 ; Bell. Jud. ii. iv. 1. In contrast with this case, the name Juda, son of Sepperaios (υἱὸς Σεπφεραίου), has nothing to do with Zeppori. This name, according to Bell. Jud. i. xxxiii. 2, was that of one of the two teachers of the law who cut down the golden eagle of Herod from the temple gate ; see also Antt. xvii. vi. 2 (which has ὁ Σαριφαίου). The resemblance is really with the Palmyrene proper name צפרא, Σεφφεράς, de Vogüé, x. 11.

[3] W. Lütgert, Das Reich Gottes nach den synoptischen Evangelien (1895), 26.

God is regarded by Jesus principally as "a gift of God." Schnedermann,[1] on the other hand, is mistaken in asserting that Jesus "adopted from the people of His time the representation of the kingdom of God with all its peculiar traits, including even the very considerable tinge of national-political elements."[2] Wellhausen has very properly struck out sentences of similar tendency to be found in the first edition of his Israelitish and Jewish History.[3] The genuine nature of the preaching of Jesus, not less than of the doctrine of Judaism, is entirely misrepresented by such statements.

It was not merely the content of the conception which forms the kernel of our Lord's teaching that was new and original, but also His application of the term, despite the fact that the phrase selected originally belonged to the religious vocabulary of the Jews. The theocracy about to make its entrance into the world was something more than a gratifying realisation of the hopes entertained regarding it; it was a creative force bringing new ideas in its train.

APPENDIX A.

Luke 16[16] ὁ νόμος καὶ οἱ προφῆται μέχρι (D ἕως) Ἰωάννου (D add. ἐπροφήτευσαν)· ἀπὸ τότε (D αποτε)[4] ἡ βασιλεία τοῦ θεοῦ εὐαγγελίζεται καὶ πᾶς εἰς αὐτὴν βιάζεται. Matt. 11[12f.] ἀπὸ δὲ (D om. δὲ) τῶν ἡμερῶν Ἰωάννου τοῦ βαπτιστοῦ ἕως ἄρτι ἡ βασιλεία τῶν οὐρανῶν βιάζεται, καὶ (D add. οἱ) βιασταὶ ἁρπάζουσιν αὐτήν. Πάντες γὰρ οἱ προφῆται καὶ ὁ νόμος ἕως Ἰωάννου ἐπροφήτευσαν.

---

[1] Jesu Verkündigung und Lehre vom Reiche Gottes, i. 152.

[2] See also *Schnedermann's* sentence, Wissenschaftl. Beilage zur Leipz. Zeitung, 1897, No. 44, "The kingdom preached by Jesus was none other than that so long desired by His people, the kingdom of God for Israel."

[3] Cf. Israelitische und jüdische Geschichte, ed. i. (1894) 308, with edition iii. (1897) 374.

[4] *Blass* rejects ἕως and ἐπροφήτευσαν, but adopts ἀφ' ὅτου (instead of αποτε), as required by the Roman recension.

In the first place, we have to ask what Aramaic word may be the antecedent of βιάζειν. A. Meyer[1] recommends חֲסַן, the Aphel form of which, by analogy with Dan. 7[18. 22], would be preferable. Still אֲחְסֵן, which means merely "to take possession of," would hardly cause one who was writing in Greek to use βιάζειν. A better equivalent is found in תְּקֵף, which means in the Peal "to be strong," and in the Aphel "to hold fast." In Deut. 22[25] Onkelos has וִיתְקַף בַּהּ for the Hebr. בָּהּ וְהֶחֱזִיק, while the LXX renders by βιασάμενος. In 2 Sam. 13[25. 27] for the Hebr. פָּרַץ בְּ, "to urge upon any one," the Targum has again אַתְקֵף בְּ, and for פָּרַץ, Gen. 28[14], Ex. 1[12], Onkelos has the Peal תְּקֵף. The Ithpaal אִתַּקַּף is found in Gen. 48[2] and Num. 13[20] for the Hebr. הִתְחַזֵּק, "to strengthen one's self," and in 1 Kings 12[18] for הִתְאַמֵּץ, "to exert one's self." It is also important to note that תְּקֵף has no passive any more than חָזַק[2] in the older Hebrew. From this it would follow that the passive βιάζεται, Matt. 11[12,3] is not derived immediately from an Aramaic prototype. The same test applies to the passive εὐαγγελίζεται in Luke, since אִתְבַּשַּׂר can mean only "to receive a message." The word ἐπροφήτευσαν in Matthew, for which ὁ νόμος is an unsuitable subject, also raises suspicion. And as it is not original in Luke, and therefore need not be considered indispensable, it can hardly be attributed to the original utterance.—The more precise designation of John as "the Baptist" in Matthew is similarly to be regarded as secondary. If it had to be reproduced in Aramaic, then the Syriac מַעְמְדָנָא (as in Jerus. Gosp. Matt. 11[12]) would be as inapt as מַצְבְּעָנָא (loc. cit. Matt. 11[11]). Wellhausen,[4] indeed, supposes that "the

[1] Jesu Muttersprache, 88 f., cf. 157 f.

[2] Only the Chronicler has as passive הִתְחַזַּק, meaning "to be consolidated," 2 Chron. 1[1].

[3] *Deissmann*, Neue Bibelstudien, 85 f. [Bible Studies, 258], recalls the fact that βιάζομαι may also be used as a middle voice, and absolutely, meaning "to appear with force." But one can here found nothing on the "exercise of compulsion" in the theocracy.

[4] *J. Wellhausen*, Der arabische Josippon (1897), 43.

word ' Schmatten ' in colloquial Jewish usage has been derived from עָמַד," and thus proves the occurrence of this verb among the Jews, with the meaning " to baptize." But the Jewish שָׁמַד, as may be seen from the use of the word in the Talmud, has nothing whatever to do with " baptizing," and עָמַד in this sense is quite unknown among the Jews. " To make one take a bath by immersion " is expressed among them by אַטְבֵּל, b. Yeb. 45ᵇ; Hebr. הִטְבִּיל, j. Yeb. 8ᵈ; b. Nidd. 32ᵃ. The corresponding Aram. noun would be מַטְבְּלָנָא, formed like מוֹרְיָנָא, " teacher of the law "; מִתְנְיָנָא, " teacher of the Mishna "; מַלְפָנָא, " teacher "; מְרַבְּיָנָא, " tutor."

We conclude accordingly that the first sentence (in Luke) might be presented as follows :—

אוֹרַיְתָא וּנְבִיאַיָּא עַד יוֹמֵי יוֹחָנָן. מִן הָכָא וּלְהָלָא מַלְכוּתָא דִשְׁמַיָּא.

The second sentence admits of being retraced to כָּל מַן דְּמִתְקֵף בַּהּ יַתְקֵף. This can mean " every one can lay hold of it," i.e. " it is attainable for every one." It may also, however, imply : " He who does not shun the requisite effort may take possession of it." Further, in case of need one might also read : כָּל מַן דְּמִתַּקֵף יַתְקֵף בַּהּ, " every one who exerts himself possesses himself of it." Somewhat thus it may have been understood by Matthew. And, finally, there remains the possibility of attaching the second half of the first clause to the second clause, so that the latter should then read : מִן הָכָא וּלְהָלָא מַלְכוּתָא דִשְׁמַיָּא כָּל מַן דְּמִתַּקֵף בַּהּ יַתְקֵף, " from that time and onwards the sovereignty of God—every man who will lay hold upon it lays hold of it." This perhaps may be presupposed in Luke.

To all this it may, however, be objected that the Greek form of our Lord's saying does not after all in either case tally closely with the Aramaic expression. A solution which should be in congruity with the tenor of the Greek would merit the preference. Such a solution for the wording of the phrase in Matthew may be arrived at, provided אֲנַס be made the starting-point, for this word can mean " to use force " and " to rob." In that case the original utterance would be: מַלְכוּתָא דִּשְׁמַיָּא מִן יוֹמֵי יוֹחָנָן וְעַד [1] בְּעָן מִתְאַנְסָה וְאָנוֹסִין [2] אַנְסוּהָא. The text thus refers to that period of the theocracy which was introduced by the imprisonment of the Baptist; it is its peculiarity that the theocracy suffers violence, not, of course, from believers, but from those in authority. The words ἁρπάζουσιν αὐτήν, corresponding to אֲנְסוּהָא, are not intended to suggest that the violent rulers seize the theocracy, but merely that they maltreat it in the persons of its representatives.

The utterance is found in Luke in an entirely different connection. According to him, it is applied in opposition to the Pharisees, who despised the admonition of Jesus in regard to the right use of money. Jesus declares to them that the proclamation of the theocracy since the time of John made it possible for any one to intrude himself violently into it; but nevertheless it was not their own estimate, but the judgment of God, that decided who was worthy of entrance. The context, however, in Luke may be pronounced peculiarly Greek. Neither the passive εὐαγγελί-ζεται (see above) nor εἰς αὐτὴν βιάζεται are capable of being directly rendered into Aramaic, especially not in case אָנַס is used. If it be supposed that, by using (vv.[15-18]) sayings of our Lord which originally had a quite different association, Luke obtains the transition to a new parable, then it may be surmised that he himself has given to v.[16] its present form, so as to accommodate the saying to the context. The saying which Matthew and Luke found in their sources made mention only of the violent treatment of the theocracy since the time of John. Luke thought upon attempted entrance into it, and thus found it natural to insert it in the position which it occupies in his Gospel; Matthew—with greater reason—understood it to refer to the violent treatment of the preachers of the theocracy, and has therefore connected

[1] Galil. כְּדִין.   [2] Galil. אֲנַסְתַּהּ.

it with the answer sent by Jesus to John. Neither by Jesus
nor by the evangelists is the statement intended to suggest
that any one could actually appropriate the theocracy through
the exercise of force. Unless absolutely driven to it, we
ought not to try to discover beneath these words an idea so
distinctly at variance with the whole style of our Lord's
teaching.

APPENDIX B.

Luke 17[20, 21] οὐκ ἔρχεται ἡ βασιλεία τοῦ θεοῦ μετὰ παρατηρήσεως, οὐδὲ ἐροῦσιν· ἰδοὺ ὧδε ἤ (D add. ἰδού) ἐκεῖ (D
add. μὴ πιστεύσητε).[1] ἰδοὺ γὰρ ἡ βασιλεία τοῦ θεοῦ ἐντὸς
ὑμῶν ἐστίν.

For μετὰ παρατηρήσεως Delitzsch puts בְּמַרְאֶה עֵינַיִם in his
translation of the New Testament into Hebrew—not, indeed,
without much misgiving, as may be seen from his private
copy. The Talmudic בְּפוֹמְפֵּי, " in triumphal parade," πομπή,
had appeared to him not impossible ; but in publishing the
11th edition the present writer did not venture to adopt
it. Salkinson renders it by לְעֵינֵי הַפַּבִּיט, Resch by בְּשִׁמּוּרִים, the
Syriac version, Sin. Cur. Pesch. has בנטורתא, " with observation." Meyer [2] proposes בְּנִמְטִיר, which, according to the Targ.
Job 4[12], he takes to mean " in secret." In that case the
evangelist misunderstood the word. But בְּנִמְטִיר, even in Job
4[12], can mean merely " by lying in wait for," i.e. as robbers
lie in wait for any one; cf. Targ. Job 10[14]. It is not amiss
to adduce as a parallel topic a certain Baraitha given b.
Sanh. 97[a]. Rab Zera there appeals to those who busy
themselves speculating about the date of the redemption :
" By your leave ! hinder it not, I beseech you (by your in-
quiries) ; for we have it by tradition : שְׁלֹשָׁה בָּאִין בְּהֶסֵּחַ הַדַּעַת
אֵילּוּ הֵן מָשִׁיחַ מְצִיאָה וְעַקְרָב, there are three things which come

---

[1] Both insertions in D are omitted by Blass in his so-called Roman recension
of the text of Luke.
[2] Jesu Muttersprache, 87.

unexpectedly (literally, while the attention is diverted) ; what
are they ? the Messiah, treasure-trove, and a scorpion." The
Palestinian Talmud generally uses 'הד בְּהֶסֵּעַ for 'הד בְּהֶסֵּחַ, putting ע instead of ח. The expression is also quite possible in
Aramaic, as may be seen from j. Taan. 67ᵇ (j. Meg. 75ᶜ):
" I looked up (at the priests pronouncing the benediction),
but my attention was not thereby diverted, דַּעְתִּי מַסְּעָה וְלָא ";
and again in j. Taan. 64ᵇ מַסַּע דַּעְתִּי מִן פֵּעֲלוֹתִי [1] מָה הֲוֵינָה, " why
was I to turn away my attention from my work ? " The
contrary of דַּעְתֵּיהּ אַסַּע is properly perhaps דַּעְתֵּיהּ כַּוֵּן, b. Ber.
30ᵇ; cf. simply כַּוֵּן, j. Ber. 5ᵃ, or דַּעְתֵּיהּ יְהַב, j. Sabb. 10ᵈ " to
pay regard to anything." But it is the unexpected and
startling aspect of Messiah's coming that is emphasised in
the Baraitha; whereas Jesus appears to have in view the
unostentatious advent of the theocracy. It is certainly not
" attention " which He wishes to exclude. This being so, the
words μετὰ παρατηρήσεως require no other term than נְטַר, for
this, without doubt, has the force of " to observe, watch for " ;
see Onk. Gen. 3¹⁵, Targ. Jer. 8⁷, Eccles. 11⁴, Ber. R. 78, and
the corresponding Hebr. שָׁמַר, Siphre, Deut. 127 (ed. Friedm.
100ᵇ). It had at the same time the meaning " to wait for " ;
see the phrase of the Mishna, יָבָם שׁוֹמֶרֶת, " the widow who
waits for her husband's brother," Yeb. iv. 3, and the parallels
in the Targum Jerus. I. Num. 27⁴, Ruth 1¹³. Consequently,
it is only the context of our Lord's saying that can determine the precise sense in which נטר is there used. And the
context favours " to watch for, to be on the outlook for."
The literal translation of μετὰ παρατηρήσεως, which would
have to be by בְּנַטִּירוּתָא or בְּנַטִּירוּ,[2] sounds to me unidiomatic.
Might not לֵהּ כִּדְנַטְרִין, " if one lies in wait for it," meet the
case ? The future ἐροῦσιν is distinctly unsuitable where it

---

[1] So it should be read. The emendation מְסַעַר, proposed in my " Aram.
Dialektproben," 29, is erroneous.

[2] The substantive נְטִיר, " observation," given in the Lexicon of Levy and
Jastrow, is doubtful. In Ex. 12⁴² Onk. נְטִיר is in both cases of its use the
Passive Participle, as may be seen in Jerus. I. II. בְּנָטִיר occurs only Job 4¹².

stands, whereas in v.[23] it is quite in its place. The whole clause v.[21a] is probably an interpolation introduced from v.[23].

The following would be a possible retranslation : מַלְכוּתָא דִשְׁמַיָּא לֵית הִיא אָתְיָא בִּנְטִירוּ (וְלָא יֵימְרוּן עֲלַהּ הָא [1] כָּא הִיא אוֹ הָא תַּמָּן הִיא).

For ἐντὸς ὑμῶν, the Syriac, Sin. Cur. Pesch. has בינתכון, "among you," Delitzsch and Salkinson have בְּקִרְבְּכֶם, Resch (following Ephrem) בִּלְבַבְכֶם, Meyer לְגוֹ מִנְּכוֹן. In Meyer's opinion the phrase is meant to indicate the sudden manifestation of the theocracy. But the most important element in that view—the suddenness—would fail to be expressed in the phrase, so Meyer conjectures that בגוכן was perhaps miswritten for בתכוף. As to the Aramaic term in question here, it is a striking circumstance that the Hebr. בְּקֶרֶב, in the sense of "among," is rendered in the Targums by בְּגוֹ when it is followed by a substantive, but generally by בֵּינֵי when it is attached to a pronominal suffix. Thus in Deut. 18[2] Onkelos has: "he shall have no inheritance among his brethren (בְּגוֹ אֲחוֹהִי)," but Ex. 17[7] "Is, then, the presence of God among us (בֵּינָנָא)?" Specially significant is Targ. Jud. 1[29] "the Canaanites dwelt among them, בֵּינֵיהוֹן," and 1[33] "they dwelt among the Canaanites (בְּגוֹ כְנַעֲנָאֵי)." The same rule applies to בְּתוֹךְ. Thus בְּקֶרֶב and בְּתוֹךְ, having suffixes attached, can be rendered by בְּגַוֵּהּ, בְּגַוַּהּ, only when they mean "within"; see for בְּקֶרֶב, Onk. Gen. 18[24]; for בְּתוֹךְ, Onk. Gen. 41[48], Lev. 11[33], Num. 35[34]; cf. Gen. 23[9] 35[2].

Thus there are only two options possible for Luke 17[21].[2] The reading is either בֵּינֵיכוֹן, and this meant "among you," or else בְּגַוְּכוֹן, with the sense of "within you." With the

---

[1] The double use of בְּרָא would also be possible, as in Vay. R. 34 : אִין הֲוָה אָזֵיל בְּרָה הָא אָזֵיל בְּרָה וְאִין לָא הֲוָה אָזֵיל בְּרָה אֱמוֹר הָא אָזֵיל בְּרָא (ed. Constant. wrongly בראי), "when he (who flees before the Roman power) is come here (say): Lo, he goes there! and when he has not come here, say: Lo, he is come here!"

[2] For the simple בְּ, which can also mean "in" and "among," we should expect ἐν in Greek.

latter compare Ezra 5⁷ בִּנְיָה, and בִּנְיָה, j. Ned. 39ᵇ, j. Keth.
31ᶜ, where in each case the reference is to the matter contained " in " a written document. Both words are found
j. Taan. 66ᶜ. Khanina dwells בְּנַוָּיה, " in it," *i.e.* in a certain
street, and he is בְּינַיכוֹן,[1] " among you," *i.e.* the inhabitants of
Zeppori. Against בִּנַוְכוֹן it appears an objection that it is the
Pharisees who are addressed ; but this cannot be considered
a final criterion, for the historical situation, where the
saying of the Lord is introduced, cannot lay claim to the
same degree of certitude as the saying itself. A complete
negation of μετὰ παρατηρήσεως required the affirmation of
an advent of the theocracy in the secrecy of men's hearts.
In other places Luke has ἐν μέσῳ for " among " ; see Luke 2⁴⁶
8⁷ 10³ 22²⁷·⁵⁵ 24³⁶, Acts 1¹⁵ 2²² 27²¹. When he writes
ἐντός in this case, he certainly means something more than
" among," namely, " within." Hence the closing phrase would
run : דְּהָא מַלְכוּתָא דִשְׁמַיָּא בְּנַוְכוֹן הִיא. Ephrem is therefore quite
right with his rendering " in your heart," although his exemplar can hardly have been so expressed. What Jesus had
in view in this utterance was the unseen genesis of the
theocracy caused by the " Word," and its effectual working, as
the latter is set forth in the parables of the Sower (Luke 8⁴ᶠᶠ·),
the Grain of Mustard-seed, and the Leaven (Luke 13¹⁸ᶠᶠ·).
Such an inner advent of the sovereignty of God realised itself
in all those to whom the teaching of Jesus had access. Jesus
might, therefore, in the word for ἐντὸς ὑμῶν have in view
the general company of His hearers. Even Luke felt no
necessity to exclude the Pharisees, and thus remained free
to place this paradox, tending rather to veil than to explain
the dictum, as an answer to the Pharisees in clear contrast
with the very different instruction communicated by Jesus
to His own disciples. Again, in Luke 11²⁰ (Matt. 12²⁸)
Jesus says even to the Pharisees when they had obdurately

---

[1] The proper reading is בֵּינַיכוֹן. In the Venice edition ביניכון יתב should be
read instead of ביני ויתב.

refused to recognise the divine power as effectual through Him: ἔφθασεν ἐφ᾽ ὑμᾶς ἡ βασιλεία τοῦ θεοῦ, " the theocracy is come upon you." [1]   In that case it is the power of Jesus against evil spirits which makes the theocracy recognisable even to outward vision; in the passage under consideration, it appears through the power of the Word invisibly, but not, therefore, less effectually.

II. THE FUTURE AGE, THE AGE (ÆON).

1. ITS OCCURRENCE IN THE DISCOURSES OF JESUS.

To him who speaks against the Holy Ghost forgiveness is denied, both ἐν τούτῳ τῷ αἰῶνι as well as ἐν τῷ μέλλοντι, Matt. 12[32]. But v.[32] is merely a repetition of v.[31], which, like Luke 12[10], mentions the unpardonable sin, omitting the addition, while Mark 3[29] states that the non-remission is valid " for evermore " (εἰς τὸν αἰῶνα); cf. the phrase: אֵין לוֹ מְחִילָה עוֹלָמִית, " there is no forgiveness for him for ever," j. Bab. b. 6ᶜ (Josa).[2]   The more detailed statement of Matt. 12[32] appears to have grown out of the shorter form, εἰς τὸν αἰῶνα, in Mark.   Hence no certain inference can be drawn in this instance as to the precise words used by Jesus Himself.

In Mark 10[30] (Luke 18[30]) ἐν τῷ καιρῷ τούτῳ and ἐν τῷ αἰῶνι τῷ ἐρχομένῳ are placed in contrast, while in Matt. 19[29] neither one or other is found.   In Luke 20[34f.] οἱ υἱοὶ τοῦ αἰῶνος τούτου are found alongside of οἱ καταξιωθέντες τοῦ αἰῶνος ἐκείνου τυχεῖν; but Matt. 22[30], Mark 12[25] have nothing corresponding.   Elsewhere, again in Luke (16[8]), οἱ υἱοὶ τοῦ αἰῶνος τούτου occurs as antithesis to the υἱοὶ

---

[1] O. *Schmoller*, Die Lehre vom Reiche Gottes (1891), 140 ff., successfully draws attention to the inner connection between Luke 11[20] and Luke 17[20].

[2] The shorter form, אֵין לוֹ מְחִילָה, is seen, *e.g.*, Ab. d. R. Nathan (39) (Akiba); cf. *Bacher*, Ag. d. Tann. i. 287.

τοῦ φωτός—without any parallel in the other Synoptists. In addition to these, we have also ἡ μέριμνα τοῦ αἰῶνος, Matt. 13²² (Mark 4¹⁹ αἱ μέριμναι τ. α.), but not in Luke, and the expression peculiar to Matthew, ἡ συντέλεια τοῦ αἰῶνος. Hence it is clear that the ideas, "this age," "the future age," *if Jesus used them at all*, were not of importance in His vocabulary. As observed above (p. 135), the idea of the "sovereignty of God" filled the place of that of the "future age."

Paul also speaks, and that frequently, of "this age" (ὁ αἰὼν οὗτος), see Rom. 12², 1 Cor. 1²⁰ 2⁶.⁸ 3¹⁸, 2 Cor. 4⁴, Eph. 1²¹; "this present age" (ὁ νῦν αἰών), 1 Tim. 6¹⁷, 2 Tim. 4¹⁰, Tit. 2¹², cf. Gal. 1⁴; "the time that now is" (ὁ νῦν καιρός), Rom. 8¹⁸; "this world" (ὁ κόσμος οὗτος), 1 Cor. (1²⁰) 3¹⁹ 5¹⁰ 7³¹, Eph. 2²; but only in Eph. 1²¹ is "the future age" (ὁ αἰὼν μέλλων, cf. Eph. 2⁷ "the ages to come") spoken of. The place of the latter is elsewhere occupied by ἡ βασιλεία τοῦ θεοῦ. The same holds good of the Johannine Gospel. The correlative of "this world," "this age," is properly not "that æon," and never "that other world," but "the sovereignty of God," and the "eternal life."

2. ORIGIN OF THE EXPRESSION.

In pre-Christian products of Jewish literature there is as yet no trace of these ideas to be found. Cremer, in the "Wörterbuch der Neutestamentl. Graecität," gives Tob. 14⁵ as the solitary instance of this conception to be found in the Apocrypha. Cod. Vat. has in the verse in question καιροὶ τοῦ αἰῶνος, Alex. εἰς πάσας τὰς γενεὰς τοῦ αἰῶνος, Sin. ὁ χρόνος τῶν καιρῶν, Itala "tempus maledictionum," while the Hebr. and Aram. texts present no equivalent. The original reading is therefore uncertain in this case; and, further, ὁ αἰών by itself does not necessarily presuppose an antithesis of two epochs. Even in Sir. 18¹⁰ ἐν ἡμέρᾳ αἰῶνος

means no more than "during one's lifetime," although the
translator into Syrian here makes a distinction between עלמא
הנא, "this age," and עלמא דזדיקא, "the age of the pious."
Moreover, the whole verse is an interpolation foreign to the
original document of the son of Sirach. The same holds of
"sæculum" in relation to "ævum sanctum"[1] in the Latin
version, 17^{25} 24^{33}.[2] The Ethiopic Book of Enoch speaks of
the "future age" only once, 71^{15}, and of "this unrighteous
age,"[3] 48^7, both late additions. The Assumptio Mosis and
the Book of Jubilees never mention either idea. The Apocalypse of Baruch, in its older sections, takes no notice of these
ideas. They are first mentioned in the more recent elements,
belonging to the period after the destruction of Jerusalem.
The "age that is promised" to the pious (Syr.[4] עלמא דמלכת
להון) appears there, contrasted with "this age" (Syr. עלמא
הנא), 14^{13}; "the age to come" (Syr. עלמא דעתיד, דאתי) appears
alongside of "this age," 15$^{7f.}$ 44^{15}; "that endless age" (Syr.
עלמא הו דסוף לית לה) beside "this passing age" (Syr. הנא עלמא
דעבר),[5] 48^{50}, cf. 40^3;[6] see also "the new age" (Syr. עלמא
חדתא), 44^{12}; "the deathless age" (Syr. עלמא דלא מאית), 31^3.
"Æon" is further used as a time-concept in 16^1 44$^{11ff.}$ 51$^{8.7}$
In 2 Esd.[8] 7^{50}, cf. 8^1, it is said that God has made, not
one world, but two. In that book are found the expressions

---

[1] Cf. Barn. 10^{11} ἐν τούτῳ τῷ κόσμῳ—τὸν ἅγιον αἰῶνα.

[2] See *A. Schlatter*, Das neugefundene hebr. Stück des Sirach. Der Glossator
des griechischen Sirach (1897), 145, 147 f.

[3] Cf. עֹלָם דִּשְׁקַר, Vay. R. 26; ὁ αἰὼν ὁ ἐνεστῶς πονηρός, Gal. 1^4; ὁ κόσμος τῆς
ἀδικίας, Jas. 3^5.

[4] According to the Syriac version published by *A. M. Ceriani* in the Monu-
menta sacra et profana, v. 2.

[5] Cf. עֹלָם עֲבֵיר (to be read thus, instead of עֲבֵיד 'y), Jerus. I. Gen. 38^{25}.

[6] That 40^3 does not belong to the older sections of Bar. Apoc., I have maintained against R. H. Charles in a review of his edition of Baruch, Theol. Litbl.
xviii. (1897), No. 15.

[7] Cf. also Bar. Apoc. 42^{13} "These are they who will inherit the time which
was spoken of, and whose is the earth in the age that is promised," with 42^{15}
"to them is given the age to come."

[8] Edition of the Latin version by *R. L. Bensly* and *M. R. James* (1895), of
the Syriac version by *A. M. Ceriani* in Mon. sacr. et prof. v. 1.

"hoc (præsens) sæculum" (Syr. עלמא הנא), "futurum sæculum"
(Syr. עלמא דעתיד), 4². ²⁷ 6⁹ 7¹². ⁴⁷. ¹¹² 8¹ᶠ.; "hoc tempus,"
"futurum tempus" (Syr. עלמא דעתיד, הנא עלמא), 7¹¹³ 8⁵² (cf.
Bar. Apoc. 44¹¹⁻¹³). The Slavonic Enoch also mentions "the
future age," according to Morfill's translation,[1] 56⁴ and 61²,
though the text does not seem to be certain in these passages.

The Targum of Onkelos makes no use whatever of the
ideas "this age," "the future age."[2] Even in the Targum
to the prophets they are infrequent. There are found בְּעָלְמָא
הָדֵין, 2 Sam. 22²⁸, 1 Kings 5¹³, Mal. 3⁶; לְעָלְמָא דְאָתֵי, 2 Sam.
7¹⁹ 23⁵, Jer. 50³⁰; בְּעָלְמָא דִמְשִׁיחָא[3] בְּעָלְמָא דַעֲתִיד, 1 Kings 5¹³; בְּעָלְמָא
לְמֵיתֵי, 2 Sam. 22²⁸.

If the addition to a saying of Hillel, given in Ab. ii. 7,
be genuine, then Hillel would be the earliest witness for the
use of the expressions. The passage runs : "He who acquires for himself the words of the law, acquires for himself
the life of the age to come (קָנָה לוֹ חַיֵּי הָעוֹלָם הַבָּא)."[4] A second
witness is next found in Yokhanan ben Zakkai[5] (fl. c. 80 A.D.),
who declared that God had revealed to Abraham "this age"
(הָעוֹלָם הַזֶּה), but not "the age to come" (הָעוֹלָם הַבָּא). A third
example may be taken from Eleazar of Modiim, who lived
slightly later, who enumerates among the six good gifts
received by Israel, "the age to come" (עוֹלָם הַבָּא), and "the
new world" (עוֹלָם חָדָשׁ).[6] See also the saying of Eleazar ben
Zadok given on p. 121, and the prayer of Nekhonya ben ha-
Kanna, j. Ber. 7ᵈ.

There is no value in the notice (Ber. ix. 5 ; Tos. Ber.
vii. 21) to the effect that in the temple no more than עַד
הָעוֹלָם[7] used to be pronounced in the benedictions, until the

---

[1] W. R. Morfill and R. H. Charles, The Book of the Secrets of Enoch (1896).

[2] See, however, Fundamental Ideas, III.

[3] This is the reading of the Venice edition of 1517, and Cod. Reuchl. without
insertion of דְּאָתֵי, which appears in the Venice edition of 1525.

[4] The saying is found also without mention of its author, Vay. R. 34.

[5] Ber. R. 44 ; cf. Bacher, Ag. d. Tann. i. 36.

[6] Mechilta, ed. Friedm. 50ᵇ on Ex. 16²⁵ ; cf. Bacher, Ag. d. Tann. i. 202.

[7] So it should be read as in Tosephta. כִּן הָעוֹלָם would be meaningless.

longer formula, כִּן הָעוֹלָם וְעַד הָעוֹלָם, was instituted to combat the sectaries who acknowledged one single æon only. This longer form is already found in Neh. 9[5], 1 Chron. 16[36], Ps. 41[14] 106[48]; the shorter, לְעוֹלָם, Ps. 72[19] 89[53]. Such a tradition merely suggests a historical sequence for the two formulæ. Carried out in practice, the prescription would have had no result. He who did not think on "the future age" when the shorter form was used, would not do so even with the longer form.

The currency of the expressions "this age," "the future age," is at all events established by the end of the first Christian century. This reservation should probably be made, that for that period the expressions characterised the language of the learned rather than that of the people. As for the sense imputed to the terms, J. H. Holtzmann[1] says: "The earlier representation simply makes the world to come to coincide with the 'days of the Messiah,' or at least to be inaugurated by that period (Dan., the 'Similitudes' of Enoch, Ps. Sol., Targum, and Mishna); a later view, on the other hand, reckons those Messianic days as part of the present world, and in this way distinguishes them from the final world-renovation (2 Esdras and Apoc. Bar., Midrash and later Theology)." But this hardly represents the true state of the case. Both "the days of the Messiah" and "the future age" are terms unfamiliar in the earlier period. When, subsequently, the world-renovation was located, not before, but after the Messianic epoch, there arose the controversy whether the phrase הָעוֹלָם הַבָּא, which meantime had come into use, should be made to include the Messianic age or not. The Targum in this regard represents the former view, it is true, but in the Mishna, Talmud, and Midrash the expression everywhere definitely implies no more than that the time of salvation is set forth as one sharply marked off from the present. Any fuller significance always requires

[1] Lehrb. der Neutestamentl. Theologie, i. 80.

to be ascertained with special reference to each statement and document.

The origin of the expression cannot be explained, as by von Orelli,[1] on the supposition that the idea of different ages was derived from the plural עוֹלָמִים, which originally was intended merely to enhance the idea, and that thus it came to pass that עוֹלָם was used to designate the now current age. This explanation is too ingenious to be considered probable. And the Old Testament בְּאַחֲרִית הַיָּמִים has not even indirectly served as a connecting link, for the Targums reproduce it by בְּסוֹף יוֹמַיָּא; see Gen. 49[1], Num. 24[14], Deut. 31[29], Isa. 2[2]. Reference could be made with better reason to the rendering given in the Targum for יוֹם יְהוָֹה, viz. יוֹמָא דַעֲתִיד לְמֵיתֵי מִן קֳדָם יְיָ, "the day destined to come from God"; see Isa. 2[12], Amos 5[18], Joel 1[15], Zeph. 1[7. 14], Mal. 3[23]: for the comprehensive idea of יוֹם יְהוָֹה is the real historical precursor of the idea of "the future age." The differentiating cause must probably have been that, during the development of a doctrine regarding the substance of the prophetic promises, comprehensive terms were a necessity for the instruction of the people. In these circumstances nothing was easier than to set in contrast the imperfect present with the perfect future. Further, to express "future," there were available the terms דְּאָתֵי, "that which is coming," or דַּעֲתִיד לְמֵיתֵי, "that which is destined to come." For these, see Hebr. הֶעָתִיד לָבוֹא, "the future," Ber. ix. 4; Mechilta, ed. Friedm. 37ᵃ; Siphre, ed. Friedm. 140ᵇ; j. Shebi. 35ᵃ; also merely הַבָּא, j. Shebi. 35ᵈ; Samaritan, דְּאָתֵי, Commentary of Marka;[2] Aram. מָה דַעֲתִיד לְמֵיתֵי Targ. Eccl. 3[11]. Further, as a matter of fact, the Hebr. לֶעָתִיד לָבוֹא became in Palestine a favourite expression for the Messianic future; for examples see pp. 108, 116, 127, 153.

Contact with Greek modes of thought, moreover, introduced the idea of the αἰών, i.e. "lifetime," "the age," and

---

[1] Die hebr. Synonyma der Zeit und Ewigkeit, 80 ff.
[2] *Heidenheim*, Bibliotheca Samaritana, iii. 69ᵇ.

"the temporary," into the circle of Jewish thought, either directly or through the medium of the Syrians. And when a term corresponding to αἰών was wanted, it would be readily remembered that the Aramaic לְעָלַם, was equivalent to the Greek εἰς αἰῶνα, "for ever," and thence easy to attribute to this עָלַם the special meanings of the Greek αἰών. Thus עָלַם became "age"; and it cannot excite surprise that Jewish scholarship adopted it as a most convenient designation for comprising "future" and "present."

To illustrate the new use of עָלַם (Hebr. עוֹלָם) as occasioned by the Greek αἰών, reference can be made to b. Ber. 17ª עוֹלָמְךָ תִּרְאֶה בְּחַיֶּיךָ, "mayest thou enjoy thine age during thy lifetime"; Vay. R. 32: יָצָא מֵעוֹלָמוֹ, "he departed from his generation"; b. Yeb. 63ᵇ (ascribed to Ben Sira) נִמְצָא מִצְטָעֵר עַל עוֹלָם שֶׁאֵין לוֹ, "he is found encumbering himself for the sake of an age which does not belong to him"; Koh. R. 1³ שִׁבְעָה עוֹלָמוֹת, "seven generations" (of men), and עוֹלְמֵי הַשָּׁנָה, "the seasons of the year," in the Samaritan Marka.[1]

Beyond question the idea of the κόσμος, which was afterwards combined with עָלַם, in many respects displaced the idea of the αἰών. But this does not apply so early as the time of Jesus, though Paul in 1 Cor. uses ὁ κόσμος οὗτος in juxtaposition with ὁ αἰὼν οὗτος.[2] Thus in the discourses of Jesus the rendering of αἰών by "world" should be avoided, because that term usually suggests the locus of all created things, or else the creation in its entire extent.

A point to be noted in the use of the word is that Aram. and Hebr. constantly have בָּעוֹלָם הַזֶּה, בְּעָלְמָא הָדֵין, "in this age," but almost always "for the age to come," with לְ—לְעָלְמָא דְאָתֵי לְעוֹלָם הַבָּא, just as it is also said לְעָתִיד לָבוֹא, "in the future."

---

[1] M. Heidenheim, Bibliotheca Samaritana, iii. p. xxii. For "age," Marka further uses readily דָּר, properly, "generation"; see loc. cit. 67ª f.

[2] See above, p. 148. Even in Greek αἰών sometimes denotes that which constitutes the contents of transitory time; see Heb. 1² 11³, which represent God as having made the αἰῶνες; and cf. 2⁵ τὴν οἰκουμένην τὴν μέλλουσαν, with 6⁵ μέλλοντος αἰῶνος.

Here also it is evident that עֲלַם in these phrases is a time-concept. Examples for the Aramaic usage: Targ. Lam. 3²⁸; Eccl. 1³ 7¹¹ᶠ·¹⁵ 8¹⁴ 9⁶; j. Schebi. 35°; j. Taan. 66°; j. Meg. 72ᵇ; b. Kidd. 81ᵃ; b. Ab. z. 65ᵃ: for the Hebrew usage, Ab. vi. 4, 9; for לָבוֹא לֶעָתִיד, j. Sanh. 28°; Ruth R. 3¹; b. Bab. m. 85ᵇ. For the uncommon בְּעָלְמָא דְאָתֵי, see Targ. Eccl. 5⁹·¹⁰; j. Dem. 22ᵃ.

Both ὁ αἰὼν ὁ μέλλων and ὁ αἰὼν ὁ ἐρχόμενος have their counterpart in עָלְמָא דְאָתֵי. And ὁ αἰὼν ἐκεῖνος also finds its equivalent in עָלְמָא הַהוּא, Targ. Eccl. 6⁹ 7¹⁴.

On the expression καταξιωθῆναι τοῦ αἰῶνος ἐκείνου τυχεῖν, see above, p. 119 f.; for οἱ υἱοὶ τοῦ αἰῶνος τούτου, see p. 115.

3. THE SIMPLE ὁ αἰών.

In the phrase ἡ μέριμνα τοῦ αἰῶνος, Matt. 13²², ὁ αἰών denotes "that which is temporal," without implying that the term is a contraction for ὁ αἰὼν οὗτος. Even if it were desired to supply τούτου as in some texts, then the antithesis between the current epoch and a future period of a different character would in this passage be needlessly introduced. Cognate Jewish phrases are: מִלֵּי דְעָלְמָא, "affairs of this life," b. Pes. 113ᵃ; b. Sabb. 82ᵃ;[1] עִסְקֵי דְעָלְמָא הָדֵין, "the concerns of this age," Targ. Eccl. 7¹⁸; מִלֵּי דִידֵיהּ, "his own concerns," in contrast with מִלֵּי דִשְׁמַיָּא, "the things of God," b. Ber. 7ᵇ; b. Meg. 6ᵇ;[2] חֶפְצֵי שָׁמַיִם, b. Sabb. 113ᵃ, 114ᵃ. According to j. Ber. 11ᵃ, food has relation to the "transitory life" (חַיֵּי שָׁעָה),[3] but the study of the law has relation to "the ever-enduring life" (חַיֵּי עַד לֹא כְשָׁעָה). To gain the "transitory life" (חַיֵּי שָׁעָה) is placed alongside of the gaining of "the life of the world to

---

[1] b. Sabb. 82ᵃ expresses blame that any one should call the "life of men" (חַיֵּי דְבִרְיָתָא) the same thing as occupation with מִלֵּי דְעָלְמָא. Palestinian parallels to this expression are wanting.

[2] Cf. μεριμνᾶν τὰ τοῦ κόσμου (in apposition with τὰ τοῦ κυρίου), 1 Cor. 7³⁴.

[3] שָׁעָה חַיֵּי means, Vay. R. 32, in an Aramaic passage "maintenance." b. Yom. 85ᵃ it has the literal meaning of the words: "the life of an hour," i.e. a brief interval; cf. Jerus. I. Gen. 49¹⁸ פֻּרְקָן דְשַׁעְתָּא, "a temporary redemption."

come" (הַבָּא הָעוֹלָם חַיֵּי), Vay. R. 34. See also p. 157. Whether "anxiety" should really be rendered by the Targumic יְצָפָא may be left undecided. In Sir. 42⁹ anxiety on behalf of the daughter (ἡ μέριμνα αὐτῆς) is expressed in Hebr. דַּאֲנָתָה, Syr. צפתה, which tends to support the rendering by יְצָפָא. Still יְצָפָא דְעָלְמָא appears suspicious; מַרְחוּתָא דְחַיֵּיהוֹן, "the troubles of their life," might perhaps be the right phrase.

ἡ συντέλεια τοῦ αἰῶνος occurs in Matt. 13³⁹ᶠ· ⁴⁹ ¹ 28²⁰ without parallel in Mark and Luke. The same phrase in Matt. 24³ is replaced in Mark 13⁴ by ὅταν μέλλῃ ταῦτα συντελεῖσθαι πάντα, and in Luke 21⁷ by ὅταν μέλλῃ ταῦτα γίνεσθαι (cf. v.³⁶). The theme in the context is the conclusion of the current world-epoch. Hence ὁ αἰών is here also no abbreviation for ὁ αἰὼν οὗτος, but a designation of time as transitory, of the world's course. As the term occurs only in Matthew, it will belong not to Jesus Himself, but to the evangelist, who has it in common with the Hellenistic author of the Epistle to the Hebrews (9²⁶): ἐπὶ συντελείᾳ τῶν αἰώνων. Paul also writes, 1 Cor. 10¹¹ τὰ τέλη τῶν αἰώνων. There is here a close relationship with τὸ τέλος, Matt. 24⁶· ¹⁴ (Mark 13⁷, Luke 21⁹); cf. εἰς τέλος, Matt. 10²² 24¹³ (Mark 13¹³). This rests again upon the Hebr. קֵץ עֵת, LXX ἕως καιροῦ συντελείας, Dan. 12⁴; הַיָּמִים לְקֵץ, LXX εἰς συντέλειαν ἡμερῶν, 12¹³; Aram. סוֹפָא עַד, LXX ἕως τέλους, Dan. 7²⁶·². One might therefore with some probability refer ἡ συντέλεια τοῦ αἰῶνος as expressed by Jesus to the simple סוֹפָא. Nevertheless the phrase in Matthew has also its Jewish parallels; see "exitus sæculi," Ass. Mosis 12⁴; "the end of the age" (Syr. דעלמא שולמה), Bar. Apoc. 54²¹ 69⁴ 83⁷; "the end of the ages" (Syr. דעלמא שולמהון), loc. cit. 59⁸; "finis temporis hujus" (Syr. עלמא דהנא שולמה), 2 Esd. 7¹¹³; עָלְמָא סוֹף, Targ. 2 Sam. 23¹. See also Bar. Apoc. 27¹⁵ דזבנא שולמא, "completion of

---

¹ Matt. 13³⁹ without the article, v.⁴⁹ according to some MSS. with τούτου.
² Cf. also in OT. הַיָּמִים בְּאַחֲרִית, for which the Targums have יוֹמַיָּא בְּסוֹף; see above, p. 152.

the times," cf. 29⁸ 30³; Ass. Mosis 1¹⁸ "in consummatione exitus dierum."

III. ETERNAL LIFE, LIFE.

1. ITS POSITION IN THE DISCOURSES OF JESUS.

ζωὴ αἰώνιος (always without the article) is spoken of by Jesus as the possession in which the righteous will one day have part, while the godless are subject to perdition.

ζωὴ αἰώνιος is the object of κληρονομεῖν, Matt. 19²⁹ (where Mark 10³⁰ has λαμβάνειν, Luke 18³⁰ ἀπολαμβάνειν), as also in the question addressed to Jesus, Mark 10¹⁷ (Luke 18¹⁸, cf. 10²⁵), where Matt. 19¹⁶ has ἔχειν. In these cases ζ. a. is regarded as a possession. It is a certain status, when mention is made of an "attaining to" it, Matt. 25⁴⁶ (ἀπέρχεσθαι εἰς ζ. a.). This status is also on several occasions referred to as merely ἡ ζωή (this always with the article). Again, in Matt. 7¹⁴ ἡ ζωή is anticipated by ἡ ἀπώλεια in the previous verse (Luke 13²⁴ contains neither). "Ways" lead in this instance to "life" and "destruction." One can "enter into," εἰσέρχεσθαι, life εἰς τὴν ζωήν, Matt. 18⁸ᶠ· (Mark 9⁴³· ⁴⁵). The antithesis to this is "to go away," ἀπέρχεσθαι, "into hell" (εἰς τὴν γέενναν), Matt. 5³⁰, Mark 9⁴³, or "to be cast into hell" (βάλλεσθαι), Matt. 18⁸ᶠ· (Mark 9⁴⁵· ⁴⁷). In Mark 9⁴⁷ there stands in place of εἰς τὴν ζωήν the obvious equivalent, εἰς τὴν βασιλείαν τοῦ θεοῦ. εἰσελθεῖν εἰς τὴν ζωήν is found Matt. 19¹⁷ as a repetition of ἔχειν ζωὴν αἰώνιον.

2. THE JEWISH USAGE.

The "eternal life" (חַיֵּי עוֹלָם) of the pious is first mentioned in the Book of Daniel (12²), next during the first century before Christ in the Psalter of Solomon 3[16], cf. 13[9]; Enoch [1] 37[4] 40[9] "to take possession of eternal life," cf. 58[3] 62[54] (see also Slavonic Enoch 65[10], cf. 50[2] "to take possession of the endless life to come"); 2 Macc. 7[9] (αἰώνιος ἀναβίωσις ζωῆς), 7[26] (ἀέναος ζωή); 4 Macc. 15[3]. The idea has also found admission into the Targum of Onkelos, though it is not spoken of as "the age to come," for חַיֵּי עָלְמָא, Lev. 18[5], Deut. 33[6] (where the Jerus. Targ. incorrectly thinks of the life of this age), is intended for "eternal life." Further, the association with יֵחֵי בְּחַיֵּי עָלְמָא in the passages adduced and Targ. Ezek. 20[11. 13. 21], Hos. 14[10], makes it clear that חַיֵּי עָלְמָא is there regarded as equivalent to עָלְמָא דְאָתֵי. The Targum to 1 Sam. 2[6] also says that God will cause a resurrection from the realm of the dead "in the" eternal life (בְּחַיֵּי עָלְמָא), and Jerus. Targ. I. on Deut. 13[19] straightway changes it in this connection into עָלְמָא דְאָתֵי. See also Targ. 1 Sam. 25[29], which tells that the soul of David is hidden before God "in the security of the eternal life" (בִּגְנַט חַיֵּי עָלְמָא), i.e. in the safe keeping of those who are destined to life eternal.

Elsewhere throughout the older Jewish literature the term "eternal life" is found almost only in a case where it stands in contrast with "transitory life." Eliezer ben Hyrkanos (c. 100 A.D.) speaks reproachfully of such as neglect the eternal life (מַנִּיחִין חַיֵּי עוֹלָם) and "occupy themselves with the transitory life" (עוֹסְקִין בְּחַיֵּי שָׁעָה).[2] The same terms are afterwards imputed also to Simeon ben Yokhai[3] (c. 130) and to Simeon ben Gamliel II.[4] (c. 160). The school of Shammai (first century) makes use, according to Tos. Sanh. xiii. 3, of חַיֵּי עוֹלָם in a passage containing allusions to Dan. 12[2]. An appendix to a statement of Yehuda ben Ilai (c. 150)[5] contains the words חַיֵּי עוֹלָמִים, Tam. vii. 4. The Aramaic prayer

---

[1] In Enoch 10[10] ζωὴ αἰώνιος is meant merely of a "life without death."
[2] b. Bez. 15[b]; *Bacher*, Ag. d. Tann. i. 108 (cf. 62).
[3] b. Sabb. 33[b]; *Bacher*, op. cit. ii. 89.
[4] j. Mo. k. 82[b]; *Bacher*, op. cit. ii. 330.
[5] *Bacher*, loc. cit. i. 336.

beginning מַחֵי וּמְםֵי says,[1] "he who brings forth out of Sheol
into the eternal life" (לְחַיֵי עָלְמָא), and a similar formula in the
Kaddish prayer used after an interment[2] appears in לְאַפָּקָא
יָתְהִין לְחַיֵי עָלְמָא, "to raise them (the dead) up to the eternal life."

In general, however, "the life of the world to come,"
חַיֵי הָעוֹלָם הַבָּא, has taken the place of the shorter "eternal life,"
חַיֵי עוֹלָם. Examples of the former, see pp. 103, 118, 125, 150,
155, 160.

3. THE VERBS CONNECTED WITH IT.

As for the combinations in which ζωὴ αἰώνιος is found,
the verb κληρονομεῖν is, in Aram., יְרַת or אַחֵם; see, for these
terms, p. 125.[3] λαμβάνειν and ἀπολαμβάνειν, Mark 10[30],
Luke 18[30], are both to be referred to נְסַב. For ἔχειν, on the
contrary, Matt. 19[16], no equivalent need be sought, since the
parallels in Mark and Luke have here, as one would expect,
κληρονομεῖν. The verb ἀπέρχεσθαι, Matt. 25[46], is modified
by the adjacent εἰς κόλασιν αἰώνιον, cf. Matt. 5[30]. Yet אֲזַל
is the only word that can be proposed to render it; and to
the same verb—to אֲזִילוּ or זִילוּ (Galil. אִזְלוּ), "go ye," the δεῦτε,
v.[34], addressed to the righteous — must also be referred.
Thus it can also be said concerning them, יֵיזְלוּן לְחַיֵי עָלְמָא, "they
go away (from the judgment) into eternal life." To "attain
unto" the eternal life (εἰσέρχεσθαι) would, on the other
hand, be expressed by אֲתָא לְחַיֵי עָלְמָא; see above, p. 116 f.

4. THE SIMPLE ἡ ζωή.

In the Old Testament the scope of expressions like הַחַיִּים,
"the life," Deut. 30[13. 19]; דֶּרֶךְ הַחַיִּים, "the way of life," Jer.
21[8]; אֹרַח חַיִּים, "path of life," Prov. 2[19], does not extend be-

---

[1] Seder Rab Amram, ii. 21b.
[2] According to Baer's Seder Abodath Yisrael, 588. But the formula is
wanting in Seder Rab Amram and in Maimonides.
[3] The "heir" (cf. κληρόνομοι ζωῆς αἰωνίου, Tit. 3[7]) would be יַרְתָא. On the
"promise" of the life, see above, p. 103.

yond earthly life and well-being. The last-named phrase as used in Ps. 16¹¹ already seems to contain the idea of a happy existence after death. At a later date the idea of the life eternal of those risen from the dead attached itself to these verses, so that "life" could be put shortly for "eternal life." Thus the Psalter of Solomon (14⁶) says of the pious: κληρονομήσουσιν ζωήν, and speaks of ζωή, 9⁹, without qualification, meaning thereby, according to 3¹⁶, the "eternal life." In 2 Macc. 7¹⁴ there is also found the abbreviated ἀνάστασις εἰς ζωήν alongside of εἰς αἰωνίου ἀναβίωσιν ζωῆς ἡμᾶς ἀναστήσει, in 7⁹. The treatise of the "Two Ways,"[1] generally supposed to be of Jewish origin, alone contains the expression "way of life." The Slavonic Enoch (ed. Morfill and Charles) 30¹⁵ also speaks of these ways. A detailed description of them is given in the Testament of Abraham,[2] not, however, without marked Christian influence, which shows itself in the use of expressions from the Synoptists. Bar. Apoc. 42⁷ represents that "perdition" and "life" one day will claim what pertains to each.

The later Jewish literature has given the preference to the clearer appellation, "life of the age to come." Nevertheless there are found occasionally as correlatives: חיין, "they attain to the (eternal) life," and מדונין, "they are judged (pass to eternal punishment)," Tos. Sanh. xiii. 2; b. Sanh. 103ᵇ.[3] It is only when "life" and "death" form parts of the same picture that they are always left without qualification. Thus Yokhanan (c. 260 A.D.) declares that those who are pious to perfection receive[4] the "Judge's award (ἀπόφασις) of life" (אַיפּוֹפְסִי שֶׁלְּחַיִּים); and in the prayer

<hr>

[1] See A. Harnack, Die Apostellehre und die jüdischen beiden Wege ² (1896), 57. As to the Jewish origin of the "Two Ways," I have, however, grave doubts. It could hardly have been intended for the instruction of proselytes.

[2] M. R. James, The Testament of Abraham (Texts and Studies, ii. 2), 88 ff., 112 ff.; cf. 51 ff.

[3] Cf. Bacher, Ag. d. Taan. i. 140.

[4] So in j. R. h. S. 57ᵃ, while b. R. h. S. 16ᵇ speaks of a recording and sealing "unto life," לחיים.

which begins רַחֲמָנָא אִדְּכַר,[1] it is said עֲלָן גְּזוֹר דְּחַיֵּי דִּינָא, "may the award of life be pronounced over us!"[2] The principle that "the medicine which brings life" (סַם חַיִּים) may also be "the poison which brings death" (סַם מִיתָה), is observed first of all by Benaya (c. 200 A.D.),[3] and afterwards by others, as Joshua ben Levy (c. 240).[4] In the Samaritan author Marka,[5] God refers to Himself as פרנס חייה ואריסה דמותה, "the stay of life, and the poison of death." There should also be added the Pauline expression: ὀσμὴ ἐκ θανάτου εἰς θάνατον, ὀσμὴ ἐκ ζωῆς εἰς ζωήν, 2 Cor. 2¹⁶.

It is quite conceivable that the detailed Greek phrase: ἡ ὁδὸς ἡ ἀπάγουσα εἰς τὴν ζωήν, Matt. 7¹⁴, may be derived from the simple ἡ ὁδὸς τῆς ζωῆς; cf. Aram. אוֹרַח חַיֵּי, Targ. Jer. 21⁸; אוֹרְחָא דְחַיֵּי, Targ. Jerus. I. Deut. 30¹⁵· ¹⁹. The Old Testament never contemplates a way as "leading" to some destination. But in post-biblical literature we have Bar. Apoc. 85¹³ "the way of the fire, the path which leads to Gehinnom" (Syr. אורחא דנורא ושביל דמקרב לגהנא); and Ber. R. 9: אֵיזֶה דֶרֶךְ מְבִיאָה אֶת הָאָדָם לְחַיֵּי הָעוֹלָם הַבָּא, "which way is it that leads to the life of the age to come?" The Jerus. Gospel in Matt. 7¹⁴ uses אובל, which is likewise known to the Jewish Aramaic of Palestine. Recourse is thus open to the Aramaic אַיְתִי or אוֹבֵל, and if need be to קְרֵב. "The way that leads to the life" would in Aramaic be: אָרְחָא דִּמְטֵיתֵיהּ (דִּמוֹבְלָה)[6] לְחַיֵּי[7]

εἰσέρχεσθαι εἰς τὴν ζωήν (Matt. 18⁸, Mark 9⁴⁵) would be אֲתָא לְחַיֵּי, cf. p. 116, since עַל לְחַיֵּי עָלְמָא, being in the late Targum to the Psalms (40⁸), should not determine the selection. It may well be asked, however, whether the

---

[1] Seder Rab Amram, ii. 20ᵃ.   [2] Cf. δικαίωσις ζωῆς, Rom. 5¹⁸.
[3] Siphre, Deut. 45, ed. Friedm. 82ᵇ; cf. Bacher, Ag. d. Taan. ii. 540.
[4] b. Yoma 72ᵇ; cf. Bacher, Ag. d. p. Am. i. 137; see also ibid. pp. 37, 262. The Aramaic form is סַמָּא דְחַיֵּי and סַמָּא דְמוֹתָא, as in b. Yom. 72ᵇ (Raba).
[5] Heidenheim, Bibl. Samarit. iii. 7ᵃ.
[6] ארח in Aramaic is at least generally fem. not masc., as Gesenius-Buhl and the dictionaries of Levy represent.
[7] That חַי is readily used as the defined form, see above; also Onk. Deut. 30¹⁵· ¹⁹, where חַי is put for the Hebrew הַחַיִּים, and Targ. Mal. 2⁵.

simple ἡ ζωή is original in this connection. Judging from Matt. 19¹⁷, where ἡ ζωή represents ζωὴ αἰώνιος, and Mark 9⁴⁷, cf. vv.⁴³˙⁴⁵, where ἡ βασιλεία τοῦ θεοῦ is used in its place, it is not improbable that as used in the words of Jesus—excepting, perhaps, Matt. 7¹³˙¹⁴—it might throughout be represented by חַיֵּי עָלְמָא or מַלְכוּתָא דִּשְׁמַיָּא.

5. THE SIGNIFICANCE OF THE IDEA.

With Jesus " eternal life " and " life " form the correlative idea to expressions which denote eternal perdition. The popular Jewish term גֵּיהִנָּם (Aram. form of גֵּיהִנֹּם), Greek ἡ γέεννα, is the one term whose use by Jesus is assured, since all three Synoptists record it among the words of Jesus. Less certain is τὸ πῦρ τὸ ἄσβεστον, based upon Isa. 66²⁴, as it occurs among the words of Jesus only in Mark 9⁴³˙ (⁴⁵). Peculiar to Matthew are: τὸ πῦρ τὸ αἰώνιον (18⁸), κόλασις αἰώνιος (25⁴⁶), ἡ κάμινος τοῦ πυρός (13⁴²),—this being occasioned by the imagery of the parable,—and ἡ ἀπώλεια (7¹³). The last-named is required as antithesis to ἡ ζωή (7¹⁴), and can therefore be reckoned as certain. Both " eternal life " and " Gehenna " have as necessary presupposition a judgment which awaits all men, in which the fate of men is for ever decided. There is thus involved a symbolism derived from a judicial process. The penalty of death threatens him who has been found guilty at the bar of justice ; the gift of life is bestowed on him who is acquitted. In the final judgment, it is not the ending or continuation of earthly existence that constitutes the decisive issue ; but either, on the one hand, the penalty of an eternal death by fire, the scene of which is Gehenna, which involves permanent exclusion from the theocracy ; or, on the other hand, appointment to the eternal life which is consummated in the theocracy, or, in rabbinical terms, in the age to come. Hence " eternal life " radically means participation in the " theocracy " ; and it is substan-

tially the same thing whether it be the entrance into the
theocracy or into eternal life that is spoken of. The forgiveness of sins should not be regarded, as by Holtzmann,[1] as " the
negative counterpart of the beatitude (of the kingdom of
God), the primary foretaste of the positive possession of life " ;
it is rather the indispensable condition for entrance into "life,"
but not a constituent element of the life itself. Nor is there
any call for peculiar speculations in regard to the conception
of " the life," as being, according to Haupt's definition [2] of
ἡ ζωή, " the sum-total of all that constitutes life in its fullest
sense,—the true life." The difference between the preaching
of Jesus and Jewish views consists not in the idea of the
" life," but in what Jesus has to say of the theocracy, and of
that righteousness without which life in the theocracy can
never be attained.

IV. THE WORLD.

1. BOOKS IN WHICH THE TERM IS STILL UNKNOWN.

Old Testament Hebrew has no term which would quite
correspond to the Greek ὁ κόσμος. The *Alexandrian Version*
of the biblical books renders the " host " of heaven (צָבָא) by
ὁ κόσμος in the Pentateuch, Gen. 2¹, Deut. 4¹⁹ 17³. This
Greek usage, which belongs to an earlier period, is also
adopted by the LXX in Isa. 24²¹, elsewhere they use κόσμος
merely for " ornament." The Book of Daniel still has בָּל
אֲרָעָא, where a term for world might be expected, Dan. 2³⁵. ³⁹
3³¹ 4⁸. ¹⁹ (without בָּל) 6²⁶. The Book of Sirach has κόσμος,
43⁹, for the Hebr. עֲדִי, " ornament," and 50¹⁹, probably for
תִּפְאֶרֶת, with the same meaning ;[3] and αἰών occurs 43⁶ 46¹⁹,[4]

---

[1] Lehrb. d. Neutest. Theol. i. 202.

[2] *E. Haupt*, Die eschatologischen Aussagen Jesu, 85.

[3] So *S. Schechter* conjectures, Jew. Quart. Rev. x. 206. The MS. Hebrew
Text published by Schechter has לְשָׁרֵת מְקוֹם נֶזֶר, " to serve the altar."

[4] Here without equivalent in the Hebrew text.

for עוֹלָם, "eternity."[1] In the Syriac version κτίσμα αἰῶνος
also appears 38³⁴ as עבידתא דעלמא, but can scarcely be correct.
The original might probably have here used עוֹלָם adverbially
to mean "always."[2] In 39² ἀνδρῶν ὀνομαστῶν (Syr. אנשא
דעלמא) apparently reproduces אַנְשֵׁי עוֹלָם, "the men of olden
time"; cf. אֲבוֹת עוֹלָם, 44¹, or even אַנְשֵׁי שֵׁם, also occurring in 44³.
And just as עוֹלָם, in the sense of world, is absent from the
original of the Wisdom of the Son of Sirach, so it is not
to be found in 1 Macc., Ps. of Solomon, nor in the Books of
Tobit and Judith. No importance need be attached to the
saying attributed to Simeon the Just (c. 280 B.C.) concerning
the three things on which "the world" (הָעוֹלָם) rests.[3] The
substance and the form of the expression are equally unfavourable to its authenticity.

Nor, again, did the first[4] section of the *Book of Enoch*
(chaps. 1–36), the original of which was probably in
Hebrew,[5] contain עוֹלָם, in the sense of world. The terms of
the Greek version: ὁ θεὸς τοῦ αἰῶνος, 1³; ὁ βασιλεὺς τῶν
αἰώνων, 12³; κύριε ὁ τῆς δικαιοσύνης κυριεύων τοῦ αἰῶνος, 22¹⁴;
ὁ κύριος τῶν αἰώνων, 9⁴; ὁ βασιλεὺς τοῦ αἰῶνος, 25³·⁵·⁷ 27³,
cannot be dissociated from the biblical expressions: אֵל עוֹלָם,
Gen. 21³³; אֱלֹהֵי עוֹלָם, Isa. 40²⁸; צוּר עוֹלָמִים, Isa. 26⁴; מֶלֶךְ עוֹלָם,
Jer. 10¹⁰ (Targ. Venice 1517, מֶלֶךְ עֲלַם; Venice 1525, Cod.
Reuchl. מֶלֶךְ עָלְמִין); מַלְכוּת כָּל עוֹלָמִים, Ps. 145¹³. In any case it
may be assumed that the Hebrew original, from which the
Greek version was made, everywhere employed the article,
i.e. had מֶלֶךְ הָעוֹלָם, אֱלֹהֵי הָעוֹלָם. But the article, of course, may

---

[1] In additions to the Book of Sirach there occur κόσμος, "world," 16¹⁸ 18¹;
κτίσις, 16¹⁴ 24³, on which see *A. Schlatter*, Das neugefundene hebr. Stück des
Sirach. Der Glossator des griech. Sirach (1897), 133, 136, 140 f.
[2] Cf. Ps. 61⁸.   [3] Aboth i. 2.
[4] The first part of the Book of Enoch can scarcely be the oldest, and at least
it cannot have originated at the beginning of the second century B.C., as R. H.
Charles holds. The divine names θεός, βασιλεύς, κύριος, τοῦ αἰῶνος, τῶν αἰώνων,
currently used by the author, are scarcely in keeping with so early a date.
[5] The decisive proof lies in the Hebrew words contained in the Greek version;
see *R. H. Charles*, The Book of Enoch, 325; *A. Lods*, Le livre d'Hénoch, lvi ff.

merely be intended to render the general conception more
definite. It is not impossible that the article coupled with
עוֹלָם in composite expressions, gives the sense of "eternal."
It occurs Dan. 12[7], Hebr. חֵי הָעוֹלָם; Dan. 4[31], Aram. חֵי עָלְמָא,
meaning: "He that liveth eternally"; Onk. Lev. 18[5] חַיֵּי עָלְמָא,
"the eternal life"; Gen. 9[12] לְדֹרֵי עָלְמָא, "for perpetual generations"; Palmyr. בֵּת עלמא, "the eternal house" (grave), de
Vogüé, 32, 34 (Galil. בֵּית עָלַם, "cemetery," Vay. R. 12); Palmyr.
לְעָלְמָא, "for ever," de Vogüé, 21, 23; and also לְעָלְמָא, Targ. Isa.
28[28]; עַד עָלְמָא, "for evermore," Onk. Gen. 13[15], cf. Dan. 2[20];
but elsewhere always undefined לְעָלַם, "for ever," e.g. Onk.
Deut. 15[17]; לְעָלְמִין, Dan. 5[10], Targ. Isa. 25[8].

Still, it is perhaps more probable that עוֹלָם when united
with the article in the Book of Enoch does not merely represent the adjective "eternal." מֶלֶךְ עוֹלָם means "eternal
King"; מֶלֶךְ הָעוֹלָם is "the King who as ruler controls the im-
measurable duration of the world." The Greek translator
by his choice of αἰών in preference to κόσμος, shows he too
was conscious of a time-concept. Thus הָעוֹלָם in this section
of the Book of Enoch has the same sense as it bears in
Eccl. 3[11], where the second half of the verse makes it clear
that the idea in view is the incomprehensible range of time—
the consideration of which God has imposed upon the heart
of man, despite man's impotence to survey completely the
works of God therein comprised.—With ὁ αἰών ὁ μέγας, Enoch
16[1], little indeed can be done. The Greek text for that
passage is doubtless in confusion. Perhaps עַד יוֹם סוֹף הָעוֹלָם
הַגָּדוֹל stood in the original, and הַגָּדוֹל by mistake was taken
with הָעוֹלָם; or else the variants: עַד יוֹם הַדִּין הַגָּדוֹל and עַד סוֹף
הָעוֹלָם, were blended with each other. Since, however, the
context contemplates in any case an end of the עוֹלָם, it is
evident that the author did not regard עוֹלָם as signifying an
entirely unlimited range of time.

He can thus have in view the world-epoch extending
from the creation to the judgment, and עוֹלָם, in that case, is

differentiated from the idea of the "world" solely by its
temporal element. But he may also, disregarding the "end,"
give prominence to the infiniteness of the עוֹלָם; and this he
does intentionally, especially where the plural is used. מֶלֶךְ
הָעוֹלָמִים is "the King of the endless succession of ages," though,
of course, even מֶלֶךְ הָעוֹלָם is not "the King of the world," but
He who controls infinite time. There is, then, no great difference between the "God of the collective ages" and "the
eternal God"; cf. Ass. Mos. 10[7] "deus æternus"; 1 Tim. 1[17]
ὁ βασιλεὺς τῶν αἰώνων; Susanna LXX [35], Theod. [42], ὁ θεὸς ὁ
αἰώνιος; Rom. 16[26] ὁ αἰώνιος θεός.

Here may also be named certain expressions which con-
tain עוֹלָם in the plural: רִבּוֹן הָעוֹלָמִים, "the Lord of the ages,"
b. Yom. 87[b] (Yokhanan, c. 260); the liturgical phrase רִבּוֹן כָּל
הָעוֹלָמִים, "Lord of all the ages," Seder Rab Amram, i. 2[a], 12[a],
27[a]; צוּר הָעוֹלָמִים, "Rock of the ages," ibid. 3[b]; תַּקִּיף עָלְמַיָּא, "the
Strong One of the ages," Targ. Isa. 26[4]; מֶלֶךְ עָלְמַיָּא, "the King
of the Ages," Targ. Isa. 6[5] 30[33], Ezek. 1[24], Zech. 14[16].

Of a similar nature are the expressions: εἰς πάσας τὰς
γενεὰς τοῦ αἰῶνος, Enoch 9[4] (beside εἰς πάντας τοὺς αἰῶνας),
10[3. 22] (εἰς πάσας τὰς ἡμέρας τοῦ αἰῶνος), 14[5] 15[6]; cf. Gen.
9[12] לְדֹרֹת עוֹלָם; Onk. לְדָרֵי עָלְמָא; Targ. Eccl. 7[29] כָּל דָּרֵי עָלְמַיָּא;
Eph. 3[21] εἰς πάσας τὰς γενεὰς τοῦ αἰῶνος τῶν αἰώνων. All
the generations of "the world" are not here meant, but all
the generations of "the current age" of the "world-period."
In Enoch 9[6], according to the correct text, τὰ μυστήρια τοῦ
αἰῶνος, which are preserved in heaven, must signify "the
mysteries of primæval time"; cf. μυστήριον χρόνοις αἰωνίοις
σεσιγημένον, Rom. 16[25].

The Greek version of Enoch has also used ὁ κόσμος, 20[2. 4].
There, however, it is the host of the stars that is in consideration, so that κόσμος will be derived from צְבָא; cf.
p. 162.

The section of Enoch called the Book of Similitudes,
chaps. 37–71, the date of which is uncertain, mentions the

"creation of the world" only in later additions, 48⁶ 69¹⁶· ¹⁷· ¹⁸
71¹⁵. Further, 48⁶· ⁷ must be considered an interpolation,
because (1) it disturbs the connection between vv. ⁵ and ⁸,
(2) v.⁶ merely repeats with variations the substance of v.³,
and (3) v.⁷ contains terms which suggest affinity with those
of the late addition in 108⁸· ⁹· ¹⁰.

The section, chaps. 83–90, containing the Book of Visions,
contains the phrase "God of the whole world," 84². It
occurs in a very ornate doxology which belongs to the introduction to the Visions, and this part may very likely have
been more recent than the Visions themselves.

For the other sections of Enoch, see, further, under 3.

From this review it appears that the use of עָלַם or עֹלָם
for "world" in pre-Christian times must at least be gravely
doubted. It is also obviously improbable that the use of
κόσμος for world, which even among the Greeks did not
originate early, should have prematurely modified the phraseology of the Syrians and the Jews.

2. THE IDEA OF THE "WORLD" IN THE SYNOPTISTS.

Jesus says: τὸ φῶς τοῦ κόσμου, Matt. 5¹⁴, in proximity
with τὸ ἅλας τῆς γῆς, v.¹³; but the cognate passages, Luke
11³³, Mark 4²¹ (Luke 8¹⁶), have no corresponding term.
Still the phrase in the account of the Temptation : πάσας τὰς
βασιλείας τοῦ κόσμου, Matt. 4⁸ (Luke 4⁵ π. τ. β. τῆς
οἰκουμένης), may be brought into comparison; and in it
κόσμος could easily be referred to אַרְעָא, "the earth"; cf.
Targ. Jer. 34¹ אַרְעָא מַלְכְוָת כָּל. All the Synoptists have
κερδαίνειν τὸν κόσμον ὅλον, Matt. 16²⁶ (Mark 8³⁶, Luke 9²⁵).
In Matt. 18⁷ occurs οὐαὶ τῷ κόσμῳ, but the parallel in Luke
17¹ omits τῷ κόσμῳ. The gospel will be preached ἐν ὅλῳ
τῷ κόσμῳ, Matt. 26¹³ (Mark 14⁹ εἰς ὅλον τὸν κόσμον), ἐν ὅλῃ
τῇ οἰκουμένῃ, Matt. 24¹⁴ (Mark 13¹⁰ εἰς πάντα τὰ ἔθνη; cf.
Luke 24⁴⁷); see also πορευθέντες εἰς τὸν κόσμον ἅπαντα—

πάσῃ τῇ κτίσει, Mark 16¹⁵, and μαθητεύσατε πάντα τὰ ἔθνη, Matt. 28¹⁹. The field in the parable, Matt. 13³⁸, is the world (Epiphanius: ὁ κόσμος οὗτος), but the interpretation is not given in Mark 4 and Luke 8. Luke 12³⁰ speaks of τὰ ἔθνη τοῦ κόσμου, but Matt. 6³² has only τὰ ἔθνη. The world over which the signs of the end come is called ἡ οἰκουμένη, Luke 21²⁶, but no parallels appear in Matt. 24²⁹ᶠᶠ· or Mark 13²⁴ᶠᶠ·. Lastly, there occur also the expressions: ἀπὸ καταβολῆς κόσμου, Matt. 25³⁴, Luke 11⁵⁰ (but not in Matt. 23³⁵); ἀπ᾽ ἀρχῆς κόσμου, Matt. 24²¹ (Mark 13¹⁹ ἀπ᾽ ἀρχῆς κτίσεως), ἀπὸ (δὲ) ἀρχῆς κτίσεως, Mark 10⁶ (Matt. 19⁴· ⁸ only ἀπ᾽ ἀρχῆς).

In this it is surprising that Matthew alone uses ὁ κόσμος with any frequency, its appearance in Mark and Luke being only intermittent. The only expressions common to all the Synoptists are ἀπὸ καταβολῆς (ἀρχῆς) κόσμου (κτίσεως), and κερδαίνειν τὸν κόσμον ὅλον. As for the first, the citation from Scripture in Matt. 13³⁵ refers it to Ps. 78², where the LXX puts ἀπ᾽ ἀρχῆς for the Hebr. מִנִּי קֶדֶם. Thus it would be just the favourite term of the Targ. of Onkelos מִלְּקַדְמִין, "in former times"; see Gen. 2⁸ 3¹⁵, Deut. 2¹² 33²⁷.¹ As for ἀπ᾽ ἀρχῆς, Matt. 19⁸, it may reproduce בְּקַדְמֵיתָא or מִן קַדְמֵיתָא. For the former, see Onk. Gen. 13³; for the latter, j. Kidd. 64ᶜ.

Hence there appears to be some degree of certainty that Jesus employed the term עָלַם in the sense of κόσμος only in the one instance, κερδαίνειν τὸν κόσμον ὅλον.

In the case of "gaining" the whole world, as in that of "losing" one's soul, there is involved a metaphor drawn from commercial dealings. This consideration will determine the Aramaic words to be presupposed. For "gain" and "loss" the Mishna uses שָׂכַר and הֶפְסֵד, Ab. ii. 1, v. 11; Bab. m. v. 4; cf. j. Bab. m. 10ᶜ. In Aramaic "gain" is אֲגַר, j. Bab. m. 8ᶜ 10ᵇ. To "make profit" and to "suffer loss" are Hebr.

---

¹ Cf. Targ. Isa. 41⁴ where שְׁרָא is rendered by מִלְּקַדְמִין. Of course מִן עָלְמָא is also possible.

נִשְׁבַּר and נִפְסַד, b. Pes. 50ᵇ (Baraitha); but also הִשְׁתַּבֵּר and הִתְחַפֵּר, Vay. R. 34. In Ber. i. 2 to "suffer loss" is הִפְסִיד. In Aramaic the equivalent of the last is אַפְסֵיד, j. Ned. 38ᵈ, while the Peal פְּסַד, as it seems, j. Keth. 30ᵈ, means "to end in ruin." A verb for "to gain" other than אֲרַוַח, j. Ned. 39ᵇ, is not known to me; and this verb does not properly admit of taking an object with it. Hence there may be put [1] for Matt. 16²⁶ וּמָה ² מַהֲנֵי לֶאֱנָשָׁא אִין הֲוָה לֵיה אֲגַר כָּל עָלְמָא וְאַפְסִיד נַפְשֵׁיה.

The Palestinian proverb, b. Ned. 41ᵃ, applied to knowledge (דֵּעָה), has some resemblance: דְּדָא בֵיה כֻּלָּה בֵיה דְּלָא דָא בֵיה מָה בֵיה דָא קָנֵי מָה חָסַר דָא לָא קָנֵי מָה קָנֵי, "he in whom it (knowledge) resides has everything: he in whom it does not reside, what (after all) has he? this attained, what more is lacking? if he has not attained this, what (after all) has he attained?" Here we have the antitheses "to possess" and "not to possess," "to acquire" and to "fail to acquire," but they do not admit of being transferred to the saying of our Lord. Still the common correlatives "to gain" and "to lose" may quite well be inserted without injury to the sense. For these, Aramaic offers קְנָא and אוֹבֵד, and the saying of Christ would be: וּמָה מַהֲנֵי לֶאֱנָשָׁא אִין קְנָא כָּל עָלְמָא וְאוֹבֵד נַפְשֵׁיה. With אוֹבֵד נַפְשֵׁיה may be compared Ab. ii. 35 [3] R. Nathan: "Every one who keeps a precept of the Law, keeps his own soul (נַפְשׁוֹ הוּא מְשַׁמֵּר); and every one who destroys one precept of the Law, destroys his own soul (נַפְשׁוֹ הוּא מְאַבֵּד)."

The "whole world" is similarly referred to as a possession in the dictum of Meïr (c. 160 A.D.):[4] "When man comes into the world, his hands are folded together as if he would say, 'The whole world is mine, and I take possession of it'" (כָּל הָעוֹלָם כֻּלוֹ שֶׁלִּי הוּא וַאֲנִי נוֹחֲלוֹ). On the other hand,

---

[1] Jerus. Gospel has, Mark 8³⁶ Vat. : מא גר מתהני ברנש אן יתגר כולה עלמא ונפשיה יכסר (read יחסר).

[2] Cf. Vay. R. 20 : אם הָדֵן דּוּחֲכָא מְעוֹרָב מָה הֲרָוְחָא כְּתַנְיָא, "If the laughter is not unqualified, what good is there in merriment?"

[3] Ed. Schechter, 39ᵃ.

[4] Koh. R. 5¹⁴ ; cf. Bacher, Ag. d. Tann. ii. 19.

עוֹלָם is understood to denote "age" in the statement of Simeon ben Shetach (c. 80 B.C.), who maintained[1] that the praise of the God of the Jews (on the part of heathen who esteemed the integrity of Simeon) was dearer to him than "the gain of this whole age" (מֵאֲגַר כָּל הָדֵין עָלְמָא).

Of course the possibility also exists of setting aside even this solitary instance in the words of Jesus of the use of עֹלָם = κόσμος. That might be done either by taking עָלְמָא in the sense of "transitory time," or else by substituting terms such as כָּל אַרְעָא, "the whole earth"; שְׁמַיָּא וְאַרְעָא, "heaven and earth."

3. INSTANCES OF THE USE OF THE IDEA "WORLD."

It is not surprising that Hellenistic compositions, such as 2 Macc. (5 times), 4 Macc. (4 times), Wisdom (19 times), should use the conception and the term ὁ κόσμος. Among the New Testament writers, the extensive use of ὁ κόσμος by John in the Gospel and Epistles is specially worthy of note—a use which forms an essential part of this writer's nomenclature. It is much less frequently used by Paul, not being found at all in his Epistles to the Thessalonians; it occurs also in Peter and James, in the Epistle to the Hebrews, and in the Apocalypse. Of the Synoptists, Matthew, as remarked above, p. 167, has it most frequently (9 times); Mark, apart from 16[15], only once; and even Luke only 3 times in the Gospel, and once only, 17[24], in the Acts. The cognate term οἰκουμένη is found in Matthew only once, 24[14]; in Mark not at all; in Luke, however, 3 times in the Gospel (2[1] 4[5] 21[26]), and 5 times in Acts; and elsewhere only in Romans once, Epistle to the Hebrews twice, and in Revelation 3 times. This choice of terms by Luke must be attributed to his desire of writing in biblical style. Despite the influence of the earliest Christian tradition in regard to the words of

[1] j. Bab. m. 8ᶜ.

Jesus, Paul in the Epistles to the Thessalonians did not yet require to use ὁ κόσμος; and thus his testimony agrees with that of the Synoptists in proving that for Jesus the idea had not attained to any importance.

If we turn to the Hebrew compositions of Jewish litera-ture as yet unnoticed, we find that in the *Book of Enoch,* chaps. 72–82, the idea of the "created world," 72^1 $75^{3.\ 8}$ $82^{1.\ 5.\ 7}$, is certainly recognised. It may be left undecided whether in 81^3 "the King of the glory of the world," 81^9 "the Lord of the world," really meant "the eternal King of glory," as in 75^3, and "the eternal Lord."

Enoch, chaps. 91–104, contains the expression "to all the generations of the world," 103^8 104^5, where no time-limit is admissible, and the translation must therefore be "to all generations in perpetuity." In 91^{14a}, however, mention is made of the revelation of the righteous judgment before "all the world"; while the reference to "the world," 91^{14b}, as destined to destruction, is probably an interpolation, be-cause this apocalypse is not apparently cognisant of any destruction of the world.

The *Assumption of Moses* speaks of the "world" (orbis terrarum) only in its framework, namely, $1^{2.\ 11.^1\ 12.\ 13.\ 14.\ 17}$ $11^{8.\ 16.\ 17}$ 12^4, and not in the proper prophetic part, chaps. 2–10. It is worthy of note that 11^{16} and 12^4 have in juxta-position "orbis terrarum" and "sæculum." For these, Hebr. offers תֵּבֵל and עוֹלָם.

In the *Apocalypse of Baruch* two of the parts (chaps. 27–29, 36–40), dating from before 70 A.D., do not mention the "world." It occurs, however, in the third of the older sections (chaps. 53–74) several times (54^1 $56^{2.\ 3}$ $73^{1.\ 5}$). In the more recent sections the world is the subject of remark, $3^{1.\ 7}$ 4^1 $14^{2.\ 13.\ 18.\ 19}$ $21^{4.\ 24}$ 48^{15} 49^3 $83^{2.\ 8}$ 85^{10}. In general עלמא is the corresponding Syriac word, so that the Hebr. may be taken to be עוֹלָם. Only in 3^7, where the Syriac version

---

[1] Dominus orbis terrarum.

has תצביתא beside עלמא, the Greek ὁ κόσμος must have stood as parallel to ὁ αἰών. In this passage עוֹלָם and תֵּבֵל might be proposed as the Hebrew original.

In the *Book of Jubilees* [1] it appears doubtful whether עוֹלָם has been used for the idea of the " world." Reference is indeed made to " the generations of the world," 10^{17}, but also to " the perpetual generations," 4^{25} $8^{12.\ 21}$ 33^{16}, and to " all the generations of the earth," 6^{10} 12^{24} 19^{20} (which has also the reading " omnes generationes sæculi "); cf. above, pp. 164 f., 170. God is called " Lord of the world," 25^{23}, but 25^{15} " God of the ages " (אֱלֹהֵי הָעוֹלָמִים), 13^{8} " eternal God " (where there is another reading at least in the Latin version), and with special frequency " the Creator of all things " (see 2^{32} 11^{17} 17^{3} $22^{4.\ 27}$). " Heaven and earth," not " the world," constitute His creative work, 2^{25}. In the Flood the water fills " the whole world," 5^{24}.

In the *Second Book of Esdras*, " sæculum " (Syr. עָלְמָא) occurs with extraordinary frequency in the sense of the created " world," *e.g.* $3^{9.\ 18.\ 34}$ 4^{24} $5^{44.\ 49}$ $6^{55.\ 59}$ $7^{11.\ 30.\ 31.\ 70.\ 74.\ 132.\ 137}$ $8^{20.\ 41.\ 50}$ $9^{2.\ 5.\ 8.\ 13}$ 11^{40}. These passages cannot in every case be distinctly separated from those in which " sæculum " represents the idea of the " Æon." A Greek original would necessarily have had αἰών throughout, and Heb. 1^{2} 11^{3} confirms this likelihood. The Hebrew original had עוֹלָם.

The later Jewish literature abounds in instances of the use of עוֹלָם = world. It must, indeed, be observed from the outset that a clear distinction of the meanings " age," " eternity," and " world " is not everywhere practicable. As soon as the geographical connotation of κόσμος had been transferred to עוֹלָם, the speaker could at will apprehend it as a magnitude either of space or of time. Whether the school of Shammai really originated the statement [2] that " the

[1] See the translation by R. H. *Charles* in Jew. Quart. Rev. vi. (1894) 184 ff., 710 ff., vii. (1895) 297 ff.

[2] Eduy. i. 13 ; cf. *Bacher*, Ag. d. Tann. i. 20.

world has been created" (נִבְרָא הָעוֹלָם) solely with a view to propagation, is immaterial. But from the end of the first century עוֹלָם is so commonly used for "world," that it cannot be doubted that this name for the idea was then in general use. It has found its way even into the older Targums; see Onk. Gen. 3²²; cf. Targ. Isa. 51² יְחִידִי בְּעָלְמָא, "the only one in the world"; Deut. 33²⁸ בְּמֵימְרֵיהּ אִתְעֲבֵיד עָלְמָא, "through His (God's) word the world was made";[1] in the Targ. to the prophets, Isa. 41⁴ אֲנָא יְיָ בְּרֵית עָלְמָא, "I, Jehovah, created the world." Joshua ben Khananya and Eliezer ben Hyrcanus (c. 100 A.D.) dispute concerning the mode of origin and the form of the earth, and the word they use is עוֹלָם.[2] Both agree that God has created[3] "the world" (הָעוֹלָם). A proclamation finds its widest extension if it goes "from one end of the world to the other" (מִסּוֹף הָעוֹלָם וְעַד סוֹפוֹ), according to Joshua ben Khananya.[4] Eliezer ben Hyrcanus uses the same phrase to indicate the utmost range of vision.[5] According to Joshua ben Khananya,[6] "to destroy," "to ruin," may be expressed by "to put out of the world" (הוֹצִיא—מִן הָעוֹלָם). The "fathers of antiquity" (אֲבוֹת עוֹלָם) are now become "the fathers of the world" (אֲבוֹת הָעוֹלָם) according to Simeon ben Yochai;[7] and the "primeval mountains" (הֲרֵי עוֹלָם) are the "mountains of the world."[8] Compare גִּבְעוֹת עוֹלָם, Gen. 49²⁶, for which Onkelos has רַבְרְבַיָּא דְּמִן עָלְמָא, "the mighty ones of old"; Targ. Jerus. I. רַבְרְבָנֵי עָלְמָא, "the great ones of the world"; in Marka, זכאי עלמה, "the pious of the world," Bibl. Sam. iii. 3ᵇ; נביאה דעלמה, "the prophet of the world," ibid. 9ᵇ. One encounters such expressions as: "to come into the world" (אֲתָא בְעָלְמָא),

---

[1] Cf. John 1¹⁰ ὁ κόσμος δι' αὐτοῦ (τοῦ λόγου) ἐγένετο.
[2] b. Yoma 54ᵇ; b. Bab. b. 25ᵃ f.; cf. Bacher, Ag. d. Tann. i. 136, 139.
[3] Midr. Psalms 104¹; Bacher, loc. cit. i. 134. See also j. Ab. z. 42ᶜ, which says God rules "the world," whose shape is a globe.
[4] Mechilt. 56ᵇ f.; Bacher, loc. cit. 153.
[5] Siphre, Num. 136; Bacher, loc. cit. 154.
[6] Aboth ii. 11; Bacher, loc. cit. 162.
[7] j. Chag. 77ᵈ; Bacher, loc. cit. 18.
[8] Shir. R. 1¹²; Bacher, loc. cit. 134.

Targ. Eccl. 3¹⁴ 4² ;¹ " to come into this world " (אָתָא לְעָלְמָא הָדֵין),²
ibid. 5¹⁵ ; " to come upon the world " (אָתָא עַל עָלְמָא),³ ibid. 1⁴,
Jerus. I. Deut 5²¹ ; " to be in the world " (הֲוָה בְעָלְמָא),⁴ Targ.
Eccl. 1⁸ ; " to go out of the world " (אֲזַל מִן עָלְמָא),⁵ ibid. 1⁴ ;
" to judge the world " (לְמִדָן עָלְמָא),⁶ Targ. 2 Sam. 23⁷. רֹאשׁ
הַשָּׁנָה שֶׁלָּעוֹלָם is, according to j. Shebi. 35ᵈ, the first day of
the month Tishri, the day of the world's creation. Lastly,
" world " can sink down to the mere meaning, " the people."
מָה קָלָא בְּעָלְמָא,⁷ literally, " what is the voice in the world ? "
really means : " what do people say ? what is being talked
about ? "

Of the world in its fullest sense, God is readily referred
to as the Ruler, Hellenistic expressions no doubt helping as
models ; cf. ὁ τοῦ κόσμου βασιλεύς, 2 Macc. 7⁹ ; ὁ κύριος τοῦ
κόσμου, 2 Macc. 13¹⁴ ; δεσπότης πάσης τῆς κτίσεως, 3 Macc.
2². Even in Palmyra the " Lord of Heaven " (בעלשמן) is called
" Lord of the world," מָרֵא עָלְמָא, on an inscription of the year
114 A.D. (de Vogüé, 73) ; and the Samaritan author Marka
uses as names for God not only מרה דעלמה, " Lord of the
world," ⁸ מרה דכל עלמה, " Lord of the whole world," ⁹ but also
מלכה דעלמה, " King of the world," ¹⁰ and אלהה דעלמה, " God of
the world." ¹¹ These three Samaritan appellations, which recall biblical prototypes (see above, p. 163), were in use also
among the Jews.

For " Lord of the world," see besides Enoch 81¹⁰,
Ass. Mos. 1¹¹, Jubilees 25²³ (cf. above, p. 171), a dictum
of Eliezer ben Hyrcanus (c. 100) רִבּוֹנוֹ שֶׁלָּעוֹלָם ;¹² in the

---

¹ ἔρχεσθαι εἰς τὸν κόσμον, John 1⁹, Rom. 5¹².
² ἔρχεσθαι εἰς τὸν κόσμον τοῦτον, John 9³⁹.
³ ἐπέρχεσθαι τῇ οἰκουμένῃ, Luke 21²⁶.
⁴ εἶναι ἐν τῷ κόσμῳ, John 9⁵.
⁵ ἀφιέναι τὸν κόσμον, John 16²⁸ ; ἐκ τοῦ κόσμου ἐξέρχεσθαι, 1 Cor. 5¹⁰.
⁶ κρίνειν τὸν κόσμον, John 12⁴⁷, Rom. 3⁶.
⁷ j. Taan. 66ᵈ.
⁸ *Heidenheim*, Bibl. Samarit. iii. 10ᵇ, 11ᵃ.   ⁹ Ibid. 5ᵃ.
¹⁰ Ibid. iii. 10ᵇ.   ¹¹ Ibid. iii. 14ᵃ.
¹² Mechilta 56ᵃ ; *Bacher*, Ag. d. Tann. i. 152.

Targums, רִבּוֹן עָלְמָא in place of the simple הָאָדוֹן, Onk. Ex.
34²², Targ. Isa. 3¹ ; רִבּוֹנֵי עָלְמָא, Targ. Eccl. 4¹³ (cf. רִבּוֹנֵיהּ
דְּעָלְמָא, j. Taan. 68ᵈ) ; רִבּוֹן כָּל עָלְמָא, Targ. Cant. 5². Subsequently the synonymous עָלְמָא (מָרֵא) מָרֵי came into use side
by side with רִבּוֹן עָלְמָא, and appears, e.g. Targ. Eccl. 5¹¹ ;
Cant. 2¹³ 8³ ; Targ. Jerus. I. Gen. 22¹ ; Tob. 8¹⁴ (Aram.
text).

As " King of the world" God is called מֶלֶךְ עָלְמָא (Cod.
Reuchl. מ' עָלְמַיָא), Targ. Zech. 14¹⁷, מַלְכָּא דִי עָלְמָא in the prayer
beginning יְקוּם פֻּרְקָן ; in Hebrew, chiefly in the blessings מֶלֶךְ
הָעוֹלָם, e.g. Seder Rab Amram, i. 1ᵇ.

" God of the world" appears as אֱלָהּ עָלְמָא, Onk. Gen. 21³³ ;
Targ. Isa. 40²⁸ 42⁵ ; cf., however, above, p. 163 ff.

It is remarkable that none of these designations has
found an entrance into the New Testament. Jesus says,
Matt. 11²⁵ (Luke 10²¹), in an invocation of God, not κύριε
τοῦ κόσμου, but κύριε τοῦ οὐρανοῦ καὶ τῆς γῆς. Elsewhere
we find : ὁ αἰώνιος θεός, Rom. 16²⁶ ; ὁ βασιλεὺς τῶν αἰώνων,
1 Tim. 1¹⁷. Only Rev. 11¹⁵ speaks of ἡ βασιλεία τοῦ κόσμου
as having become the portion of God and His Anointed. In
2 Cor. 4⁴ Satan is called by Paul : ὁ θεὸς τοῦ αἰῶνος τούτου,
and by John (12³¹) : ὁ ἄρχων τοῦ κόσμου τούτου.

A mode of expressing the same idea without the use of
the conception κόσμος is exemplified in אֲדוֹן כָּל הָאָרֶץ, " Lord of
the whole earth," Zech. 4¹⁴ 6⁵ ; קֹנֵה שָׁמַיִם וָאָרֶץ, " possessor of
heaven and earth," Gen. 14¹⁹·²² ; ὁ κύριος τοῦ οὐρανοῦ καὶ
τῆς γῆς, Tob. 8²⁰ Vat. ; δεσπότης τῶν οὐρανῶν καὶ τῆς γῆς,
Judith 9¹⁷ ; מָרֵא דִשְׁמַיָא וְאַרְעָא, " Lord of heaven and earth,"
in the prayer דְּבָךְ טָב¹ and in the Prayer for the Dead ;²
אֱלָהָא דִשְׁמַיָא וְאַרְעָא, " God of heaven and earth," Tob. 8¹⁵
(Aram.).

Of similar nature are the common designations : " God of
heaven," " Lord of heaven," " King of heaven," which have

---

¹ Zunz, Nachtrag zur Litgesch. d. syn. Poesie (1867), 1 : מָרֵיהּ שְׁמַיָא וְאַרְעָא.
² L. M. Landshuth, Seder bikkur cholim, etc. (1867) 49.

originated not so much with the motive of sharply separating[1] between God and the world, as of emphasising His power as Controller of the whole earth. Even the Phœnicians and Palmyrenians had a "Lord of heaven" (בעל שמן), see above; and a "Queen of heaven" (מלכת השמים) was known in Judah even before the Babylonian Exile (Jer. 44[18]). It was quite a common predicate of Deity which the Jews applied to the God of revelation, when they began after the Exile to style Him "God of heaven." This is found notably in Nehemiah (1[4] 2[4. 20]); see also ὁ θεὸς τοῦ οὐρανοῦ, Judith 6[19]; אֱלָהּ שְׁמַיָּא, Dan. 2[18]; אֱלָהָא דִשְׁמַיָּא, Tob. 8[20] 10[11. 12] (Aram.); for "Lord of heaven," see Enoch 106[11]; Ass. Mos. 4[4]; מָרֵא שְׁמַיָּא, Dan. 5[23]; מָרֵי שְׁמַיָּא, Vay. R. 25; מָרֵיהּ דִשְׁמַיָּא, Koh. R. 3[2]; for "King of heaven," see Dan. 4[34] מֶלֶךְ שְׁמַיָּא; 3 Macc. 2[2] βασιλεὺς τῶν οὐρανῶν; Tob. 13[11], Vat. Sin. 16 Sin. βασιλεὺς τοῦ οὐρανοῦ. A rare parallel form to אֱלָהָא דִשְׁמַיָּא appears in מֵימְרָא דִשְׁמַיָּא, the "Word of heaven," Targ. Eccl. 4[4], 11[3].

It is clear that the form of Judaism which readily chose to denominate God as "Lord of the world" cannot fairly be credited with the belief that the world was "altogether fallen into the power of the demons and ripe for judgment." Holtzmann[2] holds that this became the average sentiment among the Jews, whereas in contrast therewith Jesus preferred to adopt a positive attitude with relation to the created world and its blessings. But the pessimism of later Judaism, which expelled the joy of life, is connected with the thought of exile and not with a gloomier view of the condition of creation. The Israel which had produced Ps. 104 and the Song of Solomon was not yet extinct in the time of Jesus. And one must beware of supposing that the mixed population of Galilee was dominated by a conception of life which was peculiarly rabbinic.

In the later Jewish literature there are likewise found

---

[1] Maintained by Holtzmann, Lehrb. d. Neutest. Theol. i. 50.

[2] Lehrb. d. Neutest. Theol. i. 179.

parallels to those expressions whose real use by Jesus was found open to question. The phrase: $\phi\hat{\omega}\varsigma$ $\tau o\hat{v}$ $\kappa\acute{o}\sigma\mu ov$, Matt. 5[14], so freely used by John (8[12], cf. 3[19] 9[5] 12[46]), is Hellenistic. John 11[9] speaks of the sun as $\tau\grave{o}$ $\phi\hat{\omega}\varsigma$ $\tau o\hat{v}$ $\kappa\acute{o}\sigma\mu ov$ $\tau o\acute{v}\tau ov$. The light of the sun is referred to figuratively, Wisd. 18[4], where the Law is called $\phi\hat{\omega}\varsigma$ $\tau\hat{\omega}$ $a\grave{\iota}\hat{\omega}\nu\iota$, " a Light for the age." Similarly Israel is styled (Shir. R. 1[3]) a " light for the world " (אוֹרָה לָעוֹלָם), and according to Tanchuma, ed. Buber, Bem. 24[a], God is " the Light of the World " (אוֹרוֹ שֶׁלָּעוֹלָם). It was said [1] of Eliezer ben Hyrcanus that he excelled the sun, which gives its light to this world only, whereas the light of the teacher illuminated both this and the other world. A similar figure is employed by the disciples of Yokhanan ben Zakkai in calling their teacher נֵר הָעוֹלָם, " the lamp of the world " (so in Ab. R. Nath. 25), or נֵר יִשְׂרָאֵל, " the lamp of Israel " (so in Ber. 28[b]). The lamp illuminating the darkness occupies the place of the light of the sun.

" In the whole world " (Matt. 26[13], cf. 24[14]) would be expressed by בְּכָל עָלְמָא. As for $\epsilon\grave{\iota}\varsigma$ $\acute{o}\lambda ov$ $\tau\grave{o}v$ $\kappa\acute{o}\sigma\mu ov$, Mark 14[9], it may be recalled that בְּכָל עָלְמָא is used to denote "everybody " in Babylonian Aramaic. The Galilean dialect has, however, only כָּל עַמָּא, properly, " every people," in the same sense.[2] Hence in that dialect " the whole world " will also stand for " the whole earth."

Again for $\pi\acute{a}\sigma\eta$ $\tau\hat{\eta}$ $\kappa\tau\acute{\iota}\sigma\epsilon\iota$, Mark 16[15], it may be pointed out that בְּרִיתָא, literally, " created beings," was a passable term for " mankind." The corresponding Hebr. הַבְּרִיּוֹת was used as early as, by Hillel, c. 10 A.D. " Love mankind " is expressed in his formula by הֱוֵי אֹהֵב אֶת הַבְּרִיּוֹת [3]

---

[1] Mechilta, ed. Friedm. 73[a]; *Bacher*, Ag. d. Tann. i. 352.

[2] The כל עלמא cited under the word עלם by *Levy* in Neuhebr. Wörterbuch from j. Sabb. 10[c] is, on the authority of the Venice edition, to be taken as כל עמא. j. Bab. m. 8[d] really contains כולי עלמא; but as it there points back to the immediately preceding כל עמא, it should be amended accordingly. So, too, in j. Ber. 4[b] כולי עלמא does not seem to be original.

[3] Ab. i. 12, see also Ab. iii. 10, iv. 1, iv. 2; and for the Aramaic term בְּרִיתָא, Esth. R. 1[1]; Vay. R. 22.

The "peoples of the world" (Luke 12³⁰) are termed in Hebr. אֻמּוֹת הָעוֹלָם, as by Gamaliel II.[1] and Akiba (both c. 110 A.D.);[2] and in Aramaic this would be אֻמֵּי עָלְמָא, though instances to verify it are awanting.

And here הָעוֹלָם contains no suggestion, as Holtzmann [3] supposes, that the peoples are regarded as alienated from God. The "peoples of the world" is a name for the sum-total of the peoples existing upon the earth, just like מִשְׁפְּחוֹת הָאָרֶץ, "the families of the earth," in Zech. 14¹⁷. "Since the beginning (creation) of the world" (see above, p. 167) recalls מִתְּחִלַּת בְּרִיָתוֹ שֶׁלְעוֹלָם, Ber. R. 3 ; Vay. R. 25 ; Aram. מִן יוֹמָא דְּאִתְבְּרִי עָלְמָא, Targ. Ruth 1¹; Targ. Cant. 8²;[4] cf. יוֹמָא תִנְיָנָא לִבְרִיַת עָלְמָא, "the second day in the creation of the world," Targ. Cant. 8⁶; "since the beginning of the creation," Jubil. 1²⁷.

4. THE NEW WORLD.

The unusual expression ἐν τῇ παλινγενησίᾳ, Matt. 19²⁸ (for which Luke 22³⁰ has ἐν τῇ βασιλείᾳ μου), is distinctly Greek, and cannot be literally translated either into Hebr. or Aram. It must be attributed to the evangelist himself. The Jerus. Gospel ventures to replace it by the peculiar בתולודתא דמן ריש, "in the regeneration." The East Syrian version (Cur. Sin. Pesh.) despaired of a verbal reproduction, using בעלמא הדתא, "in the new world." This, in fact, is what would have to be proposed in Jewish Aramaic also. The Apoc. of Baruch already uses, 44¹², the term "the new world" (Syr. עלמא חדתא), and 57² "the world that is to be renewed" (Syr. עלמא דמתחדת). Eleazar of Modiim (c. 100 A.D.), in the citation given on p. 150) mentions "the new world" (עוֹלָם חָדָשׁ). The Targums also know the term, see

---

[1] Pesikt. 12ᵇ.
[2] Mechilta on Ex. 15², ed. Friedm. 37ᵃ.
[3] Lehrb. d. neutest. Theologie, i. 179.
[4] The Targ. Isa. 41⁴, Hab. 1¹² even says מִבְּרָאשִׁית.

Onk. Deut. 32¹² בְּעָלְמָא דְהוּא עָתִיד לְחַדְתָא, "in the world which
He (God) will renew"; Targ. Mic. 7¹⁴ בְּעָלְמָא דְהוּא עָתִיד
לְאִתְחַדָתָא, "in the world which will be renewed"; cf. Targ.
Hab. 3²; Jerus. I. Deut. 32¹. The phrase used by Onkelos is
also found in the Kaddish prayer; see Seder Rab Amram, i.
55ᵃ, and Sopher. xix. 12.¹ The renewal of the world is
spoken of in ancient traditions given in b. Sanh. 92ᵇ, 97ᵇ, the
latter passage being based upon a Hebrew document which is
said to have been found in the archives (treasures) of Rome.²

This "renewal" of the world has nothing to do with ἄχρι
χρόνων ἀποκαταστάσεως πάντων in Acts 3²¹. This is suitably rendered by the Syriac version in keeping with the context: עדמא למוליא דזבנא דבלהין אלין ד, "until the fulness of the
times, touching all that" (God has spoken). The matters
predicted by the prophets shall in their entirety be "established," i.e. realised, but not all things in general. Palestinian
Aramaic would say: עַד זְמָנָא דְיִתְקַיְמוּן כָּל מֻלַיָּא דְ.

Unlike the verse just mentioned, the idea of the "new
creation (creature)" is here in place—Enoch 72¹, Jubil. 1²⁹,
of the time when God "renews His creation" (Syr. נהדת
בריתא), Bar. Apoc. 32⁶; cf. 2 Esdras 7⁷⁵ incipies creaturam
renovare (Syr. עתיד אנת דתחדת בריתך). Just as Paul, Gal. 6¹⁵,
2 Cor. 5¹⁷, speaks of a καινὴ κτίσις, so, too, Jewish literature
is able to say that God fashions any one into a new creature
(בְּרָא — בְּרִיָה חֲדָשָׁה), Vay. R. 29. 30; Pes. Rabb., ed. Friedm.
146ᵇ; Midr. Ps. 2⁹.³ While these instances have in view
the real renewal of a person, the position of one who has been
acquitted after judgment by God is merely likened to such
a renewal by the Amora Yizkhak (c. 280), when he represents God as saying to Israel:⁴ "do penance in the ten

¹ See Dalman, Messianische Texte (1898), 25 f.
² A. Wünsche, Neue Beiträge, 233, renders according to the reading substituted by the censor, "Persian treasures"; and M. Buttenwieser, Die hebr. Elias
Apokalypse (1897), 59, even speaks of a "Parsee" tradition.
³ See my treatise, "Der leidende und der sterbende Messias," 52, 66, 73.
⁴ Pes. Rabb., ed. Friedm. 169ᵃ; Bacher, Ag. d. p. Am. ii. 261.

days between New Year and the day of Atonement; then may I pronounce you free on the day of Atonement, and transform you into a new creature." The address by God to Israel, given by Yose bar Kezarta, is very much alike, namely,[1] "When ye are come before me for judgment at the New Year, and have passed out thence in peace, I reckon it to you as if ye were formed into a new creature."

V. "THE LORD" AS A DESIGNATION FOR GOD.

1. NOT A NAME FOR GOD TO BE FOUND IN ORDINARY USE.

Only in a few passages do the Synoptists put ὁ κύριος as a name for God into the mouth of Jesus; and even in these the evidence is uncertain. Mark 5¹⁹ has ὁ κύριος, but the parallel, Luke 8³⁹, has ὁ θεός, and conversely Luke 20³⁷ has κύριος, while Matt. 22³¹ (Mark 12²⁶) has ὁ θεός. Matt. 24²², by inverting the sentence through the use of the passive voice, dispenses with the κύριος used in Mark 13²⁰. The fact may thus be inferred from the Gospels that in His own discourses Jesus did not apply to God any Aramaic name equivalent to κύριος. The usage in quotations from Scripture will be specially considered under 2. In this respect Jesus did not adopt a mode of speech quite peculiar to Himself. For an Aramaic name for God, directly answering to ὁ κύριος, never did exist among the Jews. When ὁ κύριος or *dominus* is met in Apocrypha and Pseudepigrapha, that implies merely that the divine name יהוה was written in the original, which might be in Hebrew, and hence that there was no scruple in writings of this kind against employing the sacred name. It does not, however, follow that "the Lord" was a divine appellation really found in ordinary use. The significant transition from the divine name "Jahve" to the

[1] j. R. h. S. 59ᶜ.

divine name "Lord" did not take place in the region of
Hebraic Judaism.[1] It is rather a peculiarity of Jewish
Hellenism, and from that source found its way into the
language of the Church, even of the Semitic-speaking part of
it. For מָרְיָא in the Syriac of Edessa, and for מָרֵא in the
Christian Palestinian, there is no Jewish parallel. Not till
a very late period was the Greek κύριος in the form קִירִיס
adopted also among the Jews who spoke Aramaic. The
Jerusalem Targums on the Pentateuch,[2] and the Targums on
Job and the Psalms, do indeed employ קִירִים; still it never was
a term popularly used.

The facts above stated do not exclude the possibility of
designating God upon occasion as Lord of a particular person
or persons. The Targum illustrates this by rendering אָבִי
"my Father," Jer. 3[4. 19], by means of רִבּוֹנִי, "my Lord." In
addition, there may be given the following examples, which
at the same time supply evidence that the suffix of the Old
Testament אדני, in speaking of and to God, was by no means
otiose. In prayer, God is addressed in Aram. as מָרִי, Ber.
R. 13; in Hebr. as רִבּוֹנִי, j. Ber. 7[d]; Siphra, ed. Weiss, 112[a].
Similarly in the Aramaic prayer, beginning בַּת צִיּוֹן עֵינֵהּ,[3] the
daughter of Zion calls her God אֱלָהִי וּמָרִי, "my God and my
Lord." The phrase מָרַן דְּבִשְׁמַיָּא, "our Lord, who art in heaven,"
is used when Israel turns to God in יְקוּם פֻּרְקָן,[4] as also in the
prayer[5] prefaced by the same words; and the older form
מָרְנָא is seen in the prayer מָה נִפְתַּח.[5] The Levites say to
Nebuchadnezzar, Targ. Sheni Esth. 1[2]:[6] "How can we sing
the praise of ' our Lord ' (מָרִינַן) before thee ? " after the king
had just spoken of God as "your mighty Lord of Jerusalem"

---

[1] This has not been sufficiently emphasised in my "Der Gottesname Adonaj
und seine Geschichte," 80 f.

[2] See also Machzor Vitry, 337, 341.

[3] Roman Machzor (Bologna, 1540), Selikhoth for the days before New Year;
cf. *Zunz*, Litteraturgeschich. d. synagog. Poesie, 18, 74.

[4] *Baer's* Seder Abodath Yisrael, 229.

[5] Roman Machzor, loc. cit.

[6] See *M. David*, Das Targum scheni nach Handschriften herausgegeben (1898).

(מָרֵיכוֹן רַבָּא דִירוּשְׁלֵם).   In words addressed to an Israelite, the
Jews are called בְּנֵי מָרֵיךְ, "the sons of thy Lord," j. Khag. 77ᵈ;
j. Sanh. 23ᶜ; j. R. h. S. 58ᵃ.   In relation to the community
of Israel, God is "its Lord," מָרַהָא, Targ. Cant. 8¹⁰, and מָרַהּ in
the prayer mentioned above, בַּת צִיּוֹן עַיְנַהּ.   In a popular way
of speaking, b. Yom. 86ᵃ, God is called מָרֵיהּ, "his Lord," *i.e.*
of any one whose sins He forgives.   Nimrod's being styled
"a hunter before the Lord," Gen. 10⁹, implies, according
to Siphra 111ᵇ, that he knew "his Lord" (רִבּוֹנוֹ), and
rebelled against Him intentionally.   In an address to King
Nebuchadnezzar, the temple of God is called בֵּיתֵיהּ דְּמָרָךְ,
"the house of thy Lord," Ech. R. Peth. 23; and even of
the locust it is said, j. Taan. 66ᵈ, that it bears the name גּוֹבַי,
"because it executes the punishment decreed by its Lord"
(דְּהוּ גָבֵי דִינָא דְמָרֵיהּ).

While the designation of God as "Lord of any one" is
comparatively rare in Jewish literature, the Samaritan Marka
makes a copious use of it.   According to him, Moses, in the
presence of Pharaoh, calls God not only מָרִי, "my Lord," but
also מָרַן, "our Lord"; and the sea in an address to Moses
calls God מָרָךְ,[1] "thy Lord."   In his narrative the God of
Moses is called מרה.[2]   That may be pointed so as to read
מָרֵהּ, "his Lord," but also מָרָה, "the Lord."   The latter must
be assumed where מרה is vocative.[3]   In general, however, it
is מָרֵהּ that is intended, since Marka, when speaking for himself as an author, usually writes מָרַן,[4] "our Lord," for God.

Even on an Egyptian papyrus written in Aramaic a heathen
god is spoken of as מָרְאִי, "my Lord"; see CIS, ii. 1. 144.

To this use of "Lord" the Gospels have no real parallel;
for the similar expressions in the parables, which treat of the
relation between master and servant, as in Matt. 24⁴⁶ (Luke
12⁴³), do not belong to this category.   It is not in itself impossible that the Hellenistic (ὁ) κύριος should have in some

[1] *Heidenheim*, Bibl. Sam. iii. 48ᵃ f.   [2] Ibid. 9ᵃ.
[3] Ibid. 6ᵃ.   [4] Ibid. 139ᵇ, 163ᵃ.

measure supplanted the Aram. מָרֵא when coupled with suffixes ;
but in any case Jesus did not make an extensive use of מָרֵא,
for His preference was to speak of God as " Father."

2. SUBSTITUTE FOR THE TETRAGRAMMATON (יהוה).

Another question arises as to what Jesus actually said
when occasion required the expression of the tetragrammaton
in quotations from the Old Testament, e.g. Matt. 22³⁷ (Mark
12³⁰, Luke 10²⁷); Matt. 22⁴⁴ (Mark 12³⁶, Luke 20⁴²). It
may be accepted as certain that by the time of Jesus the
divine name יהוה had long disappeared from popular use, and
that in the public reading of Holy Scripture the word was
replaced by אדני.[1] It may be added that this practice,
strangely enough, was followed in rendering the Scriptures
into Aramaic in the worship of the synagogue,—a custom
which the vocalised Targum texts indicate by the expedient
that, along with the symbol commonly used for יהוה, vowels
are given which require the word אדני to be pronounced, and
also by the fact that they also put this same symbol for אדני.

From this it must not be inferred that אדני, apart from
the public reading of Scripture, was used in mere quotations
from Scripture.   Among the Samaritans[2] the custom is to
substitute שְׁמָא, " the Name," for the tetragrammaton ; and
this holds invariably, even in reading the Law.   A. Geiger[3]
was of opinion that the original Jewish usage was the same,
and that later on, in imitation of the Hellenistic κύριος,
אדני was introduced instead of שְׁמָא. This, however, is incapable of proof.   All that is assured is merely the Jewish
custom of saying in citations from Scripture not אדני, but
הַשֵּׁם, " the Name."[4]   Early examples of the use of הַשֵּׁם for

---

[1] See my treatise, "Der Gottesname Adonaj und seine Geschichte" (1889), 36 ff.
[2] See J. H. Petermann, Ling. Samarit. Gramm. (1873) 78.
[3] Nachgelassene Schriften, iii. 261.
[4] Cf., e.g., the model given by M. Grünwald, Spagnolische und spanisch-
türkische Schrifttafeln (1894).

the tetragrammaton—apart from Lev. 24[11. 16]—may be illustrated by the phrases: פֵּרֵשׁ הַשֵּׁם, "to pronounce clearly the
tetragrammaton," Sanh. vii. 5 ; הָגָה הַשֵּׁם, "to read the tetragrammaton," Sanh. x. 1 ; קִלֵּל בַּשֵּׁם, "to curse by (using) the
tetragrammaton," Sanh. vii. 8 ; שָׁאַל שָׁלוֹם בַּשֵּׁם, "to greet by
(using) the tetragrammaton, Ber. ix. 5 ; cf. בֵּרַךְ אֶת־הַשֵּׁם, "to
curse God," b. Sanh. 46[a], 56[a]. From Yoma iii. 8, iv. 2, vi. 2,
the high priest, in the temple on the day of Atonement, even
appears to have begun the confession of sins with the words
אָנָּא הַשֵּׁם representing אָנָּא יהוה.[1]   לְשֵׁם means "for God," Shek.
vi. 6 ; Yoma iv. 1.

It may accordingly be inferred that in citations of
Scripture Jesus was wont to use הַשֵּׁם when He quoted in
Hebrew, and שְׁמָא when Aramaic was used, but not אֲדֹנָי, despite the fact that the Gospels contain no trace of this
usage,—which, indeed, would be unintelligible to Hellenists
and Greeks.

The biblical style of Hellenistic authors but not the
Jewish-Hebrew type of language is marked by expressions
such as ἄγγελος κυρίου,[2] Matt. 1[20. 24] 2[13. 19] 28[2], Luke 1[11] 2[9] ;
ὁ ναὸς τοῦ κυρίου, Luke 1[9] ; (ὁ) νόμος κυρίου, Luke 2[23f. 39] ;
δικαιώματα τοῦ κυρίου, Luke 1[6] ; δουλὴ κυρίου, Luke 1[38] ; χεὶρ
κυρίου, Luke 1[66] ; δόξα κυρίου, Luke 2[9] ; δύναμις κυρίου, Luke
5[17] ; ὁ Χριστὸς κυρίου, Luke 2[26]. A Hebraist, indeed, might
also have written these expressions — which are mostly
peculiarities of Luke—if he were consciously imitating the
language of the Old Testament; but the popular mode of
speech was quite different. In such locutions the name of
God was either entirely omitted, as in בֵּית הַמִּקְדָּשׁ, הַתּוֹרָה, הַהֵיכָל,
or else replaced by mere suggestions of the divine name.

---

[1] On the other hand, the reading הַשֵּׁם, adopted by H. L. Strack, Yoma iii. 8,
in the citation Lev. 16[30], on the basis of MSS. collated by Rabbinovicz, and of
old prints, is incorrect, and should be replaced by יי.

[2] One must not seek to find in this "the angel of the Lord" of the Old
Testament. ἄγγελος is defined by κυρίου as a messenger of God. The reference
is to one of the ἄγγελοι (τοῦ) θεοῦ, Matt. 22[30], Luke 12[8f.]. See also p. 197.

VI. THE FATHER IN HEAVEN.

1. THE ISRAELITISH-JEWISH USAGE.

That God is the father of Israel is attested for the first time, Ex. 4[22], in the words: "Israel is my son, my firstborn." But while Israel here receives merely the first rank among the peoples, who all are sons of God, other passages refer to the Israelites as sons of God, in the idea that this can be predicated of them alone: Deut. 32[5], Isa. 1[4] 30[9], Hos. 2[1,1] Deut. 14[1], Jer. 3[14] 31[20], Isa. 43[6] 45[11], Mal. 2[10]. Correspondingly, God is called "father" of the Israelites: Deut. 32[6], Jer. 3[4, 19] 31[8], Isa. 63[16] 64[7], Mal. 1[6], 1 Chron. 29[10]. The significance of this relation lay chiefly in the solicitude which the Israelites might expect on the part of God, and in the obedience which they were bound to yield to Him. The assumption is that the Israelites are the servants of God, and members of His family; God on His part recognises the rights and obligations of the head of a household in relation to the members of the house.[2] In Jeremiah (cf. 3[4] with 2[27]), the Second Isaiah (43[6] 64[7]), and in Malachi (2[10]), it is also affirmed that the "father" is the originator of the existence of the son, and hence God as the creator of Israel is his father.

The son of Sirach has obviously maintained the exceptional position of his people, whom God has likened to a first-born son, 36[17]. At the same time he makes an application of the idea of the fatherhood to the position of the individual Israelite. The individual is a being who has been called into existence by God, 23[1, 4]. In this passage κύριε πάτερ καὶ δέσποτα (v.[4] θεέ) ζωῆς μου is to be retraced to יהוה אָבִי וְאֵל[3]

---

[1] In Hos. 11[1] בְּנִי should be read for בְּנַי. Further, the term in Hosea and Isaiah appears to have been one already current, not first introduced by these prophets.

[2] Israel as the "house" of God (בֵּית יְהֹוָה), Hos. 8[1], Jer. 12[7].

[3] Cf. Ps. 42[9] אֵל חַיָּי.

חַיָּי, in which I cannot, like Cremer,[1] detect any influence of heathen views. The same applies to Sir. 51¹⁰. In κύριον πατέρα κυρίου μου we have only to replace κυρίου by κύριον. The original may have had: יהוה אָבִי וַאדֹנָי, "Jehovah my Father and my Lord."[2] The Book of Wisdom insists strongly on the idea that the *righteous* man has God for his father, not only by calling God, 2¹⁶, "the father of the pious," but also by its predilection for παῖς κυρίου (see, *e.g.*, 2¹³) and υἱὸς θεοῦ (2¹⁸) as designations of the righteous man. God is addressed as πάτερ, 14³. This application to the individual does not prevent the author from also calling the nation Israel the "son of God" (θεοῦ υἱός, 18¹³). According to 3 Macc. 5⁷, God is for Israel a "father."

In Palestinian circles, in harmony with the Old Testament view, it is generally the *Israelites* as such who have God in relation to themselves as "their father,"—an idea which implies the love that God bears, in a special sense, to His own people in distinction from other peoples,—a love which has to be requited with obedience and trust on the part of its members. Thus the goal of Israel's history is described, Jubil. 1²⁴ᶠ·, in these terms: "Their souls (of the Israelites) will attach themselves to Me and to all My commands, and My commands will return to them; and I will be to them a father, and they shall be My children. And they shall all be called children of the living God ; and every angel and every spirit shall surely recognise that these are My children, and that I am their father in sincerity and righteousness, and that I do love them." In Tob. 13⁴ God is termed "our Father"; "His sons" are the pious Israelites according to Enoch 62¹¹. In Ps. Sol. 17³⁰ it is said of them that they will be recognised by the Messiah as "sons of their God." In the Pseudepigrapha the name of father is nowhere

---

[1] Bibl. theol. Wörterbuch,⁸ 752.

[2] The Syriac version has : אבי מן כרומא מריא נגברא ופרוקא, which admits of being referred to : אָבִי מְקָדוֹם יְהֹוָה גִּבּוֹר וּמוֹשִׁיעַ.

used as a designation of God. The dicta of the Rabbis from the end of the first Christian century onwards, are the earliest source of instances. The "heavenly Father," *i.e.* God, is conceived as the counterpart of the "earthly father," as appears from a saying of Simeon ben Yokhai, *c.* 130 A.D. He declares that a wise son not only makes "his earthly father" (אָבִיו שֶׁבָּאָרֶץ) glad, but also "his heavenly Father" (אָבִיו שֶׁבַּשָּׁמַיִם).[1] The love of his child is here the chief mark of the father. Akiba (*c.* 120 A.D.) says :[2] " The Israelites are beloved (by God), for they are called God's children (בָּנִים לַמָּקוֹם) [it is due to] the exceptional love [of God that[3]] it was made known to them that they are called God's children, as it is said, Deut. 14[1] 'Ye are the children of Jehovah, your God.'" The same idea is expressed by Gamaliel II. (*c.* 100 A.D.), who declared concerning Israel :[4] מִדְאַרְגִּיזוּ בְּנַיָּא חֲבִיבַיָּא קֳדָם אֲבוּהוֹן דְּבִשְׁמַיָּא[6] אֲקֵים עֲלֵיהוֹן מַלְכָּא חַנְפָּא, "since the beloved children provoked their heavenly Father to anger, He set over them an impious king." The Israelites are full of confidence in having recourse to this "heavenly Father." It is said in Rosh ha-Shana iii. 8, no author being named, that during the battle with Amalek it was not the uplifting of the hands of Moses that procured the victory for Israel, nor yet the serpent set up by Moses that brought them healing, but the fact "that the Israelites lifted up their eyes and directed their heart towards their heavenly Father" (שֶׁיִּשְׂרָאֵל מִסְתַּכְּלִין כְּלַפֵּי מַעֲלָה וּמְכַוְּנִין לִבָּם לַאֲבִיהֶם שֶׁבַּשָּׁמַיִם).[7] He it is who hears the prayer of Israel; hence the Kaddish[8] says: תִּתְקַבַּל צְלוֹתְהוֹן

---

[1] Siphre, Deut. 48, ed. Friedm. 84[b] ; cf. *Bacher*, Ag. d. Tann. ii. 131.
[2] Aboth iii. 14.   [3] Read נוֹדַעַת for נוֹרַעַת.
[4] Midr. Abba Gorjon 1[1] ; cf. *Bacher*, loc. cit. i. 96.
[5] Esth. R. 1[1] has the Galilean form כַּן דְּאַכְעְסוּן, and inserts עֲבָדֵיהוֹן in front of קֳדָם.
[6] Thus in Est. R. 1[1].
[7] So it should be read according to Manuskr. München, see *Rabbinovicz*, Variæ Lectiones zu b. R. h. S. 29[a]. Cf. Targ. Jerus. I. Num. 21[9] : אִין מְכַוֵּן לִבֵּיהּ לְשׁוּם מֵימְרָא דַיְיָ, "If he direct his heart to the Name of the Word of Jehovah."
[8] Seder Rab Amram, i. 13[b].

וּבְעִיתְהוֹן דִּי אֲבוּהוֹן קֳדָם יִשְׂרָאֵל דְּכָל, "may the prayers and tears of all Israel be accepted before their heavenly Father!" When every other refuge and hope fails, there remains for Israel nothing but the cry :[1] עַל מִי לָנוּ לְהִשָּׁעֵן עַל אָבִינוּ שֶׁבַּשָּׁמַיִם, "upon whom shall we put our trust? upon our Father in heaven." It was not unknown to the Jews that the Christians claimed God for themselves as their Father. Thus Juda ben Shalom (c. 300) said :[2] " God foresaw that the Gentiles would translate the Law, and read it in Greek and say, 'we are Israel.' Then spake God to him (Moses), 'See, Moses, the Gentiles will say, we are Israel, we are the sons of God' (אָנוּ בָּנָיו שֶׁלַּמָּקוֹם)." See also p. 190 f.

The following examples, which might easily be multiplied, illustrating the fatherly relation of God towards the individual Israelite, may here be adduced. Only two persons are addressed in the astonished exclamation of an aged man, j. Maas 50ᶜ "To your heavenly Father (לַאֲבוּכוֹן דְּבִשְׁמַיָּא) ye give it not (an offering due to Him); yet ye give it to me!" Eleazar ben Azarya (c. 100 A.D.) speaks of the things which "his Father in heaven" has forbidden to him.[3] Yehuda ben Tema (before 200) gives the exhortation :[4] "be bold as a leopard, quick as an eagle, swift as a gazelle, and strong as a lion 'to do the will of thy heavenly Father' (לַעֲשׂוֹת רְצוֹן אָבִיךָ שֶׁבַּשָּׁמַיִם)." Of the same nature are also the words of Nathan[5] (c. 160) commenting upon Ex. 20⁶, in the light of the period of religious persecution under Hadrian: "'those who love me and keep my commandments'—these are the Israelites who dwell in Palestine and give up their life for the commandments. Why art thou slain?—because I have circumcised my sons. Why art thou burned?—because I have read in the Law. Why art thou crucified?—because I have eaten

---

[1] Sot. ix. 15 (anonym.).   [2] Pes. Rabb. 14ᵇ.
[3] See above, p. 96 f.
[4] Aboth v. 20 ; b. Pes. 112ᵃ ; cf. Bacher, Ag. d. Tann. ii. 556.
[5] Mechilta, ed. Friedm. 68ᵇ ; Vay. R. 32 ; Midr. Ps. 12⁵ ; cf. Bacher, Ag. d. Tann. ii. 437.

unleavened bread.　Why art thou scourged ?—because I have done the 'will of my heavenly Father' (רְצוֹן אַבָּא שֶׁבַּשָּׁמַיִם).[1] This is that which is written (Zech. 13⁶): And they say to him, what mean these wounds ? and he answers, they were inflicted upon me in the house ' of those who caused me to be beloved ' (מְאַהֲבַי)—these wounds have brought it about ' that I am beloved by my Father in heaven ' " (לֵיאָהֵב לְאָבִי שֶׁבַּשָּׁמַיִם). Simeon ben Eleazar (c. 200) explained the statement in the Law regarding mixed textures (שַׁעַטְנֵז), as implying that who-soever wears such a vestment " is perverted " (נִלּוֹן) and " alienates " (מְלִין)[2] from himself " his heavenly Father."　In an Aramaic Haggada for the Feast of Weeks,[3] it is said of the Joseph of the Old Testament story : אַפֵּיהּ לְמָרָתֵיהּ וְלִבֵּיהּ לַאֲבוּהִי דִּשְׁמַיָּא, " his face was turned towards the wife of his master, but his heart was directed to his heavenly Father."

The gradual adoption of the divine name " our Father in heaven " as a popular substitute for the then obsolete tetra-grammaton, is a clear proof that the view represented by H. H. Wendt requires considerable restriction.　" In later Judaism," he says,[4] " up to the time of Jesus there had been no development in the conception of God, in the sense that grace and truth were more strenuously insisted on as para-mount elements in the divine nature and character, leading in consequence to a greater readiness to apply the name of Father to God."　But " a greater readiness to apply the name of Father to God " on the part of the Jews is a historical fact ; and Jesus adopted this term for God from the popular usage of His time.　Judaism, above all, as it existed in the time of Jesus, must not be depicted according to the de-veloped system of subsequent Rabbinism, least of all when the excrescences in the latter are set up as the norm of

---

[1] So in Vay. R. 32.

[2] Kil. ix. 8 ; cf. *Bacher*, Ag. d. Tann. ii. 433.

[3] Machzor Vitry, 342.　　　　[4] Die Lehre Jesu, ii. 144.

Judaism, and when all traces of genuine religious feeling which it exhibits are either overlooked or eliminated.[1]

The instances cited above also show the incorrectness of the idea that the relation of God to the individual was not set forth until the New Testament revelation. Of course the individual Israelite was aware that it was only as a member of his people that he possessed the claim to and prospect of God's help and patronage. But the Old Testament shows abundant traces of the conviction that God's providence is directed not only to the people as a whole, but also to every single member of the nation. It was therefore nothing novel when the fatherly relation of God was also applied within the Jewish community to the individual.

2. THE USAGE IN THE LANGUAGE OF JESUS.

(a) My, your heavenly Father.

The current designation of God, ὁ πατὴρ ὁ ἐν (τοῖς) οὐρανοῖς (ὁ οὐράνιος), which never appears without an accompanying pronoun (μου,[2] ἡμῶν, ὑμῶν), occurs among the words of Jesus in Matthew 20 times, in Mark only once, 11²⁵, in Luke not at all—although in Luke 11¹³ his use of ὁ πατὴρ ὁ ἐξ οὐρανοῦ betrays his acquaintance with the title. The same motive which caused Luke to change ἡ βασιλεία τῶν οὐρανῶν into ἡ β. τοῦ θεοῦ has here, too, been at work. A mode of speech distinctively Jewish and not at the same time biblical had to be avoided. The Jewish carefulness always to make it clear through the addition of " in heaven " that " Father " referred to God, might seem superfluous to the Hellenist.

The conception of God as father of the Israelites was not altogether unrecognised even by Jesus. In Matt. 15²⁶

---

[1] I have sought to urge a juster estimate of the religious condition of the Jewish community in the time of the second temple, in "Das Alte Testament ein Wort Gottes," Leipzig, 1896.

[2] σου is accidentally absent, as ὁ πατήρ σου precedes in Matt. 6¹⁸.

(Mark 7²⁷) He compares in a figurative way the Israelites to "the children" (τέκνα), the heathen to "the dogs" (κυνάριοι), which latter, indeed, also belong to the household, but must not be maintained at the expense of children.[1] But this point of view is by no means decisive in His designation of God as Father. Much rather is God regarded either as the Heavenly Father of *His own disciples*, Matt. 5¹⁶· ⁴⁵· ⁴⁸ 6¹· ⁹· ¹⁴ (Mark 11²⁵) 6²⁶· ³² 7¹¹ 18¹⁴ 23⁹, or else as the Heavenly Father *of Jesus Himself*, Matt. 7²¹ 10³²ᶠ· 12⁵⁰ 15¹³ 16¹⁷ 18¹⁰· ¹⁹· ³⁵. He thus indicates the unique personal relation which subsists between God and, in the first place, Jesus Himself, but also between God and those who are His, who can be spoken of as "sons of the theocracy," Matt. 13³⁸. At the same time, Jesus draws a sharp line of distinction between Himself and the disciples in purposely setting aside the usual Jewish "our Father in heaven," where He Himself is concerned, and yet prescribing its use for His disciples, Matt. 6⁹. From this, too, it may be perceived that it was not the veneration of those who came after that first assigned to Him an exceptional relation to God, incapable of being transferred to others. On the Sonship of Jesus see, further, Fundamental Ideas, X.

(b) My, your Father.

In Jewish parlance it is unusual to refer to God in common discourse informally as Father without adding the epithet "heavenly." It is only in prayers that a different course is followed. The fifth and sixth petitions of the "Eighteen Supplications"[2]—the daily prayer which took form *c.* 110 A.D.—entreat the working of penitence and the forgiveness of sins by God, whom Israel ventures to name,

---

[1] In a somewhat different sense, Matt. 8¹², the Israelites as "sons of the kingdom" (υἱοὶ τῆς βασιλείας) are distinguished from strangers ; cf. p. 115.

[2] The "Shemoneh Esreh" (eighteen), for which see *Schürer*, Hist. of the Jewish People, Div. II. vol. ii. p. 85 f. ; and *Dalman*, Messianische Texte aus d. nachkanon. jüd. Litt. (1898), pp. 19–24.

firstly אָבִינוּ, " our Father," and then מַלְכֵּנוּ, " our King." The
petitions begin הֲשִׁיבֵנוּ אָבִינוּ לְתוֹרָתֶךְ, " bring us back, Our
Father, to Thy Law ! " and סְלַח לָנוּ אָבִינוּ כִּי חָטָאנוּ, " forgive us,
Our Father, for we have sinned ! " So, too, a prayer in
Tob. 13⁴ Vat. has θεὸς αὐτὸς πατὴρ ἡμῶν εἰς πάντας τοὺς
αἰῶνας (absent from Hebr. and Aram.). Akiba (c. 120) once
brought rain in answer to a short prayer which began :
אָבִינוּ מַלְכֵּנוּ, " Our Father and our King." [1] The biblical
phraseology was obviously the model in prayers, and in them
there was no danger of ambiguity.

Apart from prayers, the Targums show that great care
was exercised against the use of the single word " father " for
God. The Targ. Jerus. II. Exod. 15², it is true, makes young
children in presence of their fathers say, in reference to God,
" *He* is our Father," דֵין הוּא אֲבוּנָן.[2] In that case the narrower
designation by בִּשְׁמַיָּא did not suit the occasion. Again, in
Deut. 32⁶, where God calls Himself the Father of Israel,
Onkelos renders אָבִיךְ literally by אֲבוּךְ, while Targ. Jerus. II.
is singular in giving אֲבוּכוֹן דְּבִשְׁמַיָּא. But when Israel calls
God his Father, the Targumist does not venture to give a
literal reproduction.[3] For אָבִינוּ, Isa. 63¹⁶ 64⁷, he puts the
whole sentence: דְּרַחֲמָךְ עֲלָנָא סַגִּיאִין כְּאַב עַל בְּנִין, " Thou, whose
mercy towards us abounds as that of a father to sons "; and
in Jer. 34. 19 he changes אָבִי into רִבּוֹנִי, " my Lord." He had,
however, no scruple in rendering the אָבִי as used by an
idolater 2²⁷ by אֲבוּנָא, " our Father."

Jesus never, as it seems, addressed God in prayer as
" My Father in heaven," but only as " My Father." It
makes no difference whether the Greek has merely πάτερ, as
in Matt. 11²⁵ (Luke 10²¹), Luke 22⁴² 23³⁴. ⁴⁶; or ὁ πατήρ, as
in Matt. 11²⁶ (Luke 10²¹), Mark 14³⁶; or πάτερ μου, as in
Matt. 26³⁹. ⁴². For in each case the word to be presupposed

---

[1] b. Taan. 25ᵇ ; *Bacher*, Ag. d. Tann. i. 330.

[2] Jerus. I. Lev. 22²⁸ אֲבַתּוּן, which has no meaning if uttered by God, should
be changed into יָת, according to j. Meg. 75ᶜ.

[3] Still in Mal. 2¹⁰ אַב without suffix is replaced by אַבָּא.

on the testimony of Mark 14[36] (cf. Rom. 8[15], Gal. 4[6]) is ἀββᾶ
(אַבָּא). This is just the definite form, and therefore means
strictly " the Father "; but during the obsolescence of the
form with the pronominal suffix (אָבִי still to be seen Dan. 5[13])[1]
it became the regular form for " my Father," just as אִמָּא,
" the mother," was also said for " my mother." [2] This Aramaic
idiom has even found its way into the Hebrew of the Mishna.[3]
There, too, it appears that אַבָּא could be said in the name of
several children, thus acquiring the force of " our Father." [4]
Hence it would not be impossible to derive πάτερ in the
Lord's Prayer, Luke 11[2], from אַבָּא, although in a prayer the
more solemn form אֲבוּנָא, Galil. אֲבוּן, " Our Father," has
greater probability in its favour.

אַבָּא, אֲבוּנָא as a title of address to God meant something
different when used by Jesus to what was implied by מַלְכֵּנוּ,
qualified though it was by אָבִינוּ of the Shemoneh Esreh and
Akiba. The usage of family life is transferred to God : it is
the language of the child to its father.

Jesus also speaks of God as ὁ πατήρ μου, Matt. 11[27]
(Luke 10[22]) 20[23] 25[34] 26[29. 53]. The Father of the Son
of man, He calls ὁ πατὴρ αὐτοῦ (i.e. Aram. אֲבוּהִי), Matt. 16[27]
(Mark 8[38]). The Father of the disciples is ὁ πατὴρ ὑμῶν
(אֲבוּכוֹן), Matt. 6[8] 10[20. 29] ; ὁ πατὴρ αὐτῶν (אֲבוּהוֹן), Matt. 13[43] ;
ὁ πατήρ σου (אֲבוּךְ), Matt. 6[4. 6. 18]. It must be conceded that,
for each particular instance, there is no certitude that even
here Jesus used the appellation of Father without addition.
It might be that every instance of ὁ πατήρ μου, σου, ὑμῶν,
not addressed directly to God, ought to contain the addition
ὁ ἐν οὐρανοῖς. This alone would correspond to the terminology
of Rabbinic literature. Nevertheless the existence of a well-

---

[1] אֲבִי also occurs once Targ. Esth. ii. 1[1], according to MS. Orient 2375 in the
British Museum.

[2] See Gramm. des jüd. pal. Aram. 157 f.

[3] E.g. Keth. ii. 6, xiii. 5 ; Ned. ii. 1. See A. Geiger, Lehrbuch zur Sprache
des Mischnah, 50.

[4] Bab. b. ix. 3 ; Shebu. vii. 7.

founded tradition remains quite possible, to the effect that Jesus did not closely adhere to the Jewish phraseology on this point, and that He did, in fact, sometimes speak exclusively of the Father, of Himself and those that were His. On this hypothesis the consistent omission of the supplement in Luke would appear to have some historical justification.

(c) The Father.

A special consideration is required for those passages in which, excluding cases of address, the simple ὁ πατήρ appears with no pronoun added.

Luke 9²⁶ should be brought into agreement with Matt. 16²⁷ (Mark 8³⁸). Jesus can surely not have said that the Son of Man will come ἐν τῇ δόξῃ αὐτοῦ καὶ τοῦ πατρὸς καὶ τῶν ἁγίων ἀγγέλων, but ἐν τῇ δόξῃ τοῦ πατρὸς αὐτοῦ μετὰ τῶν ἁγίων ἀγγέλων. Moreover, αὐτοῦ is omitted in Luke merely for the sake of euphony, as it has been used just before.

In the saying of our Lord Acts 1⁷, ὁ πατήρ as uttered by Jesus would have to be retraced to אבא, which might just as well represent ὁ πατήρ μου. The saying would thus have been: " It is not for you to know times or seasons which My Father determined in the exercise of His own authority." Still we may here have an expression which just slipped from the pen of the author, because it was otherwise familiar to him.

There remain now only the passages in which ὁ πατήρ and ὁ υἱός mutually condition each other, where no pronoun is admissible, namely, Matt. 11²⁷ (Luke 10²²), Matt. 24³⁶ (Mark 13³²), and Matt. 28¹⁹. Of these the first vindicates itself as an utterance of Jesus. When Jesus testifies that all things are delivered unto Him by "His Father," and adds that only " the Son " and " the Father " are mutually known to each other, the statement may be understood as a reference

13

to a real relationship which exists universally between a father and a son, and thus finds also an application as between Jesus and His Father. In that case ὁ πατήρ and ὁ υἱός were not used as theological terms, and אַבָּא and בְּרָא are not unlikely equivalents.

It is different with Matt. 24³⁶ (Mark 13³²), where the angels and "the Son" are ignorant of something which only "the Father" knows. In this case the terms ὁ υἱός and ὁ πατήρ are not due to comparison with each other, but appear as a ready-made formula, and are therefore to be attributed to the influence of the Church vocabulary on the text. If οὐδὲ οἱ ἄγγελοι—οὐδὲ ὁ υἱός were taken separately as a supplementary illustration of the preceding οὐδείς, then ὁ πατήρ, which alone would remain, could be referred to אַבָּא = ὁ πατήρ μου, as the form used by Jesus, just as in the similar case Acts 1⁷. It is, however, more probable that the original was, "not even the angels know it," and that the ending, "nor the Son, but the Father only," should be regarded as an accretion.

A similar amplification of an originally shorter expression presents itself also in the baptismal commission, Matt. 28¹⁹, of which it is intended to treat specially in a later volume.

VII. OTHER DIVINE NAMES.

1. GOD (ὁ θεός).

All three Synoptists record the use by Jesus of ὁ θεός. This must appear somewhat surprising, if the language of the Mishna be brought into comparison. The tractate which most frequently afforded occasion for the use of divine names—Pirke Aboth—has שָׁמַיִ, "Heaven," 8 times; הַמָּקוֹם, "the Place," 5 times; הַקָּדוֹשׁ בָּרוּךְ הוּא, "the Holy One, blessed be He," 3 times; and אָבִיךָ שֶׁבַּשָּׁמַיִם "heavenly Father," הַשֵּׁם

"the Name," הַשְּׁכִינָה "the Dwelling-place," once each. But, on the other hand, אֱלֹהִים no less than יְיָ (יהוה) occurs only in quotations from the Bible, the latter appearing also in a form of prayer. The tractate Berakhoth has שָׁמַיִם twice, הַמָּקוֹם once; and הַשֵּׁם and יְיָ appear only in prayers and quotations. Similarly the tractate Yoma has once each: הַקָּדוֹשׁ בָּרוּךְ הוּא, הַמָּקוֹם הוּא, שֶׁבַּשָּׁמַיִם אֲבִיכֶם; in prayers הַשֵּׁם; in Bible quotations יְיָ, but never אֱלֹהִים. Frequently the divine name is entirely evaded by circumlocutions, or simply omitted. In a quotation, Gen. 1²⁷ would have been written בְּצֶלֶם אֱלֹהִים, "in the image of God"; but where it does not form part of a quotation, e.g. Ab. iii. 15, בְּצֶלֶם alone is expressed, the reader being expected to know that the image of God is meant. "Distinguished are the Israelites," חֲבִיבִין יִשְׂרָאֵל, says Akiba, Ab. iii. 14, meaning "distinguished by God." In Ber. ix. 2 appears the prayer יְהִי רָצוֹן, "may it be well-pleasing," without, however, expressing the necessary complement "*before God*"; and in Yoma i. 5 the high priest takes an oath for the due performance of his duties in the temple " by Him who causes His name to dwell in this house."

That this mode of procedure in the Mishna was no innovation, is evident from the fact that the Book of Esther entirely omits the divine name—not, as is sometimes supposed, owing to the irreligious disposition of the author, but as a result of his reverence for divine things. Again, the First Book of Maccabees, despite frequent mention of religious matters, has used שָׁמַיִם, "Heaven," as a designation of God, only nine times in all, and never speaks of "God." The Aramaic part of Daniel (Dan., chaps. 2–7) avoided the use of יהוה, and denoted the true God by אֱלָהּ שְׁמַיָּא, "God of heaven" (for which 4³⁴ has מֶלֶךְ שְׁמַיָּא, 5²⁵ מָרֵא שְׁמַיָּא), and by אֱלָהָא עִלָּיָא or עִלָּיָא, "the Most High God," or "the Most High," more rarely by אֱלָהָא חַיָּא, "the living God," 6²⁷; חַי עָלְמָא, "the Ever-living," 4³¹. The simple אֱלָהָא (= הָאֱלֹהִים) occurs only in 2²⁰ 5²⁶.

The course followed in other writings is not in every

case so consistent. But there was a means of guarding against possible profanation of the divine name by writing it so as merely to suggest it. The manuscripts represent יהוה by writing Yod two, three, or four times, also by modifications like ידוד and יקוק, and by putting 'ה or 'ד for הַשֵּׁם when pronounced in place of יהוה; אלהים appears as אלדים or אלקים, and אלהא as אלקא, אלדא. In view of this expedient, it does not mean so much that the Apocrypha and Pseudepigrapha should use the biblical names for God. Least of all must it be assumed that the popular usage is reflected in these books. In regard to the tetragrammaton alone can the proof be shown that—through the influence probably of Egyptian religious customs—it had really vanished from common use among the people. But we may well assume that it was not very different with regard to the other special names for God, and that apart from prayers and benedictions they were little used. Jesus Himself indicates[1] that the ordinary custom in taking an oath was not to name God, but heaven, Jerusalem, the temple, the altar, the offering, one's own head. He does not, however, sanction the opinion that, supposing an oath should have to be taken, God must be named in it, but teaches that it is better not to swear at all. Even He appears to approve the non-pronunciation of the name of God, and He at least conformed to the custom by avoiding the tetragrammaton, and preferring the substitute " Heavenly Father."

In these circumstances it must be questioned whether the Gospels, in ascribing to Jesus a frequent use of ὁ θεός, really reproduce the original form of what was said by Jesus. It is not unlikely that the evangelists set aside such terms as would have been unintelligible to the Greek and the Hellenist.

Of course, " Father in heaven " cannot in every case be inserted for " God." When, e.g., mention is made of ὁ θεός alongside of ἄνθρωπος, Matt. 19⁶ (Mark 10⁹), and of ὁ θεός

[1] Matt. 5³⁴ᶠ· 23¹⁶⁻²².

in contrast with μαμωνᾶς, Matt. 6²⁴ (Luke 16¹³), we must probably substitute—supposing אֱלָהָא, "God," were to be avoided—either שְׁמָא, "the Name," [1] or שְׁמַיָּא, "Heaven." [2] In some other cases it is possible to omit the divine name. When the accusation is brought against Jesus, Matt. 26⁶¹, that He had said : " I am able to destroy the temple of God," there is every probability that His words had really been " this temple" (τὸν ναὸν τοῦτον) as in Mark 14⁵⁸, or " the temple" (τὸν ναόν) as in Matt. 27⁴⁰ (Mark 15²⁹). Again, Jesus says, Mark 12²⁵, that they who are risen from the dead will be as " the angels in heaven" (ἄγγελοι ἐν τοῖς οὐρανοῖς). The Aramaic for this would be מַלְאֲכַיָּא בִשְׁמַיָּא, which is certainly more original than the wording in Matthew (22³⁰): ἄγγελοι θεοῦ ἐν τῷ οὐρανῷ, and much more so than Luke's amplification (20³⁶): ἰσάγγελοι καὶ υἱοὶ θεοῦ.—In order to avoid the expression " in the presence of God," we have in Luke 12⁸· ⁹ 15¹⁰ " before the angels of God " (ἔμπροσθεν—ἐνώπιον—τῶν ἀγγέλων τοῦ θεοῦ). In these cases τοῦ θεοῦ should clearly be erased, as it partially defeats the intention of the phrase. The occurrence of ἔμπροσθεν τοῦ πατρός μου τοῦ ἐν οὐρανοῖς in Matt. 10³²· ³³ as parallel to Luke 12⁸· ⁹ shows how the same point may be reached in another fashion. See also under 5.

On the other hand, no scruples need attach to the use of ὁ θεός in the prayers which Jesus, Luke 18¹¹· ¹³, puts into the mouth of the Pharisee and the publican—even although, in the case of the Pharisee especially—a more elaborate form of address to God might be expected. But ὁ θεός must not, as is done by Delitzsch and Resch, be rendered by אֱלֹהִים, which would be a very uncommon form of address. If one assumes Hebrew as the language of the Pharisee's prayer, the word used would be אֱלֹהַי, " my God"; if the publican prayed in Aramaic, the word would be אֱלָהִי. That Jesus Himself, though using Aramaic while praying on

[1] Cf. p. 182 f. [2] Cf. Fundamental Ideas, VIII. 7.

the Cross, said [1] אֵלִי, was due to the fact that His prayer was expressed in the words of a psalm. אַבָּא, "Father," was the form of address to God in prayer which was peculiar to Jesus.[2]

2. THE HIGHEST (ὕψιστος).

The divine appellations אֵל עֶלְיוֹן and עֶלְיוֹן first appear in the mouth of non-Israelites, being used by Melchizedek, Gen. 14[18ff.], and by Balaam, Num. 24[16]. The author's intention of implying that the Deity revered by these men was the true God, is by this means realised. Thereafter, in the Psalms, עֶלְיוֹן is not infrequently adopted by Israelites,[3] e.g. יְהוָה עֶלְיוֹן, Ps. 47[4]; אֱלֹהִים עֶלְיוֹן, Ps. 57[3]; אֵל עֶלְיוֹן, Ps. 78[35]; עֶלְיוֹן, Ps. 9[3]. The son of Sirach has אֵל עֶלְיוֹן, 46[5] 48[20]; while in dependence on a preceding noun, he prefers the simple עֶלְיוֹן, 41[4. 8] 42[2] 44[20] 49[4]. The Aramaic part of Daniel has עֶלְיָא and אֱלָהָא עִלָּאָה, and also makes use of the Hebrew עֶלְיוֹן in the combination קַדִּישֵׁי עֶלְיוֹנִין, 7[18. 22. 25. 27]. Further, the "Most High," as a divine title, occurs Tob. 4[11], Judith 13[8] (ὁ θεὸς ὁ ὕψιστος), Ass. Mos. 10[7], in all the sections of the Book of Enoch (see Charles on 9[93]), often in the Bar. Apoc. (see Charles on 17[1]), and repeatedly in 2 Esdras. Onkelos puts עִלָּאָה for עֶלְיוֹן in Gen. 14[20], Num. 24[16]. In Rabbinic literature, on the contrary, this name for God is extraordinarily rare. The Palestinian Abbahu (about 300 A.D.) is said, b. Sot. 40[a], on one occasion to have styled God עִלָּאָה. There is thus good ground for the opinion that עֶלְיוֹן did not really belong to the popular speech, but characterised the language of religious poets and authors following a biblical style.

Holtzmann [4] detects in עֶלְיוֹן, as a divine title, a symptom of the "abstract colourlessness of the conception of God in the post-prophetic age" (der Epigonen), inasmuch as he holds

---

[1] On this verse see above, p. 53 f.   [2] See above, p. 191 f.
[3] Cf. T. K. Cheyne, The Origin and Religious Content of the Psalter, 83 f.
[4] Lehrb. d. neutest. Theologie, i. 49.

that Judaism in its use of אֱלֹהִים, the divine title of the legalistic period, had already begun to accentuate the metaphysical
idea of God to the detriment of the religious contents of the
prophetic conception of God. But אֱלֹהִים is in no way the
name of God which distinguished the so-called legalistic
[nomistisch] period. The Priests' Code makes it quite clear
that the God of Israel and of the Law chooses to be known
as יהוה. And how עֶלְיוֹן or אֱלֹהִים should be more colourless
than the Tetragrammaton as understood by the Jews according to Ex. 3¹⁴, it would be hard to tell. Moreover, it does
not agree with Holtzmann's theory of a retrogression that
עֶלְיוֹן in the time of Christ should be replaced by designations
like "the Holy One," "our Father in heaven," the first of
which is of prophetic origin, while the second even implies
an advance beyond the prophetic mode of speech.

Only once, Luke 6³⁵, is ὕψιστος ascribed to Jesus; and
the expression there is υἱοὶ ὑψίστου, for which Matt. 5⁹ has
υἱοὶ θεοῦ, and Matt. 5⁴⁵ υἱοὶ τοῦ πατρὸς ὑμῶν τοῦ ἐν οὐρανοῖς.
According to Mark 5⁷ (Luke 8²⁸), a man with an unclean
spirit addressed to Jesus the words: υἱὲ τοῦ θεοῦ τοῦ ὑψίστου.
But Matt. 8²⁹ does not give τοῦ ὑψίστου. Luke, however,
delights in ὕψιστος as a name for God. He says: υἱὸς ὑψίστου, Gospel 1³²; δύναμις ὑψίστου, 1³⁵; προφήτης ὑψίστου, 1⁷⁶;
ὁ ὕψιστος, Acts 7⁴⁸; δοῦλοι τοῦ θεοῦ τοῦ ὑψίστου, 16¹⁷.
So, too, we may suppose υἱοὶ ὑψίστου, Luke 6³⁵, is due to his
personal predilection. The hypothesis is probable that the
expression υἱοὶ ὑψίστου in Ps. 82⁶ LXX (Heb. 81⁶), which,
indeed, in its context has quite another sense, indicating the
exalted rank of those so entitled, was in his mind when he
chose this epithet. The primitive wording of the expression
is preserved in its earliest form by Matthew—υἱοὶ τοῦ πατρὸς
ὑμῶν τοῦ ἐν οὐρανοῖς, Aram. בְּנֵי אֲבוּכוֹן דְּבִשְׁמַיָּא.

3. THE BLESSED ONE (ὁ εὐλογητός).

The high priest uses the words ὁ υἱὸς τοῦ εὐλογητοῦ, Mark 14⁶¹, for which Matt. 26⁶³ gives ὁ υἱὸς τοῦ θεοῦ. The construction in Mark, assuming the intention was to refer to the Messiah as the Son of God, would, in fact, be more prob- able than that in Matthew on the lips of the high priest. "The Blessed," however, is, as a rule, in Jewish literature only added to "the Holy One" as an appendix¹ in the formula : הַקָּדוֹשׁ בָּרוּךְ הוּא, "the Holy One, Blessed is He," Aram. קֻדְשָׁא בְּרִיךְ הוּא, on which see below. The simple הַמְבֹרָךְ, "the Blessed One," Ber. vii. 3, forms an exception. Even in Palmyra, indeed, God can be spoken of as : בְּרִיךְ שְׁמֵהּ לְעָלְמָא, "He, whose name is to be praised for ever," de Vogüé, 74, 76 (111 A.D.), 77 ; see also Enoch 77¹ "the Ever-Blessed."

4. THE POWER (ἡ δύναμις).

The Synoptists with one consent relate (Matt. 26⁶⁴, Mark 14⁶², Luke 22⁶⁹) that Jesus was condemned by the Sanhedrim when He announced that He should sit "at the right hand of the Power" (ἐκ δεξιῶν τῆς δυνάμεως). In the interest of his readers Luke adds τοῦ θεοῦ by way of explanation, and thereby obscures, as in other cases (see p. 197), the nature of the idiom. Hegesippus (in Eusebius, ii. 23), in an allusion to this statement, attributes to James the words ἐκ δεξιῶν τῆς μεγάλης δυνάμεως, with which may be compared Acts 8¹⁰, where Simon Magus is called ἡ δύναμις τοῦ θεοῦ ἡ καλουμένη μεγάλη. The sorcerer was really spoken of as "God," and τοῦ θεοῦ as well as καλουμένη are additions due to Luke. The adjective "great" marks the "Power" as super- human, just as "the great Holy One" in the Book of Enoch (see below) is the unique possessor of this attribute, i.e. God.

---

¹ Paul also has as an appended epithet εὐλογητὸς εἰς τοὺς αἰῶνας, Rom. 1²⁵ 9⁵, 2 Cor. 11³¹.

On the other hand, the exclamation on the Cross, ἡ δύνα-μίς μου ἡ δύναμίς μου, as found in the "Gospel of Peter," is probably occasioned by Aquila's version of Ps. 22² (according to *Eusebius*, Demonstr. Evangel. x. 8, either ἰσχυρέ μου or ἰσχύς μου). The sense is not that the strength which was His own, but the Power which for Jesus is God, had left Him; cf. the address to God "my strength," עֻזִּי, Ps. 59¹⁸; see also Ex. 15², Ps. 46² 81². One need not therefore assume, as Harnack [1] does, that the author had taken offence at the confession of being forsaken by God.

The statement in Matt. 14² (Mark 6¹⁴) that "the powers do work in Jesus" (αἱ δυνάμεις ἐνεργοῦσιν ἐν αὐτῷ), may arise through a misunderstanding of its Aramaic antecedent: גְּבוּרְתָא מִתְעַבְדָן בֵּהּ, "mighty deeds are done by Him"; cf. Matt. 11²¹· ²³.

To show that ἡ δύναμις, in the saying of our Lord previously mentioned, really stands for "God" and is based upon גְּבוּרְתָא in Aramaic, we may cite the following instances from Jewish literature, which at the same time will indicate the extent to · which the literal meaning of the term has disappeared from view. Ishmael (*c.* 100 A.D.) begins a quotation of words spoken by God with the formula: it was said "by the mouth of the Power" (מִפִּי הַגְּבוּרָה).[2] In Aboth d. R. Nathan, 37, appears the expression: it seemed good in his eyes and "in the eyes of the Power" (בְּעֵינֵי הַגְּבוּרָה). Meïr (*c.* 160 A.D.) says, b. Sot. 37ª, that, owing to the situation of the temple in his territory, Benjamin was "the host of the Power" (אוּשְׁפִּיזְכָן לַגְּבוּרָה). An anonymous saying in Siphre [3] has in place of "God" "the Power that is above," כֹּחוֹ שֶׁל מַעֲלָה. There may also be compared Targ. Isa. 33²¹, which has גְּבוּרְתָא דַיְיָ for the simple יהוה, and Targ. Isa. 48¹³ where גְּבוּרְתִי appears for "יְמִינִי, My right hand" (*i.e.* God's).

[1] *A. Harnack*, Bruchstücke des Evangeliums und der Apokalypse des Petrus ², 65.

[2] Siphre, Num. 112, ed. Friedm. 33ª. For the same expression, see j. Sanh. 28ª.

[3] Siphre, Deut. 319, ed. Friedm. 136ᵇ.

A kindred expression, not, however, to be found in the
Gospels, may also be adduced: דַּעַת עֶלְיוֹנָה, "the Most High
Knowledge" (= God), Mechilta, ed. Friedm. 89[b], Aram.
דַּעְתָּא דִלְעֵיל, Jerus. I. Num. 27[5]; cf. μόνῳ σοφῷ Θεῷ, Rom.
16[27].

5. THE HOLY ONE (ὁ ἅγιος).

Although ἅγιος as a name for God is found in the New
Testament only once, 1 Pet. 1[15], where it is suggested by a
quotation from the Old Testament, it does not seem irrelevant
to observe that there was a divine title הַקֹּדֶשׁ, "the Holiness";
see, e.g., Siphre, Num. 112, ed. Friedm. 33[a].[1] Of the same
nature is the much used קֻדְשָׁא בְּרִיךְ הוּא, "the Holiness, Blessed
be He"; see j. Makk. 31[d], j. Bab. mez. 12[a], Ber. R. 78, Targ.
Isa. 50[11], Targ. Esth. ii. 5[1], Kaddish. The Hebrew equivalent, curiously enough, is הַקָּדוֹשׁ בָּרוּךְ הוּא, "the Holy One,
Blessed be He"; see, e.g., Aboth iii. 1, 2, iv. 22. The prototype
of the latter appears in the biblical קְדוֹשׁ יִשְׂרָאֵל, e.g. Isa. 10[17]
49[7], and קָדוֹשׁ, Isa. 40[25], and occurs frequently also in the
Book of Enoch, as "the Holy One," Enoch 1[2] 93[11]; "the
Holy One who is great," 1[3] 10[1] 14[1] 25[3] 84[1] 92[2] 97[6] 98[6]
104[9].

It might readily be supposed that in the term רוּחַ קֻדְשָׁא,
"the Holy Spirit," the word קֻדְשָׁא became in reality a name
for God, so that τὸ πνεῦμα τοῦ θεοῦ would represent it more
accurately than τὸ πνεῦμα τὸ ἅγιον. But in that case terms
like רוּחַ קָדְשְׁךָ, "Thy Holy Spirit," Ps. 51[13], רוּחָא דְקָדְשִׁי, "My
Holy Spirit," Targ. Isa. 42[1], would be impossible. And yet
it must be maintained that the addition of קֻדְשָׁא is expressly
meant to specify Divinity as an attribute of the Spirit. As
regards content, therefore, there is no difference between "the
Spirit of God" and "the Holy Spirit." Moreover, רוּחַ קֻדְשָׁא,
not רוּחַ אֱלָהָא, is the common Jewish expression; and when
Jesus uses ἐν πνεύματι θεοῦ, Matt. 12[28], the original would

---

[1] Cf. מִפּוּם קֻדְשָׁא, "from the mouth of the Holiness," Targ. Lam. 3[38].

be the Aram. בְּרוּחַ קֻדְשָׁא, unless the preference were given to
the fuller form suggested by Matt. 10²⁰ בְּרוּחֵהּ דְּאַבָּא דְּבִשְׁמַיָּא,
" by the Spirit of My Father in heaven."

The Targums have conjoined רוּחַ, wherever in the Old
Testament it is not expressly called the Spirit of God, either
with קֹדֶשׁ or נְבוּאָה to make it clear what Spirit was contemplated; see רוּחַ קֻדְשִׁי for רוּחִי, Jerus. I. Gen. 6³, Targ. Isa. 59²¹,
Targ. Joel 3²; רוּחַ נְבוּאָחֵיהּ for רוּחוֹ, Onk. Num. 11²⁹; רוּחַ קֻדְשָׁא
for רוּחַ, Onk. Gen. 45²⁷ (Jerus. I. רוּחַ נְבוּאָה). In Jewish
literature it is so unheard of to speak of " the Spirit " (הָרוּחַ),
when the Spirit of God is meant, that the single word " spirit "
would much rather be taken to mean a demon or the wind.[1]
In the account of the Baptism, where Luke (3²²) has τὸ
πνεῦμα τὸ ἅγιον, while Matthew (3¹⁶) has πνεῦμα θεοῦ, and
Mark (1¹⁰) τὸ πνεῦμα, it is only the first that would be
probable in a Hebrew primitive gospel as רוּחַ הַקֹּדֶשׁ; while
הָרוּחַ[2] based on Mark, as proposed by Resch in his דִּבְרֵי יֵשׁוּעַ,
would be quite impossible. Resch's Hebrew in (2⁸): וַיִּרְא
אֶת־הָרוּחַ יוֹרֶדֶת בִּדְמוּת יוֹנָה, could at best only signify: "and he
saw the wind coming down in the form of a dove." Again, in
Matt. 4¹ τὸ πνεῦμα cannot be simply reproduced in Hebrew.
What is offered by Resch (2¹⁰): אָז הוּבַל יֵשׁוּעַ הַמִּדְבָּרָה בְּרוּחַ, would
have to be translated, " then was he carried into the wilder-
ness in spirit." In the same way ἡ τοῦ πνεύματος βλασ-
φημία, Matt. 12³¹, is unsuitable on the lips of Jesus, and τοῦ
ἁγιοῦ, as in v.³², must be supplied. Similarly ἐν πνεύματι,
Matt. 22⁴³, should be supplemented as in Mark 12³⁶ ἐν τῷ
πνεύματι τῷ ἁγίῳ.

---

[1] It may perhaps be mentioned that even in recent times a missionary
evoked the scorn of the Jews by using the term הָרוּחַ without qualification in
his address.

[2] Such translations could not be avoided by Franz Delitzsch, as he had to
copy the idiom of the Synoptic texts with all their variations; but in a pro-
fessing Hebrew original they are intolerable.

6. THE MERCIFUL ONE.

Only in Rom. 9^{16} ὁ ἐλεῶν θεός does "the Merciful" appear in the New Testament as a designation of God; cf.
3 Macc. 5^7 ὁ ἐλεήμων θεός. The son of Sirach (50^{19}) already
had the simple רַחוּם as a name for God. On the inscriptions
of Palmyra, רַחֲמָנָא occurs as an epithet applied to deity (de
Vogüé, 75, 77, 79); and in Jewish literature it often appears
as an independent title, e.g. j. Sabb. 3^b (Simeon ben Yokhai,
c. 140 A.D.). See also the prayers, רַחֲמָנָא עֲנֵינוּ and רַחֲמָנָא אִדְּכַר,
Roman Machzor, for the days before New Year. It was
thus an obviously natural thought that the children of the
Heavenly Father ought to be "merciful," to be in accord
with the fact that God is "merciful," οἰκτίρμων, Luke 6^{36}.
Similar admonitions are, accordingly, often given by the
Rabbis; see, e.g., j. Meg. 75° כְּמָא דַאֲנַן מְרַחֲמִין בִּשְׁמַיָּא בֵּן תִּהְווֹן
רַחֲמִין בְּאַרְעָא, "according as We are moved to mercy in heaven,
so should ye be merciful on earth"; cf. Jerus. I. Lev. 22^{18},
where the protasis runs: הֵיכְמָא דַאֲבוּנָן רַחֲמָן בִּשְׁמַיָּא, "as our
Father is merciful in heaven."

VIII. EVASIVE OR PRECAUTIONARY MODES OF REFERRING TO GOD.

1. THE VOICE.

To the evangelic narrative and not to the words of Jesus
belong the expressions : φωνὴ ἐκ τῶν οὐρανῶν, Matt. 3^{17} (Mark
1^{11}, Luke 3^{22} ἐξ οὐρανοῦ), and φωνὴ ἐκ τῆς νεφέλης, Matt.
17^5 (Mark 9^7, Luke 9^{35}). The mention of heaven and of the
cloud, in these cases, is due to the fact that, immediately
before the voice is alluded to, the heaven and the cloud are
involved in the context. Luke speaks only of a "voice"
(φωνή), Acts $10^{13.\ 15}$ $11^{7.\ 9}$ and in 7^{31}, after the biblical

manner of a "voice of the Lord" (φωνὴ κυρίου). It is only in John 12²⁸ and Rev. 10⁴· ⁸ 14¹³ that the source of the voice ἐκ τοῦ οὐρανοῦ is not suggested by the context.

This "voice" is heard when God is said to speak audibly to the sense of hearing. It is obviously a means of avoiding the notion that God should speak without any medium in the world. And hence it is not meant that the "voice" is any peculiar "being" or mediating hypostasis.

Nor again is any idea entertained of an imperfect type of divine revelation. The phrase is merely precautionary. Its aim is to indicate that the incident is miraculous, and it does not warrant any direct inference as to the nature of the supramundane God.

The expression appears first of all Dan. 4²⁸ קָל מִן שְׁמַיָּא נְפַל, "a voice fell from heaven"; see also Bar. Apoc. 13¹ "a voice came from on high" (Syr. קלא אתא מן מרומא), cf. 22¹. Instead of the simple קָל, later Jewish literature inserts the fuller בְּרַת קָלָא, Hebr. בַּת קוֹל, which, however, means no more than "sound, voice,"[1] though, as a rule, it causes the omission of "the heaven." The ordinary form here is: נִפְקַת בְּרַת קָלָא, Hebr. קוֹל מִן הַשָּׁמַיִם, "a voice came forth," the mention of heaven being unusual, as b. Sanh. 11ᵃ נִתְּנָה בַּת קוֹל מִן הַשָּׁמַיִם, "a voice was given from heaven." In this literature also the voice was not at the first regarded as an inferior form of revelation,[2] since we have here to do with the one and only mode of divine intimation. The endowment with the Holy Spirit, in the sense of the old prophecy, was something more exalted,[3] only because the divine element in it assumed a permanent relation to the inner life of an individual, and did not make itself heard merely from without and at intervals.

[1] See my article "Bath Kol," PRE ii.³ 443 f., where details are given to show that two species of the voice must be distinguished, (1) one which was really and miraculously caused by God directly, (2) one which was a human utterance, heard by some chance, to which was attributed the significance of a divine intimation.

[2] Incorrectly advanced in my "Der Gottesname Adonaj," 58, note 1.

[3] See the Baraitha, b. Sot. 48ᵇ; j. Sot. 24ᵇ.

2. SWEARING BY HEAVEN.

Swearing by heaven, ἐν τῷ οὐρανῷ, Matt. 5³⁴ 23²², is looked upon by Jesus as equivalent to swearing by God. He thus implies that a real name of God was being intentionally avoided, whenever the throne of God was named instead of God Himself, but not that " heaven " itself is meant as a divine name. Jesus affirms that an oath of such a kind is still an oath, which, if once taken, must be kept (23²²), though it is better to avoid it in general (5³⁴). Against the form of the expression as such, Jesus urges no objection.

In Siphre, Deut. 304, ed. Friedm. 147ᵃ,[1] הַשָּׁמַיִם appears as an asseveration. As a matter of fact, swearing in the name of "heaven and earth," according to Shebu. iv. 13, is not regarded as the oath of a witness; hence refusal on the latter's part to give evidence is not regarded as a culpable offence. On the position of Judaism in relation to oaths, see " Der Gottesname Adonaj," 60 ff., 68 ff.

3. REWARD, TREASURES IN HEAVEN.

Jesus speaks of a reward ἐν τοῖς οὐρανοῖς, Matt. 5¹² (Luke 6²³ ἐν τῷ οὐρανῷ), of treasures ἐν οὐρανῷ, Matt. 6²⁰ (Luke 12³³ ἐν τοῖς οὐρανοῖς), 19²¹ (Mark 10²¹, Luke 18²² ἐν οὐρανοῖς). Here " in heaven " stands for " with God "; cf. Matt. 6¹ παρὰ τῷ πατρὶ ὑμῶν τῷ ἐν οὐρανοῖς; and Jesus merely means that the recompense of completed work or the compensation for what is sacrificed in this world, is made ready by God even now, in so far as the " theocracy " is assuredly destined to come for the righteous. Any mystical pre-existence of " reward " or " treasure " is in no way contemplated. Cf. above, p. 129 f.

In agreement with texts of Scripture like Ps. 31²⁰

---

[1] See also *E. Landau*, Die dem Raume entnommenen Synonyma für Gott (1888), 16.

מָה רַב טוּבְךָ אֲשֶׁר צָפַנְתָּ לִירֵאֶיךָ, "how great is Thy goodness which Thou hast laid up for them that fear Thee," and Prov. 2[7] יִצְפֹּן לַיְשָׁרִים תּוּשִׁיָּה, "He layeth up salvation for the upright,"[1] Tobit (4[14]) speaks of divine remuneration for him who pays wages when they are due, and (4[9]) of a "goodly provision" (θέμα ἀγαθόν)[2] which man by the exercise of benevolence makes for himself against the day of necessity. "He who practises righteousness, lays up (θησαυρίζει) for himself with the Lord 'life,'" Ps. Sol. 9[9]. Bar. Apoc. 14[12] says that the pious forsake this present age without fear, because they have with God "a provision of works, kept in treasure-chambers" (Syr. חילא דעבדא דנטיר באוצרא). See also 2 Esdr. 7[77] "est tibi thesaurus operum repositus apud altissimum" (Syr. איתהו לך—אוצרא דעובדא דסים לות מרימא), cf. 8[33]. It is to be observed, in these cases, that the treasure is laid up "with God," which also confirms the view that "in heaven" in the words of Jesus is a mere synonym for this expression.

Later Jewish literature also affords in this connexion the expression : סֵגֶל מִצְוֹת וּמַעֲשִׂים טוֹבִים, "to lay up the fulfilment of commandments and good deeds";[3] see Ber. R. 9; Vay. R. 4; Deb. R. 1. According to Peah i. 1 (anonym.), there are certain pious services, the interest of which is enjoyed in this age, while the capital (קֶרֶן) remains over for the future age.[4] King Monobazos (c. 10 A.D.) retorts to his relatives, who find fault with his beneficence:[5] "My fathers gathered treasures

---

[1] See also Targ. Isa. 33[6] עָתִיד טוּבֵיהּ דַיָי אוֹצַר דַיָי לִדְחָלַיָּא, "to them that fear God is the treasure of His goodness appointed."

[2] Syr. סימתא רבתא, Aram. דרופתק טב, for which read טב הופתק (ὑποθήκη), Hebr. עישר ואוצרות כסף וזהב.

[3] See the definition of סְגֻלָּה Pes. Rabb. 43[a] : "To him who possesses it, it is disagreeable to disturb it : if he is forced by need to deduct from it, then he is ever busy to make up what was taken away." Hence סְגֻלָּה is an inalienable capital.

[4] For the idea of reward in Rabbinic doctrine, see F. Weber, Jüdische Theologie[2] (1897), 279 ff., 302 ff. That there also exist in it opinions which tend to mitigate the insistent attitude in the idea of recompense, will be shown elsewhere.

[5] j. Peah 15[b] ; b. Bab. b. 11[a].

upon earth; I, in heaven: my fathers gathered treasures which yield no interest; I, such as yield interest: my fathers gathered them into a place over which the hand of man has power; I, into a place over which man's hand has no power: they gathered gold, I gather souls; they gathered for others, I for myself; they for this age, I for the age to come." All these passages merely have in view some form of book-keeping on the part of God. The good words recorded by Him are merely so many claims to future recompense. Even the Targ. Isa. 24[16] is not, as Meyer[1] holds, intended to suggest things really existent in the other world. According to the Targumist, the prophet says: רָז אֲמַר לְצַדִּיקַיָּא אִתְחֲוִי לִי רָז פּוֹרְעָנוּת לְרַשִּׁיעַיָּא אִתְגְּלִי לִי, "the mystery of a recompense for the righteous was revealed to me, the mystery of a chastisement for the wicked was made manifest to me." That is, the prophet learned what the things are which the righteous and the wicked have to expect as reward and punishment.

In contrast with this, a celestial pre-existence of the reward might *possibly* be presupposed in Shem. R. 45, where God is represented as having shown to Moses "all the treasure-chambers of reward" (כָּל אוֹצְרוֹת שֶׁל מַתַּן שָׂכָר) pre-pared for the righteous; and also in Shir. R. 7[14], Deb. R. 7, where Abba bar Kahana (c. 300)[2] represents God as address-ing the Jews thus: "Preserve ye yourselves by fulfilling the law and by good works, and I will preserve for you treasure-chambers overflowing with all the blessings of the world";[3] of the same nature is also Targ. Jerus. II. Num. 23[33] טוּבֵיכוֹן צַדִּיקַיָּא מָה אֲגַר טָב מְתַקַּן לְכוֹן נַבֵּי אֲבוּכוֹן דְּבִשְׁמַיָּא לְעָלְמָא דְאָתֵי, "Blessed are ye righteous! what a noble reward is prepared for you with your Father in heaven for the age to come!" Still, in this case, the other sense is possible.

[1] Jesu Muttersprache, 83.

[2] Cf. *Bacher*, Agada d. pal. Am. ii. 499 f.

[3] For the term אוצר זכיות, "treasure of merits," *Charles* in Bar. Apoc. 14[12] cites Sabb. 31[b]. He is misled, however, perhaps through *Weber's* Jüd. Theo-logie, 279.

4. WRITTEN IN HEAVEN.

The names of the disciples are written ἐν τοῖς οὐρανοῖς (ἐν τῷ οὐρανῷ), Luke 10²⁰, *i.e.* the disciples as such are known to God and are kept in remembrance. " In heaven " stands for " with God." The allusion is to the " book of God " in Ex. 32³²ᶠ·, and the " book of the living " in Ps. 69²⁸, in which all the righteous are enrolled; cf. Isa. 4³, Dan. 12¹·¹ Of this the Book of Enoch also speaks, 47³ 104¹: " your names stand inscribed before the majesty of the Exalted"; 108³ " the book of life and the books of the holy ones." Jubil. 30²⁰ has: " he is entered in the heavenly tablets as a friend and an upright man "; cf. 30²². The Targum to the prophets supplements Isa. 4³ in the sense in which Jesus also appears to have interpreted the text, making the life הַחַיִּים to be " the eternal life " (חַיֵּי עָלְמָא). The school of Shammai would seem to have spoken of a registration unto life and unto death,[2] b. R. h. S. 16ᵇ; but in Tos. Sanh. xiii. 3 the requisite terms for this sense are wanting. On the other hand, Yokhanan[3] (*c.* 260) takes note of three " lists " (פִּינְקְסָיוֹת)—one for the righteous, one for the wicked, and the other for an intermediate class—into which, as it seems, names are from year to year entered afresh at the beginning of the year.

5. BEFORE THE ANGELS, BEFORE GOD.

Over the sinner that repents there is joy ἐνώπιον τῶν ἀγγέλων τοῦ θεοῦ, Luke 15¹⁰, or ἐν τῷ οὐρανῷ, ibid. v.⁷. By that is meant that there will be joy in the presence of God, or, strictly : God will rejoice.

---

[1] This book resembles the list of citizens among the nations and cities on earth, and must be kept distinct from the book of good and evil deeds ; see R. H. *Charles* on Enoch 47³.

[2] See *Bacher*, Agada d. Tann. i. 18 f.

[3] j. R. h. S. 57ᵃ ; cf. *Bacher*, Agada d. p. Am. i. 331.

14

The Son of Man will acknowledge His confessors and disown those who have denied Him, ἔμπροσθεν (ἐνώπιον) τῶν ἀγγέλων τοῦ θεοῦ, Luke 12⁸ᶠ. The reproduction in Matt. 10³²ᶠ. ἔμπροσθεν τοῦ πατρός μου τοῦ ἐν οὐρανοῖς, shows what is really meant, namely, an acknowledgment in the presence of God, for whom the angels are substituted merely to avoid the use of the divine name. In Jewish literature this idiom is unfamiliar. It is exceedingly probable that it should not be assumed as falling from the lips of Jesus either, and that it was Luke who inserted " the angels " in place of a term which appeared to him less intelligible. In his source he will have found the expression " before Heaven " (Judæan קֳדָם שְׁמַיָּא, Galil. קֳמֵי שְׁמַיָּא), an echo of which occurs Luke 15⁷ " in heaven." The Palestinian Talmud Kidd. 64ᶜ shows that קֳמֵי שְׁמַיָּא was in actual use.

Even the sparrows are not forgotten " in the sight of God " (ἐνώπιον τοῦ θεοῦ), Luke 12⁶, i.e. God does not forget them. To get the words of Jesus here, ὁ θεός would have to be converted into " heaven," or, following the parallel in Matt. 10²⁹, into " your Heavenly Father." The former is recommended by the saying which shows some affinity with Matthew's mode of expressing the idea : צִפּוֹר מִבַּלְעֲדֵי שְׁמַיָּא לָא יַבְדָא, " not a bird perishes apart from Heaven," j. Shebi. 38ᵈ ; cf. Ber. R. 79. Luke's form of the expression is recalled by the dictum of Ishmael ben Elisha (c. 110 A.D.):[1] " there is joy in the presence of ' the Place ' (יֵשׁ שִׂמְחָה לִפְנֵי הַמָּקוֹם), when those who provoke Him to anger disappear from the world." So, too, it is said, Siphre, ed. Friedm. 139ᵃ : " when ' the Place ' (הַמָּקוֹם) judges the peoples, there is joy in His presence (שִׂמְחָה הִיא לְפָנָיו); but when He judges Israel, it is, as it were, with regret (כִּבְיָכוֹל יֵשׁ תָּהוּת לְפָנָיו)." " There is no forgetfulness before the throne of Majesty," according to a saying of Simeon ben Lakish (c. 250 A.D.).[2] In j. Maas. sh. 56ᵈ the question is

---

[1] Siphre, Num. 117, ed. Friedm. 37ᵃ ; cf. Bacher, Agada d. Tann. i. 256.
[2] b. Ber. 32ᵇ ; cf. Bacher, Agada d. pal. Am. i. 397.

asked : " is there then sleep before God ? " and Midr. Ps. 121[3]
positively affirms : " there is neither sleep nor sitting ' on
high ' (לְמַעֲלָה)." In Ab. v. 2 it is pointed out how God de-
ferred the Flood " in order to show how great is longsufferance
' in His presence.' " Speaking generally, the accomplishment
of actions is attested or denied *before* God, when those
activities are in question which God Himself either does or
does not do.

Even " volition " might not be directly predicated of God.
It is true, Luke 12[32] has : εὐδόκησεν ὁ πατὴρ ὑμῶν, but Matt.
18[14] gives : οὐκ ἔστιν θέλημα ἔμπροσθεν τοῦ πατρὸς ὑμῶν
τοῦ ἐν οὐρανοῖς, " it is not the will of (before) your Father
in heaven." Instead of " it has pleased Thee," Jesus says
in addressing God, Matt. 11[26] (Luke 10[21]): οὕτως εὐδοκία
ἐγένετο ἔμπροσθέν σου, " so it was well-pleasing in Thy sight."
These are not Old Testament usages. The last-named in-
stance recalls the formula often used in prayer : יְהִי רָצוֹן מִלְּפָנֶיךָ,
" may it be well-pleasing in Thy sight "; see, *e.g.*, j. Ber. 7[d];
Aram. יְהֵא רַעֲוָה מִן קֳדָם יְיָ, Targ. Cant. 7[14]; יְהֵא רַעֲוָה מִקַּמֵּי קֻדְשָׁא
בְּרִיךְ הוּא, " may it be well-pleasing before the Holiness, Blessed
be He," Koh. R. 3[2,1] One may also compare Onk. Gen.
28[17] אַתְרָא דִּרְעָוָה בֵּיהּ מִן קֳדָם יְיָ, " a place, which has regard
from before Jhvh "; and Numb. 14[8] אִם רַעֲוָא בָּנָא קֳדָם יְיָ, " if we
find favour before Jhvh."

To the expression of Matt. 18[14] there corresponds in the
Targums : רְעָוָא קֳדָם יְיָ לְ ?, " it is the will of (before) Jhvh, to
. . ." This phrase is used to replace the Hebr. יהוה חָפֵץ,
" Jhvh was pleased to," Targ. Judg. 13[23], 1 Sam. 2[25], and
Isa. 53[10], which has the form : מִן קֳדָם יְיָ הֲוַת רַעֲוָא ?. Though
not suggested by the Hebrew text, it appears in Ezek. 1[25].
Its antiquity appears from its use in 1 Macc. 3[60] ὡς δ' ἂν ᾖ
θέλημα ἐν οὐρανῷ, Syr. איך דאית צבינא קדם עמורא דשמיא, " as
may be the decision before Him who dwells in heaven."

---

[1] According to Midrash Khamesh Megilloth, ed. Salonica, 1593, not in ed.
Pesaro, 1519, nor Venice, 1545.

As divine honours are rendered to a king, so it comes to pass that in Egypt men spoke only " in the presence of the king," not " to " him.[1]   One speaks " before " the king (לִפְנֵי, Aram. קֳדָם), also in Esth. 1[16] 7[9] 8[3], Dan. 2[9. 10. 11. 27. 36] 5[17]. That prayer is offered " before " God is stated more frequently in the younger books of the Old Testament than in the earlier books.   And consistently with this tendency, the Targums never represent man as speaking " to," but " before " (קֳדָם) God ; men blaspheme and provoke to anger not " Him," but " in His presence."[2]   Hence it is not surprising that it is also said that man sins not " against " God, but " before " God.   In Gen. 20[9], which treats of a matter between two men, the Hebr. חָטָא לְ is rendered in the LXX by ἁμαρτάνειν εἰς, and in Onkelos by חָב לְ; but in Ex. 32[33], where the sin is against God, the same Hebr. חָטָא לְ is rendered in the LXX Alex. ἁμαρτάνειν ἐνώπιον, and Onkelos חָב קֳדָם.   Daniel (6[23]) affirms that he has done no wrong " before " the king. According to j. Sanh. 28[b], King Ahab complained to Levi, the Amora, whose teaching was prejudicial to the character of that king : מֶה חֲטֵית לָךְ וּמֶה סְרָחִית קֳדָמָךְ, " what is my sin against thee, and what ill have I done before thee ? "   This reverent mode of address is here used to an ordinary man. With respect to God, the prayer מַחֵי וּמַפֵּי [3] has, as a matter of course : חֲטֵינָא לְקַפָּךְ, " we have sinned before Thee."   It is different in the statement of Ps. 51[6] לְךָ לְבַדְּךָ חָטָאתִי וְהָרָע בְּעֵינֶיךָ עָשִׂיתִי; for here בְּעֵינֶיךָ goes with הָרָע, and the rendering should be : " against Thee alone have I sinned, and that which is evil in thine eyes I have committed."   Luke, however, conforms to the usage under consideration, when in his Gospel 15[18. 21] the prodigal son says to his father : " I have sinned even against heaven (εἰς τὸν οὐρανόν) and before thee (ἐνώπιόν σου)."   The motive here is not that the father in the

[1] A. Erman, Ägypten, 109.

[2] M. Ginsburger, Die Anthropomorphismen in den Targumim, 22 f., 32 f., 41 ; G. Dalman, Der Gottesname Adonaj, 57.

[3] Seder Rab Amram, ii. 21[b].

parable stands for God, but that the son speaks with befitting reverence towards his father. Luke will thus have interchanged the prepositions εἰς and ἐνώπιον for reasons of style.

6. BOUND, LOOSED IN HEAVEN.

What the disciples of Jesus bind upon earth is reckoned "in heaven" also as bound; what they loose upon earth is also loosed "in heaven," Matt. 18¹⁸. The same is said in regard to Peter, Matt. 16¹⁹ (with ἐν τοῖς οὐρανοῖς). The antithesis is doubtless here intended to lie between the disciples, or Peter, on the one side, and on the other [not heaven, but] God. Even when Jesus says that He has power "on earth" (ἐπὶ τῆς γῆς) to forgive sins, Matt. 9⁶ (Mark 2¹⁰, Luke 5²⁴), the meaning is that He does so here on earth just in the same way as is done by God in heaven.

With the foregoing use of the phrase "in heaven," the Rabbis are not always in agreement when they speak of "the court of justice which is on high," שֶׁלְמַעְלָה דִין בֵּית, as, e.g., in j. Ber. 14ᶜ; j. R. h. S. 58ᵇ; j. Bikk. 64ᶜ. Often, indeed, that is also a mere phrase intended to avoid naming God;[1] but sometimes, too, the idea entertained is, that God with the angels forms a real court of justice. The principle, which Holtzmann in his Commentary on Matt. 16¹⁸f.[2] refers to as generally acknowledged, that the heavenly Sanhedrim will confirm the conclusions of the earthly, does not, however, hold so extensively. Certain specified matters, such as the regulation of the Calendar, have been entrusted by God to the supreme council in Israel, and by this agreement He too appears to be bound.[3] In the Targum Cant. 8¹³ God says to the community of Israel: "let me hear the Law, the sound of thy words, when thou sittest to acquit and to condemn;

---

[1] Cf. e.g. Midr. Ps. 57² where הוּא בָרוּךְ הַקָּרוֹשׁ takes the place of שֶׁלְמַעְלָה דִין בֵּית, j. Ber. 14ᶜ.

[2] See also *Holtzmann*, Lehrb. d. neutest. Theol. i. 50.

[3] j. R. h. S. 57ᵇ; Pesikt. 53ᵇ f.; cf. j. Ber. 14ᶜ.

and I will consent to all that thou doest." That does not mean that in all things God subordinates His resolution to that of the community of Israel; it is merely the interpretation and application of the Law that He has placed in their hands.

According to Tanna Eliyyahu rabba 29,[1] a ban pronounced on earth has even enhanced validity before God. It is there said, " to any one who is excommunicated ' below ' (מִלְּמַטָּה) for *one* day, even if he has been freed from the ban, there is ' on high ' (מִלְּמַעְלָה) no release for seven days." Here " on high " quite corresponds to the expression in Matthew. On the other hand, " Heaven " stands directly for " God " in the epithet מְנַדִּין לִשְׁמַיָא, " banned by Heaven," b. Pes. 113[b].

This recognition on God's part of earthly decisions of justice, attested by the Rabbis, is left far behind when the belief is expressed that in certain circumstances the divine authority must even give way before that of the pious person. In dependence upon such biblical passages as 2 Sam. 23[3], Job 22[28], Eccles. 8[4, 5], it is made out, j. Taan. 67[a] (cf. b. Sabb. 63[a]), that " the Holy One, Blessed be He, makes His determination invalid, if it contradict the determination of a pious person "; b. Mo. k. 16[b],[2] " I, God, rule over men; who rules over Me? The pious—for I enact and he annuls," and j. Taan. 67[a] " Even if I (God) say thus, and thou sayest otherwise, then thy word is valid and Mine invalid."

The terms δέειν and λύειν used in Matthew can be referred only to אֲסַר and שְׁרָא in Aramaic. As may be seen j. Ber. 5[b], *e.g.*, these are the technical forms for the verdict of a doctor of the law who pronounces something as " bound " (אֲסִיר, j. Ber. 6[c]), *i.e.* " forbidden," or else as " loosed " (שְׁרֵי, j. Sanh. 28[a]), *i.e.* " permitted "—not, of course, in virtue of his own absolute authority, but in conformity with his knowledge of the oral law. Consequently the statement of

---

[1] Cf. Yalk. Shimeoni, i. 745.
[2] Cf. *Bacher*, Ag. d. pal. Am. ii. 127.

Jesus would mean that His disciples—in virtue of their knowledge of His oral teaching—will be able to give an authoritative decision in regard to what the adherents of the theocracy may do and may not do. To this it must, however, be objected, (1) that Matthew can hardly have understood the saying of our Lord in that sense, because δέειν and λύειν do not in his Greek mean "forbid" and "permit"; and (2) that the context, at least in Matt. 18¹⁸, has in view an exclusion from the community. If the supposition be rejected that Matthew has misunderstood the statement and has set it in a connection originally foreign to it, the only remaining option is that the terms "bind" and "loose" were really taken from the aforesaid use of the legal schools, but that here no emphasis falls on "permitting" and "forbidding" as such, but only on the final significance universally attaching to the word of him who has authority to "permit" and "forbid." The context goes on to say in what direction that verdict is regarded as being operative.

The thought is similar to that associated with the figure of the keeper of the keys. Isa. 22²² shows how Shebna [for the time being] has the key of the house of David upon his shoulder; if he opens, none shuts; if he shuts, then no one opens. That does not mean that Shebna is the palace door-keeper, but that he is comptroller of the household, to whom the management of all the king's domestic concerns is entrusted.[1] In allusion to this passage, it is said in Rev. 3⁷ᶠ· of Christ, that He has the key of David, and that He, as rightful possessor of this key, has power to open and to shut; in virtue of this authority He can pronounce sentence upon the status and value of any community, while no other power whatever can avail in opposition. In the same way הַפִּפְסֵר,

---

[1] So, too, in the old story, according to which the priests of the temple then doomed to destruction threw the keys towards the heavens, because they had been unworthy keepers, it is not the opening and shutting that are in consideration, but the general supervision of the sanctuary. See Bar. Apoc. 10¹⁸, the rest of the words of Baruch, 4³ᶠ·; b. Taan. 29ᵃ; j. Shek. 50ᵃ; Vay. R. 19.

"the locksmith," 2 Kings 24[14], suggests in Siphre, Deut. 311, ed. Friedm. 138[a], the teacher of the law: "all sit before him and learn from him; if he has opened no one shuts,"— *i.e.* his instruction has indisputable authority. In the same sense, Peter, Matt. 16[19], has the keys of the theocracy, and, as keeper of the keys, is the fully authorised steward of the house of God upon earth. Since, moreover, it is the community of Jesus that is here concerned, in which Peter is to exercise this office, and as no sort of limitation to a defined sphere is indicated, it follows necessarily that the control of teaching and of discipline are regarded as entrusted to him. Peter had just shown that he understood his Master better than the others. He, therefore, shall it be, who will one day assume in the fellowship that position which Jesus then occupied in relation to His disciples. Again, in Matt. 18[18] the same plenary power is vested in the disciples collectively, in the case when the special application of that authority is made in respect of the discipline of the community. Accordingly, the application which is given in John 20[23] to this saying is not unwarranted. For exclusion from the community on account of some offence includes the "retaining" of the sins; the readmission of the sinner includes the "remission" of his sins. The only remark to be made here is that the term κρατεῖν in John has no Jewish parallel. שִׂית עַל, which Salkinson puts for it, means, according to Num. 12[11] "to impute something (as a sin) to any one." In Delitzsch, too, הֶאֱשִׁים is merely a make-shift.

That שְׂרָא, "to loose," if not the companion term, can also be used figuratively in various connections in Jewish Aramaic, may also be demonstrated here.

(*a*) "To ban" is in Hebr. נִדָּה, "to loose" from the ban Hebr. הִתִּיר, Mo. kat. iii. 1, 2; Aram. נַדִּי, חֲרֶם (אַחְרֵם) and שְׂרָא, j. Mo. kat. 81[d]. In that passage Simeon ben Lakish (*c.* 260) calls out to some fruit-stealers: "Let those people be banned (מַחְרְמִין)!" They reply: "Let that man be banned!" He

hastens after them and entreats them: "Loose me (שְׁרוֹן לִי)!"
They reply: "Loose us, and we will loose thee."

(b) "To render spellbound" through sorcery is אֲסַר, b.
Sabb. 81ᵇ, and correspondingly "to loose," i.e. "to set the
spellbound person free," is שְׁרָא, ibid. and j. Sanh. 25ᵈ. F. C.
Conybeare[1] is of opinion that it was from the phraseology of
magic that Jesus selected His terms, and that the power
transmitted by Him to the disciples was like a magical influence, supposed to confer ability to work miracles. But
the context in Matthew, like everything else we know about
Jesus, is opposed to this supposition.

(c) "To loose" (שְׁרָא) can also be said for "to forgive."
According to Midr. Ps. 19⁷,[2] David said to God: "the trans-
gressions wherein I have trespassed before Thee, I pray Thee,
forgive me" (תִּשְׁרֵי לִי)![3] And the answer received was: "lo!
it is forgiven unto thee; lo! it is remitted unto thee (הָא שְׁרֵי
לָךְ וְהָא שְׁבִיק לָךְ)." The month Tishri is called by this name,
according to Vay. R. 29, because at that time God "forgives,
remits, expiates" (תִּשְׁרֵי תִּשְׁבּוֹק תְּכַפֵּר) the sins of His people.
Those who have beaten Tarphon (c. 110), not knowing who
he was, call to him, j. Shebi. 35ᵈ: שְׁרִי לֹן, "forgive us!" Nachman bar Yizkhak (c. 350) quotes b. Yom. 86ᵃ the Babylonian
phrase: שְׁרָא לֵהּ מָרֵיהּ דִּפְלַנְיָא[4], "forgive him, O Lord of such an
one!" In Jerus. I. Num. 14¹⁸ God is called שְׁרֵי לְחוֹבִין, "One
who forgives the guilty."

7. HEAVEN.

It may be doubted whether Luke ever consciously used
"Heaven," meaning "God." The solitary passage which can
be adduced in support of that view is Luke 15¹⁸· ²¹ ἥμαρτον

---

[1] Jew. Quart. Rev. ix. 468 ff.

[2] The saying is here attributed to Simeon ben Yokhai (c. 140 A.D.), but in
Vay. R. 5 to Khoni, in b. Sanh. 107ᵃ to Dosithai.

[3] This appears only in ed. Buber, not in ed. Const. 1512, Venice, 1546.

[4] So it should be read instead of לפלניא in the text.

εἰς τὸν οὐρανὸν καὶ ἐνώπιόν σου, assuming the translation to
be: "I have sinned *against* Heaven and before Thee." As
has been said above, under 5, we should expect preferably
"*before* Heaven" to have been said by Jesus. Still it may
be that this was the original, and that εἰς τὸν οὐρανόν should
mean for Luke, "even unto Heaven."

The examples already given, under 5, of the corresponding rabbinic usage may here be supplemented. We have
the phrase: הֵטִיחַ דְּבָרִים כְּלַפֵּי מַעֲלָה, "to make reproaches towards
heaven," said, b. Ber. 31[b], b. Taan. 25[a], to have been used by
Eleazar ben Pedat (*c.* 290).[1] The Babylonian Nachman
(*c.* 300) made bold to say:[2] "Even insolence in the face of
heaven (כְּלַפֵּי שְׁמַיָא) has its use"; cf. Targ. Eccl. 7[9] מֵימַר
שְׁמַיָא כְּלַפֵּי סַרְבָּנוּתָא פִּתְגָמֵי, "to speak words of insubordination
in the face of heaven." The Palestinian Khanina (*c.* 210)[3]
distinguishes sins as "upon the earth" (בְּאָרֶץ), or "in heaven"
(בִּשְׁמַיִם), *i.e.* against men or against God.

In all probability Jesus made a more extensive use of
שְׁמַיָא as a divine name than the Gospels would lead us to
suppose. This need not seem surprising. The antiquity of
the popular custom to which He adhered, which arose probably through the impulse of Greek influence, is proved, so far
as Hebraists are concerned, by Dan. 4[23], 1 Macc. 3[18. 19. 50. 60]
4[10. 24. 55] 12[15]; and for Hellenists by 2 Macc. 7[11] 8[20] 9[4. 20].
The cases are not here distinguished, where "heaven" must
necessarily stand for the Person of "God," and where phrases
like "to heaven," "from heaven," are due to the desire not
to name the Person of God in any way. Examples of the
use of שָׁמַיִם for "God" in the rabbinic literature, especially
the Mishna, have been collected by *E. Schürer*, Jahrbb. f.
prot. Theol. 1876, 166–187, and by *E. Landau*, Die dem

---

[1] Cf. the expressions הִתְפַּלֵּל כְּלַפֵּי לְמַעֲלָן, "to direct one's prayer on high (to
God)," j. Ber. 8[b]; הִסְתַּכֵּל כְּלַפֵּי מַעֲלָה, "to direct one's look upwards (to God),"
R. h. S. iii. 8.

[2] b. Sanh. 105[a].

[3] Koh. R. 9. 12; cf. *Bacher*, Agada d. pal. Am. i. 10.

Raume entnommenen Synonyma für Gott (1888), 14–28. Here we may name such cases only as have clearly put "heaven" in place of the divine name. Composite expressions of this kind are: מוֹרָא שְׁמַיָּא, "the fear of God," Ab. i. 3; מַלְכוּת שָׁמַיִם, "the sovereignty of God," Ber. ii. 2; שֵׁם שָׁמַיִם, "the name of God," Sanh. vi. 4; דִּינֵי שָׁמַיִם, "the decrees of God," b. Bab. k. 55[b]; רַחֲמֵי שְׁמַיָּא, "the mercy of God," Jerus. I. Num. 26[19]; מֵימְרָא דִשְׁמַיָּא, "the word of God" (God), Targ. Eccl. 4[4] 11[3]; and in the prayer תִּשְׁתַּלַּח אָסוּתָא.[1] Prepositions are conjoined with שָׁמַיִם in בִּידֵי שָׁמַיִם, "by the hand of God," Sanh. ix. 6; לְשֵׁם שָׁמַיִם, "for God" (in the name of God),[2] Ab. ii. 2; לְשָׁמַיִם, "for God," Men. xiii. 1, j. Ned. 37[a]; קַמֵּי שְׁמַיָּא, "before God," j. Kidd. 64[c]. "Heaven" is the subject of the verb in שְׁמַיָּא מֶעֱבַד נִפִּין, "God does wonders," j. Taan. 66[d].

8. FROM HEAVEN.

In Matt. 21[25] (Mark 11[30], Luke 20[4]) Jesus requires an answer to the question whether the baptism of John was "from heaven" (ἐξ οὐρανῶν) or " of men " (ἐξ ἀνθρώπων). Of the same nature are John 3[27] "to have been given from heaven," ἐκ τοῦ οὐρανοῦ; 19[11] "to be given 'from above,' ἄνωθεν"; 3[7] "to be born 'from above'"; 3[31] "to come 'from above,' to come 'from heaven'"; Jas. 1[17] 3[15] "to come 'from above.'" What is meant throughout is derivation from God, though it must be granted that "heaven" did not in these cases stand pure and simply for the divine name (cf. above, p. 92).

Beside these instances may be set the following: ἔχομεν τὴν ἐξ οὐρανῶν βοηθίαν, "we have the help which comes from heaven," 1 Macc. 12[15], cf. 3[19]; ἐξ οὐρανοῦ ταῦτα κέκτημαι, "from heaven have I received these as my possession," 2 Macc. 7[11]; אֵין תּוֹרָה מִן הַשָּׁמַיִם, "the law is not from heaven,"

---

[1] Seder Rab Amram, i. 52[b].
[2] Cf. G. A. Deissmann, Bibelstudien, 143 ff. ; Neue Bibelstudien, 24 ff.

Sanh. x. 1; יְהֵא שְׁלָמָא רַבָּא מִן שְׁמַיָּא, "may there be (come) peace abounding from heaven," Kaddish;[1] יְקוּם פֻּרְקָן מִן שְׁמַיָּא, "may redemption arise from heaven," in the prayer that begins with these words:[2] אֵין מִן הַשָּׁמַיִם מוֹחֲלִין לָהֶן, "there is no forgiveness from heaven for them," Tos. Shebu. iii. 1 (Joshua ben Khananya, c. 130 A.D.); תֵּיתֵי עֲלָךְ אוֹבַחְתָּא מִן שְׁמַיָּא, "there shall come upon thee correction from heaven," Targ. Eccl. 7⁹; אִתְיְהֵב לֵיהּ מִן שְׁמַיָּא, "it was given to him from heaven," ibid. 8¹⁵; מִן שְׁמַיָּא אִתְגְּזַר, "it was decreed from heaven," ibid. 9²; אִשָּׁה שֶׁהִקְנוּ לוֹ מִן הַשָּׁמַיִם, "a wife whom men have assigned to him from heaven,"[3] Ned. x. 6. The use of "above" in the same sense is closely related; examples: מַזָּלָא דִלְעֵילָא, "the destiny which is above," Targ. Eccl. 3⁹; מֵימְרָא דִלְעֵיל, "the word which is above," Jerus. I. Lev. 24¹²; דַּעַת עֶלְיוֹנָה, "the knowledge which is above," Mechilta, ed. Friedm. 89ᵇ, Aram. דַּעְתָּא דִלְעֵיל, Jerus. I. Num. 27⁵; בּוֹחוֹ שֶׁל מַעֲלָה, "the power that is above," Siphre, ed. Friedm. 137ᵃ; עֵינוֹ שֶׁלְּמַעֲלָה, "the eye that is above," Mechilta, ed. Friedm. 91ᵇ; "there is no release of the ban from above" (מִלְּמַעֲלָה), Tanna El. Rabb. 29; "if thou orderest well thy prayer, disfavour shall not be thy portion from on high (צָרֵי עַיִן מִלְּמַעֲלָה), j. Taan. 66ᵈ. See also under Nos. 5, 6, and 10.

9. HOSANNA IN THE HIGHEST.

In the mouth of the multitude we find the cry ὡσαννά, Matt. 21⁹ (Mark 11⁹ᶠ·) On this occasion Matthew and Mark have it twice, and the second time they couple with it ἐν τοῖς ὑψίστοις. At the first occurrence here and also in 20¹⁵ Matthew adds τῷ υἱῷ Δαυείδ.

Guillemard [4] finds this Dative surprising, since both הוֹשִׁיעָה

---

[1] *Baer*, Seder Abodath Yisrael, 153.

[2] Ibid. 229.

[3] What is alluded to is a consort whom a man has acquired through Levirate liabilities, not by his own choice.

[4] *W. H. Guillemard*, Hebraisms in the Greek Testament (1879), i. 44.

and σῶσον are transitive, and would require the Accusative. His statement does not quite hold of הוֹשִׁיעַ, which may also be followed by לְ, Ps. 72⁴ 116⁶; but it cannot, after all, be supposed that a Greek author, to whose mind σῶσον occurred as the meaning of ὡσαννά, would have followed it up with the Dative.[1] ὡσαννά cannot therefore be taken, as by Holtzmann, in the sense : " give greeting to." Inasmuch as the Teaching of the Twelve Apostles, 10⁶, substitutes ὡσαννὰ τῷ θεῷ Δαβίδ, it cannot be doubted that ὡσαννά was understood to be a cry of homage in the sense of "glory" or "hail to the Son of David." This sense will further hold of Matthew's Gospel also, *whose author consequently can have been no Hebraist, and cannot have been the apostle.*[2] And again the connection of ὡσαννά with ἐν τοῖς ὑψίστοις in Matthew and Mark creates surprise. As regards Matthew, it follows from what has just been said that ὡσαννά will here also signify "glory" or " praise." The evangelist takes ὡ. ἐν τοῖς ὑψίστοις to mean the same thing as Ps. 148¹ LXX αἰνεῖτε αὐτὸν (τὸν κύριον) ἐν τοῖς ὑψίστοις, Hebr. הַלְלוּהוּ בַּמְּרוֹמִים, that is, the song of adoration which the angels are to sing to God. This is the sense attributed to it by Luke also, who, in 19³⁸, has : ἐν οὐρανῷ εἰρήνη καὶ δόξα ἐν ὑψίστοις. He too, therefore, did not understand Hebrew. The way in which Mark apprehended the utterance may remain open to question. One might conceivably hold that ἐν τοῖς ὑψίστοις had been a substitute for the name of God, which, from the tenor of Ps. 118²⁵, ought properly to have been expressed here. But deliverance ought, of course, to have come " from the highest," and not be given " to the highest." In the former sense only could parallel Jewish expressions be found.[3] And hence the source of the addition ἐν ὑψίστοις in Mark also is presumably the mistaken view of ὡσαννά to be found in the early Church.

[1] Cf. Ps. 20¹⁰ הוֹשִׁיעָה הַמֶּלֶךְ, LXX σῶσον τὸν βασιλέα σου.

[2] Of course a collection of the sayings of our Lord forming the basis of the "Matthew" Gospel may nevertheless originate from the apostle.

[3] Cf. p. 220.

It must also be said that, in the mouth of those who accompanied Jesus in His entry into the city of Jerusalem, הוֹשַׁע נָא בַּמְּרוֹמִים is but little probable, inasmuch as Ps. 118 did not directly furnish this expression. The mere הוֹשַׁע נָא בָּרוּךְ הַבָּא בְּשֵׁם יְהֹוָה, as Mark 11⁹ records it, in the first instance will have been the real cry of the multitude. All else in Mark and Matthew is explanatory amplification. In that case the cry requires discussion here only in so far as the divine name has been dropped after הוֹשַׁע נָא. How the יהוה, which comes at the end, was expressed, we do not know. הַשֵּׁם being impossible, שָׁמַיִם might preferably be proposed. But probably, in this case, there would be less hesitation in using the אֲדֹנִי of public worship, since the state of feeling which prompts the exclamation is quite devotional in character. The shout of homage rendered to a king would have to be expressed by Hebr. יְחִי הַמֶּלֶךְ, as in 1 Kings 1³⁹, for הוֹשַׁע הַמֶּלֶךְ, 2 Sam. 14⁴, is not homage, as Nowack[1] supposes, but an entreaty for help. Thus, too, it becomes clear why the entry of Jesus into Jerusalem was not made a ground of accusation against him before Pilate. Wellhausen[2] rightly supposes that the procession on Palm Sunday did not acquire its pronounced Messianic colouring till a later period. The Teacher and Miracle-worker from Nazareth was then welcomed with jubilation, and accompanied with invocation of blessings. Of the entry of the King, as depicted in Zech. 9⁹, few will have thought, and this thought will have occurred to them probably at a later date, rather than on the day itself.

There is no occasion whatever for reverting to the Aram. אֹושַׁעְנָא, "help us," as the prototype of ὡσαννά, because, indeed, the shorter form, הוֹשַׁע, must itself be reckoned the regular form, even in Hebrew, see Jer 31⁶, Ps. 86². Moreover, the abbreviated form, הוֹשַׁע נָא, can be verified in Jewish liturgies. The earliest witness for it is the name given to

---

[1] W. Nowack, Hebräische Archäologie, i. 307.

[2] Israelit. u. jüd. Geschichte,³ 381, note 2.

the seventh day of the Feast of Tabernacles, יוֹמָא דְּהוֹשַׁעֲנָא, Vay.
R. 37, and the designation of the branches used for that
festival by הוֹשַׁעֲנָא, Sukk. 30ᵇ. From a later time come the
processional songs with the refrain הוֹשַׁע נָא, see Seder Rab
Amram, i. 51ᵇ; Machzor Vitry, 447–456.

10. FROM ON HIGH.

In Luke 24⁴⁹ the reception of the Spirit by the disciples
is referred to as an endowment with "power from on high"
(ἐξ ὕψους δύναμιν). Acts 1⁸ says: λήμψεσθε δύναμιν ἐπελ-
θόντος τοῦ ἁγίου πνεύματος ἐφ᾽ ὑμᾶς. Both are an echo of
Isa. 32¹⁵ עַד יֵעָרֶה עָלֵינוּ רוּחַ מִמָּרוֹם, LXX ἕως ἂν ἔλθῃ ἐφ᾽ ὑμᾶς
πνεῦμα ἀφ᾽ ὑψηλοῦ; cf. Wisd. 9¹⁷ ἔπεμψας τὸ ἅγιόν σου
πνεῦμα ἀπὸ ὑψίστων. The phrase ἐνδύεσθαι δύναμιν originates in Old Testament passages like Ps. 92¹ LXX: ἐνεδύσατο
κύριος δύναμιν. For ἐξ ὕψους, see Lam. 1¹³ LXX. ὕψος is
there an equivalent for "heaven": "from on high" is the
same as "from God." In Old Testament expressions of this
kind an intentional evasion of the name of God cannot be
imputed. Probably, however, the use of these terms in Luke
springs from this motive.

Similarly, Onkelos does not venture to translate כֹּחַ אֲדֹנָי,
"the power of God," Num. 14¹⁷, literally, but replaces it by
חֵילָא קֳדָמָךְ יְיָ, "the power in Thy presence, Jhvh." The spirit
of Jhvh, which is to rest upon the Messiah, Isa. 11², is in the
words of the Targum "a spirit of prophecy from before Jhvh"
(רוּחַ נְבִיאָה מִן קֳדָם יְיָ), cf. Targ. Isa. 61¹. The "Spirit of God"
in Gen. 1² is for Onkelos רוּחָא מִן קֳדָם יְיָ (cf. Targ. Isa. 40⁷),
and for Targ. Jerus. I. רוּחַ רַחֲמִין מִן קֳדָם יְיָ, "a spirit of mercy
from before God."

Further, in ἀνατολὴ ἐξ ὕψους [the dayspring from on high],
Luke 1⁷⁸, ἐξ ὕψους represents "from God." Delitzsch renders
literally נֹגַהּ מִמָּרוֹם; Resch, copying but not improving upon
Delitzsch, הַנֹּגַהּ מִמָּרוֹם. But the association with ἐπεσκέψατο

(Hebr. פֶּקַד), which mixes the metaphor based on the light, would be admissible in Hebrew only if נֹגַהּ מִמָּרוֹם were a title coined to denote a definite person. Salkinson has perceived this, and therefore speaks only of " the rise of the dayspring from on high." Still, daylight does not arise from on high. As Bleek has already remarked, the evangelist starts from the assumption that ἀνατολή, in accordance with LXX Jer. 23⁵, Zech. 3⁸ 6¹², is a name for the Messiah. The version of the LXX obviously comes very near to identifying the Messianic advent with the appearance of light, when they render יְהוָה צֶמַח יִהְיֶה, Isa. 4², by ἐπιλάμψει ὁ θεός.

For Luke, therefore, ἀνατολὴ ἐξ ὕψους is simply " God's Messiah," מְשִׁיחָא דַיְיָ, with which the Targum renders צֶמַח יְהוָה, Isa. 4³. As the Hebrew צֶמַח excludes the allusion to the light, which follows in v.⁷⁹, it is clear that in Luke, chap. 1, an original in Greek lies before us.

11. USE OF THE PASSIVE VOICE.

Sometimes the passive voice of the verb is preferred, on the ground that, if an active voice were used, it would be necessary to name God as the subject. Thus we have : παρακληθήσονται, Matt. 5⁵; ἐλεηθήσονται, 5⁷; κληθήσονται, 5⁹; κριθῆτε, 7¹ (Luke 6³⁷); 7² κριτήσεσθε, μετρηθήσεται (Mark 4²⁴, Luke 6³⁸ ἀντιμετρηθήσεται); δοθήσεται, 7⁷ (Luke 11⁹ 6³⁸); 7⁷·⁸ ἀνοιγήσεται (Luke 11⁹ᶠ· ἀνοιχθήσεται); 12³¹ᶠ· (Luke 12¹⁰) ἀφεθήσεται; 21⁴³ (cf. Mark 4²⁵, Luke 8¹⁸) ἀρθήσεται, δοθήσεται; Luke 14¹⁴ ἀνταποδοθήσεται; Matt. 23¹² (Luke 14¹¹ 18¹⁴) ταπεινωθήσεται, ὑψωθήσεται; see also Mark 4²⁴, Luke 6³⁷.

In these cases, then, the passive, as a rule, is retraceable to an active whose subject is not specified, as happens in Luke 6³⁸ (δώσουσιν). In the same way in the translation of Dan. 4²⁸ᶠ· Kautzsch has rendered the active clauses : לָךְ אָמְרִין מִן אֲנָשָׁא לָךְ טָרְדִין, and וְיַטְעֲמֻן לָךְ עִשְׂבָּא, in which the subject

would have been God, by the use of the passive : " it is made
known to thee " ; " from among men thou shalt be cast forth " ;
" herbage will be given thee for food." The LXX also has
here at least σοὶ λέγεται, whereas Theodotion renders word
for word throughout.

Some instances of this construction from rabbinic litera-
ture may be given : כָּל הַמְרַחֵם עַל הַבְּרִיוֹת מְרַחֲמִין עָלָיו מִן הַשָּׁמַיִם,
" whosoever pities men, for him there is compassion from
heaven,"[1] b. Sabb. 151ᵇ (Gamaliel III. c. 220). כָּל הַמַּעֲבִיר עַל
מִדּוֹתָיו מַעֲבִירִין לוֹ עַל כָּל פְּשָׁעָיו, " whosoever is forbearing, for him
they overlook all his offences," b. R. h. S. 17ᵃ ; b. Yoma 23ᵃ
(Raba, c. 340). הֲוֵי אֶת חֲבֵרוֹ לְכַף זְכוּת דָּנִין אוֹתוֹ לִזְכוּת, " he who
judges his neighbour charitably, is judged charitably," b. Sabb.
127ᵇ (Baraitha). כָּל הַמְחַלֵּל שֵׁם שָׁמַיִם בַּסֵּתֶר נִפְרָעִין מִמֶּנּוּ בַּגָּלוּי,
" whosover secretly profanes the name of God, him do men
punish openly," Ab. iv. 4 (Yokhanan ben Baroka, c. 130).
בָּא לְטַמֵּא פּוֹתְחִין לוֹ בָּא לְטַהֵר מְסַיְעִים אוֹתוֹ, " if one goes to con-
taminate himself, a way is open to him ; if one goes to cleanse
himself, he is helped," b. Sabb. 104ᵃ (Simeon ben Lakish,
c. 260). בַּמִּדָּה שֶׁאָדָם מוֹדֵד בָּהּ מוֹדְדִין לוֹ, " with the measure
wherewith one measures, therewith is it measured in return,"
Sota i. 7 (anonym.). הַלָּמֵד עַל מְנָת לְלַמֵּד מַסְפִּיקִין בְּיָדוֹ לִלְמוֹד וּלְלַמֵּד,
" he who learns in order to teach, to him is given the power
to learn and to teach," Ab. iv. 5 (Ishmael ben Yokhanan,
c. 160). A passive construction is found in Akiba's saying :
חֲבִיבִין יִשְׂרָאֵל שֶׁנִּקְרְאוּ בָּנִים לַמָּקוֹם, " highly favoured are the Israelites
because they are called the sons of God."

Part of such sentences, as with those of Jesus, may depend
on popular ways of speaking, which originally referred solely
to relations between man and his fellows, e.g. Hillel's dictum
[on seeing a skull floating in the water]: עַל דַּאֲטֵיפְתְּ אֲטִיפוּךְ,
" because thou didst immerse others, men have immersed
thee," Ab. ii. 6 ; and Akiba's admonition : עֲבֵד דְּיַעֲבְדוּן סְפוֹר דְּיִסְפְּדוּן

---

[1] Cf. Tos. Shebu. iii. 1 : אֵין מִן הַשָּׁמַיִם מוֹחֲלִין לָהֶן, "one forgives them not
from heaven."

קְבוֹר דְּיִקְבְּרוּן לָךְ דִילַוּן, "do thou, that others may do; weep, that they may weep; bury others, that men may bury thee; accompany others, that they may accompany thee!" j. Keth. 31ᵇ;[1] or the statement of Bannaa (c. 200): אָם יָרְתִּק יִפְתְּחוּ לוֹ, "if one knocks, they shall open to him."[2] But this explanation does not apply generally, and we cannot avoid the conclusion that hesitation to use the divine name has had an influence on the style. Through a similar tendency in Egypt, in order not to have to express the title, far less the name of the king, there was a predilection for phrases like "one has ordered," "one is now residing (at Thebes)," for "the king has ordered, the king is now residing."[3]

12. AMEN.

It has already been frequently pointed out that the mode in which Jesus uses ἀμήν is unfamiliar to the entire range of Jewish literature. Even Sota ii. 5, cf. Jerus. I and II, Numb. 5²², cannot really be forced into comparison. In that passage the repeated Amen pronounced by the woman suspected of adultery is explained as a protestation of her innocence, as if she were to say: "Amen [= I protest] that I have not polluted myself! Amen that I will not pollute myself!" But a literary explanation of this sort must not be made an index to the real colloquial usage. In the latter, אָמֵן never is a corroboration of one's own word, but always of the word, prayer, blessing, oath, or imprecation of some other person. A dictum ascribed to various Palestinian Amoraim says:[4] "Amen is confirmation, Amen is protestation, Amen is assent." From the accompanying comments it may be seen that what is meant is confirmation of the word of

---

[1] Cf. Bacher, Ag. d. Tann. i. 331.
[2] Vay. R. 21 ; cf. Bacher, ibid. ii. 540 f.
[3] See A. Erman, Ägypten, 92, Eng. trans. 58.
[4] j. Sot. 18ᵇ ; b. Shebu. 36ᵃ ; Midr. Ps. 89⁴ ; cf. Bacher, Agada d. pal. Am. i. 112 f.

another, affirmation to the oath prescribed by another, submission of oneself to the declaration of another. He who says "Amen" thereby asserts that the statement of the other is binding also for the speaker. On the other hand, אָמֵן is not an assertion of assured conviction that what has been said by the other will be accomplished,[1] not even in the instance Tob. 8[8], where Sarah, by pronouncing "Amen," takes for her own the prayer of her husband, which, indeed, had been made in her name as well as his.

If Amen be thus synonymous with a corroborative "yes," it becomes clear how ναί and ἀμήν are treated as identical 2 Cor. 1[20], and are coupled together Rev. 1[7]; and how, even in the words of Jesus, ναί appears several times in passages where ἀμήν might have been expected, as Matt. 11[9] (Luke 7[26]), Luke 11[51] (Matt. 23[36] ἀμήν), Luke 12[5]. ἀμήν is replaced by ἀληθῶς, Luke 9[27] (Matt. 16[28], Mark 9[1] ἀμήν), Luke 12[44] (Matt. 24[47] ἀμήν), Luke 21[3] (Mark 12[43] ἀμήν); by ἐπ' ἀληθείας, Luke 4[25], cf. v.[24]; and by πλήν, Luke 22[21] (Matt. 26[21], Mark 14[18] ἀμήν). Luke is here the one who uses ἀμήν most sparingly, namely, 6 times; whereas in Matthew it appears 30 times, and in Mark 13 times. Just as in the phrases "sovereignty of heaven," "Father in heaven," so here also Luke has avoided as much as possible what would be unfamiliar to his readers.

The double ἀμήν, occurring 25 times in John, cannot be used as evidence of the terms used by Jesus. Nor can it be accounted for, as by Delitzsch,[2] through the אָמֵינָא, "I say," of the Babylonians,—a term quite unfamiliar in Pales-

---

[1] Otherwise represented in *Cremer*, Bibl. theol. Wörterbuch,[8] 141, who further makes the mistake that Amen as an ending for prayers in the synagogue is unusual. But the following prayers all end with Amen : קַדִּישׁ (Seder Rab Amram, i. 13[b]), יְהִי רָצוֹן (ibid. 24[a], 33[a]), מִי שֶׁעָשָׂה (33[b]), לְרָצוֹן יְהִי (48[a]), אֲסוּתָא תִּשְׁלַח (52[b]), תַּעֲנוּ (ii. 21[b]), פִּרְקָן פּוּם (Machzor Vitry, 172), שֶׁבֵּרַךְ מִי (ibid. 173), besides the priestly benediction, on which see b. Ber. 55[b].

[2] First expressed by *F. Delitzsch*, Zeitschr. f. luth. Theol. 1856, 422 ff., and often repeated since in opposition to the theory of Delitzsch, that Jesus spoke Hebrew.

tine.[1] It is evident, however, from the Johannine usage that ἀμήν introducing a statement was regarded as an interjection, and as such it is capable of repetition. Other instances of repetition may be compared: אָמֵן אָמֵן, Num. 5²², Neh. 8⁶; ναὶ ναί, Matt. 5³⁷; κύριε κύριε, Luke 6⁴⁶; Μάρθα Μάρθα, Luke 10⁴¹; Σίμων Σίμων, Luke 22³¹; ῥαββὶ ῥαββί, Matt. 23⁷ D; פַּרְמָא פַּרְמָא, "Vineyard!" Koh. R. v. 14; סָבָא סָבָא, "old man!" j. Sabb. 11ᵃ; בַּר יוּדִי בַּר יוּדִי, "son of a Jew!" j. Ber. 5ᵃ; גְּלִיל גְּלִיל, "Galilee!" j. Sabb. 15ᵇ; רַבִּי רַבִּי, "teacher!" b. Makk. 24ᵃ.

With Jesus, then, there is this peculiarity, that the Hebr. אָמֵן, which in His time was usual only in response to benedictions or oaths, was employed by Him in the Aramaic language as a corroboration of any statement [2] of His prefaced by this word; and this despite the fact that other terms, e.g. בְּקִשְׁטָא[3] or קְשִׁיטָא מִן, "verily," were available for the same purpose. This seemed so strange, that Matthew and Mark, as a rule, left the foreign word untranslated. The strangeness of the expression is not felt by Germans, merely because Luther's inexact rendering by "wahrlich" (verily) has effaced its peculiarity.

Clearly an enforcement of what He said by a mere appeal to its truthfulness was not felt to be sufficient by Jesus. With that end in view, no other resource remained open for Him than an averment with the use of an oath, after the manner, say, in which Yokhanan ben Zakkai (c. 80 A.D.) confirmed a principle of his teaching before his pupils with חַיֵּיכֶם, "by your life." [4] But an oath had been

---

[1] To one approaching this question from a study of the Babylonian Talmud, this solution seems very natural; but to one proceeding from the Palestinian literature, such an idea would never have suggested itself. See Gramm. d. jüd.-pal. Aram. 193.

[2] H. W. Hogg, "Amen," Notes on the significance, etc., Jew. Quart. Rev. ix. (1896) 1–23, unsuccessfully tries to prove that in the use of ἀμήν by Jesus there is always a retrospect to what has preceded with a view to its confirmation.

[3] See Onk. Gen. 42²¹ בְּקִשְׁטָא for the Hebr. אֲבָל.

[4] Pes. d. Rab Kah. 40ᵇ; cf. for this specially popular mode of protestation, Gramm. d. jüd.-pal. Aram. 193.

pronounced by Jesus, Matt. 5[37], as displeasing to God ; He had therefore to seek for some other mode of emphasis, and found it in the solemn " Amen." This is not an oath, yet more potent than a simple " verily," because it gives the hearer to understand that Jesus confirms His own statement in the same way as if it were an oath or a blessing. Thus did He fulfil His own injunction to make the simple " yea, yea " take the place of an oath. But as Jesus, in forbidding the oath, had in view the guarding against a misuse of the divine name,[1] so here, too, one may speak of a conscious avoidance of the name of God.

The nearest cognate construction in Jewish literature appears in the Babylonian הֵימָנוּתָא, " in truth." Juda ben Ilai (c. 150), b. Ned. 49[b], says to a woman : " Truth into the hand of this woman (הֵימָנוּתָא בִּידָא דְהָדָא אִתְּתָא), if I shall have any enjoyment !" Instead of this, the same story in j. Sabb. 11[a] has the Palestinian imprecation : " May the spirit of this woman breathe its last (תִּפַּח רוּחַהּ דְהָדָא אִתְּתָא)!" Of this הֵימָנוּתָא we are told, b. Sabb. 10[b], that it is permissible to utter it in a place which is not ceremonially clean, because the term does not contain the name of God. It is also used as a protestation by Iddi, b. Sanh. 38[b], where, however, the הימנותא ביך of the Venice ed. 1520 is represented in the Munich MS. by הֵימָנוּתָא בִּידָךְ, " (my) truth into thy hand ! "

13. THE DWELLING (SHECHINAH), THE GLORY, THE WORD.

In the Synoptic Gospels we find no representatives of these expressions used in the Targum of Onkelos : שְׁכִינְתָּא דַיְיָ, " the dwelling of Jhvh "; יְקָרָא דַיְיָ, " the glory of Jhvh "; מֵימְרָא דַיְיָ, " the word of Jhvh " (as to which it may be remarked that מֵימַר is different from פִּתְגָם, the latter being the word in Onkelos for the Hebr. דָּבָר). Besides these, more

---

[1] For the Jewish view of the commandment of Ex. 20[7] see my treatise, Der Gottesname Adonaj, 51 f., 60 ff., 66 ff.

recent Targums offer דְּבֵרָא דַיְיָ (דִּבּוּרָא), "the word of Jhvh," which is properly the Aramaicised *Hebrew* equivalent of מֵימְרָא דַיְיָ, and found its way into these Targums from rabbinic Hebrew. All these ideas which do not denote concrete hypostases of the Deity, but abstractions, originally served the single purpose of guarding, during the reading of Scripture in the synagogues, against sensible representations of God, such as the Bible text might have aroused among the common people. They were products of the reflection of the scribes, and we do not know in regard to them whether they really were general characteristics of the style of Targum exposition in the Palestinian synagogues, having nothing directly to do with the philosophic speculation of Philo, apart from the common motive which inspired both movements. Apart from the biblical text, which they were intended to preserve from misconception, there was no great occasion for their use. Besides, the spoken language was rich in cautious circumlocutions for God. It is thus quite natural that in ordinary life their use should be comparatively limited. But in use they actually were, subject only to the usual evasion of the divine name outside of public worship; and, as a rule, the form used was Hebrew: (הַדִּבּוּר) הַדִּבֵּר, הַכָּבוֹד, הַשְּׁכִינָה.[2] Aramaic examples, apart from the Targums, are rare; still see מֵימְרָא דִשְׁמַיָא, "the word of heaven," in the prayer beginning תִּשְׁתַּלַּח אָסוּתָא, Seder Rab Amram, i. 52ᵇ; cf. Targ. Eccl.

---

[1] דְּבַר occurs Jer. 5¹⁵ in the biblical text, and *Giesebrecht* (Comm.) finds the reason for the punctuation there unintelligible. Though neither Gesenius-Buhl nor Siegfried-Stade adduce it as a noun in the Lexicons, it is a word certainly verifiable in Jewish diction, from which Levy curiously has made רְבִיר. See, *e.g.*, Hebr. הדיבר, Vay. R. 1, ed. Constant. 1512; j. Sabb. 10ᶜ, ed. Venice, 1524; Aram. דִּי בֵּירָא, Targ. Ez. 1²⁴·²⁵, ed. Venice, 1517, 1525 (ed. Buxtorf דִּיבּוּרָא); דִּיבְּרָא, Targ. Cant. 1¹¹, MS. Lond. Or. 2375; דיבירא, j. Taan. 65ᵈ. *Ginsburger*, Die Anthropomorphismen in den Targumim (1896), 9, is surprised that in the Paris MS. of the Fragmentary Targum he should find רברא. It is, however, just the ancient דְּבְרָא, subsequently extruded as a rule by דִּבּוּרָא.

[2] *Holtzmann's* statements, Lehrb. d. neut. Theol. i. 57 f., on these topics are quite erroneous. In contrast to the Memar,—the special intermediary proper,— Shechinah, according to H., is an impersonal representation of God, which in the Talmud, has taken the place of the Memar.

4⁴ 11³; and מֵימְרָא דִלְעֵיל, "the word that is above," Jerus. I
Lev. 24¹². Here too, of course, one is far removed from the
idea of divine hypostases. The name used is הַדִּבֵּר and מֵימְרָא,
but the reality meant is "God." Jesus may have been
acquainted with these Targumic terms; but no necessity for
using them presented itself.

In the New Testament we have suggestions of the phrase
of the Targums: יְקָרָא דַיְיָ, "the glory of God," in Rom. 9⁴, where
ἡ δόξα is reckoned among the prerogatives peculiar to Israel,
Heb. 1³ ἀπαύγασμα τῆς δόξης, 9⁵ χερουβεῖν δόξης, John 12⁴¹,
where it is said of Isaiah : εἶδεν τὴν δόξαν αὐτοῦ (Χριστοῦ),
while the Targum reproduces Isa. 6⁵ by " mine eyes saw the
glory of the dwelling (Shechinah) of the King of the ages
(יְקָר שְׁכִינַת מֶלֶךְ עַלְמַיָא), Jhvh Sebaoth"; and in 2 Pet. 1¹⁷,
according to which the voice at the Transfiguration of Jesus
proceeded ὑπὸ τῆς μεγαλοπρεποῦς δόξης. In the last-named
passage, however, it should be remarked that a Targum would
preferably have named the Memar of God. מֵימַר, as well as
יְקָר and שְׁכִינָה, appear to be represented in John 1¹⁴ καὶ ὁ λόγος
σὰρξ ἐγένετο καὶ ἐσκήνωσεν ἐν ἡμῖν καὶ ἐθεασάμεθα τὴν δόξαν
αὐτοῦ δόξαν ὡς μονογενοῦς παρὰ πατρός. ὁ λόγος is מֵימְרָא;
ἐσκήνωσεν represents שְׁכִינְתָא; δόξα stands for יְקָרָא. All the
three entities became incarnate in Jesus; and in this, at
least, a use is made of these ideas which is at variance
with their primary application.

14. THE PLACE.

Wholly absent from the New Testament is the Jewish
designation of God as הַמָּקוֹם, "the Place." This term G.
Buchanan Gray¹ mistakenly tries to find as early as Sirach
41¹⁹, Ryle and James² as early as Ps. Sol. 16⁹. According
to the Mishna Taan. iii. 8, Simeon ben Shetakh (c. 80 B.C.)

---

¹ Jew. Quart. Rev. ix. 567 ff.
² In their edition of the Psalter of Solomon.

had already used it, but its evidence in reference to the linguistic form of sayings from so remote a period is of little value. It is certain only that in the Mishna, by 200 A.D., the designation of God by הַמָּקוֹם is quite current. It is the most colourless appellation for God which the Mishna contains.

In הַמָּקוֹם it appears that men were not content to name instead of God, His dwelling-place heaven; but as this itself had become a divine name, they desired when possible only to allude obscurely to it, so that only the place (*i.e.* of God) was mentioned, when the intention was to name "Heaven," meaning "God." In the choice of the term the efficient cause was not the philosophic idea that God is the locus of the world,—though this had been expressed as early as by Ammi (*c.* 280 A.D.),[1]—but the language used in the Old Testament where the "place" of God is frequently spoken of while heaven is meant;[2] see Hos. 5¹⁵ מְקוֹמִי, "My place"; Targ. מְדוֹר קֻדְשִׁי דִבְשְׁמַיָּא, "My holy dwelling in heaven"; Isa. 26²¹ מְקוֹמוֹ, "His place"; Targ. אֲתַר שְׁכִינְתֵּיה, "the place of His dwelling." The casual expression, מְקוֹם שֵׁם יְהֹוָה צְבָאוֹת, "the place of the name of Jhvh of hosts," by which the temple was originally meant, may also have played its part in creating the usage. In itself מְקוֹם יְיָ ought to mean "the place of God"; but just as הַשְּׁכִינָה, "the dwelling-place," הַדִּבֵּר, "the Word," were said in place of דִּבֵּר יְיָ, שְׁכִינַת יְיָ, so here also the name of God is omitted and replaced by the article. הַמָּקוֹם is "*the* place" κατ᾽ ἐξοχήν, that is, of God.

No Aramaic equivalent for הַמָּקוֹם ever presents itself. The term thus belonged entirely to the Hebrew language of the legal schools, and never became popular. This being so, it is not to be expected that it should be used by Jesus, even supposing it should have already been used in the legal schools of His time.

[1] Ber. R. 68; cf. *Bacher*, Agada d. pal. Am. ii. 163 f.
[2] Already maintained by *A. Geiger*, Jüd. Zeitschr. ii. 228. *Landau*, Die dem Raume entnommenen Synonyma für Gott. 41 ff., errs in supposing Parsee influences as contributory.

15. CONCLUDING STATEMENT.

Religious custom among the Jews, in respect to the use and avoidance of the name of God, has been found, according to what has been said under VI.–VIII., to constitute the standard followed by Jesus; but, of course, in such a manner that, in conforming to it, He preserved a peculiar position of His own by His marked preference for the appellation of God as Father.

It would certainly be a mistake to regard all the other evasive locutions for God which have the sanction of Jesus as mere accommodation on His part to prevalent custom. Superstitious ideas, foreign to the true Revealed Religion, in regard to the character of the divine name, may have contributed to the formation of the current custom. When it was supposed that the enunciation of God's name would bring down into this world the divine Person magically associated[1] with that name, there were strong objections against taking it upon one's lips. But the decisive element in the circumstances was, of course, the commandment of the Decalogue (Ex. 20^7): "Thou shalt not needlessly pronounce the name of Jhvh thy God";[2] and beneath that there lay a genuine religious reverence, inspired by the thought of the Judge of the worlds, enthroned in heaven. This reverence Jesus did not choose to set aside, Matt. 10^{28} (Luke 12^5); He even intensified it. The Heavenly Father, whom He declared, remained always the Omnipotent Lord. The archaic position of authority ascribed in the family to the father, who, above all things has an unlimited paternal control, was firmly maintained. There is nothing in the teaching of Jesus to favour the idea of a mystical absorption in the Deity, such as obliterates the distinctions between Creator and creature.

---

[1] See on this point *F. C. Conybeare*, Jew. Quart. Rev. ix. 581 ff.

[2] On the Jewish interpretation of this commandment see my treatise, "Der Gottesname Adonaj," 51 f., 60 ff., 66 ff.

Still, matters must not be represented as if the deeper insight gained by Israel after the exile in Babylon into the transcendent majesty of God, were nothing but a relapse in comparison with the knowledge of God in the older prophecy, so that Jesus was under the necessity of reverting to the earlier prophetic standpoint. Directly opposed to such a view is the peculiar significance attached by Jesus to the Book of Daniel as well as to the writing of the second Isaiah, although Daniel obviously bears the impress of a new epoch in the process of Revelation, widely separated from the earlier prophecy.[1]

IX. THE SON OF MAN.

1. THE LINGUISTIC FORM OF THE EXPRESSION.

To understand the designation which Jesus chose to apply to Himself: ὁ υἱὸς τοῦ ἀνθρώπου, it is important to observe the way in which the corresponding terms in Hebr. בֶּן אָדָם, and Aramaic בַּר אֱנָשׁ are used.

In *biblical Hebrew*, אָדָם (as also אֱנוֹשׁ) is nearly always used as a collective expression, and can therefore stand beside the collectives בְּהֵמָה, "quadrupeds," and בָּקָר, "cattle,"[2] often having to be rendered in German by the plural "men." If it be necessary to specify a plurality of individual men, Hebrew can only say בְּנֵי אָדָם or בְּנֵי הָאָדָם, for which see Gen. 11[5], Deut. 32[8] (with גּוֹיִם), 2 Sam. 7[14] (with אֲנָשִׁים), Mic. 5[6], Isa. 52[14] (with אִישׁ). In later times, from the evidence of the Psalms and of Ecclesiastes,[3] this appears to have become a common term for "mankind," not belonging exclusively to poetry. For the single human being, it is generally אִישׁ or אִשָּׁה that is used.

---

[1] The writings of the pre-exilic prophets are, on the other hand, of slight importance for Jesus.

[2] See Ex. 9[19], Num. 31[23. 47].   [3] See also Dan. 10[16], Sir. 40[1].

On the other hand, the singular form בֶּן אָדָם, apart from its frequent use as a nominative of address in Ezekiel,[1] was always rare.[2] It is found only in poetic language where parallelism supplies a motive for its use, see Num. 23[10] (with אִישׁ); Isa. 51[12] (with אֱנוֹשׁ), 56[2] the same; Jer. 49[18. 33] 50[40] 51[43] (all with אִישׁ); Ps. 8[5] (with אֱנוֹשׁ), 80[18] (with אִישׁ), 146[3] (with נְדִיבִים); Job 16[21] (with גֶּבֶר), 25[6] (with אֱנוֹשׁ), 35[8] (with אִישׁ); cf. בֶּן אֱנוֹשׁ, Ps. 144[3] (with אָדָם). In the Apocrypha בֶּן אָדָם is found only in allusion to Old Testament phrases. In Judith 8[16] υἱὸς ἀνθρώπου occurs in a statement which depends upon Num. 23[19]. An echo of the same scriptural passage will be found in Sirach 17[30], if υἱὸς ἀνθρώπου is there a literal rendering of the original.[3] A similar echo is unmistakable in the solitary instance of υἱὸς ἀνθρώπου in the Testaments of the XII Patriarchs (Joseph 2).

This generic scope of אָדָם has, as its natural corollary, the fact that בֶּן אָדָם denotes, not "the son of a certain man," but the member of the genus man; cf. אַחַד הָאָדָם, "one of the genus man," i.e. "an ordinary man," Judg. 16[7].

The *biblical Aramaic* does not differ from the usage in Hebrew. The simple אֱנָשׁ, not בַּר אֱנָשׁ, is the word for "man." In the next place, in Aramaic אֱנָשׁ is also the term for the generic conception "mankind," and can stand where we should say "men." Hence בְּנֵי אֱנָשָׁא, "the sons of man," is equivalent to the simple אֱנָשָׁא; cf. מִן אֱנָשָׁא טְרִיד, Dan. 4[30], with מִן בְּנֵי אֱנָשָׁא טְרִיד, 5[21].[4] Both mean "he was driven out from among mankind." When there comes with the clouds of heaven one כְּבַר אֱנָשׁ, Dan. 7[13], he is described as resembling one of the human species, or as one who had in himself the nature of a human being; just as in 3[25] the fourth in the

---

[1] Daniel also is once named in this way (8[17]).

[2] It is a defect in *Lietzmann's* researches on "Der Menschensohn" (1896) 30 ff., that he has not investigated separately the use of singular and plural. The representation given of the Old Testament usage in *H. Appel*, Die Selbstbezeichnung Jesu: Der Sohn des Menschen (1896), 28–48, is quite erroneous.

[3] The Syriac version is considerably different.

[4] Similarly דְּמוּת בְּנֵי אָדָם, Dan. 10[16], and כְּמַרְאֵה אָדָם, 10[18], are identical.

fiery furnace is described דָּמֵה לְבַר אֱלָהִין, as one who resembles the gods. In substance, though not in verbal form, a unit of the species is also meant, when in 7⁴ it is said of a beast that it was made to stand upon two feet, כֶּאֱנָשׁ, "as a man." An individual man is גְּבַר (2²⁵).

In the *Hebrew of the Mishna*, which, being Aramaic in the guise of Hebrew, affords important testimony for our present purpose, הָאָדָם is "the human being," Ab. ii. 1, 11, iii. 10, 14; אָדָם אֶחָד is "a man," Ab. vi. 9. "Mankind" is not infrequently בְּרִיּוֹת, "creatures," Ab. i. 12, ii. 11, but also בְּנֵי אָדָם. This last expression is used to denote ordinary "men," "the people," Ber. i. 3; Taan. i. 7, and b. Mo. k. 19ᵃ (Simeon ben Yokhai, c. 130). In Ned. viii. 5, 6, דֶּרֶךְ בְּנֵי אָדָם means "the common custom"; and לְשׁוֹן בְּנֵי אָדָם is "the common parlance," Siphre, ed. Friedm. 33ᵃ (Ishmael, c. 110). The singular בֶּן אָדָם is altogether uncommon.

The *Targum of Onkelos* generally conforms to the Hebrew text. In Gen. 11⁵, Deut. 32⁸ it has בְּנֵי אֲנָשָׁא for אָדָם (הָ) בְּנֵי; Gen. 6¹, בְּנֵי אֲנָשָׁא for the simple הָאָדָם; the same again, Num. 23¹⁹, both for אִישׁ and for בֶּן אָדָם, and in Deut. 32²⁶ for אֲנוֹשׁ. The singular number בַּר אֱנָשׁ, which is twice used in Targ. Jerus. I Num. 23¹⁹ appears to be intentionally avoided by Onkelos. Moreover, "a human being" is always אֱנָשׁ, and not בַּר אֱנָשׁ. In this respect Onkelos and the Mishna agree.

In the *Samaritan Pentateuch* אנש is also the word for "a human being." Only in Num. 23¹⁹, conformably with the Hebrew, do we find בר אנש. The plural forms appear בני אנשא, Gen. 11⁵; ברי אדם, Deut. 32⁸. Marka also, where he does not use אדם, has אנש; see *Heidenheim*, Bibl. Sam. iii. 2ᵇ, 59ᵃ, 130ᵃ, 131ᵇ; *Munk*, Des Sam. Marqah Erzählung über d. Tod Mose's, 44, 48. The form ברנשיתה in Munk, p. 48, is unusual, and, of course, should be corrected into ברנשיה.

The *Targum to the Prophets*, which is of minor consequence

for Aramaic usage, has in Mic. 5⁶ בַּר אֱנָשׁ, replacing בְּנֵי אָדָם. Elsewhere בַּר אֱנָשׁ is found in agreement with the Hebrew text, Isa. 51¹² 56², Jer. 49¹⁸. ³³ 50⁴⁰ 51⁴³.¹ When the Targumist uses בַּר אָדָם to represent בֶּן אָדָם in Ezekiel, it is clear that he takes the meaning to be "son of Adam." The plural בְּנֵי אֱנָשָׁא is often used.—Nor do the Aramaic *Inscriptions* attest a single instance of בַּר אֱנָשׁ for Palestine. The Palmyra customs tariff, of date 137 A.D., puts אניש מדעם for "any person whatever." אנוש appears for "any one" in Nabatæan inscriptions, CIS II. i. 197, 209 f., 212, 214, 220, 223 f.; and in the inscription from Tema, ibid. 113ᵃ, אניש stands for "men."

The *Jewish-Galilean*, along with the *Christian-Palestinian*, are the earliest dialects to contain בַּר אֱנָשׁ in the sense of "a human being," although in both these types of language the simple אֱנָשׁ remains current for "any one": for the former dialect see, *e.g.*, j. Ber. 13⁴, j. Sanh. 25ᵃ, Ber. R. 69; for the latter see *Lietzmann*, Der Menschensohn, 32. בַּר אֱנָשׁ for "a human being" then made its way also into the Jerusalem Targums on the Pentateuch, Jerus. I Num. 9¹⁸ 23¹⁹. Even the Aramaic recension of the Book of Tobit² has twice (8¹⁸ 12¹) put בַּר נָשׁ for "any one," while elsewhere it uses אֱנָשׁ (3⁸ 4¹⁹), בְּנֵי אֱנָשָׁא (8⁴), plur. const. אֱנָשֵׁי (1¹⁹ 12¹).

As a result of the general situation here reviewed, it must be concluded that the Jewish Palestinian Aramaic of the earlier period possessed the term אֱנָשׁ for "a human being"; while, to indicate a number of human beings, it employed occasionally בְּנֵי אֱנָשָׁא. The singular number בַּר אֱנָשׁ was not in use; its appearance being due to imitation of the Hebrew text, where בֶּן אָדָם is confined to poetry, and, moreover, uncommon in it. The case in Dan. 7¹³, where the person coming from heaven is described as כְּבַר אֱנָשׁ, "one like unto a son of man," is just as uncongenial to the style of prose as the designation of God in the same verse as עַתִּיק יוֹמַיָּא, "the

---

¹ *Lietzmann*, Der Menschensohn, 31, appears to have overlooked this.
² See on this point Gramm. d. jüd.-pal. Aram. 27 ff.

advanced in days," " the aged,"[1] the ordinary prose for " old "
being, of course, סָבָא. Further, according to the theory proposed on p. 13, the original of Dan. 7 was Hebrew, in support
of which we may refer to the occurrence of עֶלְיוֹן peculiar to this
chapter. If this theory be correct, then בַּר אֱנָשׁ in Dan. 7[13], as
in other cases, is simply the translation of the Hebr. בֶּן אָדָם.

It is in keeping with the peculiar nature felt to be inherent in בַּר אֱנָשׁ that, like the Hebr. בֶּן אָדָם, it never occurs
in the definite form. בַּר אֱנָשָׁא, just like בֶּן הָאָדָם, is quite
unheard of in the older Jewish Aramaic literature. " The
human being" is there called merely אֱנָשָׁא. If, however,
Judæans, Samaritans, and probably also Nabatæans and
Palmyrenians, had this expression in use, it may be supposed
that in this respect the Galileans in the time of Jesus formed
no exception; and that the use of בַּר אֱנָשָׁא, בַּר נָשָׁא in the
Jewish-Galilean and Christian-Palestinian literature, which at
a later time was probably common to all Aramaic-speaking
Palestinians, was an innovation introduced into Palestine
from the north-east along with many other influences affecting
the use of terms and the vocabulary.[2]

A final testimony for the terms used by Jesus is afforded
by His own words as reported in the Gospels. " Man," both
in the singular and in the plural, is frequently enough the
subject of remark. How is it that υἱὸς ἀνθρώπου never
occurs for " man," and οἱ υἱοὶ τῶν ἀνθρώπων only in Mark
3[28] ? Can the Hellenistic reporters—apart from the self-
appellation of Jesus—have designedly avoided it, although
Jesus had on all occasions said nothing but " son of man " for
" man " ? That cannot be considered likely.

Holtzmann[3] calls it a " discovery " that " son of man "

---

[1] The rendering " the Ancient of days " is inexact, and would require עַתִּיקָא
דְיוֹמַיָּא. From עַתִּיק יוֹמִין also, v.[9], it is apparent that the ending does not define
יוֹמִין, but the compound expression.

[2] Lietzmann omits all proof that the Galilean, with its use of בַּר אֱנָשׁ, must be
valid for the time of Jesus.

[3] Lehrb. d. neutestamentl. Theol. i. 256.

would be the only available term for "man" in the mother-
tongue of Jesus. Wellhausen affirms : [1] " the Aramæans have
no other term for that conception "; and Lietzmann, agreeing
with Eerdmans,[2] on this topic constructs the thesis : [3] " Jesus
never applied to Himself the title ' Son of man,' for this term
does not exist in Aramaic, and *for linguistic reasons is an impossible term.*" [4] Nevertheless it is a grievous error, which
careful observation of the biblical Aramaic alone would have
rendered impossible.

When the composite expression בַּר אֱנָשׁ, "son of man,"
had to be made definite, the determinative could attach only
to אֱנָשׁ, as to אָדָם in the Hebr. בֶּן אָדָם. Thus arises בַּר אֱנָשָׁא,
בֶּן הָאָדָם, which must not be rendered simply by " the human
being " (" der Mensch,"—as by de Lagarde, Wellhausen, Lietzmann), but only by " the son of man," if the essential character of the expression is not to be entirely obliterated.

If, again, " the son of the man " had to be expressed in
Aramaic, it would have been necessary to say בְּרֵהּ דֶּאֱנָשָׁא (literally, " his son, that of the man "). The Mishna Hebrew would
say בְּנוֹ שֶׁלְאָדָם. It is therefore in no way surprising that the
Christian-Palestinian version of the Gospels renders ὁ υἱὸς τοῦ
ἀνθρώπου by בְּרֵהּ דְּבַר נָשָׁא, or sometimes, to escape the incon-
venient repetition of בַּר, by בְּרֵהּ דְּגַבְרָא. The principle of
literal faithfulness in the translation led naturally to the
production of this expression, which the same dialect further
used for בֶּן אָדָם in Job 16²¹, as remarked by Nestle.[5] In a
dialect where בַּר נָשָׁא was the common word for " man," this
term would be no equivalent for the peculiar expression in
question. Certainly בְּרֵהּ דְּבַר נָשָׁא tended to the error, which
the German " der Sohn des Menschen " also suggests, that the
person so entitled was the *son* of some one. In this sense the

[1] Israelit. und jüdische Geschichte,³ 381.
[2] Theol. Tijdschr. 1894, 165 ff.   [3] Der Menschensohn (1896), 85.
[4] The italics of the last clause are due to me.
[5] See *A. S. Lewis*, A Palestinian Syriac Lectionary (1897), xxxi ; cf. p. 56,
ברה דבר נשא.

translator will also have understood the Greek ὁ υἱὸς τοῦ ἀνθρώπου.

But the Greek expression is itself merely the outcome of sore embarrassment. ὁ υἱὸς τοῦ ἀνθρώπου can indeed be regarded as the Greek singular for οἱ υἱοὶ τῶν ἀνθρώπων, which the LXX has coined for בְּנֵי אָדָם, and which occurs Mark 3²⁸ and Eph. 3⁵. But while the plural substantially corresponds to the Hebr. בְּנֵי אָדָם, the expression " the sons of men " of course signifying men in general, in the singular form an unnatural stress was laid upon both members of the phrase. No assistance could be got from ὁ υἱὸς ἀνθρώπου, for this would have meant merely " the son of a man." In Greek, then, ἄνθρωπος is neither a generic conception like אֱנָשׁ, אָדָם, nor is υἱός the term for an individual endowed with the nature implied in the generic term. The readiest substitute for בַּר אֱנָשָׁא would still have been ὁ ἄνθρωπος with no addition. But then, what disastrous misunderstandings would have been occasioned by the change in the Gospels of the uncommon expression of the original into an ordinary expression! In view of this, it was therefore preferred to convey the impression, suggested in Aramaic by בַּר אֱנָשָׁ when made definite, by the utmost possible definiteness in the composite expression. Thus was avoided at least the error of supposing that " the man " merely as such was meant, and there was acquired the possibility of using this expression as a self-appellation of Jesus. That the Hellenists from the beginning apprehended the term, not in a Semitic, but in a Greek sense, with the feeling that Jesus in some sense had pronounced Himself on the human side of His nature as " descended from men," is all too probable. To this point we refer later.

In these circumstances it can be seen why the Christian Hellenists avoided the term as much as possible, and did not adopt it into their religious phraseology. In Aramaic, indeed, בַּר אֱנָשָׁא was perfectly suitable as the special name of a definite personality; but its reproduction in Greek would be as defectively inaccurate as it would—though for different reasons—be in Syriac and Christian-Palestinian. In German, "des Menschen Sohn" is a correct rendering of ὁ υἱὸς τοῦ ἀνθρώπου, but the Aramaic בַּר אֱנָשָׁא is represented with some degree of success only by "der Menschensohn."

2. "SON OF MAN" WAS NOT A CURRENT JEWISH NAME FOR THE MESSIAH.

There is no need to begin by proving here that for the author of the Book of Daniel, "the one resembling a son of man" in chap. 7¹³ is a personification of the "people of the saints of the Most High" (v.²⁷, cf. v.²²), who are destined one day to receive an imperishable dominion as an award from God. The vision, in which the one like unto a son of man is seen, is a parallel to Dan. 2⁴⁴ᶠ·, where the establishment by God of an eternal sovereignty is the explanation of the stone[1] which shatters the great statue without any assistance from man. In contrast with the beasts emerging from the sea, types of preceding secular powers, the one like unto a son of man, type of the future possessor of universal dominion, comes "with the clouds of heaven" (עִם עֲנָנֵי שְׁמַיָּא). The expression is surprising because the judicial session of the "Advanced in days," in which He Himself appears, is held in the place where the animals have their being, i.e. upon the earth.[2] Besides, it would be more appropriate if the one like to a son of man were to come "*upon* the clouds of heaven."

[1] This stone is interpreted as referring to the sovereignty of the Messiah, Tanchuma, ed. Buber, Ber. 70ᵇ; Bemidb. R. 13. 2 Esdras connects with the stone its own peculiar representation of the mountain which "that man" brings with him; see 2 Esdr. 13⁶ᶠ· 12³⁶.

[2] No change of scene is suggested in 7⁹. The divine chariot furnished with wheels and a throne is that described by Ezekiel which was to serve God at His appearance upon earth. There is therefore no occasion for the view brought forward by *Holsten*, Zeitschr. f. Wiss. Theol. 1891, 62, and by *Appel*, Die Selbstbezeichnung Jesu : der Sohn des Menschen, 40 ff., that the scene of the judgment is conceived as being above the earth, and that the one like to a son of man comes thither from the earth.

16

A reading עֲנָנֵי שְׁמַיָּא עַל[1] appears to be presupposed by ἐπὶ τῶν νεφελῶν, LXX Dan. 7¹³; cf. Matt. 24³⁰ 26⁶⁴, Mark 13²⁶ D, Rev. 14¹⁴⁻¹⁶, Teaching of the Apostles 16⁸ (ἐπάνω), Justin, Apol. 1⁵¹ (ἐπάνω), Hegesippus in Euseb. Hist. Eccl. ii. 23. On the other hand, the reading of the Massoretic text (עִם) is represented in Theodotion, Mark 14⁶², Rev. 1⁷, 2 Esdr. 14³. The words ἐν νεφέλαις, Mark 13²⁶, ἐν νεφέλῃ, Luke 21²⁷, similarly imply accompaniment, and presuppose μετά = עִם. It belongs to God only to move upon the clouds; see Isa. 19¹, Ps. 104³. In the endeavour to minimise the divine manifestation in the one like to a son of man, a subsequent writer will have changed עַל into עִם. But even if one reads עִם, the fact remains that the destined possessor of the universal dominion comes, not from the earth, far less from the sea, but from heaven. He is a being standing in a near relation to God, well fitted to typify the people of the saints of God. It is noteworthy that nothing more is said of him than that he resembles man. He is distinguished from the four beasts, not because he alone possesses reason; the first beast, according to 7⁴, receives " a man's heart," the last has " the eyes of a man," and can speak (v.⁸). The emphasis rather lies on the fact that in contrast with the winged lion, the devouring bear, the four-headed leopard, the fourth beast with ten horns terrible exceedingly beyond its predecessors, he appears unarmed and inoffensive, incapable through any power of his own of making himself master of the world; he is only as a son of man. If ever he is to be master of the world, God must make him so.

From the first Christian century there are only two Jewish writings known which deal with Dan. 7¹³, the Similitudes of the Book of Enoch, and the Second Book of Esdras. The two agree in regarding the one like to a son of man as an individual person. And as they combine

[1] E. Nestle, Marginalien und Materialien, 1893, i. 40, remarked upon the importance of this reading.

Dan. 7 with Messianic prophecies from the Old Testament, they clearly show that they regard this individual as the Messiah. Special attention must be given to the name they use in this connection for Messiah.

The *Similitudes of Enoch* (chaps. 37–71), whose Jewish character need not be doubted,[1] though it cannot be proved that they originate from a pre-Christian period, introduce 46^1 a being, partaking of the nature of angels and of men, to whom reference is afterwards made as " that son of man," $46^{2. 4}$ 48^2 $62^{5. 9. 14}$ 63^{11}, while only " the son of man " is said in 46^3 $62^{7 2}$ $69^{26. 27. 29}$ 70^1 71^{17}. N. Schmidt,[3] however, says that little stress can be laid on the use or non-use of the Ethiopic demonstrative, so that throughout ὁ υἱὸς τοῦ ἀνθρώπου may be what is represented. Similarly no importance attaches to the fact that the Ethiopic version vacillates in its choice of a term for " son of man," sometimes even putting " son of a man," " son of a woman."[4] It is clear, at all events, that " son of man " is not taken for granted by the author as an already established title for the Messiah. But it is not to be denied that the author, though in this part of the Similitudes he avoids every other Messianic title, really imputes to " the son of man " a Messianic significance. This is seen most obviously in 46^3. The " son of man who has righteousness " is certainly not a periphrasis for " the righteous man," but is meant to recall 38^2 39^6, where the Messiah bears the name, " the chosen one who is righteous," or " the elect of righteousness." That again, on its part, must be considered an allusion to צֶמַח צַדִּיק, Jer. 23^5; צֶמַח

---

[1] A Christian author or interpolator should above all things have made it clear in some way that the " son of man " coming to the judgment was Jesus of Nazareth. But the " son of man " in this case appears never to have been upon earth, far less to have passed through the state of death.

[2] This passage is highly uncertain.

[3] See his essay, " Was בר נשא a Messianic title ? " Journal of Bibl. Lit. xv. (1896) 48.

[4] That these really refer to " son of man," see *R. H. Charles* on Enoch 46^2, and *N. Schmidt*, op. cit. 46 ff.

צְדָקָה, Jer. 33[15], for which the Targum has מְשִׁיחַ דִּצְדְקָה,
" Messiah of righteousness." [1]

Probably the author of the Similitudes, in using " son of
man," did not intend to introduce any new designation for
the Messiah. Still it is significant that he consistently
applies this name exclusively to the mysterious personality
who never was upon earth, and yet is not God. If the
original was Hebrew, we should here have בֶּן הָאָדָם (with the
article) as an exceptional instance in the earlier Jewish
literature ; and it would also represent a considerable development beyond the stage seen in the Book of Daniel, which
uses, 10[16. 18], the terms כְּמַרְאֵה אָדָם, כִּדְמוּת בְּנֵי אָדָם, meaning
" the one resembling man," to denote a definite personality.

In an interpolation in the Similitudes it is Enoch himself
who is the son of man, brought according to Dan. 7 before
the ancient of days. By this name he is addressed 60[10], and
in 71[14] the words are used to him : " thou art the son of man
who art born for righteousness," in which there is evident
at least an allusion to צֶמַח צְדָקָה, " the righteous Branch."

Turning now to the Second Book of *Esdras*, we find in
chap. 13 a different style of language. Here a wind causes
to rise up from the sea " as it were the likeness of a man "
(Syr. איך דמות דברנישא). He is then referred to in v.[3] as
" ille homo " (Syr. הו ברנישא),[2] in v.[5] as " homo, qui ascenderat
de mari " (Syr. ברנישא הו דסלק מן ימא), in v.[12] as " ipse homo "
(Syr. הו ברנישא), and in vv.[25. 51], cf. v.[33], as " vir ascendens de
corde maris " (Syr. גברא דסלק מן לבה דימא). If the original
was Hebrew, the Syriac נברא would represent הָאִישׁ; the Syriac
ברנישא, Lat. " homo," would, on the other hand, be הָאָדָם, and
correspondingly in v.[3] we should have כִּדְמוּת אָדָם, not כִּדְמוּת בֶּן
אָדָם, cf. Dan. 10[18]. The author's dependence upon Dan. 7
must be admitted, although he represents—doubtless not

---

[1] Cf. under XI. 1.
[2] The Latin version has ''convolabat ille homo cum nubibus,'' but the
beginning is lost.

unintentionally—the figure in human form as rising from the sea. But for בַּר אֱנָשׁ he has put אָדָם, the term proper to prose style, and from that, of course, a Messianic title could not well be formed.

A Messianic interpretation of Dan. 7¹³ appears to have been assumed by Akiba (c. 120 A.D.), when he spoke of the "thrones" of Dan. 7⁹ as prepared for God and for David, b. Sanh. 38ᵇ. This statement of Akiba then gave rise to the description of the Sepher Hechaloth,[1] which says that David, adorned with a crown in which are embedded the sun, the moon, and the twelve signs of the zodiac, takes his seat in heaven upon a throne which is erected for him in front of the throne of God. Joshua ben Levy (c. 250)[2] brought forward the alternative that, if Israel were worthy, then the Messiah would come, as in Dan. 7¹³, with the clouds of heaven; but if Israel were unworthy, he would come riding upon the ass, as said in Zech. 9⁹. Samuel ben Nachman (c. 270)[3] says that, according to Dan. 7¹³, the angels accompany the Messiah as far as their precincts allow, while God then conducts him to Himself, according to Jer. 30²¹. Other late testimonies are referred to in Dalman, "Der leidende und der sterbende Messias," 38 note.[4]

It is a mere suggestion of Dan. 7¹³ that appears in Targ. Jerus. II on Ex. 12⁴², which says that the Messiah will lead His people like Moses, בְּרֵישׁ עֲנָנָא, "on the summit of the cloud." The cloud is there conceived as accompanying the Messiah during His activity. On account of the "cloud" (עֲנָן) in Dan. 7¹³, it is said that the person named עֲנָנִי, who is the last in the Davidic line in 1 Chron. 3²⁴, will be the Messiah, Midr. Tanchuma, ed. Buber, Ber. 70ᵇ, and in the Targum on the passage. Probably we should also mention here the Messianic name בר נפלי, though it is otherwise

[1] Seder Rab Amram, i. 13ᵃ; *Jellinek*, Beth ha-Midrasch, v. 168, cf. vi. 150 f.
[2] b. Sanh. 98ᵃ; cf. *Bacher*, Ag. d. p. Am. i. 152.
[3] Midr. Psalms, 21⁷, cf. *Bacher*, Ag. d. p. Am. i. 548.
[4] The citation of Dan. 7¹³ in the Midrash on Ps. 2⁷ is probably spurious.

explained by the Babylonian Nachman b. Sanh. 96ᵇ, provided נבלי stands for νεφέλη, which is very doubtful.[1]

Along with these indications of a Messianic interpretation
of Dan. 7¹³, we find traces of a different exposition of the
passage in the anonymous saying, Midr. Tanchuma, ed.
Buber, Vay. 36ᵇ:[2] "What mean the 'thrones' (Dan. 7⁹)?
One day God will be seated, and the angels will give thrones
to the great ones of Israel that they too may sit, while God
sits among them as president of the court of justice, and
thus they judge the peoples of the world"; cf. Matt. 19²⁸
(Luke 22³⁰).

Again we have a divergence from Dan. 7¹³ in the statement of the Palestinian Amora, Abbahu,[3] who lived in
Cæsarea about 280 A.D. Intending to controvert the divinity
of Christ, he asserted, j. Taan. 65ᵇ, basing his words on
Num. 23¹⁹:[4] אִם יֹאמַר לְךָ אָדָם אֵל אֲנִי מְכַזֵּב הוּא בֶּן אָדָם אֲנִי סוֹפוֹ
לְהִתְחוֹת בּוֹ שֶׁאֲנִי עוֹלֶה לַשָּׁמַיִם הַהוּא אָמַר וְלֹא יְקִימֶנָּה, "if any one say
to thee, 'I am God,' he speaks falsely; 'I am the son of
man,' his end is to regret it; 'I ascend to heaven'—he who
has said so will not verify his word." Only thus can the
passage be translated.[5] בֶּן אָדָם is here equivalent to אֵל. It
has no article, because Num. 23¹⁹ has none. The "ascending
into heaven" depends, as it seems, upon Isa. 14¹³ᶠ·, where the

---

[1] On both names see "Der leidende und der sterbende Messias," 37 f.

[2] Cf. Shem. R. 5, the similar saying of Abin.

[3] As to Abbahu, see *Bacher*, Ag. d. p. Am. ii. 88–142.

[4] Allusion is made to this passage in a late addition to a saying of Eleazar
ha-Kappar, Yalk. Shim. (ed. Salonica, 1526) on Num. 23⁷; see *Dalman-Laible-
Streane*, Jesus Christ in the Talmud, Midrash, Zohar, and the Liturgy of the
Synagogue (1893), 10* Text, 33* Translation. As doubts have arisen on the
subject, it may here be remarked in passing that the translations there given,
pp. 21*–47*, were made by me, while *Laible's* contribution appears only in the
rendering of Streane.

[5] The dictum forms a *crux interpretum* only for those who find the obvious
sense disagreeable. It is correctly rendered by *Laible*, Jesus Christ im Talmud
(1891), 48, and by *Bacher*, op. cit. 118 ; incorrectly, by *Levy*, Neuhebr. Wörterbuch under אָדָם ; *Wünsche*, Der jerus. Talmud, 141 ; *M. Schwab*, Le Talmud
de Jérusalem, vi. 156. The explanation of *F. Cohn* given by *Lietzmann*, Der
Menschensohn, 50, is quite impracticable.

king of Babylon says: "I will ascend into heaven . . .; I will ascend above the cloudy heights, like to the Most High." Compare Mechilta, ed. Friedm. 39ᵇ: "Said Nebuchadnezzar: 'I will make me a little cloud and dwell therein.'"[1] As Abbahu can be proved to have come into contact with Christians, it is most natural to suppose that his statement was meant to refer to Jesus, and was not an admonition, practically useless in his time, against any other persons claiming to be God. The motive which leads him to make Num. 23¹⁹ the basis of his assertion, despite the change of what he must have known to be the natural sense, can only be that the association of אֵל and בֶּן אָדָם seemed to him fitted to produce an allusion to Jesus. In that case he will have been aware that Jesus had called Himself " Son of man " in some exclusive sense. Of course it does not follow from the statement that " son of man " had become a Jewish name for the Messiah. Moreover, no reference is made to Dan. 7¹³.

It may be noted that in the *Zohar*, the principal product of the Kabbala in the Middle Ages, vol. iii. 144ᵃ, a distinction is drawn on one occasion, with the help of a reference to כְּבַר אֱנָשׁ, Dan. 7¹³, and כְּמַרְאֵה אָדָם, Ezek. 1²⁶, between the " higher Adam " (אָדָם דִּלְעֵילָא) and the " lower Adam " (אָדָם דִּלְתַהְתָּא). This, however, has no relation either to the first man or to the Messiah. The " higher Adam " is, on the contrary, the highest form of the self-revelation of God; the " lower Adam " is a synthesis of all the inferior stages of revelation subsumed under the former. This may in some way, no longer demonstrable by us, be historically connected with the doctrine of the Ophites, which gave to the primordial light the name of Πρῶτος ῎Ανθρωπος, and to the ῎Εννοια, which emanated from him, the name of Δεύτερος

---

[1] On account of Isa. 14¹³ᶠ· Nebuchadnezzar is supposed to stand for those who have given themselves out to be God, Tanchuma, ed. Buber, Schem. 12ᵃ f.; Schem. R. 8 ; cf. Ber. R. 9. An ascension of King Alexander is related by Jona (c. 330), j. Ab. z. 42ᶜ ; Bem. R. 13.

"Ἄνθρωπος or υἱὸς ἀνθρώπου.[1] Its genesis is doubtless to be found in Ezekiel's vision of the royal chariot, in which God appears in human semblance, to which a welcome parallel appeared for Jews in the heavenly בַּר אֱנָשׁ of Dan. 7[13], and for Christians in the self-designation of Jesus. The common opinion that Paul " simply " adopted [2] his designation of Christ as ὁ ἔσχατος 'Αδάμ or ὁ δεύτερος ἄνθρωπος [3] from the rabbinic theology is, however, erroneous, for their theology knew nothing of such a comparison between Adam and the Messiah. The proof-passages adduced by Schöttgen, Hor. hebr. et talm. 670 ff., and by J. Rhenferdius in Meuschen, Nov. Testam. ex Talmude illustr. 1048 ff., to support this idea, belong to the Middle Ages, and are influenced by the Kabbala.[4]

It may be set down as our result, that the son of man in Dan. 7[13] was certainly understood sometimes to denote the Messiah; that, further, there were two apocalyptic fragments of an early period which used this name, excluding all other designations; but that a regular Jewish name for the Messiah never was formed from the passage in question.[5] There was no intrinsic hindrance to such a development. Why should " the son of man " be less adapted to become a Messianic title than the Jewish name חִוָּרָא, " the leprous," [6] for the Messiah, or הַמָּקוֹם, " the place," [7] for God, or the Samaritan תָּהֵבָה, " He who will come again," for the Messiah ? But " son of man " as a Messianic title among the Rabbis

---

[1] Irenæus, i. 28 ; cf. *Lietzmann*, Der Menschensohn, 62 ff.

[2] See, *e.g.*, *Holtzmann*, Lehrb. d. neutest. Theol. ii. 55 ; *Lietzmann*, Der Menschensohn, 64.

[3] 1 Cor. 15[45, 47].

[4] This is the subject of remark also by *G. F. Moore* in "The last Adam," Journ. Bibl. Lit. xvi. (1897) 158-161.

[5] From the intermittent testimonies in Enoch and 2 Esdras, which were soon superseded among the Jews, one must not, of course, manufacture, like *Baldensperger*, Das Selbstbewusstsein Jesu, 170 f., a "synagogal usage," which prevailed "almost universally in the religious works of the scribes."

[6] See "Der leid. u. d. sterb. Messias," 36.

[7] See above, p. 231 f.

was to be expected, solely on the condition that they had formed their conception of the Messiah principally from Dan. 7. As they did not do so, "the son of man" did not become a Messianic title.

3. "SON OF MAN" IS NO EMPTY FORMULA.

Beza, Cocceius, H. E. G. Paulus, and Fritzsche[1] had already put forward the view, which A. Meyer[2] revives, in regard to certain cases of the use of ὁ υἱὸς τοῦ ἀνθρώπου, namely, that among the Jews it was simply a common substitute for the pronoun of the first person. Commenting on Matt. 8[20], Beza says: "(addo,) propterea quod familiare est Hebræis, ut de se loquantur in tertia persona, ideo accipi loco pronominis primæ personæ in evangelica historia." Still the custom of speaking of oneself in the third person was by no means general among the Hebrews. But it did happen that a man should speak of himself as הָהוּא גַּבְרָא, "this man," or a woman as הָהִיא אִתְּתָא, "this woman." Examples are seen in Vaj. R. 30; j. Maas. sch. 55[b]; j. Sabb. 15[c]; j. Sukk. 55[b]; j. Mo. k. 81[d]; j. Taan. 66[d] 69[a]; j. Kidd. 64[b]; j. Keth. 29[b]; b. Bab. b. 4[a]; b. Sanh. 46[b].[3] The incentive to this mode of speech will have arisen in cases where something disagreeable had to be said,[4] although its use did not remain confined to such cases. A man, who is dying, gives instructions that something should be handed over to "the wife of this man," j. Kidd. 64[b]. The Emperor Trajan, speaking of himself, j. Sukk. 55[b], says to the Jews whom he had taken by surprise: "This man, who proposed to come after ten days,

[1] See the references in *Appel*, Die Selbstbezeichnung Jesu: Der Menschensohn, 5 f.

[2] Jesu Muttersprache, 95.

[3] See also Gramm. d. jüd.-pal. Aram. 77 f., and Aram. Dialektproben, p. 18, lines 9, 12; p. 29, lines 7, 11, 13 f.

[4] "Thou" was also readily avoided; cf. the form of imprecation, "may the spirit of this man expire!" *e.g.* j. Bez. 14[b], and *Goldziher*, Abhandlungen zur arab. Philologie, i. 39.

has already arrived in five days." There is, however, no
instance to show that הַהוּא אֲנָשָׁא or הַהוּא בַר אֲנָשָׁא was used in
the same fashion. Still less would the simple בַּר אֲנָשָׁא be
possible for this purpose. Any connection between the usage
in question and the self-designation of Jesus is all the harder
to establish, in view of the fact that at that time, as concluded above, under § 1, אֲנָשׁ and not בַּר אֲנָשׁ was the common
term for "man."

The Hebrew אוֹתוֹ הָאִישׁ, "that man,"[1] had just as litttle to
do with the title "son of man" as its Aramaic equivalent
הַהוּא נַבְרָא. Cremer[2] believes that the term "son of man,"
Enoch 69²⁹, may have arisen through opposition to the
Jewish habit of referring to Jesus as אוֹתוֹ הָאִישׁ. But this
way of alluding to Jesus is unknown in the ancient Rabbinism,
and cannot be verified till the Middle Ages. This term implies only that the discussion treats of the person whose name
the speaker does not wish, or in view of the Christian censor-
ship does not dare, to mention.

What has been said tends only to prove that it should
not seem specially remarkable, if Jesus showed a preference
for speaking of Himself in the third person. But the term
He employed for that purpose was an uncommon one; and
it requires a special explanation.

4. "SON OF MAN" IS A SELF-APPELLATION OF JESUS USED
EXCLUSIVELY BY HIMSELF.

In all three Synoptists ὁ υἱὸς τοῦ ἀνθρώπου as a title of
Jesus appears only in the words of Jesus Himself. Once
indeed the fourth evangelist, 12³⁴, represents the people as
speaking of the "Son of man," but only so as intentionally
to attribute to them a repetition of the words of Jesus.
According to Acts 7⁵⁶, Stephen at his martyrdom used the
words; and according to Hegesippus (in Eusebius, Hist. Eccl.

---

[1] See Ber. R. 36.   [2] Bibl. Theol. Wörterbuch,⁸ 966.

ii. 23), James also used the title in like circumstances. Both these instances, however, contain an unmistakable allusion to the language used by Jesus before the Sanhedrim, that of Stephen agreeing with Luke 22⁶⁹, that of James with Matt. 26⁶⁴. Nowhere else is Jesus named ὁ υἱὸς τοῦ ἀνθρώπου,[1] not even in Revelation, although it speaks on two occasions, in allusion to Dan. 7, of one who resembles a son of man. The seer beholds 1¹³ Jesus as ὅμοιον υἱὸν ἀνθρώπου in a picture which recalls not Dan. 7, but Dan. 10⁵·⁶, and hence the term must be borrowed from Dan. 10¹⁶·¹⁸, where the narrative mysteriously speaks of "one like the appearance of a man." In Rev. 14¹⁴ the seer again beholds "one like unto a son of man," this time on a white cloud with a crown and a sickle about to "reap" the harvest of the earth. That Christ is referred to is not clearly stated; v.¹⁷ implies that it was an angel. The scene is not that of Dan. 7, which has only the cloud in common. Nevertheless the thought of the "one like to a son of man" of Dan. 7¹³ may here have floated before the mind of the writer. Although the seer depicts the heavenly aspect of Jesus and of an angel as being in the "form of a man," one cannot, of course, draw the conclusion that he was ignorant of the fact that Jesus, during His life on earth, had called Himself the "Son of man." One can only see a corroboration of the fact that even he, like the other New Testament writers, never uses ὁ υἱὸς τοῦ ἀνθρώπου as a name for Jesus.

In 1 Thess. 4¹⁶, 2 Thess. 1⁷, Paul, having in view the kindred statements of Jesus in regard to the second coming of the Messiah, does not even here call Jesus "the Son of man," but ὁ κύριος. It is true he terms Christ ὁ δεύτερος ἄνθρωπος ἐξ οὐρανοῦ (ὁ ἐπουράνιος), 1 Cor. 15⁴⁷ᶠ·; but this expression, which Paul probably used here for the first time,

---

[1] With the same motive, however, the Liturgy of St. James in the ritual of the Eucharist, having treated 1 Cor. 11²⁶ as an utterance of Jesus, has changed Paul's τοῦ κυρίου, which could not be supposed to have been said by Jesus, into τοῦ υἱοῦ τοῦ ἀνθρώπου.

is occasioned by the contrast, which substantially determines
the entire passage, instituted between the earthly nature
represented in Adam and his posterity, and the heavenly
nature bequeathed by Christ to them that are His. In this
connection there is no more need to detect a reference to the
self-designation of Jesus, than there is to see a use of the
ideas of Philo or the Kabbala in regard to an ideal primitive
man.[1]

The expression has clearly remained restricted to its use
by Jesus Himself, and the Synoptists are themselves witnesses confirming this usage as a historical fact, as they never
by any chance allow the term to glide into their own language.
Even to the evangelists themselves it did not seem to be a
regular Messianic title. The main point is to understand
that Jesus alone called Himself "the Son of man," and that
no one else did so. It is not a sign of a sound historical
method to give up the attempt to solve this problem and to
seize upon the contention of Oort[2] and Lietzmann, that the
non-use of the term by the New Testament writers is a sign
that it did not really belong to Jesus either, and further, that
somewhere or other there had been an early community of
Christian Hellenists which delighted in this name, and in
order to find occasion for its use, represented Jesus in the
evangelic narrative as frequently speaking of Himself in the
third person. But any such assertion should have been pre-
vented by the mere observation, that although the Gospels
have proclaimed Jesus to the Church as "the Son of man"
for 1800 years, yet the name has never to this day become
a common title of Christ, and in books and sermons the "Son
of man" is not usually spoken of save when the words
of Jesus Himself are the cause. It is probable that substantially the same feeling, which to-day deters the Church

---

[1] That there can be no question of borrowing from the rabbinic theology, see
above, p. 247 f.

[2] *H. L. Oort*, De uitdrucking ο υιος του ανθρωπου in het nieuwe Testament
(1893).

from naming and invoking Jesus as "the Son of man," will have been active from the beginning.

The true reason for the non-use of ὁ υἱὸς τοῦ ἀνθρώπου in the Greek-speaking Church is disclosed by Lietzmann himself, through the instances he has given to illustrate the sense attached to the title.[1] Ignatius, Justin, Irenæus, Origen, Eusebius, Athanasius, Gregory of Nyssa, Gregory Nazianzus, Cyril of Alexandria, Chrysostom, as well as Tertullian, Ambrose, Cyprian, Augustine, with one consent, though in variously conceived modes, have seen in this title a reference to the human side in the descent of Jesus. As observed at the end of § 1, this interpretation of the name is not surprising. ὁ υἱὸς τοῦ ἀνθρώπου could not be understood by Greeks otherwise than as referring to one who desires to be known as son of a man. A name of this sort for Jesus might, in the Greek-speaking Church, be regarded from a dogmatic standpoint; but it was not adapted for practical use.

5. THE MEANING ATTACHED TO THE TITLE BY THE SYNOPTISTS.

The first appearance of ὁ υἱὸς τοῦ ἀνθρώπου is found, for Matthew in 8[20] (cf. Luke 9[58]), for Mark as early as 2[10] (cf. Matt. 9[6], Luke 5[24]), and for Luke in the passage just cited 5[24]. None of the evangelists takes the trouble to explain the designation; they seem to assume that the reader would understand what was meant by it. Had they wished the reader to think of the Messiah who was to come in the clouds of heaven, one would suppose that they would at the outset have inserted an explanation declaring the Messianic majesty of the Son of man. In the case of Matthew, however, the introductory statement about the Son of man is, that He

---

[1] *Lietzmann,* Der Menschensohn, 69–80 ; see also *Appel,* Die Selbstbezeichnung Jesu, 1–3.

lacks what even wild beasts possess; in Mark and Luke, that
the Son of man has authority on earth to forgive sins. This
latter the readers could not have understood as signifying
that this power belonged of right to Jesus in virtue of His
being the "Son of man," but as signifying that one, who was
content to call Himself merely "a son of man," had received
such absolute power. Matthew explicitly says as much in
recording this incident, Matt. 9^8, when he represents the
multitude giving praise because God had given such power
"unto men." The same evangelist, by the modifications
peculiar to himself which he introduces in his account of
Peter's confession ($\tau\grave{o}\nu$ $\upsilon\acute{i}o\nu$ $\tau o\hat{\upsilon}$ $\dot{a}\nu\theta\rho\acute{\omega}\pi o\upsilon$, 16^3, for $\mu\epsilon$,
Mark 8^{27}, Luke 9^{18}; $\acute{o}$ $X\rho\iota\sigma\tau\grave{o}s$ $\acute{o}$ $\upsilon\acute{i}os$ $\tau o\hat{\upsilon}$ $\theta\epsilon o\hat{\upsilon}$ $\tau o\hat{\upsilon}$ $\zeta\hat{\omega}\nu\tau os$,
v.[16], for $\acute{o}$ $X\rho\iota\sigma\tau\acute{o}s$, Mark 8^{29}; $\tau\grave{o}\nu$ $X\rho\iota\sigma\tau\grave{o}\nu$ $\tau o\hat{\upsilon}$ $\theta\epsilon o\hat{\upsilon}$, Luke
9^{20}), makes it clear beyond doubt that He who calls
Himself merely "Son of man" is in reality the correlative, i.e. Son of God.[1] Hence it is emphasised 16^{17} that
Peter has acquired this conviction not from men, but from
God. Even Jesus by calling Himself "Son of man" had
clearly given him no aid in coming to this conclusion. When
Mark and Luke, even sooner than Matthew, represent Jesus
as using the self-appellation "Son of man," it is clear that
they also can have seen in the title no assertion of Messianic
majesty. The injunction of Jesus not to speak to any one
of His Messianic character would, of course, seem meaningless
to them, if Jesus habitually spoke of Himself in public as the
Messiah, and that at the summit of the Messianic power, as
inferred from Dan. 7^{13}. Again, there is also present an indication that "Son of man" refers to the Messiah in His
estate of humiliation, in the account of Matthew and Mark
concerning the unpardonable blasphemy against the Holy
Spirit. The primary form of the utterance is seen in Mark,
who merely contrasts blasphemy in general with blasphemy
against the Spirit which inspired Jesus, $3^{28f.}$. Luke 12^{10} speaks

---

[1] *Holtzmann*, Lehrb. d. neutest. Theol. i. 257 f., rightly emphasises this.

of blasphemy of the " Son of man " and of the " Spirit ";
Matt. 12³² is similar, but the statement to this effect is annexed
to another, which corresponds to the form found in Mark. It
is impossible that Matthew and Luke should here intend to
make a distinction between two Persons of the Godhead, as
if it were a venial sin to blaspheme the " Son." The distinction is, on the contrary, between Jesus as man and the
divine Spirit working through Him. Invective against the
man Jesus may be forgiven ; blasphemy against the divine
power inherent in Him is unpardonable, because it is blasphemy
against God.

Mark alone draws the inference, 2²⁷ᶠ·, that the " Son of
man " is lord even of the Sabbath, on the ground that the
Sabbath was instituted for the sake of men. Hence, in the
reasoning of Mark, what applies to mankind in general, applies
pre-eminently to the " Son of man." In describing the trial
of Jesus (Luke 22⁷⁰), Luke alone has the explanatory question :
σὺ οὖν εἶ ὁ υἱὸς τοῦ θεοῦ; which evidently connects itself
with ὁ υἱὸς τοῦ ἀνθρώπου in the acknowledgment of Jesus.
The addition implies that Jesus, as His declaration really
means, is not indeed the " Son of man," but the " Son of
God."

We will be justified in concluding that for the Synoptists,
in harmony with the view of the early Church, " Son of man "
was not a term denoting the majesty of the Messiah ; but
that it was, what any Hellenist must necessarily have taken
it to be, an intentional veiling of the Messianic character
under a title which affirms the humanity of Him who bore
it. In their view, the prospect of sufferings foretold
by Jesus as the part of the " Son of man " was no paradox,
but the statements in regard to His exaltation were. It was
a matter of surprise, not that the " Son of man " should be
put to death, but that He should come again on the clouds of
heaven.

6. THE SENSE ATTACHED BY JESUS TO THE TERM "SON
OF MAN."

Owing to the diversified character of the sayings in which
Jesus refers to Himself as ὁ υἱὸς τοῦ ἀνθρώπου, investigation
of the substance of these sayings leads to no result. Jesus
nowhere gives any information defining the scope of the title.
Such information He seems, therefore, to have regarded as
uncalled for. One thing, however, is made clear by the testimony of the Synoptists, that, for their part, they assume that
the title consistently bore one and the same sense. Thus we
are directed in the next place to the term itself, which we
have to bring into comparison with the testimony borne by
Jesus to His own personality.

The Greek ὁ υἱὸς τοῦ ἀνθρώπου, *as understood by Greeks*,
would necessarily be traced to בְּרֵהּ דֶּאֱנָשָׁא in Aramaic (see
above, under § 1). But objections to the supposition that
Jesus really used these Aramaic words, arise from the considerations that the phrase is not Semitic; that the meaning
"the son of the man" has nowhere any support in the testimony of Jesus in regard to Himself; and that, further, no
literary source can be discovered for such an expression,
while every probability strongly favours the view that Jesus,
in virtue of the scriptural expression of God's will concerning Himself, adopted the expression from the Old Testament.
The only genuine Aramaic term which suggests ὁ υἱὸς τοῦ
ἀνθρώπου is בַּר אֱנָשָׁא. This term, we have said under § 1, did
not properly belong to the common language of the Palestinian
Jews as a term for "man"; it was characteristic rather of
the elevated diction of poetry and prophecy. To the Jews
it will have been known purely as a biblical word. The
Jewish hearer will therefore have had recourse in the first
place to Scripture for an explanation of the strange use of
בַּר אֱנָשָׁא on the lips of Jesus. And Scripture offered the
like Aramaic expression only in Dan. 7¹³ כְּבַר אֱנָשׁ, where

בַּר אֱנָשׁ denotes a definite personality, which, further, Jewish exegesis sometimes identified explicitly with the Messiah. We do not mean to say that every one would have been obliged to put this construction on the expression. The application of Dan. 7¹³ to the Messiah will not have been universal. Moreover, the " one like to a son of man " there mentioned, was to be brought down on the clouds of heaven in order to be master of the world. In the case of Jesus nothing resembling these circumstances was apparent. How could one, who moved about on earth, come down from heaven ? A transference thither must first have occurred before that could be accomplished. One who had died or who had been translated from the earth, might perchance be again introduced into the world in this fashion, or a personality which never had been on earth might so descend. Thus it seemed impossible to apply Dan. 7¹³ to Jesus. Any one who remained fixed in this idea, provided he did not know that Jesus had in fact foretold for Himself death, resurrection, and a second advent in majesty, will probably have discarded the reference to Daniel as impossible, and henceforward have regarded the designation as an enigma. If the words used by Jesus had been הָהוּא בַּר אֱנָשָׁא, " this son of man," this would have been regarded as an expression, uncommon indeed, but implying modesty in Jesus. But if He named Himself " the Son of man," בַּר אֱנָשָׁא, then it could only follow that for some reason or other He regarded Himself as a man distinct from other men. On the other hand, no one would have entertained the notion that He was in any sense " the ideal man " ; for this conception was far removed from Jewish thought, and was not brought nearer in the slightest by the teaching of Jesus.

In view of the obvious reference by Jesus to Dan. 7¹³ in His apocalyptic discourse, Matt. 24³⁰ (Mark 13²⁶, Luke 21²⁷), and in His testimony before the Sanhedrin, Matt. 26⁶⁴ (Mark 14⁶²), it can scarcely be doubted that Dan. 7¹³ was the source from which He took the self-designation. This origin is

17

further confirmed by the fact that it was also from Daniel that Jesus adapted the idea of the sovereignty of God. Nothing requires us to seek the source in the Similitudes of Enoch, especially as the "Son of man" there mentioned is never born as man;[1] while Daniel leaves this point unnoticed. Though such is the state of the case, we need not suppose that Jesus attached great importance to the intrinsic sense of the expression. His calling Himself "Son of man," בַּר אֲנָשׁ, really implied no more than that He was that one in whom this vision of Daniel was to proceed to its realisation. The term acquires its positive significance from the light in which it is placed by Daniel, and from what is said concerning it; just as the title מְשִׁיחָא, "the Messiah," derives its meaning not so much from the literal sense of the word, as from the scriptural testimony to the person thus entitled. But if all who heard the words of Jesus did not penetrate these associations, if there was a period when even the disciples of Jesus failed to understand them, the question arises, what aim Jesus had in view when He called Himself the "Son of man" before those to whom the term was an enigma? To such persons also He must, of course, have intended the term to convey some meaning. Or can it be that He never used the term at all before such persons?

Considerable difficulties stand in the way of discovering a true answer to these questions. In the first place, it cannot be said of any of the Gospels that they give us the sayings of Jesus in exact chronological sequence, especially as they differ widely one from another in this respect. From the first there will have been an earnest desire to be accurately informed as to the words and deeds of Jesus; but their succession in point of time appeared unimportant, and *in regard to sequence*, the recollection of the disciples would not always be able to furnish precise information. In the next place, their recollection, particularly in regard to the use of the title

[1] See above, p. 131.

"Son of man," cannot have been definite. It can scarcely be imagined that they should afterwards have known precisely on what occasions Jesus had and had not made use of this expression. The Synoptic tradition on this point is in itself ambiguous. The term is present in Matt. 16^{13}, but absent in the parallels, Mark 8^{27}, Luke 9^{18}; it is found in Luke 6^{22} 12^8, but not in Matt. 5^{11} 10^{33}; it occurs in Mark 10^{45} and Matt. 20^{28}, but not in Luke 22^{27}; Mark (8^{31}) and Luke (9^{22}) have it where Matthew (16^{21}) omits it. When all three Synoptists agree in using it, e.g. Matt. 9^6 (Mark 2^{10}, Luke 5^{24}), the only inference that can be drawn is that a source common to them all had contained the title, but not that the tradition is here particularly certain. Such being the state of matters, it cannot be ascertained with absolute certainty when or to what class of persons Jesus first used the title.

As for the evangelists themselves, they take the view that Jesus called Himself the " Son of man " at all times and before any company. Thus the first case of its use, alike in Mark (2^{10}) and Luke (5^{24}), takes place in public. Before his account of the same occasion, Matt. 9^6, Matthew, too, has only one instance of its use (8^{20}), in an interpolation foreign to the context of the passage; and even there the title is used in speaking to one who wishes to become for the first time a follower of Jesus. A complete understanding of His self-appellation, Jesus could certainly not, in such cases, have looked for from His hearers. Yet one may hold that in using the title He purposely furnished them with a problem which stimulated reflection about His person, and gave such a tendency to this reflection that the solution of the problem fully revealed the mystery of the personality of Jesus. But though Jesus obviously showed a predilection for speaking to the multitude in parables and leaving [1] the explanation to themselves, the objection may perhaps be made to the sup-

[1] See Matt. 13^{34}, Mark 4^{34}.

position that He had from the first called Himself " Son of man," that His disciples must presumably in that case have asked and received a special explanation of the expression. But any such private explanation is inadmissible for any time prior to the Messianic acknowledgment made by Peter, Matt. 16[16] (Mark 8[29], Luke 9[20]), especially considering the saying of our Lord, which Matthew records 16[17], to the effect that God, and not man, had revealed to Peter the Messianic dignity of Jesus, and also the injunction given in Mark and Luke against speaking to the people on the subject. Thus Jesus cannot possibly have made Himself known as the Messiah at a previous period in any fashion fully transparent to the disciples.   All the instructions concerning this subject which Matthew places earlier than the confession of Peter, must be relegated to the period following that confession; thus, above all, the exposition of the parable of the Tares in the Field, Matt. 13[36-43], on account of v.[41f.], unless it be assumed that it was originally God that was named where " Son of man " now stands; and further, Matt. 7[21-23], on account of vv.[22. 23]; while the Lucan parallel to this, Luke 6[46], by not naming Jesus as the Judge of the world, is unobjectionable from this point of view; as well as· Matt. 10[17-25] on account of v.[23b] (" till the Son of man be come "), and because the future separation of Jesus from the disciples, i.e. His death, is presupposed all through.   Mark and Luke do, in fact, place the first intimation of the advent of Jesus in majesty subsequent to its necessary presupposition, which is the open announcement of His death, and also subsequent to the confession of Peter; see Mark 8[38], Luke 9[26], cf. Matt. 16[27]. Thus, for the reasons indicated, one would be obliged to consider it probable [1] that Jesus had not previously referred to Himself as the " Son of man."

---

[1] Here I speak advisedly of probability only, because in the construction I proceed to put on the sense of the title, an absolute necessity for this supposition is *not* present.   It would be finally convincing for those who take " Son of man " to be a distinctively Messianic title.

This conjecture may be vindicated, if need be, in view of the Synoptic testimonies, which seem to oppose it. Prior to the confession of Peter, Matthew records the use of ὁ υἱὸς τοῦ ἀνθρώπου nine times. Three of these instances, 10^{23} $13^{37.41}$, are discounted by what has just been said; and 8^{20}, as just remarked, is out of place in its present position. Matt. 12^{32} is to be regarded as an explanatory duplicate of v.^{31}.[1] The "sign of Jonah," Matt. 12^{40}, is not mentioned by Luke (11^{30}) till after the Petrine confession. Luke alone has the instance, 6^{22}, ἕνεκα τοῦ υἱοῦ τοῦ ἀνθρώπου, for which, however, Matthew has only ἕνεκα ἐμοῦ (5^{11}). Matthew and Luke have each the comparison between the Baptist and the Son of man, Matt. $11^{18f.}$ (Luke $7^{33f.}$). Matthew, Mark, and Luke have a paragraph in common, Matt. 9^{1-17} (Mark 2^{1-22}, Luke 5^{17-39}), to which is directly added in Mark and Luke a section (Mark 2^{23}–3^6, Luke 6^{1-11}) which Matthew has remitted to a later position (Matt. 12^{1-14}). In these parts all three Synoptists have ὁ υἱὸς τοῦ ἀνθρώπου twice, Matt. 9^6 (Mark 2^{10}, Luke 5^{24}) and Matt. 12^8 (Mark 2^{28}, Luke 6^5). Thus we really have the title placed before the Petrine confession only three times.

J. Weiss, A. Meyer, Lietzmann, and Holtzmann have tried to set aside the evidence of two of these instances, by holding that Jesus had there spoken of mankind generally, or in such a way that something was applicable to Himself in virtue of His humanity. But this mode of interpretation would hardly have arisen unless there had been reasons independent of the passages themselves for desiring to supersede the title " Son of man " as a title. One of the two cases where Jesus claims for the " Son of man " the right to forgive sins, Matt. 9^6 (Mark 2^{10}, Luke 5^{24}), has been pronounced meaningless by Weiss,[3] on the ground that " no opponent of Jesus had any doubt that the Messiah had full power to forgive sins." But, in the first place, as a Messianic title,

---

[1] Cf. p. 255. [2] Die Predigt Jesu vom Reiche Gottes, 57.

בַּר אֱנָשָׁא would hardly have been intelligible for such opponents on this occasion ; and, besides, it is a fact which ought to have been familiar to J. Weiss, that Judaism never, from Old Testament times to the present day, has ventured to make any such assertion in regard to the Messiah. Still less does it signify anything important, that, according to Matthew (9⁸), praise is given to God because He had given such power unto men, for this language merely brings into view the evangelist's own idea of the expression "Son of man."[1] Moreover, an implicit reference to the power of remitting sins given to the disciples, John 20²³, is, in spite of Matt. 16¹⁹ 18¹⁸, inadmissible here.

With better reason, apparently, it may be said that mankind in general is meant by the "Son of man," who is Lord of the Sabbath, Matt. 12⁸ (Mark 2²⁸, Luke 6⁵), because in that case, according to Mark 2²⁷, the Sabbath has just previously been pronounced subservient to mankind. But this preceding sentence appears only in Mark ;[2] in place of it Matthew has something different ; Luke has nothing at all. If *brevior præferenda*, as standing closest to the original, is applicable here, then the shortest form is to be found in Luke, who gives us no occasion for thinking of mankind. Mark 2²⁷ is an interpolation whose position is parallel to that of Matt. 12⁵⁻⁷, which we have considered valid as indicating the sense attached by the evangelist to ὁ υἱὸς τοῦ ἀνθρώπου ; but it by no means implies that on this occasion Mark did not have in view the ordinary self-appellation of Jesus. It is also to be noted that the saying Luke 6⁵, cf. Mark 2²⁷, has a fresh form of introduction καὶ ἔλεγεν αὐτοῖς, and that Matthew, by omitting it, brings the saying to notice very disconnectedly. To all appearance the saying about the Lord of the Sabbath was an independent *Logion* which has

---

[1] In opposition to *Lietzmann*, Der Menschensohn, 89. See above, p. 254.
[2] It is worthy of note that the saying of our Lord, Mark 2²⁷, does not appear at all in Cod. D.

been added here only through affinity in sense.[1] Originally Jesus will only have said that necessity justified the breach of Sabbatic law by the disciples, as in the case of David's irregular eating of the shewbread; but not that He, as Lord of the Sabbath, had authorised the act of the disciples. A declaration of this nature would have been more in place if Jesus Himself had set aside the Sabbatic regulations. Again, as regards the theory represented by Pfleiderer, J. Weiss, and J. H. Holtzmann, in the absence of any historical warrant in its support, one cannot consent to the idea that Jesus at first had merely called Himself "the Man," and then at a later period, by combining this with Dan. 7[13], had transformed it into a Messianic designation. Besides, the objection arises that "Man" and "Son of man" are not traceable to the same Aramaic expression, and it would also have to be explained why Jesus called Himself not אֱנָשָׁא but בַּר אֱנָשָׁא. Why should "man" in Mark 2[27] be ὁ ἄνθρωπος, but in v.[28] ὁ υἱὸς τοῦ ἀνθρώπου?

A simpler and in itself an admittedly permissible method of explaining these passages satisfactorily, would be either to change the embarrassing ὁ υἱὸς τοῦ ἀνθρώπου into the personal pronoun, or else to suppose that the sayings concerned should be located after Peter's confession. In support of the latter, it could be held that the paragraph alluded to as common to the three Synoptists, includes within it the allusion to the days when the bridegroom shall be taken away, which will give his friends occasion for fasting (Matt. 9[15], Mark 2[20], Luke 5[35]). As Jesus here anticipates His death, the time of Peter's confession may be supposed to have preceded. Of course it by no means follows that Jesus Himself had only at that time acquired the knowledge of His violent death; still it does seem that He had not previously informed His disciples of it.

---

[1] Cod. D has not inserted it till the later narrative, Luke 6[10]. In this passage it is also placed by Blass in his text of Luke, and by Resch in his Λόγια Ἰησοῦ. On the other hand, in Luke 6[5] Cod. D has another Logion peculiar to itself.

Thus, then, it is not impossible, though it cannot be regarded as absolutely certain, that Jesus never called Himself the " Son of man " prior to the Messianic confession of Peter, and the instruction then given to His disciples in regard to His future destiny. From that time forward the title became significant to them as the name derived from Dan. 7¹³ for Him who was ordained to the sovereignty of the world. To the mass of the people Jesus did not manifest the full significance of the title, until in His open confession before the Sanhedrin, Matt. 26⁶⁴ (Mark 14⁶², Luke 22⁶⁹), He set all doubts at rest, and thereby supplied the judges with a possible pretext for pronouncing a sentence of death.

The more precise determination of the sense attached by Jesus to בַּר אֱנָשָׁא will have to be sought primarily, as indicated above, with the help of the Book of Daniel. Considering the general mode of thought peculiar to Jesus, the chief motive which led directly to the selection of the Book of Daniel, and the title it contains for the future lord of the world, is to be found in the fact that nowhere else is it asserted so unreservedly that the inevitable mutations of all earthly conditions are to be expected from the agency of God alone.[1] As a stone which no hand has unloosed from its native rock, so comes the sovereignty of God upon the world, in order to shatter every hostile sovereignty, Dan. 2³⁴· ⁴⁵. From heaven comes one like unto a son of man in order that God may bestow as a gift universal dominion upon him, Dan. 7¹³, cf. v.²⁷. Of the " violent " it is said, Dan. 11⁴, that they are raised up to establish the vision, but are at the same time destined to ruin. In His own immediate neighbourhood Jesus had been an eye-witness of the fruitlessness of individual aggrandisement, and thus preferred not to be regarded as " Messiah " by the people ; as they, in opposition to all Old Testament prophecy,[2] were looking for acts of political liberation and a forcible appropriation of the sove-

---

[1] Cf. above, p. 137 f.   [2] See on this point Fund. Ideas, XI. 1.

reignty by their Messiah. But there was still another reason why the title "Son of man" was specially appropriate to Jesus. The name Messiah denoted the Lord of the Messianic age in His capacity as Ruler; in reality it was applicable to the person so predestinated only when His enthronement had taken place, not before it. Suffering and death for the actual possessor of the Messianic dignity are in fact unimaginable, according to the testimony of the prophets. When Jesus attached to the Messianic confession of Peter the first intimation of His violent death, He did so in order to make it clear that the entrance upon His sovereignty was still far distant, and that the Messianic function of Jesus did not include, but distinctly excluded self-aggrandisement. But the "one like unto a son of man" of Dan. 7¹³ has still to receive the sovereignty. It was *possible* that he should also be one who had undergone suffering and death. At any rate, in disposition he is no user of force, no conqueror, no demolisher, but only a "son of man" whom God has taken under His protection and ordained to be great.[1] We find an idea somewhat akin to this conception in the Revelation of John, which delights to speak of Christ as τὸ ἀρνίον, "the Lamb," which offered itself to be slain without gainsaying. There, too, the prominent idea is the defencelessness which leads Him to endure all things which men, by the counsel of God, inflict upon Him. Jesus called Himself בַּר אֱנָשָׁא, not indeed as the "lowly one," but *as that member of the human race (Menschenkind), in his own nature impotent, whom God will make Lord of the world;* and it is very probable that Jesus found another reference[2] to the Son of man of Dan. 7 in the verses of Ps. 8⁵ᶠ·: "What is a man that Thou art mindful of him, and a son of man that Thou acceptest him, and permittest him to be but little less than God, and crownest him with glory

---

[1] Cf. the exposition of Dan. 7 given on p. 138 f.

[2] This view is supported by *V. Bartlet*, Expos., 6th Ser., iv. 435, and—excluding the reference to Dan. 7—by *F. Buhl*, Messianske Forjættelser, 236 f.

and honour, makest him to have dominion over the works of Thy hands, and hast put all things under his feet?"

If this exposition of the term be correct, it follows: (1) that the sense attached by Jesus to the title is peculiar to Him alone, and is no mere counterpart of the idea in Enoch and 2 Esdras; (2) that humility and suffering can be predicated of בַּר אֱנָשָׁא as well as majesty; (3) that the meaning suggested by the title to those who did not suspect its connection with Dan. 7 was not unwarranted, because in any case they too must have concluded that Jesus disclaimed the rôle of usurper by His own efforts; (4) that it was *possible* that at first the disciples were content with this conception, and did not ask any further explanation from Jesus; (5) that the interpretation put upon the expression by the Hellenistic Synoptists and by the primitive Church, though in the narrower sense inexact, was not erroneous in so far as they found in it a testimony of Jesus to the reality of His human nature; and, further, (6) that the Church was quite justified in refusing, on its part, to give currency to the title; for in the meantime the "Son of man" had been set upon the throne of God, and was, in fact, no longer merely a man, but a Ruler over heaven and earth, "The Lord," as Paul in the Epistles to the Thessalonians, and the Teaching of the Apostles in its apocalyptic statement, rightly designate Him who comes with the clouds of heaven.

Note.—For a long time I considered it possible that " Son of man" might be a paradoxical term for "Son of God." Various Jewish phrases might have been adduced as parallels.[1] According to Yokhanan ben Zakkai (*c.* 80 A.D.), the thief is more severely punished by the law than the robber, " because he, as it were, treats the eye of God as unseeing and the ear of God as deaf." In Tosephta Bab. k. vii. 2, the "eye of God" is in this case expressed by "the eye that is above"

[1] Cf. *E. Landau*, Die gegensinnigen Wörter im Alt- und Neuhebr. (1896).

(עַיִן הָעֶלְיוֹנָה); but Mechilta Mishp. Nez. 15 [1] and Bab. k. 79[b]
says: "the eye that is beneath" (עַיִן שֶׁלְמַטָּה). A tradition,
not included in the Mishna (Baraitha),[2] given b. Yom. 77[a],
b. Sukk. 53[b], explains Ezek. 8[16] by saying that the men
unveiled themselves "downward" (כְּלַפֵּי מַטָּה), whereas the
meaning really is "upward" (their heads), i.e. towards God.
Even in the Old Testament, e.g. 1 Kings 21[10], "to bless,"
בֵּרַךְ, is said instead of "to curse" when the malediction is
applied to God. In the same way בִּרְכַּת הַשֵּׁם, "blessing of the
Name," b. Sanh. 56[a] (Baraitha), is really "blasphemy against
God"; בְּרָכָה לְמַעֲלָה, "blessing of what is above," means "cursing God"; בְּרָכָה לְמַטָּה, "blessing of what is below," on the
other hand, means "cursing of parents," b. Yeb. 101[a]
(Chanina). A blind man was called in Galilee סַגְיָא נְהוֹרָא,
"the clear seer," Ber. R. 30, j. Peah 19[a], j. Keth. 34[b], or also
גַּבְרָא מִפַּתְּחָא, "the man whose eyes are opened," j. Kidd. 61[a].
When anything discreditable to Israel has to be said, it is
predicated of "the enemies of Israel," see in Hebr. שׂוֹנְאֵיהֶם
שֶׁלְיִשְׂרָאֵל, Mechilta, ed. Fried. 3[a], Tos. Sukk. ii. 6 (Meïr,
c. 160 A.D.[3]); in Aram. שָׂנְאֵיהוֹן דְּיִשְׂרָאֵל, j. Chag. 77[d]; j. Sanh.
23[c]; Targ. Esth. ii. 1[1]. In like circumstances a man does
not speak of himself but of "his enemy"; see b. Sukk. 52[a],
b. Sanh. 107[a], where מַאן דְּסָנֵי לִי, "he, who hates me," is
employed for "I."—All this, however, scarcely warrants the
imputation of a paradoxical use of "Son of man" by Jesus;
and as such a supposition is in no way indispensable in
explaining the designation, it must be set aside.

---

[1] Ed. Constantinople, 1515, not in ed. Friedm. (91[b]).
[2] Cf. the saying of Chijja, Schir. R. 1[6]; Bacher, Ag. d. pal. Am. ii. 195.
[3] Bacher, Ag. d. Tann. ii. 28.

X. THE SON OF GOD.

1. THE SECOND PSALM IN JEWISH LITERATURE.

The second Psalm is generally reckoned the principal biblical source of the designations, "Son of God" and "Anointed" (Messiah), as applied to the King of the Messianic age. It will therefore be appropriate to begin by tracing the influence of this psalm on Jewish literature.

In Ps. 2[7] the king of Zion, whom the poet had spoken of in v.[5] as God's "Anointed" (מְשִׁיחוֹ), is called by God His Son (בְּנִי), begotten by Him on the coronation day. This language should probably be taken in connection with the promise in 2 Sam. 7[14], which says that God will stand to the Davidic dynasty in the relation of father to son. But while in 2 Sam. 7[14] the inference from this promise is merely that God will keep the dynasty under discipline without overthrowing it, the psalm deduces from the filial relation of the king of Zion to God, that universal dominion originally proper to God is bequeathed to the Son as an inheritance, and in this respect goes further than Ps. 89[28], according to which the firstborn of God is only the highest of the kings of the earth. To me it seems likely that in both psalms, as in Isa. 55[4, 5], the king of Zion is meant as an emblem of God's people collectively. In Jewish literature, however, there are but few traces of such an interpretation. In the Midrash to Ps. 2[12] [1] it is said at the end: "Whom does this resemble? The king, who is angry with the people of the land, and the people go and appease the son of the king, that he may appease the king. And when the people go to render a song of praise to the king, he says to them: Is it

---

[1] In this comment, therefore, בַּר is actually understood to be "Son." But בַּר must apparently be regarded as the original reading. The fear that in v.[12] one might think of the anger of the Son, and of refuge with the Son, may have led to the change into בַּר, which in that case, from its first appearance, would have meant "purity."

to me that ye would sing praise ? Go and say it to my son, as, but for him, I had long ago exterminated the people of the land. Even so God says to the Gentiles when they wish to render Him a song of praise . . .: Go, say it to the Israelites, for without them ye could not endure for one hour."[1] The date and source of the saying are unknown. The meaning of another saying, given in Midr. Ps. 2^7, is ambiguous. It represents that the divine statement in this verse is qualified by statements in each of the three divisions of Scripture; in the Law Ex. 4^{22} ("Israel is my son, my firstborn"), in the Prophets Isa. 52^{13} and 42^1, and in the Hagiographa Ps. 110^1 2^7, Dan. 7^{13}.[2] Judging by the citation from the Pentateuch, it appears as if Israel were meant throughout.

The Messianic interpretation of the psalm is not found so frequently as might have been expected. The *Book of Enoch* originally contained no allusion whatever to Ps. 2, which justifies an inference that a non-Messianic view of the psalm was common enough. The Similitudes of Enoch make use of Ps. 72, but not Ps. 2, in delineating the Messianic picture. In the unique expression (48^{10}), "the Lord of spirits and His Anointed," the second part should be deleted. For if not, the language here, "they have disowned the Lord of spirits," would be inapplicable to the Messiah, see 41^2 45^2 46^7.

So, too, Enoch 52^4 is clearly an interpolation, as it breaks the natural connection between vv.[3] and [5]. Accordingly the reference to the Messiah as "His (God's) Anointed," which appears there, is also foreign to the original. Moreover, in this section of Enoch, the Messiah is elsewhere called consistently, according to Ps. $89^{4. 20}$, "the Chosen," see 49^4 $51^{3. 5}$ $52^{6. 9}$. To a later insertion we must also ascribe 105^2, in

---

[1] Thus in ed. Constant. 1512, and ed. Venice, 1546. Buber, in ed. Wilna, 1891, does not mention this reading, and has in its place "the world." According to Yalkut Shim. ii. (ed. Salonica, 1521) 624, it is said : "Ye would not continue to exist in this world."

[2] Dan. 7^{13} is not cited in the parallel, Yalk. Shim. ii. 621.

which case " I and My Son " might also, for that matter, be derived from Ps. 89²⁷ᵗ·.

Among the earlier sections of the *Apoc. of Baruch*, chap. 27–29 did not originally mention the Messiah. The name occurs, indeed, in 29³ and 30¹; but in 29³ He only " begins to become manifest," and 30¹ says that " He comes again." Of His actual governance one hears nothing. Both passages must therefore be struck out. On the other hand, the expression " mine (God's) anointed " is twice used in the section chaps. 36–40 (39⁷ 40¹), also twice in the section chaps. 53– 74 (70⁹ 72²), but no allusion is made to Ps. 2. In 70⁹ the Messiah is called " my Servant, the Anointed " (Syr. עבדי משיחא); but the whole verse may possibly be a gloss; see R. H. Charles on the passage. In 2 *Esdras* " the Messiah " (Syr. משיחא) appears in 12³² just as in Apoc. of Bar.—without allusion to Ps. 2. In 7²⁸· ²⁹ God calls the Messiah " Mine anointed Son " (Syr. ברי משיחא), but no indication is given as to the source of this language. In the vision of the " man from the sea " God further speaks of the Messiah as בְּרִי, " My Son," 13³²· ³⁷· ⁵² 14⁹. In this vision there occur references to Dan. 2, Dan. 7, and Isa. 11⁴. The stone cut out without hands, Dan. 2, which became a mountain, on which the Messiah takes up his position, and against which the peoples assemble, 13³⁵ᵗ·, must be Zion; and this identification implies the influence of Ps. 2 in this passage. Still this influence is not clearly marked.

There is, however, an indubitable reference to Ps. 2 in the *Psalter of Solomon* 17²⁶, perhaps also in 18¹⁸ (cf. Ps. 2⁹); and hence arises the possibility, though not the necessity, of tracing also the designations Χριστὸς κύριος,[1] 17³⁶; Χριστοῦ αὐτοῦ, 18⁶; Χριστοῦ κυρίου, 18⁸, back to the second Psalm. In this book, however, the Messiah is not referred to as " Son of God."

---

[1] This depends, according to 18⁶, upon the Hebr. מְשִׁיחַ יהוה, "the Anointed of the Lord," as does also Χριστοῦ κυρίου, 18⁸.

Later Jewish literature affords in a Baraitha given in b. Sukk. 52ᵃ an earlier witness for the Messianic interpretation of Ps. 2. In this case vv.[7] and [8] are attributed to Messiah, Son of David. More recent is the saying of Yonathan ben Eleazar (c. 240):[1] "of three persons it is said in Scripture, 'Ask!' Who are they? Solomon and Ahaz and the King Messiah." For the last, reference is then made to Ps. 2. From the Midrash Ps. 2[7] it appears that Judan (c. 350) applied this verse to the Messiah. From a very late period, doubtless, arises the anonymous assertion contained in the same passage, which is directed against the exposition maintained by the Church. It runs thus: "From this verse (Ps. 2[7]) we find a retort against the Minim (Christians), who say that the Holy One, Blessed be He, has a Son; and thou canst remonstrate that the words are not 'a son art thou to me,' but 'thou art my son,' like a servant to whom his lord vouchsafes encouragement, saying to him, 'I love thee as my son'!"[2] (מְחַבְּבְנָא לָךְ כְּבְרִי).[3]   In an addition to the saying of Huna about the sufferings of Messiah, which appears in the sources mentioned, the "begetting" is understood to be the "new creation"[4] undergone by the suffering Messiah, as a necessary prelude to His advent in majesty. The Targum for Ps. 80[16] has identified the "Son" with the Messiah, having clearly had Ps. 2 in view.

One may assume that as time passed the Christian ex-

[1] Ber. B. 44 ; cf. *Bacher*, Ag. d. p. Am. i. 83.

[2] So, too, the Targum of the Psalms has in 2[7] "dear as a son to a father art thou to me, innocent as if I had this day created thee."

[3] This is the reading in Yalk. Shim. ii. 621, ed. Salonica, 1521 ; Midr. Ps., ed. Constantinople, 1512, and ed. Venice, 1546. The Censor Dominico Caresso (1607) has blackened a part of the beginning in my copy of Yalkut; in ed. Frankf. a. M. 1687 the whole is omitted. Buber, who besides the old editions made use of 8 MSS. in preparing his edition of the Midrash Tehillim (Wilna, 1891), suppresses all the first part of the statement, without mentioning even its existence!

[4] See above, p. 178 f. The text of the Midrash on the Psalms would have us suppose that the creation of the hitherto non-existent Messiah is meant. It should, however, be emended in accordance with Yalk. Shim.; see my treatise, "Der leidende u. d. sterb. Messias," 52.

position of Ps. 2 became a deterrent to its common use by the synagogue. But even for the earlier period it must be recognised as certain that Ps. 2 was not of decisive importance in the Jewish conception of the Messiah, and that "Son of God" was not a common Messianic title. A hindrance to the use of בַּר אֱלָהָא or בֶּן הָאֱלֹהִים would have presented itself in the custom of not uttering the name of God ; and this afterwards shows itself when Mark 14[61] gives the words of the Jewish high priest as ὁ υἱὸς τοῦ εὐλογητοῦ—a form ill adapted to become a current Messianic title. When God calls the Messiah His Son, this is merely meant as a sign of the exceptional love with which He above others is regarded. Even the idea of the "heritage" combined with sonship in Ps. 2 is never developed by Jewish literature in its bearing on the Messiah.

It is a peculiar mark of great importance in Israel, that divine descent was never ascribed either to the people or to their kings. In naming God its Father, it may occasionally contemplate a genesis through the agency of divine power (see p. 184). But divine nature in the Son is never deduced from such expressions. If Ps. 2 and Ps. 89 refer to the people Israel, it is still a special relation to God that is thereby asserted, the originator of this relationship being God, and by no means any sort of procreation in the literal sense of the word. Even in Messianic expositions, an Israelite will always have taken the title "Son of God" in a figurative sense, there being no incentive in this connection to interpret it otherwise than was usual elsewhere.

The language used by Israel recalls that of Assyria. When Asshurbanipal in his Annals,[1] according to the inscriptions, calls himself "an offspring of Asshur and Bilit," this means no more than a being destined from birth to the royal power. The kings of Egypt, on the contrary, were reckoned to be real "descendants of the god Ra." Even the birth of

---

[1] *Schrader*, Keilinschriftl. Bibliothek, ii. 152 f.

each king seems to be regarded as a special act of the gods; the royal title might contain the sentence:[1] "on the day of his birth there was exultation in heaven; the gods said, 'we have begotten him'; the goddesses said, 'he went forth from us.'"

The royal style of old Egypt was continued by the Ptolemies. Hence one encounters in connection with them epithets like "a diis genitus," "filius Isidis et Osiris," υἱὸς τοῦ Ἡλίου,[2] θεὸς ἐκ θεοῦ καὶ θεᾶς.[3] Roman emperors also boasted frequently of divine progenitors. Sextus Pompeius called himself the son of Neptune; Domitian, the son of Minerva; Caligula and Hadrian deemed themselves to be earthly manifestations of Zeus.[4] In the royal title, however, there appeared only "Divus," in Greek θεός,[5] Aram. אלהא,[6] which, in the East, people applied without scruple to the living emperor, whereas it was originally intended to apply only to the emperor when transferred by death to a place among the gods. Augustus, it is true, called himself "Divi filius,"[7] θεοῦ υἱός;[8] but that has nothing really to do with divine sonship. It was a term due to his modesty, which prompted him to be known[9] as merely the "son of one who was transferred to a place among the gods," his father by adoption being Cæsar, now taken to be a Divus. Hence no assistance can be derived from this designation in determining the Greek conception of the term ὁ υἱὸς τοῦ θεοῦ used by Jesus.[10]

[1] A. Erman, Ägypten, 90 f. [Eng. tr. ּ].

[2] E. Beurlier, De divinis honoribus qnos acceperunt Alexander et successores ejus (1890), 47, 59.

[3] Corp. Inscr. Græc. 4697.

[4] E. Beurlier, Essai sur le culte rendu aux Empereurs Romains (1890), 10, 37 f.

[5] See, e.g., Wadd. 2075, 2076, 2380, 2585, 2598; Corp. Inscr. Græc. 2176, 2177.

[6] See de Vogüé, 15, 16.

[7] Äg. Urkunden a. d. kgl. Mus. Berlin (Greek), 628.

[8] Ibid. 174, 543; Wadd. 1476.

[9] Cf. Beurlier, Essai, 13, 15.

[10] In opposition to Deissmann, Bibelstudien, 166 f. [Eng. tr. p. 166 f.].

18

2. THE TITLE "SON OF GOD" AS APPLIED TO JESUS BY OTHER
PERSONS.

In the *Synoptic* Gospels, ὁ υἱὸς τοῦ θεοῦ is found as a
Messianic title in the confession of Peter, Matt. 16¹⁶ (ὁ Χριστὸς ὁ υἱὸς τοῦ θεοῦ τοῦ ζῶντος). Luke, however, has (9²⁰)
τὸν Χριστὸν τοῦ θεοῦ, and Mark (8²⁹) has merely ὁ Χριστός.
As the name ὁ Χριστός is the one which we should naturally
expect in the mouth of a Jew at that period, we must regard
Matthew's version as an expansion.[1]

In Matt. 14³³ it may certainly be admitted that the confession θεοῦ υἱὸς εἶ is not inappropriately attributed to the
disciples after Jesus had shown Himself to be master of wind
and waves. But as it is straightway asserted, Mark 6⁵¹ᶠ·, that
the disciples did not thus express themselves on that occasion,
a sufficiently sure foundation for the utterance disappears.
In the mouth of the high priest, Matt. 26⁶³, the designation
ὁ Χριστὸς ὁ υἱὸς τοῦ θεοῦ (like ὁ Χρ. ὁ υἱὸς τοῦ εὐλογητοῦ,
Mark 14⁶¹) is unsuitable; because the words, as given by
Luke (22⁶⁶), ὁ Χριστός, or perhaps ὁ Χριστὸς τοῦ εὐλογητοῦ,
have antecedent probability in their favour. In the second
question of the judges, "art thou then the Son of God?"
Luke 22⁷⁰, the evangelist has made the decisive element in
the acknowledgment of Jesus patent to his readers, but in so
doing has really obscured rather than elucidated the actual
circumstances.[2]

The railing addressed to Christ on the Cross is represented
in Matthew (27⁴⁰, cf. v.⁴³) by the words, "save thyself if
thou art the Son of God." Luke has (22³⁵): "if this is the
chosen Christ of God." The conditional clause does not
appear at all in Mark (15³⁰). This clause appears to be an
echo of the account of the Temptation, which also is related
only by Matthew and Luke (see below). The centurion

---

[1] See on the same point, pp. 183, 196, 200, 291.
[2] On this point see XI. 2.

makes the confession after the death of Jesus that He was the " Son of God," υἱὸς θεοῦ, Matt. 27⁵⁴, Mark 15³⁹; whereas, according to Luke (23⁴⁷), he merely calls Jesus " guiltless " (δίκαιος). While the synoptic tradition is in itself discordant as regards the instances just named, it is uniform in testifying that the demoniacs named Jesus " the Son of God," Matt. 8²⁹ (Mark 5⁷, Luke 8²⁸), Mark 3¹¹, Luke 4⁴¹. It is evident, however, from Luke 4⁴¹, that the evangelist here regards ὁ υἱὸς τοῦ θεοῦ as simply a synonym for ὁ Χριστός. Even in the country of the Gerasenes Jews would have been numerous enough, so that an appellation of Jesus as Messiah by the demoniacs settled there is not unnatural. Thus ὁ Χριστός would have to be substituted for the uncommon ὁ υἱὸς τοῦ θεοῦ. It is conceivable that in such a case the evangelic narrative should, without reserve, make use of the explanatory title " Son of God." In relation to these spirits, Jesus was conceived not so much the " Messiah " as the One in whom God appears upon earth.

From the foregoing, it appears that Jesus was not called " the Son of God " by any contemporary. Seeing that this was not in common use as a Messianic title, as demonstrated under § 1, this result is quite natural. I have not here considered Satan's designation of Jesus as " Son of God " in the account of the Temptation, Matt. 4³· ⁶ (Luke 4³· ⁹). It stands in close connection with the divine voice at the Baptism, to which the words of Satan, "if thou art the Son of God," obviously refer. The voice from heaven at the Baptism requires a separate discussion. Except for this association, it would be possible here also to put ὁ Χριστός for υἱὸς τοῦ θεοῦ.

Unnoticed still remain the words of the angel in Luke 1³² and 1³⁵. In the former verse, υἱὸς ὑψίστου taken along with μέγας merely emphasises the exalted distinction which falls to him whom the Most High deigns to name His " Son." The latter verse expressly connects υἱὸς θεοῦ with the supernatural birth of Jesus. We are not here called to consider the historical value of the narrative in Luke's first chapter. We have merely to note the fact that the wording of the angelic message is in conformity with the biblical style [1] adopted by Luke for this narrative; and it therefore serves all the more surely as a means of ascertaining the evangelist's own interpretation of the idea υἱὸς τοῦ θεοῦ. The second saying of the angel cannot in any case be brought into relation with Jewish popular notions. For the Jewish common people never expected the Messiah to be born of a virgin; and no trace is to be found among the Jews of any Messianic application of Isaiah's words (7[14]) concerning the virgin's son, from which by any possibility—as some have maintained—the whole account of the miraculous birth of Jesus could have derived its origin.

3. THE DIVINE VOICE AT THE BAPTISM AND THE TRANSFIGURATION.

On two occasions Jesus is called by God "His Son,"— at the Baptism and at the Transfiguration. The words are : ὁ υἱός μου ὁ ἀγαπητός, Matt. 3[17] (Mark 1[11], Luke 3[22]) and 17[5] (Mark 9[7], 2 Pet. 1[17]; but in Luke 9[35] Sin. B, ὁ ὑ. μ. ὁ ἐκλελεγμένος [2]). There is added, Mark 1[11] (Luke 3[22]), ἐν σοὶ εὐδόκησα (Matt. 3[17] 17[5] ἐν ᾧ εὐδόκησα, 2 Pet. 1[17] εἰς ὃν ἐγὼ εὐδόκησα). Moreover, there is a reading for Luke 3[22] which is supported by D, Justin, Clem. Alex.: υἱός μου εἶ σύ, ἐγὼ σήμερον γεγέννηκά σε. This form has been considered by Blass [3] to be the parent of both forms of the Lucan text and adopted into his text. The gospel of the Ebionites, according to Epiphanius, Hær. 30, had both forms side by side.[4] In the gospel of the Hebrews, Jerome [5]

---

[1] See above, p. 39 ; and on υἱὸς ὑψίστου, p. 199.

[2] Of the Syriac versions, only the Sinaitic has this reading; Cur., Pesh., Jerus., like ACD, have ὁ ἀγαπητός.

[3] *F. Blass*, Evangelium secundum Lucam (1897), xxxvii. f., 14.

[4] *Nestle*, Nov. Test. Suppl. 75.　　　　　[5] See Jerome on Isa. 11[4].

read : "tu es filius meus primogenitus, qui regnas in sempiternum."

The two forms represented in the canonical Gospels have both been moulded in the language of the Old Testament. The second, which is based from beginning to end on Ps. 2⁷, might be disallowed as originating in the interests of the idea that Jesus had only then become the Son of God when He was baptized.[1] But this reading may equally well have arisen as an afterthought, because, apart from the doctrinal preconception, it was all too probable that the divine words which recalled Ps. 2⁷ should be made to agree with the terms of the psalm.

In the former expression it is surprising that the divine good pleasure should be expressly declared towards the "beloved Son." Such a declaration seems superfluous, as this Son is not to be compared with other sons. In the case of a servant who is to be marked out from fellow-servants, the language is natural enough. In addition to this, the terms used by the divine voice recall Isa. 42¹² in the form in which it is reproduced[3] in Matt. 12¹⁸ ἰδοὺ ὁ παῖς μου ὃν ᾑρέτισα, ὁ ἀγαπητός μου ὃν ηὐδόκησεν ἡ ψυχή μου· θήσω τὸ πνεῦμά μου ἐπ᾽ αὐτὸν καὶ κρίσιν τοῖς ἔθνεσιν ἀπαγγελεῖ. The Targum also shows a readiness to render Hebr. בָּחַר, "to choose," by אִתְרְעֵי, "to be well-pleased with"; see Isa. 43¹⁰ עַבְדִּי אֲשֶׁר בָּחַרְתִּי, Targ. עַבְדִּי מְשִׁיחָא דְאִתְרְעִיתִי בֵיהּ, "my servant, the anointed, in whom I am well-pleased," cf. 41⁸ 44¹·². The bestowal of the Spirit, mentioned in Isa. 42¹, is clearly the motive for the allusion to this prophetic statement. What Isa. 42¹ says of the servant of God was now being fulfilled. In that case παῖς μου in

---

[1] Proposed by Conybeare, Jew. Quart. Rev. ix. 463.

[2] Prov. 3¹² sounds similar : "Whom the Lord loveth, He reproveth ; even as a father the son in whom he delighteth " (וּכְאָב אֶת בֵּן יִרְצֶה). The LXX, however, renders (cf. Heb. 12⁶): μαστιγοῖ δὲ πάντα υἱὸν ὃν παραδέχεται, and there is no reference to the gift of the Spirit.

[3] The LXX has : Ἰακὼβ ὁ παῖς μου, ἀντιλήμψομαι αὐτοῦ· Ἰσραὴλ ὁ ἐκλεκτός μου, προσεδέξατο αὐτὸν ἡ ψυχή μου· ἔδωκα τὸ πνεῦμά μου ἐπ᾽ αὐτόν, κρίσιν τοῖς ἔθνεσιν ἐξοίσει.

Isa. 42¹, which stands for the Hebr. עַבְדִּי, "my servant,"
would be taken to mean "a child." This is not surprising.
In Acts 4²⁵· ²⁶ there is a citation of Ps. 2¹ which v.²⁷ applies
to the opposition of the Jewish authorities against "τὸν ἅγιόν
σου παῖδα Ἰησοῦν, ὃν ἔχρισας." The word παῖς here applied
to Jesus, as also in v.³⁰ and in 3¹³· ²⁶, is rendered in the
Peshita by בר, "son."—And since the Teaching of the
Apostles regards Jesus (10⁶, cf. Matt. 21⁹) not as the son of
David, but as the God of David,[1] conformably with Ps. 110¹
and Matt. 22⁴⁵, it can hardly be imagined that, in the same
eucharistic prayers which so speak of Him, Jesus should,
with reference to God, be called "Thy servant."[2] The word
παῖς used concerning Jesus, Teaching Ap. 9²· ³ 10², will
therefore mean "child," despite the fact that 9² (cf. Acts 4²⁵)
contains the same term applied to David. This meaning is
unmistakable in Clement of Rome, whose letter to the Corin-
thians, 59²ᶠ·, twice has the formula: διὰ τοῦ ἀγαπημένου
παῖδος αὐτοῦ (σου) Ἰησοῦ Χριστοῦ, cf. 59⁴ Ἰ. Χρ. ὁ παῖς
σου. The rendering "His (Thy) beloved child" is here
obviously necessary, and an allusion to the voice at the
Baptism and Transfiguration cannot be doubted. See also
ὁ μονογενὴς παῖς, Clem. Alex., Strom. vii. 1.

Not less clearly does the Wisdom of Solomon[3] treat παῖς
and υἱός as equivalent. The righteous man who names
himself παῖς κυρίου (2¹³), prides himself, according to 2¹⁶,
that God is his father; and the wicked wish to test whether
he really is what he professes to be, namely, υἱὸς θεοῦ (2¹⁸).
Hence the Syriac version rightly enough has rendered both

---

[1] It is remarkable that the closing formula in the petition for redemption in
the Palestinian Shemoneh Esreh (Eighteen Benedictions) should speak of Him
who was to send the Branch of David as the "God of David" (אֱלֹהֵי דָוִד); see
j. Ber. 8ᶜ, and the Palestinian recension of the Prayer, "Messianische Texte,"
No. 6ᵃ.

[2] In itself and in another environment there would be no objection to this
designation; see עַבְדִּי מְשִׁיחָא, "My Servant the Messiah," in Targ. Isa. 42¹ 43¹⁰
52¹³, Zech. 3⁸.

[3] See "Der leid. u. d. sterb. Messias," 31.

2¹³ and 2¹⁸ by "Son of God," ברה דאלהא. The Israelites are "sons" (υἱοί) of God, 12¹⁹, and in v.²⁰ "children" (παῖδες). In this case the Syriac translator notices the difference between υἱοί and παῖδες; but just after, v.²⁵, he feels obliged to render παῖδες by טליא, "children." The attitude of the Book of Wisdom is the more important on this point, because it contains undoubted references to the "Servant of the Lord" of Isa. 53. παῖς κυρίου in this author must necessarily be traced back to the "servant" (עֶבֶד) of God in Isa. 40–66,[1] for which term the LXX, as a rule, is wont to put παῖς.[2] The same misinterpretation of the word παῖς in the Greek Old Testament, where it stands for "servant," was easily possible to any one who did not know the Bible in Hebrew. If this be the author's view of παῖς in Acts, chaps. 3 and 4, then these chapters were the work of a Hellenist who wrote in the style of the Greek Bible.

The same confusion of παῖς and υἱός cannot be asserted without further consideration in regard to the divine voice at the Baptism and Transfiguration, because in this case it is not παῖς but υἱός that is used. But it becomes comprehensible how an original designation of Jesus as ὁ υἱός μου, which must be considered as constituting the essence of the divine utterance, since it stands in both forms of the text (see also ὁ υἱὸς τοῦ θεοῦ, John 1³⁴), was susceptible of an extension on the lines not only of Ps. 2⁷ but also of Isa. 42¹, tending to make the sense of the shorter phrase clearer, and commensurate with the importance of the occasion. And since the bestowal of the Spirit, mentioned in Isa. 42¹, will have been the reason for citing this particular passage of Scripture, it need not be assumed that the conventional form of the text was originally present in the account of the Transfiguration. On the contrary, the utterance at the Baptism has exercised an influence on that at the Trans-

[1] For additional proofs of the use of Isa. 40-66, see ibid. 32.
[2] Exceptionally the LXX has δοῦλος, 42¹⁹ 48²⁰ 49²·⁵.

figuration, as even the present text of Matthew indicates by adopting in 17[5] the supplement ἐν ᾧ εὐδόκησα.

In these circumstances there is no occasion for inquiry as to the Aramaic original. A translation of the divine words (at the Baptism) based on the Greek of Mark would have to be : אַתְּ בְּרִי [1] חֲבִיבִי אִתְרְעִיתִי בָךְ.

The first conclusion to be drawn from the tenor of the divine declaration at the Baptism is that He who was exceptionally endued with the Divine Spirit is in a special sense the object of the love and good pleasure of God. The evangelists give an account of the voice, not on account of any importance which the reception of such a divine voice might possibly have for Jesus, but in the sense of impressive testimonies that Jesus really was what His disciples before the world proclaimed Him to be.

Hence it is clear that the voice is intended to signify the divine good pleasure, not towards the person of Jesus as such, but towards Him as the agent of a special mission. This view is obviously presupposed by the injunction, "hear ye Him," appended to the account of the Transfiguration. This recalls the divine mandate of Deut. 18[15], to "hearken unto," that is, to obey, the Prophet who was to be raised up by God. Thus, however, we are directed to that position which Jesus Himself felt conscious of occupying as "the Son of God."

4. JESUS' OWN TESTIMONY.

Jesus never applied to Himself the title "Son of God," and yet made it indubitably clear that He was not merely "*a*" but "*the* Son of God." The position assumed shows itself in the preference He manifested for the designation of God as "His" Father, in the use of which He never includes the disciples along with Himself. In the prayer which He gave as an example to the disciples, it is only in Matthew

---

[1] Cf. Jer. 31[19] יַקִּיר בֵּן, Targ. בַּר חֲבִיב, LXX υἱὸς ἀγαπητός.

(6⁹) that the words are : πάτερ ἡμῶν ὁ ἐν τοῖς οὐρανοῖς. But not merely Luke, as Holtzmann [1] affirms, but also Matthew, places it beyond doubt that Jesus in this case merely puts this expression in the mouth of His disciples ; He does not pray with them in these terms. This distinction is made obvious by the explanation added about forgiveness by Matthew, in which the form " your heavenly Father " is at once resumed. But the unique position assumed by Jesus also follows in other passages from the invariable separation between " my Father " and " your Father." [2]

What Jesus understands by the filial relationship peculiar to Himself is perceived with special distinctness from the parable of the Vineyard let out to Husbandmen, Matt. 21³³⁻⁴⁶ (Mark 12¹⁻¹², Luke 20⁹⁻¹⁹). Here He sharply distinguishes the only " son " as the sole heir from the whole series of servants. Mark 12⁶ calls this son ἕνα υἱὸν ἀγαπητόν ; Luke 20¹³ τὸν υἱόν μου τὸν ἀγαπητόν ; Matt. 21³⁷ has merely τὸν υἱόν μου. It should here be recalled that the LXX puts τὸν υἱόν σου τὸν ἀγαπητόν, Gen. 22², for Hebr. אֶת בִּנְךָ אֶת יְחִידְךָ ; Onk. יָת בְּרָךְ יָת יְחִידָךְ, " thine only Son," and hence there is no difference between ὁ υἱὸς ὁ ἀγαπητός and ὁ υἱὸς ὁ μονογενής of John 3¹⁶. The position of the only son is, in these cases as in Ps. 2, regarded as a lawful standing which confers a right to claim the entire household property. In the case of the Son of God the reference can only be to the sovereignty of the world, and to such a sovereignty as would be exercised not by a Jewish emperor, but by a divine Sovereign.

A kindred idea appears in Matt. 17²⁵, where Jesus asks whether the kings of the earth exact tribute from their own

---

[1] Lehrb. d. neutest. Theol. i. 268. In Holtzmann's opinion, Jesus could not have spoken as in Luke 11⁴ of real ἁμαρτίαι, but only as in Matt. 6¹² of ὀφειλήματα, in the sense of defects such as would have been inevitable in His earthly existence. But Aramaic requires חוֹב as the original ; and this term, literally meaning " guilt," is in that language quite a common term for " sins." See Ex. 10¹⁷, Hebr. שָׂא נָא חַטָּאתִי, " forgive, I pray thee, my sin " ; Onk. שְׁבוֹק כְּעַן חוֹבִי, " pardon now my guilt."

[2] See above, p. 190.

sons; and the thought is, that as this is quite unusual, even
so the heavenly King, God, will not exact tribute from His
Son.   The question whether the tax was being paid had been
asked with reference to Jesus only, and therefore the statement which followed cannot further include Peter than to
the extent that he might, as an adherent of the Son, be
reckoned as exempted like his Master from the tax.   Here,
too, Jesus separates Himself from all Israelites as belonging
not to their number, but to God.

We should also include in this connection Matt. 22²;
cf. vv.⁸· ¹⁰· ¹², so far as the contents themselves are concerned,
where the Messianic supper is regarded as a marriage feast
for the Son of the King.   But Luke 14¹⁶ does not contain this
detail in describing the supper.[1]   As even in Matthew the
Son does not enter into the supper, this feature may be considered as a later addition, and need not here be taken into
account.

According to the foregoing, the " Son " means for Jesus
the heir to the throne of God, who as such occupies a unique
position.   Of course the heir to the throne after coming into
possession, may well enough entrust to others the authority
of government (Matt. 19²⁸, Luke 22²⁹ᶠ·),[2] but they do not
thereby become what He is.   Their dignity remains ever
dependent upon His.   They have in a derivative sense what
primarily pertains to Him alone.   He receives the sovereignty
because He is the Son, they because they are followers of
the Son.

A different scope is given to the filial relationship of
Jesus to God in Matt. 11²⁷ πάντα μοι παρεδόθη ὑπὸ τοῦ
πατρός μου, καὶ οὐδεὶς ἐπιγινώσκει τὸν υἱὸν εἰ μὴ ὁ πατήρ,
οὐδὲ τὸν πατέρα τις ἐπιγινώσκει εἰ μὴ ὁ υἱὸς καὶ ᾧ ἐὰν
βούληται ὁ υἱὸς ἀποκαλύψαι.[3]   The parallel in Luke (10²²)

---

[1] See above, p. 118.   [2] See above, p. 134.

[3] The Evan. Hierosol. has at the end ולמן דיצבא ברא דינלא הו נלא, "and to
whom the Son wills to reveal (Him), he reveals (Him).   It seems to read ἀποκα-
λύψει, and takes the last part of the verse to be an independent clause.

as given in the common text has only insignificant deviations. Blass makes Luke's reading to be: ἀπὸ τοῦ πατρός (without μου)—γινώσκει τίς ἐστιν ὁ υἱός—καὶ τίς ἐστιν ὁ πατήρ (without repetition of οὐδεὶς γινώσκει). In the last part of the verse Justin and Marcion read: οὐδεὶς ἔγνω τὸν πατέρα εἰ μὴ ὁ υἱός, καὶ τὸν υἱὸν εἰ μὴ ὁ πατὴρ καὶ ᾧ ἐὰν ὁ υἱὸς ἀποκαλύψῃ. The idea here entertained is not the sovereignty committed by God to Jesus, but the whole revelation of Jesus by means of which an adequate consciousness of God is attained. The "mysteries" of the sovereignty of God (see Matt. 13¹¹, Mark 4¹¹, Luke 8¹⁰) in their utmost extent were entrusted by His Father to Jesus, and indeed to Him alone, with the obligation to deal with them according to His own discretion. And this exclusive committal to Him is also the most natural, because between Father and Son there exists a perfect mutual understanding so unique, that any other persons could participate in the complete knowledge of the Father only through the medium of the Son. The two clauses referring to the knowledge of the Son by the Father and of the Father by the Son must therefore be taken together, and not independently expounded. They really constitute a detailed Oriental mode of expressing the reciprocity of intimate understanding.[1] But in this case of mutual understanding, its thoroughness and absolute infallibility are assumed. He who stands in so uniquely close a relation to God is the only possible mediator of the kind, and also at the same time the absolutely reliable revealer of the whole wealth of the divine mysteries.

The phraseology will thus have been originally intended in a figurative sense. But that which holds between father and son in general is straightway applied in reference to Jesus and His heavenly Father. So that in this instance, too, the peculiar relation of Jesus to God is one that cannot be transmitted to others or be subject to change. His

---

[1] Cf. j. R. h. S. 58ᵇ אֵלִּין מוֹרֵי לְאֵלִּין וְאֵלִּין מוֹרֵי לְאֵלִּין, "these agree with those and those with these," *i.e.* they mutually agree.

disciples, indeed, through His means attain to the same knowledge of God that He Himself possessed. But their knowledge is derived through a medium, while His is acquired by direct intuition.

As regards the Aramaic to be presupposed here, it will be more satisfactory to change παρεδόθη into the active voice. It is possible, indeed, even in Palestinian Aramaic to connect the subject in question with the passive voice through מִן, but examples in support are uncommon.[1] It is further questionable whether we should use יְדַע or חֲכַם for "to know." Galilean Aramaic uses the former for "to know a fact," the latter for "to know a person."[2] The biblical Aramaic and the dialect of Onkelos use only יְדַע. The Present γινώσκε and the Aorist ἔγνω would have the same form in an unpointed text, as the participle יָדַע and the perfect יְדַע would have to be used. The transposition of Father and Son in Justin's text involves the advantage of an easier transition from the first clause of the verse to the second, but also the disadvantage that the revelation of the Son by the Son is an improbable idea. Both the Lucan τίς ἐστιν ὁ υἱός (πατήρ) and the shorter form in Matthew τὸν υἱόν (πατέρα), are capable of reproduction in Aramaic. See j. Ter. 48b לָא אֲנָא חָכִים לְאַבָּא, "I do not know my father"; and j. Ber. 13c לֵית אֲנָא יָדַע מָה הוּא, "I do not know what he is." For "to be willing" biblical Aramaic has צְבָא; the Judæan dialect אֲבָא and צְבָא; the Galilean בְּעָא. But βούληται ἀποκαλύψαι can also be a Greek expansion of a prior ἀποκαλύψῃ.

Hence the Aramaic may be thus constructed: a כֹּלָּא מְסַר לִי

---

[1] See *F. E. König*, Syntax der hebr. Sprache (1897), 36 f., and the passages from Genesis he cites in Onkelos. The only other example known to me is Vay. R. 34 : he regarded them "as those from whom denarii are exacted by the government" (כִּתְבְּעִין מִן סַלְכוּתָא דַּיָּרִין). On the other hand, it is said, Koh. R. 7¹¹ הֲוָה כִּתְבְּעֵי לְמַלְכוּתָא, "he was pursued by the government." In Targ. Eccl. 8¹⁵ אִתְחֲיֵיב מִן שְׁמַיָּא should be rendered : "it was bestowed from heaven"; ibid. 9² 11³ אֶתְגְּוַר מִן שְׁמַיָּא, "it was so destined from heaven"; see p. 219 f.

[2] Cf. j. Gitt. 45c אִית בַּר נָשׁ דְּחַכְמִין לְחַבְרֵיהוֹן בְּאַפִּין וְלָא יָדְעִין שְׁמָהַתְהוֹן, "there are men who know others by face yet not by name."

אַבָּא וְלֵית דִּידַע דְּלִבְרָא [b]לְאָבָא דִּידַע אַבָּא וְלֵית אֱלָהֵן אֱלָהָא בְּרָא [c]וּמַן דְּמִנֵּלֵי לֵהּ בְּרָא.

(*a*) Since πάντα refers back to ταῦτα (Matt. 11²⁵, Luke 10²¹), כֻּלְּהוֹן, " all these things," might be better than כֹּלָּא. ταῦτα might perhaps be replaced by הָלֵין מִלַּיָּא, " these things " (literally these words). (*b*) Variants in Luke: מַן הוּא אַבָּא, מַן הוּא בְּרָא. (*c*) Variants in Matthew and Luke: וּמַן דְּצָבֵי בְּרָא לְגַלָּאָה לֵהּ.

So far, we have encountered nothing to show what idea Jesus entertained in regard to the genesis of His divine Son-ship. It can only be said that the passages just cited appear to imply that Jesus had shown no cognisance of any begin-ning in this relationship. It seems to be an innate property of His personality, seeing that He, as distinct from all others, holds for His own the claim to the sovereignty of the world, and the immediate knowledge of God, just as a son by right of birth becomes an heir, and by upbringing from childhood in undivided fellowship with the father enters into that spiritual relationship with the father which is natural for the child. From the question which Jesus asked the scribes, Matt. 22⁴¹⁻⁴⁶ (Mark 12³⁵⁻³⁷, Luke 20⁴¹⁻⁴⁴), about the meaning of Ps. 110¹, one may, however, derive an explicit testimony on this point. The Synoptic accounts are here in virtual agreement. For it is of no real consequence that, according to Mark and Luke, Jesus should Himself propound the question, how the Messiah should be called a son of David, whereas in Matthew Jesus first causes the Pharisees to say that, from their point of view, the Messiah is a son of David. The aim in either case is the same—to awaken reflection in regard to the descent of the Messiah rather than to His dignity or exalted rank. There would indeed be nothing remarkable in the fact that a son should attain to a higher rank than his father, and for the scribes it would not in the least be strange that the Messiah should be greater than David. On that point they did not, in fact, require any instruction. Justin Martyr [1] says

[1] Dial. cum Tryph. 33, 83.

that the Jews of his time applied Ps. 110 to Hezekiah; so it appeared to them possible that David should call *this king* his Lord.[1]   There is something artificial in recent attempts [2] to reduce the thought of Jesus to a mere suggestion that "son of David" was altogether unsuitable as a title for him to whom David had shown deference by calling him his Lord. An unbiassed reading of the statement of Jesus cannot avoid the conclusion that the Messiah is in reality the Son of One. more exalted than David, that is, the Son of God. And in that idea there was essentially nothing extravagant.   If Jesus was conscious of no beginning in His peculiar relationship to God, it must, of course, have had its genesis with His birth; and, further, God must have so participated in assigning that position, that the human factors concerned fell entirely into the background.   The prophet Jeremiah, according to Jer. 1⁵, prided himself in his prenatal election by God to prophecy; and Isa. 49⁵ says that the servant of the Lord was formed from the womb for his appointed function.   Why should Jesus, conscious of being the servant of the Lord whom Isaiah predicted, not have had a similar consciousness in regard to Himself?   Only it would be natural that He, being "the Son," as distinguished from all servants, should presuppose, not merely selection and predestination, but also a creative act on the part of God, rendering Him what no one, who stands in a merely natural connection with mankind, can ever by his own efforts become.   This idea is no way opposed to the other, that Jesus called Himself "Son of man."   For all

[1] The Pseudepigrapha have traces of a Messianic interpretation of Ps. 110 only in the Similitudes of Enoch, in so far as it is there said that the Messiah sits upon the throne of God; see 45³ 51³ 55⁴ 61⁸ 62². Still, a direct dependence on Ps. 110 cannot be observed. In rabbinic literature the earliest dictum verifying this reference is that of Khamma bar Khanina (*c.* 260), Midr. Ps. 18³⁶; cf. *Bacher*, Ag. d. pal. Am. i. 457, see also Midr. Ps. 110¹. Later references are given in "Der leid. u. d. sterb. Messias," 7. And Jesus by no means implies that every one understood Ps. 110¹ of the Messiah; He knows, however, that His hearers, by naming any one else in place of the Messiah, would only have increased their difficulty.

[2] See, *e.g.*, *Holtzmann*, Lehrb. d. neutest. Theol. i. 244.

the sublimity of which He was conscious in regard to His past, present, and future, never excludes the idea that for the present, by decree of the Divine Providence, He moves about among mankind, defenceless and weak. We do not find expressed the idea of God's becoming man, or of a twofold nature united in a single person; but there is attested the presence of One who appears in human weakness, who is a perfect Revealer of God and the future Ruler of the world, who has been bestowed upon the world by the supernatural power of God.

Nowhere do we find that Jesus called Himself the Son of God in such a sense as to suggest a merely religious and ethical relation to God,—a relation which others also actually possessed, or which they were capable of attaining or destined to acquire.

We have not taken into consideration in this connection the saying in regard to the Son's ignorance of the date of the redemption, Matt. 24[36] (Mark 13[32]), on which see p. 194. It may, however, be remarked that Zech. 14[7] and Ps. Sol. 17[23] also represent that only God knows the time of the redemption. The Targ. Eccl. 7[24] affirms that the mystery of the day when the Anointed King comes (רָז יוֹם דְּיֵיתֵי מַלְכָּא מְשִׁיחָא) is kept secret from men. Simeon ben Lakish (c. 260 A.D.) explained Isa. 63[4] "a day of vengeance is in my heart," with the words:[1] "in my heart I have made (it) manifest, but not to the attending angels." The command to evangelise the heathen, Matt. 28[19], is reserved for special discussion. The wording of both statements, which represents a use of the name of the Son unprecedented in the other sayings of Jesus, will be determined by the diction prevalent in the early Church.

[1] b. Sanh. 99[a]; cf. *Bacher, Ag. d. pal. Am.* i. 414.

5. THE SENSE ATTACHED BY THE SYNOPTISTS TO THE TITLE "SON OF GOD."

If the Hellenistic Synoptists took the title "Son of man" to mean "one born of man," they will also have regarded ὁ υἱὸς τοῦ θεοῦ as "one born of God." The Greek, unlike the Hebrew, does not use the term "son" to denote an extensive circle of relationships. He will always be inclined to understand ὁ υἱὸς τοῦ θεοῦ in the most exact literal sense, whereas the Israelite would only accept this idea through the constraint of some special reason. As regards Matthew, reference may be made to 16[16], where ὁ υἱὸς τοῦ θεοῦ τοῦ ζῶντος points back to τὸν υἱὸν τοῦ ἀνθρώπου in v.[13]; further, to 26[63], cf. v.[64], where ὁ υἱὸς τοῦ ἀνθρώπου and ὁ υἱὸς τοῦ θεοῦ are likewise contrasted; but specially to the narrative of the birth of Jesus, which, even without explicit reference thereto, forms the commentary to the testimony of the divine voice at the Baptism (3[17]). As regards Luke, the words of the angel, 1[35], explain for the readers the meaning of ὁ υἱὸς τοῦ θεοῦ by express reference to the unique nature of the birth of Jesus. Even the human lineage of Jesus is traced back by Luke (3[38]) to God, so that from any point of view Jesus comes to the position of "Son of God." Even before the Baptism Jesus calls God His "Father," Luke 2[49], where τοῦ πατρός μου appears contrasted with ὁ πατήρ σου, v.[48], in the language of the mother of Jesus. In Luke 22[69, 70] Son of God is contrasted with Son of man. As Mark[1] gives no history of the birth, but in its place at the beginning of his Gospel narrates the spiritual endowment of Jesus, the latter will accordingly represent for him[2] the "generation" of the Son. In his account of the condemnation of Jesus, 14[61, 62], he, too, has put

---

[1] The ancient reading υἱοῦ θεοῦ appended to Ἰησοῦ Χριστοῦ, Mark 1[1], cannot be reckoned original.

[2] This will not apply to Matthew and Luke. *W. Lütgert*, Das Reich Gottes, 69, wrongly says of the Synoptists in general, that in the history of the Baptism they "narrate the act of God, through which He adopted Jesus."

in antithesis the "Son of the Blessed" and the "Son of man."

The Hellenistic explanation of ὁ υἱὸς τοῦ θεοῦ cannot, in view of the ideas expressed by Jesus Himself, be pronounced altogether unjustified. An essential difference in apprehending the idea appears, however, in so far as Jesus uses the expression with respect primarily to His present relation to God, and only gives a glimpse that His origin was also of a nature corresponding to this position; whereas, on the other hand, the Synoptists make the latter consideration the foundation of the expression. The mode of thought in their case is Greek; that of Jesus is Semitic.

XI. CHRIST.

1. THE TERM IN JEWISH USAGE.

(a) *Derivation and Form.*

If the anointed of the Lord, mentioned in Ps. 2[2], be taken as a personification of Israel,[1] there is then no Old Testament passage in which the coming Prince of Salvation was called in a historical sense "the Anointed." This, however, should be considered accidental; for there was nothing to hinder Isaiah, *e.g.*, from calling the promised King "the Anointed of the Lord."

The oldest witness for the Messianic interpretation of Ps. 2 is the Psalter of Solomon (17); see above, p. 270. There, too, we find (v.[36]; cf. 18[6, 8]) the earliest designation of the Prince of Salvation as "the Anointed of the Lord," which will accordingly have Ps. 2 as its source. It is quite likely that other Scripture passages regarded as applying to the King of salvation contributed to the formation of the title. Mention is made of help, which is the allotted portion of

---

[1] Cf. p. 268, and *H. Weinel*, משׁח and its derivatives, ZAW, xviii. (1898), 69 ff.

"Jhvh's Anointed," Ps. 18⁵¹ 20⁷ 28⁸;¹ cf. 1 Sam. 2¹⁰, 2 Sam. 22⁵¹, Hab. 3¹⁸. Still there are no adequate proofs of any ancient Messianic exposition of these passages. The words of 1 Sam. 2¹⁰ וְיָרֵם קֶרֶן מְשִׁיחוֹ, "and He shall exalt the horn of His anointed," taken in connection with Ps. 89²⁵ וּבִשְׁמִי תָּרוּם קַרְנוֹ, "and in my name shall his horn be exalted," are recalled by the Messianic petition in the Babylonian Eighteen Benedictions² (or Shemoneh Esreh). The first half of this petition is based on Jer. 33¹⁵, and the other on Ezek. 29²¹, the words being : אֶת צֶמַח דָּוִד עַבְדְּךָ בִּמְהֵרָה תַצְמִיחַ וְקַרְנוֹ תָּרוּם בִּישׁוּעָתֶךָ בָּרוּךְ אַתָּה ה' מַצְמִיחַ קֶרֶן יְשׁוּעָה, "let the Branch of David thy servant sprout forth speedily, and let his horn be exalted through thy help : Blessed art Thou, O Lord, who causest to bud forth an horn of salvation !" In this connection we have also in the prayer beginning אָבִינוּ מַלְכֵּנוּ ³ the petition : תָּרֵם קֶרֶן מְשִׁיחֶךָ, "raise up the horn of Thine anointed," which, however, does not appear in Seder Rab Amram, i. 45ᵇ. On the other hand, Ps. 132¹⁷ שָׁם אַצְמִיחַ קֶרֶן לְדָוִד עָרַכְתִּי נֵר לִמְשִׁיחִי, "there will I make the horn of David to bud : I have ordained a lamp for mine anointed," is made use of in the prayer הֲבִיאֵנוּ, which is an ancient abridged form of the Eighteen Benedictions.⁴ Its words are : יִשְׂמְחוּ כָּל חוֹסֵי בָךְ בְּבִנְיַן עִירֶךָ וּבְחִדּוּשׁ בֵּית מִקְדָּשֶׁךָ וּבְהַצְמָחַת קֶרֶן לְדָוִד עַבְדֶּךָ וּבַעֲרִיכַת נֵר לְבֶן יִשַׁי מְשִׁיחֶךָ

¹ For Ps. 21, in particular, Messianic exposition can be proved ; see for v.⁴ Midr. Teh. ; Tanch., ed. Buber, Shem. 11ᵇ ; Shem. R. 8 ; Bern. R. 14 (according to Bem. R. Abin, and Midr. Teh. Simon) ; for v.⁵ b. Sukk. 52ᵃ (Baraitha). For Mess. exposition of Ps. 89²⁸, see Shem. R. 19 (Nathan, c. 180 A.D.) ; Midr. Teh. 5¹ ; Yalk. Shim. ii. 840 (Shemuel bar Nachmani, c. 260). On Ps. 110, see above, p. 285 f.

² In Palestine, as it seems, this petition formed part of that concerning the building of Jerusalem, which, in Babylon, had a separate position ; cf. j. Ber. 5ᵃ, Tos. Ber. iii. 25 with b. Taan. 13ᵇ ; see S. Baer, Seder Abodath Yisrael, 97 ; L. Landshuth, Siddur hegyon leb, 65 ff. On the other hand, Rothschild, Der Synagogal-Cultus in hist. krit. Entwickelung, i. (1870) 62 f., erroneously maintains that in Palestine the Messianic petition had for long ceased to be used. See, however, "Messianische Texte," No. 6ᵃ.

³ Baer, Seder Abodath Yisrael, 111.

⁴ See "Messianische Texte," No. 7 ; cf. Baer, Seder Abodath Yisrael, 108 ; Seder Rab Amram, i. 54ᵃ.

"may all they who trust in Thee rejoice over the building of thy city and the renewal of Thy sanctuary, over the budding forth of an horn for David Thy servant, and the ordaining of a lamp for the son of Jesse Thine anointed!" Elsewhere, see on Ps. 132[17], Ech. R. 2[6] (Midr. Ps. 75[11]); Tanchuma, ed. Buber, Shem. 46[a] (Yalk. Shim. i. 363) 50[a] (Yalk. Shim. i. 378); Vay. R. 31 (Yalk. Shim. i. 650); Yelammedenu, Yalk. Shim. i. 47 (Simeon ben Lakish, c. 260);[1] v.[18], Pirke Eliezer 28 (Yalk. Shim. i. 76); Pes. Rabb. 159[b].

The fact is, that no single passage, on the ground of Messianic interpretation, can be made responsible for the title " Messiah." When a name was wanted for the King of salvation, as depicted especially in Isa. 11[1-5],[2] there was a title which at once recommended itself—the solemn synonym often used for the royal title, and indicating the King's relation to God; and it was all the more convenient because the divine appointment and recognition formed the vital element in the case of the expected King. Of him, therefore, it would become usual to speak as מְשִׁיחַ יְהוָֹה, Aram. מְשִׁיחָא דַיְיָ, " Jhvh's Anointed." But as the Tetragrammaton was not pronounced, and as there was a reluctance[3] to name " God," so here, as in other commonly used titles, the name of God was omitted, and only הַמָּשִׁיחַ, Aram. מְשִׁיחָא, " the Anointed," was said. The Aramaic form is the basis of the Greek transliteration which appears in John 1[42] 4[25]. The peculiar form Μεσσίας with its doubled sibilant, I have formerly[4] sought to explain through a phonetic variation in Semitic. It seems preferable to point out that in Greek μέσσος is found in use alongside of μέσος. A similar relation will hold between Μεσσίας and Μεσίας, which is intrinsically more accurate, though rarely found.

---

[1] Cf. *Bacher*, Ag. d. pal. Am. i. 403.

[2] In the Book of Enoch, Psalter of Solomon, Apocalypse of Baruch, and 2 Esdras, the passage Isa. 11[1-5] is one of the most important bases of their Messianic doctrine.

[3] See above, p. 194 ff.

[4] Gramm. d. jüd.-pal. Aram. 124, Note 3 ; cf. 261, Note 1.

The full name "Anointed of Jhvh," or "my, his anointed," is first attested, Ps. Sol. 17³⁶ 18⁶· ⁸, Bar. Apoc. 39⁷ 40¹ 72².¹ The abbreviated form—apart from the New Testament—is found first in 2 Esdr. 7²⁸ᶠ· 12³². This was the form which became usual in the mouth of the common people.

Later Jewish literature has the full name only in the Targums wherever the text gives occasion for it, and in the Liturgy. מְשִׁיחָא דַיְיָ occurs Targ. Isa. 4² 28⁵; מְשִׁיחָךְ, Targ. Hab. 3¹⁸, Ps. 18³² 84⁴⁰; מְשִׁיחֵיהּ, Targ. Zech. 4⁷ 10⁴, Ps. 2² 20⁷. The prayer beginning מַלְבֵּנוּ אֱלֹהֵינוּ ² contains the form קְרַב מְשִׁיחָךְ, "let Thine anointed draw near." With regard to the shortened form, it has been pointed out by Franz Delitzsch,³ with a view to explaining the occasional use of Χριστός ⁴ without the article, that the Rabbis also sometimes use מָשִׁיחַ without the article in the manner of a proper name. This, indeed, is the usual practice in the Babylonian Talmud when מָשִׁיחַ is not subordinated by the syntax to any other word. מָשִׁיחַ, without accompaniment, occurs Sukk. 52ᵇ; Sanh. 93ᵇ, 96ᵇ, 97ᵃ, 98ᵃ 99ᵃ; even in Aramaic מְשִׁיחַ, Erub. 43ᵇ; Yoma 19ᵇ; Bab. mez. 85ᵇ; Ab. z. 2ᵇ; Sanh. 93ᵇ, 96ᵇ, 98ᵃ, 99ᵃ; so that we have even שְׁנֵי מְשִׁיחַ, "the years of Messiah," b. Sanh. 98ᵇ, and חֶבְלֵיהּ דִּמְשִׁיחַ, "the sorrow of Messiah," b. Keth. 111ᵃ. It is also said: מָשִׁיחַ בֶּן דָּוִד, "Messiah son of David," b. Sukk. 52ᵃ; Aram. מְשִׁיחַ בַּר דָּוִד, Targ. Cant. 4⁵ 7⁴. Again it is מְשִׁיחָא which is written, b. Erub. 43ᵇ; Sanh. 51ᵇ; Chull. 63ᵃ; and הַמְּשִׁיחַ, Nidd. 13ᵇ. The phrase יְמוֹת הַמָּשִׁיחַ, "the days of the Messiah," always involves the article; see b. Sanh. 97ᵃ, 99ᵃ; cf. Ber. i. 8; j. Kil. 32ᶜ. Probably we should also read חֶבְלוֹ שֶׁלַּמָּשִׁיחַ,⁵

---

¹ Cf. above, p. 270.   ² Seder Rab Amram, i. 9ᵃ.

³ Theol. Litbl. 1889, No. 45.

⁴ Χριστός with no article occurs in the Synoptists in Ἰησοῦς Χριστός, Matt. 1¹· ¹⁸, Mark 1¹; and arising from this designation in Ἰησοῦς ὁ λεγόμενος Χριστός, Matt. 1¹⁶ 27¹⁷· ²²; also in Χριστὸς κύριος, Luke 2¹¹, besides Mark 9⁴¹, Luke 23². Otherwise uniformly ὁ Χριστός.

⁵ The plural חֶבְלֵי הַמָּשִׁיחַ, brought into notice particularly by Wünsche, is quite unknown in the ancient literature, as I have shown in "Der leid. u. der sterb. Messias," 42.

"the sorrow of the Messiah," b. Sanh. 98ᵇ; b. Sabb. 118ᵃ;
cf. Mechilta, ed. Fr. 50ᵇ, 51ᵃ; שְׁמוֹ שֶׁלַּמָשִׁיחַ, "the name of the
Messiah," b. Pes. 5ᵃ; cf. Ber. R. 1; רוּחוֹ שֶׁלַּמָשִׁיחַ, "the spirit
of the Messiah," Ber. R. 2; דּוֹרוֹ שֶׁלַּמָשִׁיחַ, "the generation of
the Messiah," Mechilta, ed. Fr. 56ᵇ. Nevertheless, the Babylonian custom of using מָשִׁיחַ as a proper name is incapable of
being verified in regard to Palestine. It cannot, therefore,
be regarded as old, or as having had a determining influence
on Christian phraseology.

The older Targums have always the definite form מְשִׁיחָא;
see Onk. Gen. 49¹⁰, Num. 24¹⁷; Targ. 1 Sam. 2¹⁰, 2 Sam. 23³,
1 Kings 4⁴³, Isa. 9⁶ 10²⁷ 11¹. ⁶ 14²⁰, Jer. 33¹³, Mic. 5², Zech.
6¹². For מְשִׁיחָא דַיָי, see above. עַבְדִּי מְשִׁיחָא, "my servant, the
anointed," occurs Targ. Isa. 42¹ 43¹⁰ 52¹³, Zech. 3⁸; מְשִׁיחָא
דְיִשְׂרָאֵל, "the anointed of Israel," Targ. Isa. 16¹. ⁵, Mic. 4⁸;
מְשִׁיחֲהוֹן, "their anointed," Targ. Isa. 53¹⁰, Jer. 30²¹, Hos. 14⁸;
מְשִׁיחָא בַּר דָּוִד, "the anointed son of David," Hos. 3⁵; מָשִׁיחַ
דְּצִדְקָא, "the anointed of righteousness," Jer. 23⁵ 33¹⁵ (ed.
Venice, 1517; but ed. Venice, 1525, מְשִׁיחַ דְּצִדִיקַיָּא). For מְשִׁיחָא
alone, see also Sot. ix. 15; j. Kil. 32ᵇ. In the younger Targums, as also in the Palestinian Midrash and Talmud, the
fuller title, מַלְכָּא מְשִׁיחָא, Hebr. מֶלֶךְ הַמָּשִׁיחַ,[1] predominates. This
should not, as is generally the case, be translated by "the
King Messiah," because מְשִׁיחָא and הַמָּשִׁיחַ are clearly not meant
as proper names. In later Jewish Aramaic, a title is regularly
placed after the proper name.[2] We have יַנַּי מַלְכָּא, "the king
Yannai," Ber. R. 91 לוּלְיָנוֹס מַלְכָּא, "the king Julian," j. Ned. 37ᵈ;
שְׁלֹמֹה מַלְכָּא, "the king Solomon"; דָּוִד מְשִׁיחָא, "David the
anointed," in the Litany[3] רַחֲמָנָא אִדְכַּר; נְשִׂיָּא יוּדָן, "the Prince
Judan," j. Taan. 65ᵃ. "King Messiah" would have to be

---

[1] הַמֶּלֶךְ הַמָּשִׁיחַ is unusual; see Seder Rab Amram, i. 53ᵃ. On the omission of
the article with definite substantives, see *F. E. König*, Syntax d. hebr. Sprache,
403 f.; *S. R. Driver*, Hebrew Tenses,³ 281 ff.

[2] Biblical Hebrew and Aramaic admit the inverted order; see *König*, op. cit.
397 f.; *E. Kautzsch*, Gramm. d. bibl. Aram. 149 f.

[3] Seder Rab Amram, ii. 19ᵇ f.

expressed by מְשִׁיחַ מַלְכָּא, whereas מַלְכָּא מְשִׁיחָא means "the king, the anointed," or "the anointed king." Examples for the Aramaic form are found j. Ber. 5ᵃ, j. Taan. 68ᵈ; and for the Hebrew form, Ber. R. 1, 98, Shem. R. 1. For מַלְכָּא מְשִׁיחָא, see also Targ. Jerus. I. Gen. 3¹⁵ 35²¹ 49¹·¹⁰·¹⁷, Ex. 40⁹, Num. 23²¹ 24²⁰·²⁴, Deut. 25¹⁹ 30⁴; Targ. Jerus. II. Gen. 3¹⁵ 49¹⁰·¹¹·¹², Ex. 12⁴², Num. 11²⁶ 24⁷, Targ. Cant. 1⁸ 7¹⁴ 8¹·²·⁴, Ruth 1¹ 3¹⁵, Eccl. 1¹¹ 7²⁴, Ps. 21²·⁸ 45³ 61⁷·⁹ 72¹ 80¹⁶. מְשִׁיחָא stands by itself in this sense only in Targ. Jerus. I. Num. 24¹⁷, Targ. Lam. 2²² 4²²; and for מְשִׁיחַ בַּר דָּוִד, as well as מְשִׁיחָךְ, מְשִׁיחֵיהּ, see the two preceding pages.

A less common title, in which מְשִׁיחַ is similarly inadmissible as a proper name, is מְשִׁיחַ צִדְקֵנוּ, "our righteous anointed." By this name the people Israel refer to the Messiah, Pes. Rabb. 162ᵇ, 163ᵃ, 164ᵃ. In a similar manner God calls Him "My righteous Anointed," מְשִׁיחַ צִדְקִי, ibid. 161ᵇ, 162ᵃ, 163ᵃ.[1] Men addressing God in prayer say: מְשִׁיחַ צִדְקֶךָ, "Thy righteous Anointed," Seder Rab Amram, i. 9ᵃ. The same name is given to David, ibid. 10ᵇ, and, apparently, also to Israel, ibid. 12ᵃ. The designation is borrowed from צֶמַח צְדָקָה, Jer. 33¹⁵, where the Targum has מְשִׁיחַ דְּצִדְקָא, and perhaps also from the Messianic name יְהוָֹה צִדְקֵנוּ, "our righteous Lord," Jer. 23⁶. There is also found מְשִׁיחַ הַצַּדִּיק, "the righteous Anointed," Agada to Shir ha-Shirim 4¹¹.[2]

(b) Signification and Content of the Title "Christ."

The name מְשִׁיחָא is one of those for which the particular term selected is of minor consequence compared to the general conception entertained in regard to the individual so designated. It is this general conception which really gives the word its full significance. Still, the literal sense of the expression cannot be neglected. The kings of Israel from the beginning were called "anointed of Jehovah," not merely to

---

[1] Cf. "Der leid. u. d. sterb. Mess." 58 f.

[2] Jew. Quart. Rev. vii. 153; cf. Yalk. Machiri (ed. Spira, 1894) on Isa. 11¹².

suggest that at their installation there had been an unction with holy oil, but to imply that in virtue of this unction they belonged to a special circle of the servants of God, their persons being sacred and inviolable. Whoever offers violence to this anointed character, commits an outrage against God. Hence cursing of God and of the king stand together, 1 Kings 21¹⁰·¹³. The character acquired through this unction is so prominently present in the thought of a Hebrew, that he can use the expression even where no actual unction had taken place. Thus Cyrus, Isa. 45¹, and the Patriarchs, Ps. 105¹⁵, are spoken of as " God's anointed ones," as being under His inviolable protection. When the king of the Messianic age is called מְשִׁיחָא, that implies that he is under God's peculiar protection ; and it should be noted that at the time the Jews coined this expression, they had no God-protected sovereign at their head. To set their hopes upon him meant the expectation of an independent kingdom protected by God. *This* is the Jewish Messianic idea, which one should beware of pronouncing " carnal " ; because, thus apprehended, the idea corresponds, on the whole, with Old Testament prophecy. In the sense meant by Jesus, such a predicate is possible only when any one, trusting to flesh as his arm, pledges himself to set in operation at his own instance processes which originate with God alone.

It must be specially observed that the " Messiah " of Old Testament prophecy was never at any time regarded as " Redeemer." In the Old Testament it is God who is for Israel גּוֹאֵל " redeemer," פֹּדֶה " liberator," מוֹשִׁיעַ " Saviour," מַצִּיל " deliverer," and never the Messiah ; and no similar agency is ever ascribed to the latter. Failure to observe this has led to many distorted pronouncements on the statements and the silence of the prophetic and apocalyptic writers in regard to the Messiah. So long ago as 1874, D. Castelli had written these weighty sentences : [1] " In no part of the Old Testament does the Messiah appear as himself the agent of

[1] Il Messia secondo gli Ebrei, 164.

redemption in virtue of his own proper power. The real redeemer is God.—The Messiah is the new king of the redeemed people." For the earlier Isaiah the Messiah was a highly important personality, because his righteous government guaranteed the abiding welfare of the redeemed Israel. As Jeremiah and Ezekiel recognised a miraculous transformation in the heart of the people of the future, the activity of a king could seem to them of no great consequence. They have therefore little to say of the Messiah. It need not be supposed that such prophets and apocalyptic writers as never mention the Messiah at all, should therefore have believed that Israel should be kingless in the age of salvation. But they considered it superfluous to speak of the king, the vital consideration being first of all the advent of redemption. There is silence on the subject of the Messianic king in Sibyll. iii. 73 f., Enoch i. (1–36) and v. (91–104), the Slavonic Enoch, Ass. Mosis, Book of Jubilees,[1] certain sections of the Apocalypse of Baruch and of 2 Esdras, also in Judith, Tobit, Sirach, and even in the primary form [2] of the Kaddish. Other books mention the Messiah, but give the impression that no definite apprehension existed as to his nature. It was sufficient to recognise that there is a Messiah. As a matter of course, his character and government are appropriate to the age of salvation. A passive part of this kind is ascribed to the Messiah in Enoch iv. (83–90), in the passage Bar. Apoc. 29^3 30^1, which is probably foreign to its present connection, and in 2 Esdras $7^{28f.}$ It is not otherwise, even in the official prayer of the synagogue, the Eighteen Supplications, which represents God as gathering together the scattered people, undoing the sovereignty of arrogance, building Jerusalem, making His habitation there once more, restoring the temple

---

[1] How *W. Singer*, Das Buch der Jubiläen oder die Leptogenesis, i. (1898), can discover in this book, with its absence of Messianic elements, a polemical document of the Jewish Christians against St. Paul, is incomprehensible.

[2] See "Messianische Texte," No. 8.

service; whereas the Messiah [1] is mentioned only at the close, apparently because the divine promise given to David cannot remain unfulfilled. God alone, according to the seventh petition, is Israel's Redeemer (גּוֹאֵל יִשְׂרָאֵל).

On the other hand, the work of redemption is assigned to the Messiah in Sibyll. iii. 652 ff., which says that the king sent by God destroys the perverse, and unites himself with the obedient, and in the Similitudes of Enoch, where the Son of man judges and overthrows the secular rulers; and similarly in Apoc. Bar. 39[7] 40[1f.] 70[9] 72[2–6], 2 Esdr. 12[32ff.] 13[9–11. 37. 38]. Thus there had arisen among the Jewish people in the time of Jesus a tendency, diverging from the older prophecy based on the Messianic picture of Isa. 11[1–5], which concerned itself with a Messiah endowed with miraculous power, who was to overthrow the secular might, and by this means to liberate the people of God. Thenceforward it became possible to transfer to the Messiah statements which the Old Testament applies to God only as the Redeemer of Israel. An interesting example of this kind in the New Testament is seen in Matt. 2[21], where the name of Jesus is explained by the words, αὐτὸς γὰρ σώσει τὸν λαὸν αὐτοῦ ἀπὸ τῶν ἁμαρτιῶν αὐτῶν. But it is of God that Ps. 130[8] says : הוּא יִפְדֶּה אֶת יִשְׂרָאֵל מִכֹּל עֲוֹנוֹתָיו, "and He shall redeem Israel from all his iniquities."

As the earlier view still persisted, there was therefore at the time in question a twofold conception of the Messiah; one, more closely attached to ancient prophecy, which regarded the Messiah merely as the Prince of the redeemed people; the other, recently developed, which took the Messiah himself to be the redeemer. In neither case was he merely a political character. Jews with purely secular interests would hardly have concerned themselves, in that age any more than now, with the Messianic hopes. But the Israelite who rested his

---

[1] The Davidic sovereignty alone is mentioned in the Palestinian recension of the Eighteen Benedictions ("Mess. Texte," No. 6a), in Habinenu (ibid. No. 7), in the Additional Prayer for New Year (ibid. No. 9), and in the Blessing at Meals.

hopes upon the divine promise to Israel felt it to be a religious necessity that God should vindicate His power against the tyrannous empires of the world, and so give to His people the position befitting them as His. And beyond this Israel also required a purification from godless elements within itself. This latter point must be emphasised against Ehrhardt's [1] strange contention, that in the view of the Apocalytic writers " the people would be justified through the observation of the law, and they looked for no other justification ; all they wanted was the possession of power, outward triumph." [2] But the idea of a separation between the righteous and the wicked, which had to be carried out in Israel, does pervade the apocalyptic writings. The moral admonitions in the son of Sirach, in the Psalter of Solomon, the Testament of the Twelve Patriarchs, and in Enoch 94–105, cannot be pronounced lacking in deep earnestness and holy zeal.[3] Any excessive insistence on the ceremonial precepts of the law cannot be observed in these books. It must be admitted, however, that in this respect the Books of Tobit, Judith, and Jubilees occupy a considerably lower position. For that reason, naturally, the Messiah does not appear as a person

[1] E. Ehrhardt, Der Grundcharakter der Ethik Jesu (1895), 27.

[2] Ehrhardt's reference to b. Ber. 34ᵇ is misleading. The passage, true enough, gives as the opinion of the Babylonian Samuel (c. 250 A.D.): "The difference between the present age and the days of the Messiah consists only in the oppression through the secular powers." But this means merely that in the time of Messiah no transformation of nature will as yet have taken place, because such transformation does not occur till the end of the world. In this connection it is asserted that all prophetic promises are valid only for the penitent. And it is often enough maintained that the redemption is postponed because Israel is not in the right condition required by the law.

[3] The inexact notions entertained about the ethics of late Judaism are illustrated in Ehrhardt, op. cit. 45, who infers from the preference assigned to גְּמִילוּת חֲסָדִים over צְדָקָה, b. Sukk. 49ᵇ, that a distinction was made between "a more formal exercise of virtue, and one directed rather to practical results." He has rightly identified צְדָקָה with "almsgiving," but has not perceived that גְּמִילוּת חֲסָדִים denotes above all things visits to the sick, attendance at funerals, and consolation of mourners. "Moral acts involving reward" (fruchtbringend) were never thought of in this context. Moral conduct is determined for Judaism by the Law; the "practice of deeds of love" exceeds what is prescribed by Law.

who strikes the dominant note in the religion. His function does not consist in being a moral example, in teaching right conduct, or in being mediator of atonement, far less in being the giver of the divine Spirit; but just in ruling over Israel as a king according to the will of God. But this also applies to the Prince of salvation as he appears in Old Testament prophecy. It was a later period that regarded the Messiah as expounder of the existing law, or even the inaugurator of a new law. Expiatory sufferings were then attributed to him, which, however, are brought into organic relation with the process of salvation only by the appendix to Pesikta Rabbati. On the other hand, the doctrine, which arose in the second century, of a Messiah ben Joseph who should suffer death, has no connection with the remission of sin. See " Der leid. u. d. sterb. Messias," 1–26.

(c) The Idea of Pre-existence.

We may recall the Jewish ideas already reviewed, p. 129 ff., which are concerned with the pre-existence of various entities, and especially of the Messiah. Harnack [1] supposes it to be an ancient Jewish conception that " everything of genuine value, which successively appears upon earth, has its existence in heaven, i.e. it exists with God, meaning in the cognition of God, and therefore really." But this idea must be pronounced thoroughly un-Jewish, at all events un - Palestinian, although the medieval Kabbala certainly harbours notions of this sort. According to Ex. $25^{9.40}$ 26^{30} 27^8, Num. 8^4, there was shown to Moses on Sinai a model of the tabernacle and its furniture. No ulterior idea is implied beyond the thought that the oral instruction given to Moses, being insufficient to guide him with precision, was supplemented by the exhibition of models. By this means the object was secured that the structure fully conformed to

[1] Dogmengeschichte,[3] i. 755 ; see also *Baldensperger*, Das Selbstbewusstsein Jesu, 89 ; *Schürer*, Gesch. d. jüd. Volkes, ii. 423, 446.

the divine intention. This case is substantially the same as that in 1 Chron. 28[11ff.], where David, appealing to a divine mandate concerning it, hands over to Solomon a model of the temple that was to be built. A house of God is not to be constructed to please human fancies, but according to exact divine prescription. A sanctuary permanently existent in heaven, of which tabernacle and temple were imperfect imitations, is never contemplated.

When one finds occasional statements about constituents so important in the scheme of the world as the Law, the Temple, Paradise, Hell, affirming a premundane existence in their case, these are to be regarded neither as a "warrant of compensation against the damages which the possessions of religion might incur in the bitter struggle against the hostile elements";[1] nor yet as bound up with the thought of the divine Omniscience "which preordains history and is never taken unawares by events."[2] Any one familiar with the discussions on these topics in the Midrash is aware that behind these utterances there lies no more than a vague notion that the most important elements for realising the world's chief end must have been provided from the first. The actual production of these things at once would be better calculated to secure the end than a mere designing of them. The Jerusalem of the consummation may fitly be said to come from heaven, being so majestically conceived that it can never be the product of human effort. The city of golden streets must, of course, have been made by God. On some occasions we have to do merely with a rabbinical combination of scriptural texts. Gen. 1[3] speaks of a "light" which thenceforward seems to have no place in the world. And when, for instance, Isa. 9[1] 60[1], Zech. 14[7] mention the appearance of a light in the Messianic age, it is said that this must be the light of Gen. 1[3] which was being kept in

---

[1] Thus *Baldensperger*, Das Selbstbewusstsein Jesu,[2] 89.
[2] *Harnack*, op. cit.

store for the pious, Ber. R. 3, 11; Pes. Rabb. 118ᵃ, 161ᵃ·ᵇ·[1] The presupposition implied is that all the primordial excellence of creation must again be restored at the end. A case of the same nature is found in the grape-juice of Paradise and the primæval monsters Leviathan and Behemoth. Paradise lost returns, bringing such things with it.

As for the Messiah, two ways of regarding him were possible. On the one hand, he might be looked upon as indispensable in the scheme of the world, so that it could be said that God had not only, long ages ago, contemplated the provision of a Messiah, but had actually created him. On the other hand, it was also possible to assume from the wonderful manner of his advent, that he was not an ordinary child of earth. As a matter of fact, the earlier rabbinism was content with holding, on the basis of Ps. 72¹⁷,[2] the pre-existence of the name only of the Messiah.[3] Since the Messiah had to appear as a fully-developed man, the opinion generally was that until his manifestation he should remain unknown upon earth.[4] Before his appearance he had then to undergo some sudden metamorphosis.[5] Others supposed that he should be translated into Paradise, and should thence make his advent.[6] This was all the more likely if he were regarded as a return to earth of David[7] or Hezekiah.[8] The celestial pre-existence of Messiah, as stated in the Simili-

[1] Cf. "Der leid. u. d. sterb. Messias," 58.   [2] Ibid. 72.

[3] The Targums do not go beyond the name; see Targ. Mic. 5¹, Zech. 4⁷, Ps. 72¹⁷. *Holtzmann*, Lehrb. d. neutest. Theologie, i. 75, finds personal pre-existence attested in Targ. Isa. 9⁶, Mic. 5² (read 5¹), and ideal pre-existence in Targ. Ps. 93¹, Prov. 8⁸. But the last two passages hardly deal with the Messiah at all; the second cited attributes pre-existence only to the name; and the first passage speaks only of an endless duration of the Messianic rule. Holtzmann's statements probably originate from *A. Edersheim*, who in "The Life and Times of Jesus the Messiah,"² i. 175, gives prominence to assertions that are inaccurate. More precise information is found in *Weber*, Jüdische Theologie,² 354 ff.

[4] See John 7²⁷; Justin, Dial. c. Trypho, viii. 110; Targ. Mic. 4⁸; j. Ber. 5ᵃ; also "Der leid. u. d. sterb. Messias," 39 ff., 73.

[5] See above, p. 178.   [6] "Der leid. u. d. sterb. Messias," 77 ff.

[7] So j. Ber. 5ᵃ (Baraitha); cf. "Der leid. u. d. sterb. Messias," 73.

[8] So b. Ber. 28ᵇ (Yokhanan ben Zakkai, c. 80 A.D.).

tudes of Enoch and in 2 [4] Esdr. 13, 14, excluding [1]—so at least it seems—an earthly origin, implies, apart from the incentive contributed by Dan. 7[13], his miraculous superhuman appearance. According to the late addition to Pesikta Rabbati, the Messiah shares his pre-existence with the souls of all men. The only difference is that he appears to exist not merely as a soul, but as a complete personality.[2] For all these ideas of pre-existence, earthly and heavenly, a potent stimulus lay in the cherished hope that the redemption was imminent, or might, at any rate, come at any moment. In that case, of course, the Messiah was already in existence; the only question was, where? The divine providence comes here into consideration, because it is due to it that all things have been so well ordered that the divine scheme of the world should realise itself without impediment.

The notion of pre-existence is entirely absent in Ber. R. 2,[3] which says that the Spirit of God, brooding over Chaos in Gen. 1[2], was "the Spirit of the Messiah." This belongs to an exposition of Simeon ben Lakish (c. 260), which applies Gen. 1[2] to the "sovereignties," מַלְכִיוֹת, of the world. The word תֹהוּ is applied by him to Babylon; בֹהוּ, to the Medes; חֹשֶׁךְ, to the Greek dominion; תְּהוֹם, the godless sovereignty (Rome); רוּחַ אֱלֹהִים, the Messiah;[4] הַמַּיִם, repentance, failing which the Messiah does not come. Edersheim[5] holds that the idea of the co-operation of the Messiah in the work of creation is

---

[1] The coming of the Messiah from the sea, 2 Esdr. 13[1], implies, according to 13[52], only his complete invisibility so far as the inhabitants of the earth are concerned. He seems from 14[9] to have stayed in Paradise.

[2] See "Der leid. u. d. sterb. Messias," 58. In Pes. Rabb. 152[b] it is said: "At the beginning of the creation of the world the Anointed King was 'born' (נוֹלָד), whose inception in the thought (of God) took place before the world was made."

[3] See Ber. R. 8, Vay. R. 14, for the same phrase; cf. Bacher, Ag. d. pal. Amor. i. 389 f. Only Pes. Rabb. 152[b] has construed from it an assertion of the pre-existence of the Messiah.

[4] The "Spirit of the Messiah" is only referred to, because Isa. 11[2] was the instrument used for bringing the Messiah into connection with "the Spirit" of Gen. 1[2].

[5] The Life and Times of Jesus the Messiah,[2] i. 178.

here indicated, or at least of a function of the Messiah in regard to the whole world, such as raised him beyond the status of men. But both inferences appear absurd when it is remembered that a corresponding pre-existence would have to be maintained for the four secular kingdoms. Ben Lakish had nothing of the kind in view, but simply found it remarkable that the words of Gen. 1² should contain such suggestions of the future history of the world.

2. THE APPLICATION OF THE NAME "MESSIAH" TO JESUS.

In Matt. 27¹⁷·²² Pilate uses the expression Ἰησοῦς ὁ λεγόμενος Χριστός. That is not intended to mean "Jesus who is supposed to be the Messiah," but with the usual sense of this idiom "Jesus surnamed Christ." The same form is seen Matt. 1¹⁶, and in Σίμων ὁ λεγόμενος Πέτρος, 4¹⁸ 10². In this case we have presumably the language of the Church, which named its heavenly head not "Jesus" merely, but either Ἰησοῦς Χριστός, as in Matt. 1¹·¹⁸, Mark 1¹, or else by the surname¹ ὁ Χριστός, as in Matt. 11². It cannot, however, be supposed that during His earthly life Jesus ever bore the title "Messiah" as a surname. According to Matt. 16²⁰ (Mark 8³⁰, Luke 9²¹), His disciples were not allowed so to speak of Him, and other persons will hardly have made use of such a surname. The more precise form of Pilate's words will be as in Mark 15⁹·¹², where the judge is represented— obviously in reference to the indictment brought against Jesus and His own averment — as calling Jesus ironically the "King of the Jews."

Still less can it be supposed that the form Χριστὸς κύριος was anywhere a common title of the Messiah. This is found, indeed, LXX Lam. 4²⁰, Ps. Sol. 17³⁶, but is no mere mistranslation of the Hebr. מְשִׁיחַ יְהוָה. For it is incredible

---

¹ On "by-names" (Kinnui) and their frequent displacement of the individual name, see my treatise "Der Gottesname Adonaj," 53 f.

that a translator should have taken יהוה to be a Messianic name by mistake. It is more reasonable to hold that the Greek Χριστὸς κυρίου was changed into Χριστὸς κύριος. In Luke 2¹¹ Χριστὸς κύριος cannot possibly arise from a Hebrew original.[1] It must be due to Luke himself, who here uses the appellation Χριστός for the first time in his writings, and required to explain the new term for his reader, in the same way as the Jews do for Pilate by saying, 23², Χριστὸς. βασιλεύς. In Acts 2³⁶ Luke also puts κύριος alongside of Χριστός, and frequently in the Gospel calls Jesus simply ὁ κύριος.

The expression ὁ Χριστὸς κυρίου is indeed biblical, and is well suited to the revelation given to Simeon by the Holy Spirit (Luke 2²⁶); but in the Petrine confession, where Luke uses it in the form ὁ Χριστὸς τοῦ θεοῦ (9²⁰), it would be out of conformity with the common parlance of the people.[2] The simple ὁ Χριστός of Mark 8²⁹ is alone free from objection. It was this term that Jesus Himself used in speaking of the Messiah, Matt. 22⁴² (Mark 12³⁵, Luke 20⁴¹).

By contemporaries Jesus was frequently called ὁ Χριστός. One instance is by Peter, Matt. 16¹⁶ (Mark 8²⁹, Luke 9²⁰). On this occasion, ὁ Χριστός, Aram. מְשִׁיחָא, given by Mark, is historically more exact; and the additions in Luke (τοῦ θεοῦ) and in Matthew (ὁ υἱὸς τοῦ θεοῦ τοῦ ζῶντος) should be discarded, as has already been demonstrated p. 274, cf. 196. And if the words υἱὸς τοῦ θεοῦ of the demoniacs, Matt. 8²⁹ (Mark 5⁷, Luke 8²⁸), Mark 3¹¹, Luke 4⁴¹, are to be traced back to ὁ Χριστός, as indicated on p. 275, this would also imply a designation of Jesus by this title. According to Matt. 27⁵⁴ (Mark 15³⁹), the Roman centurion on guard at the Cross acknowledged Jesus to be υἱὸς θεοῦ, i.e. "Messiah," but the words are otherwise given in Luke 23⁴⁷. Jesus is called derisively (ὁ) Χριστός, Matt. 26⁶⁸, Mark 15³² (Luke

---

[1] See above, pp. 38 f., 224.   [2] See above, p. 291 f.

23^{35}), Luke 23^{39}. In Matt. $27^{40.\ 43}$ υἱὸς θεοῦ likewise depends on the derisive use of ὁ Χριστός.

Jesus is indirectly referred to as Messiah where He is regarded as the future possessor of the kingdom, Matt. 20^{21} (Mark 10^{37}), Luke 23^{42}. He is mockingly called "King" Matt. 27^{11} (Mark 15^2, Luke 23^3), Mark $15^{9.\ 12}$, Matt. 27^{29} (Mark 15^{18}), Matt. 27^{37} (Mark 15^{26}, Luke 23^{38}), Matt. 27^{42} (Mark 15^{32}, Luke 23^{37}). In the last solemn entry into Jerusalem it is improbable that the multitude should have greeted Him as "King" (so Luke 19^{38}), or possessor of the Davidic kingdom (so Mark 11^{10}), or "Son of David" (so Matt. 21^9), see p. 222. Under No. XII. it will be shown that υἱὸς Δαυΐδ has likewise all the force of a Messianic title, so that invocations of Jesus by this name also meant the recognition of Him as the Messiah.

3. THE ACKNOWLEDGMENT OF THE NAME "MESSIAH" BY JESUS HIMSELF.

Meinhold [1] makes the statement that Jesus for His own part never desired to be "the Messiah of Israel, as the character is depicted in Old Testament prophecy and consistently therewith was expected by the contemporaries of Jesus." Of Him it should be said: [2] "He is not the Messiah, and did not desire to be so." Herein there is only this element of truth, that the position and work of the Messiah, as conceived by Jesus, greatly transcended the type predicted in the Old Testament. But any rejection of the prophetic ideal of the Messiah as understood by Jesus cannot come into serious consideration.

No weight, indeed, can be attached to Mark 9^{41}, where Jesus speaks to His disciples of benevolence shown to them ἐν ὀνόματί μου ὅτι Χριστοῦ ἐστέ. The words ὅτι Χριστοῦ

---

[1] *J. Meinhold*, Jesus und das Alte Testament (1896), 98 ff.
[2] Ibid. 101.

ἐστέ are here an unnecessary explanation of ἐν ὀνόματί μου
which arises from בִּשְׁמִי,[1] " with reference to me," " thinking
upon me." Again, Matt. 23[10], where Jesus speaks of the
Messiah as the καθηγητής of the disciples, cannot be made
the basis of any inference in this connection, because it is
probably just a duplicate of v.[8] leading up to v.[11] It is
true in fact that Jesus did not proclaim Himself to be the
Messiah, nor did He wish that others should make Him known
in this capacity; see Mark 1[34] (Luke 4[41]), Matt. 16[20] (Mark
8[30], Luke 9[21]), cf. Matt. 17[9] (Mark 9[9]). But it is equally
certain that the Synoptic Gospels unanimously maintain that
Jesus was the Messiah predicted by the prophets, not merely
in the opinion of the authors, but in the belief that Jesus
also shared this conviction. The grounds they had for this
belief will have been none other than those presented to us
in the Gospels, namely, (1) the self-designation " Son of
man " chosen by Jesus, including all He had declared of his
advent in majesty and especially of his kinghood; (2) His
assent to the Messianic confession of Peter; (3) His own
acknowledgment during the capital trial repeated before the
high priest and before Pilate.

As for the first point, " Son of man " was at the time an
unusual title for the Messiah, and for that reason it was
chosen by Jesus that the people might not transfer to Him
their own Messianic ideas. But that choice simply meant
a protest against the supposition that He on His own impulse
should seize the sovereignty before God should invest Him
with it;[2] and against the Messianic theory[3] that had recently
arisen, which required the Messiah to become through combat
the liberator of Israel. But He had not the slightest opposi-

---

[1] Matthew with the same meaning says (10[41t.]) with more precision εἰς ὄνομα.
Cf., further, G. A. Deissmann, Bibelstudien, 143 ff., Neue Bibelstudien, 24 ff.
[Eng. tr. pp. 146 ff., 196 ff.]; and for בִּשְׁמִי, A. J. H. W. Brandt, Theol. Tijdschrift,
xxv. (1891) 585–589, whose researches J. Böhmer in "Das biblische 'im Namen '"
(1898) has overlooked to the detriment of his subject. See also above, p. 123.

[2] Cf. above, p. 137 f.   [3] See above, p. 297.

tion to offer to the scriptural teaching about the King, who, according to Isa. 11¹⁻⁵, Mic. 5², Jer. 23⁵ 33¹⁵, Zech. 9⁹, should reign in righteousness over the redeemed people. He was conscious of being endowed with the Spirit of God; and this was a mark of the Messianic King, Isa. 11², as well as of the Servant of the Lord, Isa. 42¹ 61¹ (cf. Luke 4¹⁸ᶠᶠ·). He bore witness to Himself as God's only Son and Heir; such an one was the Messiah according to Ps. 2. He was assured that Ps. 110 spoke of Him (Matt. 26⁶⁴, Mark 14⁶², Luke 22⁶⁹); and the one who is there indicated as King of Sion, is in His view the Messiah (Matt. 22⁴¹ᶠᶠ·, Mark 12³⁵ᶠᶠ·, Luke 20⁴¹ᶠᶠ·). He spoke of the building of the temple (cf. Matt. 26⁶¹, Mark 14⁵⁸) in the same sense in which the Messiah is the builder of the temple according to Zech. 6¹². ¹³. He spoke of His "Kingdom," [1] and therefore also of His Messianic rank, for "Anointed" is, of course, only another name for the "King." He described Himself as Judge of the world (Matt. 25³¹⁻⁴⁶), whose mere word is decisive in regard to salvation and perdition, with reference primarily to the prophecy of the "Son of man," Dan. 7, but in accord also with Isa. 11¹⁻⁵ (cf. 2 Thess. 2⁸).

In connection with the Messianic confession of Peter, Matthew (16¹⁷ᶠ·) alone has added Jesus' commendation and promised recompense for Peter. But the injunction not to speak of the Messianic rank of Jesus can only signify, even in Mark and Luke, that, in view of His now impending suffering and death, a proclamation of this nature would have been out of place.

As for the acknowledgment made by Jesus before His judges, the Evangelist John (see 18²⁰ᶠ· ³⁴) appears to have had the impression from the evangelic tradition, that both before the high priest and before Pilate, Jesus had, in the first instance at least, avoided a direct answer to their question. Even Luke represents (22⁶⁷⁻⁷⁰) that at any rate before the Sanhedrin Jesus set aside as fruitless their question whether

[1] See above, p. 134 f.

He were the Messiah or not, and that only to a second question He gave the answer, ὑμεῖς λέγετε ὅτι ἐγώ εἰμι. According to the narrator, the judges assumed this to be an affirmative answer, as the condemnation is made to follow upon this admission; and it should not be said that, according to Luke, Jesus was unable to reply to the question whether He were ὁ Χριστός, with a direct affirmative.[1] For Luke by no means suggests any distinction between ὁ Χριστός and ὁ υἱὸς τοῦ θεοῦ, as if Jesus could more readily assent to the former than the latter. Moreover, the amplifying narrative of Luke cannot be reckoned as particularly faithful to the facts. He has omitted "blasphemy" as the ground of condemnation, and the situation is made more intelligible for his readers by tracing the condemnation of Jesus to His alleged assumption of the dignity of a Son of God. And the words of v.[67t.], which are peculiar to Luke, will also be an explanation due to the evangelist himself, the reason for their insertion being that he postponed the claim to divine Sonship to the end as being the decisive item in the trial, and was thus obliged to furnish a new introduction for the statement in regard to sitting at the right hand of God. Matthew, too, can only have meant the words used by him, σὺ εἶπας (26[64]), to be taken as a form of assent; since, according to his account (26[25]), Jesus gave the same answer to Judas when he asked if he were the betrayer. And again, πλὴν λέγω ὑμῖν, which serves in Matthew as a transition from σὺ εἶπας to the declaration about being seated at the right hand of God, imply no more, according to Matt. 11[22, 24], than that Jesus emphasises His first statement with a second of deeper significance. Since Mark (14[62]) has simply ἐγώ εἰμι for σὺ εἶπας, it is obvious that there existed a tradition to the effect that the answer of Jesus was understood to be a real affirmative.

---

[1] So *Meinhold*, Jesus und das Alte Testament, 98 f. ; *Grätz*, Geschichte der Juden, iii. 374 f. ; *Bischoff*, Ein jüdisch-deutsches Leben Jesu (1895), 38.

It must, however, be admitted that σὺ εἶπας was not in any case an ordinary form of assent, either in Old Testament Hebrew or in Greek.[1] But in the Jewish literature we are not altogether without corresponding examples. It is related, j. Kil. 32ᵇ, that the people of Zeppori had threatened death to him who should bring news of the decease of the patriarch Juda. Bar Kappara had consequently insinuated this occurrence in figurative language, whereupon they asked: דְּמַךְ רַבִּי, "Is the Rabbi fallen asleep?" and he replied אַתּוּן אֲמַרִיתּוּן, "ye say so." In similar circumstances, Koh. R. 7¹¹ 9¹⁰, with the Babylonian dialect it is added: אֲנָא לָא אֲמֵינָא, "I do not say so." These instances recall b. Pes. 3ᵇ, where Joshua bar Iddi announces with the same evasion the death of Kahana ; and when he is then asked, "Is his soul gone to rest?" he replies: אֲנָא לָא קָאמֵינָא, "I do not say so." He dislikes to be the bearer of so sad news. Still it is confessedly only the context that gives its peculiar meaning to "ye say so" in the case of Bar Kappara. The context for the utterance of Jesus is not of the same kind; no one will conclude from the evangelic narrative that Jesus meant to lay stress on the idea that it was merely a mode of speech on the part of the judge to call Him "Messiah," while He Himself would not have used the word. Hence Thayer[2] has rightly maintained that this instance is inapplicable as a parallel to the σὺ εἶπας of Jesus.

But another Jewish illustration of the idiom is to be found in Tosephta, Kelim, Bab. k. i. 6. The narrative there proceeds : "Simeon the modest declared before Rabbi Eliezer (c. 100 A.D.), 'I went forward into the temple to the part between the porch and the altar without (previously) washing

---

[1] *Guillemard*, Hebraisms in the Greek Testament, 56, conjectures a Græcism without being able to cite one instance in support.

[2] *H. Thayer*, σὺ εἶπας, σὺ λέγεις, in the Answers of Christ, Journ. Bibl. Bibl. Lit. xiii. (1894) 40–46. According to Thayer, σὺ εἶπας is equivalent to, "It is thy perverseness that is expressed in thy question, although I cannot resist it."

my hands and feet.' The other replied, 'Who is the more honourable, thou or the high priest' (who, in Eliezer's opinion, dared not have done so)? As he held his peace, Eliezer continued, 'Thou certainly doest well to be ashamed to say that even the high priest's dog is more honourable than thou?' Then Simeon spoke, saying, 'Rabbi, thou hast said it' (רַבִּי אָמַרְתָּ). Eliezer answered, '(I swear) by the temple service (הָעֲבוֹדָה), even a high priest (had he dared to do such a thing) would have had his head split with clubs; whatever did you do that the doorkeeper did not catch you?'" Here אָמַרְתָּ means exactly "you are right." The expression obviously is not, strictly speaking, a form of affirmation, but rather of concession.

"Thou art right" is also the meaning of σὺ εἶπας from the lips of Jesus. It was an assent, but in a form which showed that Jesus attached but little importance to this statement. He was, truly enough, the Messiah. But beyond that He signified that even then He was about to receive a position in which it would no longer be possible to oppose any doubt to His Messianic dignity, and in which even the divine power would be at His disposal for overcoming all His enemies. The idea last expressed in particular is not to be separated from σὺ εἶπας. It is a Jewish habit due to great familiarity with the Bible, to give sometimes only partial citations in the expectation that the reader or hearer will himself supply what remains, which may perhaps contain the most important point involved. In this case Jesus doubtless wished to suggest to His hearers the whole second half of Ps. 110[1], namely, "Sit thou at my right hand until I make thine enemies thy footstool." Thereby Jesus reminded His earthly judges of the heavenly tribunal whose authority should thenceforward maintain His cause against every opposition, and assuredly bring Him once more into the world to assume His Messianic throne.

The high priest's question can be represented in Aramaic

by : אֲמַר לָנָא ²אִן אַתְּ הוּא מְשִׁיחָא ¹, or simply אַתְּ מְשִׁיחָא ; and as no inter-
rogative particle is used, the utterance could the more directly
be assented to by the words of Jesus : אַתְּ אֲמַרְתְּ. πλήν in
Matthew and δέ in Luke imply no more than ו = " and " in the
mouth of Jesus, because in such cases Aramaic does not use
a special term for " but." And λέγω ὑμῖν, which appears in
Matthew only, may be omitted. Thus the other part of
Jesus' reply would be : ³וּמִכְּעַן ⁴תֶּחְזוֹן לְבַר⁵-אֱנָשָׁא יָתֵב מִן יַמִּינָא דִּגְבּוּרְתָא
⁶שְׁמַיָּא ⁶עַל עֲנָנֵי וְאָתֵי.

Again, it is merely a verbal change in this expression
that occurs in the vision of Stephen, Acts 7⁵⁶, who saw the
Son of man " standing " at the right hand of God. There is,
of course, no thought of a " rising up " after being seated. A
Jewish parallel, though less strongly marked, is afforded in
what is said of the seven classes of the pious in the future
world. At the close of the reading, as given by Buber, Midr.
Ps. 16¹¹, we find : " which (of the seven classes) is the highest
and most excellent ? It is that which stands at the right
hand of the Holy One, blessed be He (שֶׁל יְמִינוֹ עַל שֶׁעוֹמֶרֶת
הקב"ה), as it is written, Zech. 4³ ' one upon the right side of
the bowl,' and Ps. 16¹¹ ' at thy right hand pleasures for evermore.' " To this are then appended the sayings of two
Amoraim whose names are not given. The second of them
names as the highest class of the righteous in blessedness,
according to Midrash on the Psalms (ed. Constantinople,
1512), " the teachers of the Bible, and those who faithfully
instruct children, because they are destined to sit under the

---

¹ No decision need here be sought in regard to the form of adjuration used
by the judge to Jesus, which Matthew alone gives. It was not, at least, a case
in which the law of Moses and of the Rabbis would have empowered a court of
justice to put the defendant upon oath. The Abbés Lémann, who in " Valeur de
l'Assemblée qui prononça la peine de mort contre Jésus-Christ," ³1881, enumerate
the points in which the trial of Jesus was at variance with rabbinic law, have
overlooked this instance.

² Bibl. Aram. הֵן, Targ. אִם.   ³ Galil. גִּמָּן כַּדִּין.

⁴ Galil. תֶּחְמוֹן.   ⁵ Galil. לְבַר נָשָׁא.

⁶ In the Jerusalem Gospel, Matt. 26⁶⁴, is : את אמרת ברין די אמר דמן כדו לכון תחמון
לבדה דברנשא יתיב מן ימינא דחילא ואתי על עניהון דשומיא.

protection of the Holy One, blessed be He!" but according
to Vay. R. 30, "those teachers of the Bible and Mishna who
faithfully instruct children, because they are destined to stand
at the right hand of the Holy One, blessed be He!" (לַעֲמוֹד
בִּימִינוֹ שֶׁל הקב"ה).

To Pilate's question : σὺ εἶ ὁ βασιλεὺς τῶν Ἰουδαίων ; the
three Synoptists give as the reply of Jesus, σὺ λέγεις (Matt.
27¹¹, Mark 15², Luke 23³). According to Thayer (loc. cit.
43), these words were meant by Jesus as a question, implying
"sayest thou this, whose duty it is to do better than to make
thyself the mouthpiece of my enemies ?" or else "sayest thou
this of thyself?" as in John 18³⁴. But even in John the
answer of Jesus to Pilate's question : οὐκοῦν βασιλεὺς εἶ σύ ;
is σὺ λέγεις ὅτι βασιλεύς εἰμι. A Greek would at least have
put σὺ τοῦτο λέγεις ; for "sayest thou this ?" but not σὺ
λέγεις. But the real sense intended here also will rather
be that of an admission. To this extent Jesus meets the
question of His judge ; any further communication He refuses
by being silent. Clearly enough by His demeanour before
the judges, Jewish and heathen, Jesus wished to give no occasion for the opinion that in the last moments He had any
wavering thoughts in Himself, and therefore He did not deny
that He was the Messianic King of Israel. At the same
time, it had to be made known that He was not minded in
presence of such a tribunal to offer any sort of justification.
Consequently it was as the Messiah of Israel, though not in
the sense in which many Jews imagined him, that Jesus
went to death. By reason of the acknowledgment made by
Him, the Jews mocked Him as "Messiah" (Matt. 26⁶⁸, Mark
15³², Luke 23³⁵·³⁹), the heathen as "King of the Jews"
(Mark 15⁹·¹²·¹⁸, Matt. 27²⁹, Luke 23³⁷), although in the
Synoptists these appellations are not distributed on this
ground to the two classes. According to the superscription
on the Cross, He was put to death as "King of the Jews,"
i.e. in Aramaic, מַלְכָּא דִיהוּדָאֵי (Matt. 27³⁷, Mark 15²⁶, Luke

23³⁸), and certainly not because He had been falsely so considered.

There is, therefore, no doubt that Jesus solemnly acknowledged as His own that position which prophecy ascribes to the Messiah of Israel. He affirmed His Jewish kingship before Pilate, and thereby supplied the latter with the legal basis for His condemnation; and before the Sanhedrin He gave to His Messianic confession such a form as offered them a pretext for delivering Him up to death according to Jewish law. The assertion of a Messianic rank could not, indeed, in itself have straightway led to a death-sentence for Jesus. The procedure to be followed in such a case may be seen from a legend related in b. Sanh. 93ᵇ: "Bar Koziba held sway for two years and a half. When he said to the Rabbis 'I am Messiah,' they answered him, 'It is written of the Messiah that he discerns and judges,¹ let us see whether he can do so.' When they perceived that this was beyond his power, they then put him to death." A verdict such as we are dealing with would therefore not result from any stipulation of law, but from the duty of a law court to take precautions according to circumstances for the well-being of the people, even by inflicting an exceptional sentence of death. A mere claim to the Messianic title would never have been construed as "blasphemy." Holtzmann² would censure certain Protestant exegetes, naming Schanz on Matt. 26, according to whom this did take place in the trial of Jesus. But he thereby evinces merely his own ignorance of Jewish legal processes. By the heathen judge Jesus was condemned as a usurper of royalty; by the Jewish tribunal, because He claimed for Himself an exalted position such as had not been assigned even to the Messiah.³ His judges

¹ *l.c.* he can determine who is right or wrong without inquiry.
² Lehrb. d. neutest. Theol. i. 265 f.
³ The Similitudes of Enoch, which speak of the Son of man as Jesus does, although of Jewish origin, do not represent a view in any sense general. Moreover, it was one thing that any person should merely represent such a theory,

understood and were bound to understand His reference to the Son of man sitting at the right hand of God, which Jesus, according to Ps. 110[1], had applied to Himself, in the proper sense of the words, and not as a mere simile such as might have been used of every king of Israel, as in 1 Chron. 28[5] 29[23].[1] It was this that the high priest pronounced a case of blasphemy ; and he considered any further presentation of evidence as superfluous, because the capital offence had even then been perpetrated in presence of the whole court. There is thus no justification for Bleby's[2] complaint that Jesus was illegally condemned solely on His own admission without the hearing of witnesses. The proceedings were not in fact so informal. The judges considered themselves in this case to be sufficient witnesses of the criminal offence. But it is clear that their interpretation of the Mosaic law on blasphemy (Num. 15[30]) was less formally developed than the later rabbinic law (Sanh. vii. 5), which made a death-sentence for blasphemy almost impossible.[3]

It was not in consequence of a mere misunderstanding of an expression used by Him that Jesus was condemned to death. The thoughts He entertained of Ps. 110[1] are indicated by His question to the scribes, Matt. 22[45] (Mark 12[37], Luke 20[44]). He whom David called " Lord " was no mere man. The right to judge the world was assumed by Jesus

and another very different if there really was one who said that the theory was realised in himself. Cf. my treatise " Christianity and Judaism " (1901), 63.

[1] " And Solomon sat on the throne of the Lord as king instead of David his father."

[2] H. W. Bleby, The Trial of Jesus of Nazareth considered as a judicial act (1880), 31.

[3] On the Jewish conception of the Mosaic law on blasphemy, see "Der Gottesname Adonaj," 44–49. I am wrong in saying there, p. 46 f., that according to Siphre on Deut. 21[22] (ed. Friedm. 114[b]) every one is a "blasphemer" who puts forth his hand against a fundamental article of the law. What is stated is merely that the blasphemer belongs to the class of capital offenders. And in Siphre, ed. Friedm. 33[a], j. Sanh. 25[b], b. Kerit. 7[b], the verse Num. 15[3c] is explained as meaning that every wilful sin deprives God of something, and is therefore blasphemy. But all this does not prove that Jesus could *according to rabbinical law* have been condemned as a blasphemer. But cf. b. Sanh. 61[a].

when He forgave sins (Matt. 9^6, Mark 2^{10}, Luke 5^{24}), an act which was also regarded as blasphemous. He claimed to be a new lawgiver, Matt. 5^{21-48}, and that in a manner which Jewish feeling regarded as an invasion of the divine prerogative; for, unlike Moses, who spoke in the name of God, He announced in His own name what should henceforward be regarded as law. His miracles were done not through prayer, still less by muttering spells with the names of God, angels, and demons, but by bidding the lame to walk (Matt. 9^6, Mark 2^{10}, Luke 5^{24}), the deaf ear to hear (Mark 7^{34}), the leprous to be clean (Matt. 8^3, Mark 1^{41}, Luke 5^{13}), the dead to arise (Mark 5^{41}, Luke 8^{54}; Luke 7^{14}), the storm to be still (Matt. 8^{26}, Mark 4^{39}, Luke 8^{24}). To follow Him is of more consequence than even parental duties (Matt. 8^{22}, Luke $9^{60}_{f.}$; Matt. 10^{37}, Luke 14^{26}); on one's relation to Him depends eternal weal and woe (Matt. 10^{32}, Luke $12^{8f.}$; Matt. $16^{24ff.}$, Mark $8^{34ff.}$, Luke $9^{23ff.}$). He held Himself to be exempt from the payment of the temple tax because His was not a subject's position (Matt. 17^{26}); He entered into the temple as a Master (Matt. $21^{12f.}$, Mark $11^{15ff.}$, Luke $19^{45f.}$). Clothed in divine Majesty, He will in time return again (Matt. $24^{30f.}$, Mark $13^{26f.}$, Luke $21^{27f.}$). And in full agreement with this position comes the declaration of Jesus before the Sanhedrin. He was the Messiah and desired to be so, but in a sense which appeared blasphemous to the narrow horizon of contemporary Judaism.

It is a question of a more formal nature to what extent Jesus reckoned His earthly work, including His sufferings and death, as forming part of the Messianic vocation. That the time of His royal sovereignty was then anticipated by Him, implies also that the real Messianic status—which is but another name for kingship—belonged to the future. The Messianic confession of Peter will certainly be meant proleptically, as he certainly did not see the Messianic sovereignty of Jesus actually realised at the time; and even the question of the high priest really inquired whether Jesus believed Himself destined to become the Messiah. Despite the fact that the proper Messianic position of Jesus belonged to the future, it was not therefore disallowed to call Him " Messiah " in advance. Even the Rabbis of a later date have no hesitation in calling the Messiah by this name before His appearance as such. But a profound difference between the Jewish doctrine of the Messiah and the position of Jesus requires to be insisted on. Judaism is indifferent as to how the prior life of the Messiah may be passed, because his conduct, active and passive, during this time has nothing to do with the Messianic rôle. In the case of Jesus, the time before the entrance upon the sovereignty is organically bound up with the period of Kingship. The future ruler is at the same time He who, teaching, suffering, and dying, paved the way for the coming, not so much of His own sovereignty, as for that of God. Thus the picture of Israel's Messiah transforms itself into that of the Redeemer of mankind.

XII. THE SON OF DAVID.

1. THE JEWISH IDEA OF MESSIAH'S DAVIDIC ORIGIN.

Every Israelite held it for certain that the promise of an eternal sovereignty had been given to the house of David (see 2 Sam. 7^{16}). This promise forms the background of the Messianic prophecy of Isaiah, Micah, Jeremiah, Ezekiel, and Zechariah. Even on occasions when no necessity was felt to speak of a Messiah, the recollection of that promise was warmly cherished (see Sir. 47^{11}, 1 Macc. 2^{57}). It is true that it was found possible to apprehend it as in reality given to the people whose head was the Davidic king, and to apply it to the future of the people when it had pleased God to manifest that king, Isa. 55^3, Ps. 2. 89 ;[1] but this resulted

[1] See above, p. 268.

ultimately in supplying fresh sustenance to the Messianic hope, properly so called. In Ps. Sol. 17²³ we find for the first time υἱὸς Δαυΐδ as a title of the Messiah, where the designation is probably dependent upon such scriptural expressions as בֵּן, יֶלֶד, " son, child," Isa. 9⁵ ¹ (Targ. בַּר, רְבִי); יִשַׁי שֹׁרֶשׁ, " the root of Jesse," Isa. 11¹⁰ (Targ. בַּר בְּרֵיהּ דְּיִשַׁי, " son of the son of Jesse "); צֶמַח, " branch " (i.e. of David), Jer. 23⁵ 33¹⁵; cf. Zech. 3⁸ 6¹²; perhaps also זַרְעֶךָ, " thy seed (David's)," 2 Sam. 7¹² (Targ. בְּרָךְ, " thy son ").² Thereafter בֶּן דָּוִד is frequent in Jewish literature as a title of the Messiah, especially in the phrase " the son of David comes " (בֶּן דָּוִד בָּא). The first representatives of the expression are Gamaliel II. (c. 110 A.D.), b. Sanh. 97ª;³ Yose ben Kisma (c. 120), b. Sanh. 98ª;⁴ Yokhanan ben Torta (c. 130), j. Taan. 68ᵈ;⁵ Juda ben Ilai and Nechemya (c. 150), b. Sanh. 97ª;⁶ others of later date are named b. Sanh. 38ª, 98ª· ᵇ; b. Erub. 43ᵇ; b. Yoma 10ª; cf. j. Sukk. 55ᵇ. The " Branch of David " (צֶמַח דָּוִד) is spoken of in the Babylonian recension of the Eighteen Benedictions in the petition concerning the Messiah; but the Palestinian form of that prayer and the Blessing at meals⁷ do not go beyond mentioning the " sovereignty of the house of David " (מַלְכוּת בֵּית דָּוִד). The short form of the Eighteen Benedictions, beginning הֲבִינֵנוּ, also speaks only in general terms of the restoration of the Davidic royalty.⁸ The Targum to the prophets, which applies the prophecies of Isa. 9. 11, Mic. 5,

---

[1] The Messianic interpretation of Isa. 9⁵· ⁶, though represented by the Targum, does not seem to have been general. The Pseudepigrapha and the New Testament have no trace of it. Sometimes the passage was connected with Hezekiah, of whom Justin says the Jews understood the prophecy regarding Immanuel, Isa. 7¹⁴ and Ps. 110 ; see Dial. c. Trypho, 33, 43, 67, 68, 71, 77, 83.

[2] Messianic application of 2 Sam. 7¹² is attested for the contemporary Jews by Justin, Dial. c. Trypho, 68. That the builder of the temple alluded to in that verse might well be the Messiah, see Zech. 6¹²· ¹³, Targ. Isa. 53⁵.

[3] Cf. Bacher, Agada d. Tann. i. 97.
[4] Ibid. i. 402. [5] Ibid. ii. 557. [6] Ibid. 222, 236.
[7] See b. Ber. 48ᵇ, where Eliezer ben Hyrcanus (c. 120) already enjoins the mention of מַלְכוּת בֵּית דָּוִד in the Blessing at meals.
[8] This applies specially to the Babyl. recension ; cf. " Mess. Texte," 7ª· ᵇ.

Jer. 23. 33, to the Messiah, calls the Messiah in Hos. 3[5] by the name מְשִׁיחָא בַּר דָּוִד; while the Targum on Canticles and also the Jerusalem Targums have adopted the later distinction between a מְשִׁיחַ בַּר דָּוִד and a מְשִׁיחַ בַּר אֶפְרַיִם (see Targ. Cant. 4[5] 7[4], Targ. Jerus. I. Ex. 40[9-11], Targ. Jerus. on Zech. 12[10]).[1] In this duplicate form it is noteworthy that the more recent type of Messiah Ben Ephraim or Messiah Ben Joseph postulates the descent of the Messiah thus entitled from Ephraim or Joseph, and that the character in view is not merely a Messianic representative of the ten tribes.[2] Messianic hopes were associated also with the person of David himself, as shown above, p. 301. On the whole, it must be considered the general conviction, that the Messiah had to be a descendant of David, just as even the author of the Philosophoumena, ix. 30, represents to have been the Jewish expectation.

Though such was the case, it does not follow that, in speaking of the Messiah, his derivation from David should have been expressly mentioned or insisted upon. The prophet Zechariah already quotes the words of Jer. 23[5] without including the Davidic descent. In the same way this element is omitted in Enoch 83–90, Bar. Apoc. 40[72f.], 2 [4] Esdr. 12[32ff.].[3] The omission is most conspicuous in the Similitudes of Enoch (chaps. 37–71) and in 2 [4] Esdr. 13, where the Messiah, represented as in God's keeping, can hardly be a son of David, although Isa. 11, Pss. 72. 89 are used in delineating the picture of the Messiah. The authors have therefore considered it possible that the prophecy in regard to the Branch of David should be fulfilled through a person who did not spring from the lineage of David. But for this, as for other reasons, their view cannot be regarded as one which was widely diffused among the Jewish people.

[1] See "Aramäische Dialektproben," 12.

[2] So still *W. Bousset*, Der Antichrist (1895), 65 ; see, however, "Der leid. u. der sterb. Messias, 6, 16, 20.

[3] Only the Syriac version, 2 Esdr. 2[12], mentions the Davidic descent.

2. THE DAVIDIC DESCENT OF JESUS.

By His question how the Lord of David can also be his son, Matt. 22[45] (Mark 12[37], Luke 20[44]), Jesus showed that a Davidic descent, according to the flesh, was not an essential attribute of the Messiah. It follows, consequently, that it was in no sense the question of derivation from David that caused Him to turn to the subject of the Messiah. Apart from this, it is in full accord with His whole conception of Messiah's position [1] that God alone could call any one to that dignity. For Him there was no question of vindicating a claim to the kingly heritage. For all this it need not be inferred that Jesus was not a descendant of David.

The Gospels relate that Jesus was sometimes greeted with the cry υἱὲ Δαυείδ, Matt. 9[27] 15[22] 20[30f.] (Mark 10[47f.], Luke 18[38f.]). According to Matt. 12[23], the people expressed the conjecture that He might be ὁ υἱὸς Δαυείδ, and Matt. 21[9. 15] (cf. Mark 11[10]) they even rendered homage to Him under this name. The last instance has been reckoned unhistorical, as is shown on p. 222. With respect to the other passages, it has to be noted that, in calling Jesus υἱὸς Δαυείδ, they virtually appealed to Him as " Messiah." Now it is certain that this Messianic title would not have been ascribed to Him had it been believed that He did not satisfy the genealogical conditions implied by the name. Positive testimonies to the Davidic descent of Jesus are offered in the genealogies, Matt. 1[1-17]; cf. v.[20], Luke 3[23-38]; cf. in the narrative, Luke 1[27. 32. 69] 2[4], Acts 13[23], besides the statements of Paul, Rom. 1[3], 2 Tim. 2[8], and the Apocalypse, 5[5] 22[16]. The descent from David is attested by the evangelists with regard to Joseph only, and not Mary, in accordance with the view that descent on the mother's side does not carry with it any right of succession, and that her husband's recognition of Mary's supernatural child conferred upon it the legal rights

[1] See above, p. 266.

of his son. Lichtenstein [1] recalls the fact in this connection that all property acquired by a spouse becomes uniformly the possession of the husband according to Keth. vi. 1, and that in the case of any question as to one's origin, common opinion was, in point of law, the decisive consideration, b. Kidd. 80ᵃ. Nevertheless, neither of these points touches the right of succession. The criterion for this, according to Bab. bathr. viii. 6, is whether the father is willing to recognise any one as his son. A case such as that of Jesus was, of course, not anticipated by the law; but if no other human fatherhood was alleged, then the child must have been regarded as bestowed by God upon the house of Joseph, for a betrothed woman, according to Israelitish law, already occupied the same status as a wife. The divine will, in the case of this birth, conferred upon the child its own right of succession, which, once Joseph recognised it, would not have been disputed even by a Jewish judge.

The fact that the genealogies given by Matthew and Luke for Joseph are discordant, shows, indeed, that not all the names contained in them are reliable, but proves nothing against the genuine Davidic descent of Joseph. A family might, of course, be recognised as Davidic, and be really descended from David, even although it did not possess satisfactory genealogies to prove this. The most convincing evidence that the Holy Family was really possessed of Davidic descent is that of Paul. As the scribes held to the opinion that the Messiah must be a descendant of David, it is certain that the opponents of Jesus would make the most of any knowledge they could procure, showing that Jesus certainly or probably did not fulfil this condition. And there can be no doubt that Paul, as a persecutor of the Christians, would be well instructed in regard to this point. As he, after mingling freely with members of the Holy Family in Jerusalem, shows that he entertained no sort of doubt on this point, it must be

[1] Hebrew commentary on Mark and Luke (1896), 13ᵃ f.

assumed that no objection to it was known to him. Nowhere in the New Testament do we find a single trace of conscious refutation of Jewish attacks, based on the idea that the derivation of Jesus from David was defective. The proper conclusion, therefore, is to maintain, with Paul, the Davidic descent of Jesus, although the continuity of the divine revelation in the Old and New Testaments does not depend upon it.

There is, moreover, nothing very improbable in the fact that families known to be Davidic should have existed in the time of Jesus. Little stress, of course, can be laid on the pretensions to Davidic descent advanced by the Jewish families of Abarbanel and Yakhya in Spain.[1] Nor can we trust much to the pedigrees which trace the family of the princes of the captivity in Babylon back to David. Five discordant genealogies of this sort are known,[2] the most ancient among them being given in Seder Olam Zota,[3] which dates perhaps from the ninth century. But despite the worthlessness of these data, it may be concluded that at least Huna (*c.* 200 A.D.), the chief of the exiles, was really reckoned to be a descendant of David. This, indeed, is not proved by the Baraitha,[4] known even to Origen,[5] which found a fulfilment of Gen. 49[10] in the fact that the chief of the exiles in Babylon had a recognised legal authority, and that the patriarchs of Palestine possessed a faculty of teaching approved by the State. From this at most could be inferred

---

[1] See *I. da Costa*, Israel en de Volken [2] (1873), 510.

[2] These genealogies are reviewed by *F. Lazarus*, Die Häupter der Vertriebenen. Beiträge zu einer Geschichte der Exilsfürsten in Babylonien (1890), 171.

[3] For this, see *Zunz*, Gottesdienstl. Vorträge,[2] 142–147 ; editions of the text in *F. Lazarus*, op. cit. 158–170 ; *A. Neubauer*, Mediæval Jewish Chronicles, ii. 68–88 ; *Schechter* in Jüd. Monatsschr. xxxix. (1894) 23 ff.

[4] b. Hor. 11[b] ; b. Sanh. 5[a]. The same view of Gen. 49[10] forms the foundation of the statement of the sons of Khiyya, who roused the wrath of Juda I. by declaring to him in their intoxication that the chieftainship of the exile in Babylon and of the patriarchate in Palestine would have to cease before the son of David could come ; see b. Sanh. 38[a].

[5] See *Origenes*, De princip. iv. 3, where he gives as the Jewish belief: τὸν ἐθνάρχην ἀπὸ τοῦ Ἰούδα γένους τυγχάνοντα ἄρχειν τοῦ λαοῦ, οὐκ ἐκλειφόντων τῶν ἀπὸ τοῦ σπέρματος αὐτοῦ, ἕως ἧς φαντάζονται Χριστοῦ ἐπιδημίας.

merely the belief in a descent from the tribe of Judah. And Juda ı. says of his contemporary Huna, merely that on the father's side he was descended from Judah.[1] But if Juda ı. was reckoned a son of David in the judgment of Rab of Babylon (c. 220),[2] while Juda himself, on a previous occasion, called himself only a descendant on his mother's side of Judah, one might suppose that he really thought of Davidic descent in his own case, as in that of Huna. The same inference is supported by the fact that Huna was a kinsman of Khiyya, j. Kil. 32[b], who was likewise considered to be a descendant of David.

In regard to the paternal descent of Juda ı., he declared himself to be of the tribe of Benjamin; and thus, therefore, Paul,[3] being also from the tribe of Benjamin, was of kindred descent with his teacher Gamaliel, the ancestor of Juda. A family register[4] found in Jerusalem derived Hillel, a progenitor of Juda,[5] from David, and Khiyya from Shephatiah, son of David and Abital; whereas, according to b. Keth. 62[b], Juda springs directly from this son of David, while Khiyya is traced to Shimei, a brother of David (2 Sam. 21[21]). This representation admits of being reconciled with the statement of Juda himself in this fashion, that either Hillel himself was descended from David on the mother's side, or else that the patriarchs were only maternal descendants from Hillel; the latter being quite possible, because the connection between Hillel and Gamaliel ı. cannot be definitely exhibited.[6] Further, Hillel and Khiyya belonged by birth to Babylon, so that all these traditions of Davidic origin point to a region where particular certainty was attributed to family traditions.

---

[1] j. Kil. 32[b]; j. Keth. 35[a]; Ber. R. 33.   [2] b. Sabb. 56[a].
[3] Rom. 11[1].   [4] See above, p. 5.   [5] See b. Hor. 11[b].
[6] The view of Theodoret is exceptional, Dial. adv. Eutychianum, i., Orthod. : Universum Davidis genus extinctum est. Quis enim novit hodie aliquem qui de Davidica radice descenderit?—Eran. : Qui ergo dicuntur Judæorum patriarchæ non sunt ex cognatione Davidica?—Orthod. : Minime.—Eran. : Sed undenam derivantur?—Orthod. : Ex Herode alienigena qui ex patre quidem erat Ascalonites, ex matre autem Idumæus. This has rightly been pronounced incredible by *J. Morinus*, Exercit. Eccles. et Bibl. ii. 259.

From all this it need not, of course, be concluded that Khiyya, Juda I., and Huna were certainly descendants of David; but it is obvious that about 200 A.D. there were several families to which the tradition of Davidic descent still clung.[1]

The last sure notice of the descendants of David is seen in 1 Chron. 3 (c. 300 B.C.), which traces the descent down to seven generations after the Exile, thus proving the existence of sons of David for the period about 300 B.C. From a still later period may possibly arise the mention of the Davidic house in Zech. 12[7. 8. 10. 12. 13]. It is worthy of note that Luke traces the descent of Joseph from Nathan the son of David, while Zech. 12[10] mentions a house of Nathan alongside of the house of David; whence it has been conjectured that the former is meant to be regarded as a branch of the family of David. And hence also the Pseudo-philonic Breviarium Temporum [2] will not have been altogether without some historical basis in giving a line of Davidic princes (duces) reaching to the Hasmonæans. There seems, in fact, to have once been a Davidic family at the head of post-exilic Israel, although we have no precise information about it.

At all events the Book of Chronicles, which gives (1 Chron. 17) the promise of 2 Sam. 7, revived afresh the idea of the royal destiny of the family of David, and thereby contributed to the preservation of the household traditions of descendants of David. Where, in addition to proud recollections, national hopes of the greatest moment were bound up with a particular lineage, those belonging to it would be as unlikely to forget their origin as in our own days, for instance, the numerous descendants of Muhammed,

---

[1] It is, however, too much to say that "princely descent was attributed to every school president," as stated after Weber by *Holtzmann*, Lehrb. d. neutest. Theol. i. 245.

[2] Too much importance is ascribed to this document by *L. Herzfeld*, Gesch. des Volkes Jisrael (1847), 378–387 ; *F. Lazarus*, Die Häupter der Vertriebenen, 56 f. ; *J. Lichtenstein* on Luke 3[23].

or the peasant families of Norway who are descended from
ancient kings. Hence it results that no serious doubts need
be opposed to the idea of a trustworthy tradition of Davidic
descent in the family of Joseph.

XIII. "THE LORD" AS A DESIGNATION OF JESUS.

1. THE JEWISH USE OF THE TERM.

The application of אָדוֹן and אֲדֹנִי in the Hebrew of the
Old Testament is discussed in my treatise " Der Gottesname
Adonaj," 16 ff., 21 f. The biblical Aramaic uses only מָרֵא
for " lord." In Dan. 4¹⁶ the king is addressed as מָרִאי (kerē
מָרִי). The Targum of Onkelos is also acquainted with this
term, but makes use of it only to replace בַּעַל or אִישׁ, signifying the owner or possessor of anything; cf. e.g. Gen. 37¹⁹,
Ex. 21²⁹; אָדוֹן, on the other hand, always appears in
Onkelos as רִבּוֹן. The feminine form רִבּוֹנָה[1] is also found; see
Gen. 16⁸ רִבּוֹנְתִי, " my mistress." Only in the designation of
God as אֲדֹנֵי הָאֲדֹנִים, Deut. 10¹⁷, do we find מָרֵי מַלְכִין as we
have it also in Dan. 2⁴⁷. The form of address, אֲדֹנִי, is
always רִבּוֹנִי when it refers to one person, e.g. Gen. 23¹¹;
and when it refers to several, רִבּוֹנַנָא, as Gen. 23⁶. For אֲדֹנִי
pointed so as to refer to God, we find only the usual abbreviation of the Tetragrammaton.[2] The Targumic mode of
using רִבּוֹן is recalled in Mark 10⁵¹, John 20¹⁶, by the term
addressed to Jesus, ῥαββουνεί[3] (another reading ῥαββουί,
D Mark ῥαββεί, John ῥαββωνεί), and also by the strange

---

[1] For "mistress" the Targum to the Prophets puts מָרָה; see Isa. 24² קְרָתָה,
"her mistress."

[2] See "Der Gottesname Adonaj," 24.

[3] In the time of Jesus רִבּוֹן had not yet become רִבּוֹן. The interchange of u
and o in pronunciation can also be seen in other cases; see Gramm. des j.-pal.
Aram. 140 ; Cl. Könneke, Behandl. d. hebr. Namen in der Septuaginta (Star-
garder Programm), 23 ; Σουσάννα, Luke 8³, for שׁוֹשַׁנָּה, and the Palmyrenian
Ἰακούβος for the name יַעֲקֹב.

reading, רבונכן for רבכן, "your teacher," in the fragments of
the Tractate Keritot (better Kārētōt) of the Babylonian
Talmud,[1] which have recently been published by S. Schechter
and S. Singer. Otherwise it is a remarkable fact that in
the early Jewish literature, apart from the Targums, רִבּוֹן is
scarcely ever used except as referring to God, often especially
in the title רִבּוֹנֵיהּ דְּעָלְמָא; see, e.g., j. Taan. 68ᵈ, Hebr. רִבּוֹנוֹ
שֶׁלָּעוֹלָם; see, e.g., Taan. iii. 8 ; Mechilt. 56ᵃ.[2] The biblical אָדוֹן,
referring to a man, is once rendered by רִבּוֹן, Ber. R. 93 ; but
this is due to the influence of the Targum. In j. Meg. 75ᶜ,
רִבּוֹנֵיהֶם are the "masters" of slaves. With these exceptions,
the usual name for a human master, conjointly with רַב or
רַבָּן, to be discussed under No. XIV., is only מָרֵא, מָר. The
"lord" of a slave is called מָרֵיהּ, j. Gitt. 46ᵃ. For the
phrases, "if thou art lord of thy soul (passion)," "if thy
soul is thy mistress," we find in j. Ab. z. 44ᵈ, אִין אַתְּ מָרֵיהּ דְּנַפְשָׁךְ
and אִין נַפְשָׁךְ מָרָתָךְ. But even the owner of a pearl is called
מָרֵהּ, "its lord," j. Bab. m. 8ᶜ ; and the creditor is said to be
מָרֵי חוֹבָא, "lord of debt," j. Taan. 66ᶜ. The layman addresses
the learned man as מָרִי, "my lord," j. Keth. 28ᵈ ; but the
learned man also says מָרִי as a form of courtesy to the pro-
fessional man, j. Kil. 32ᵃ ; Ab. d. R. Nathan, 25 ; and a maid-
servant uses the same term of her master, Vay. R. 24.
David is called מָרִי by Abigail, j. Sanh. 20ᵇ ; King Yannai by
Simeon ben Shetach, j. Naz. 54ᵇ ; and the Roman emperor
gets the same name from Turnus Rufus, b. Sanh. 65ᵇ. The
proper style of address to the King of Israel, according to
Tos. Sanh. iv. 4, was אֲדֹנֵינוּ וְרַבֵּינוּ. Moses is also addressed by
Joshua as "lord," Ass. Mos. 11⁴· ⁹· ¹⁹. The Targum, 2 Kings
5¹³, reproduces אָבִי of the text by מָרִי in the appeal to Naaman.
According to b. Makk. 24ᵃ, b. Keth. 103ᵇ, King Jehoshaphat
greeted every learned man with the words : רַבִּי רַבִּי מָרִי מָרִי.[3]
The title to be used in speaking to the Messiah, according to

[1] Talmudical Fragments in the Bodleian Library (Cambridge, 1896), 5, 29 f.
[2] See also above, p. 173 f.   [3] See Rabbinovicz on b. Makk. 24ᵃ.

b. Sanh. 98ᵃ (ed. Venice, 1520), is רִבִּי וּמוֹרִי, which should be read as רַבִּי וּמָרִי,[1] "my master and lord." "My lord high priest," מָרִי כָּהֲנָא רַבָּא, is the real form at the root of the peculiar address to the high priest : אִישִׁי כֹּהֵן גָּדוֹל, Yoma iv. 1, in which the intention probably was to avoid אֲדֹנִי ; cf. אֲדֹנִי הַכֹּהֵן, "my lord priest," Ber. R. 71. Considering also that מָרִי can likewise be used in speaking of and to God, as shown on p. 180 f., we conclude that this is a term of deferential homage, the scope of which can vary widely, according to the position of the person addressed.

When a person so esteemed is spoken *about*, the same form of language can be used. But, in that case, the pronominal suffix is as indispensable as in the case of אָדוֹן in the Old Testament.[2] To speak of "the Lord" with no suffix is contrary to Palestinian usage. If the speaker includes others along with himself, who owe a similar deference to the superior named, then the form to use is מָרַן, "our lord," as Abigail says when speaking of King Saul, j. Sanh. 20ᵇ. Again, in a narrative with a Palestinian colouring, b. Ab. z. 11ᵇ, Esau as the ancestor of Rome is called by the Roman herald מָרָנָא. Similarly we find in Aramaic inscriptions מראנא, "our lord," CIS, ii. 1. 201, 205 (Nabatæan); מרהון, "their lord," de Vogüé, 28 (Palmyr.), said of a king ; and מראי, "my lord," CIS, ii. 1. 144 (Egyptian). In Babylon only was it customary to use מָר without suffix, even without the definite ending, of an exalted person supposed to be well known. Even with regard to the Messiah this form has been used, b. Sanh. 98ᵃ.

It is improbable that the Greek κύριος had been adopted into the language of the people at an early period.[3] Only the most recent Targums have occasionally קיריס for "lord"; see Jerus. I. Num. 11²⁶; Targ. Ps. 53¹, Job 5². The other

---

[1] The Munich MS. has, however, only רַבִּי.

[2] "Der Gottesname Adonaj," 21 f.; Gramm. d. jüd.-pal. Aram. 78.

[3] Formerly I had considered an early date possible ; see "Der Gottesname Adonaj," 81, 84.

Targums all ignore it.   As part of Greek sentences, it occurs,
b. Ab. z. 11ᵇ and j. Shebu. 34ᵈ (j. Ned. 38ᵃ).   According to
Ber. R. 89, it was known that קִירִי (κύριε) meant "lord" (אָדוֹן),
whereas כִּירִי (χείριε) meant "slave" (עֶבֶד).   It was in Babylon
considered likely enough, according to b. Chull. 139ᵇ, that
certain Palestinian doves uttered the sound קִירִי קִירִי, κύριε
κύριε; and in b. Erub. 53ᵇ—if בירי be corrected into כירי—
we hear of a story told in Babylon about a Galilean woman
who contrived to address a heathen judge with the words
מָרִי כִּירִי, "my lord slave" (χείριε for κύριε).   But the Palestinian Talmud and Midrash give no sign of so intimate a
blending of the languages.   Among uneducated Jews living
in Greek surroundings such a thing might possibly occur.
But in the absence of proof such a condition must not be
relegated to the time of Jesus.

2. THE USAGE IN THE SYNOPTISTS.

In Matthew and Luke, Jesus is often addressed as κύριε,
not only by the disciples but also by others, especially such
as appealed for His help.   Mark has this form of address
only once (7²⁸); but in general this evangelist shows reticence
in recording such forms of address.   Speaking to the disciples,
Jesus refers to Himself as ὁ κύριος ὑμῶν, Matt. 24⁴².   It is
further to be noted that parallel passages sometimes have not
the same word as the title of address.   For κύριε, Matt. 8²⁵,
we find in Luke 8²⁴ ἐπιστάτα, and in Mark 4³⁸ διδάσκαλε.
The κύριε of Matt. 17⁴ is replaced in Luke 9³³ again by
ἐπιστάτα, and in Mark 9⁵ by ῥαββεί.   Mark 9¹⁷, Luke 9³⁸
have διδάσκαλε for κύριε in Matt. 17¹⁵.   ῥαββουνί occurs in
Mark 10⁵¹ for κύριε in Matt. 20³¹·³³ (Luke 18⁴¹).   And
while Jesus in giving instructions to His disciples about the
entry into Jerusalem, Matt. 21³ (Mark 11³, Luke 19³¹),
implies that they were in the habit of speaking about Him
as ὁ κύριος, He bids them, in the charge to make ready for

the Passover, refer to Himself as ὁ διδάσκαλος, Matt. 26¹⁸ (Mark 14¹⁴, Luke 22¹¹). But despite this uncertainty in the tradition, it is impossible, with Resch in his דִּבְרֵי יֵשׁוּעַ, to trace every instance of κύριε addressed to Jesus back to διδάσκαλε or ῥαββεί. The Palestinian Jewish literature also recognises the two styles of address, מָרִי and רַבִּי.[1] The most natural supposition, therefore, is that both should be found in the case of Jesus. The designation of Jesus as ὁ κύριος ἡμῶν, which was afterwards current in the Christian community, must, of course, be explained as a continuation of the language of the disciples. In Aramaic, according to 1 Cor. 16²², Teaching of the Twelve Apostles, 10, this title was μαρανα or μαραν, i.e. מָרַנָא or מָרַן.[2] The disciples must therefore have often addressed Jesus as מָרִי, and other contemporaries will have done the same. " Our Lord," מָרַנָא, is, however, to be assumed for κύριε, where several persons are represented as speaking in common, as, e.g., Matt. 8²⁵ 20³³. In these cases the Peshita, true to the instinct of the Syriac language, correctly writes מרן.

When the disciples spoke about Jesus, it cannot be supposed, despite the occurrence of the simple ὁ κύριος, Matt. 21³ (Mark 11³, Luke 19³¹· ³⁴), Luke 24³⁴, that they used מָרָא with no suffix. As in the Jewish usage, just exhibited, so also in this case we should expect only מָרְנָא or מָרַן. And thence it follows that Luke's frequent use of ὁ κύριος in his narrative when speaking about Jesus (7¹³ 10¹ 11³⁹ 12⁴² 13¹⁵ 17⁵· ⁶ 18⁶ 19⁸ 22³¹· ⁶¹), would have to be altered into the same form, in order to agree with Aramaic idiom. And the appellation ὁ κύριος Ἰησοῦς (Luke 24³) cannot be imagined other than מָרַנָא יֵשׁוּעַ in the mouth of a Palestinian Christian.

Special mention may be made of Matt. 22⁴⁵ (Mark 12³⁷,

---

[1] *A. Wünsche's* remark, Neue Beiträge z. Erläut. de Evangelien, 278, that in Palestine רב had the same meaning as קר in Babylon, is incorrect.

[2] See Gramm. d. jüd.-pal. Ar. 120, 162, 297. מָרְנָא is the older, fuller form.

Luke 20^{44}), ϵi $o \hat{v} v$ $\Delta a v \epsilon i \delta$ $\kappa a \lambda \epsilon \hat{i}$ $a \dot{v} \tau \grave{o} v$ $\kappa \acute{v} \rho \iota o v$, $\pi \hat{\omega} s$ $v \acute{\iota} o s$ $a \dot{v} \tau o \hat{v}$ $\dot{\epsilon} \sigma \tau \acute{\iota} v$; as any one might perhaps hold that in the question of Jesus the word $\kappa \acute{v} \rho \iota o s$ was meant as a predicate of Deity. The Peshita, indeed, appears to have really taken it in this sense, as it renders $\kappa \acute{v} \rho \iota o v$ by מריא; and in support of such interpretation it can be pointed out that for the time in question, the distinction between the sacred and the secular אדני, by pointing אֲדֹנָי for the former and אֲדֹנִי for the latter, was not yet completely established,[1] so that it was possible to apprehend the unpointed אדני in Ps. 110^1 as a divine epithet. But such an interpretation of Ps. 110^1 cannot be imputed to Jesus. And further, מָר without a suffix is inadmissible in the Aramaic original. Our Lord's words (as in Mark) will therefore have been : ² אֵיכְדֵין אָמְרִין סָפְרַיָּא דִּמְשִׁיחָא בְּרֵיהּ דְּדָוִד וְהָא אָמַר דָּוִד בְּרוּחָא דְקֻדְשָׁא נְאֻם יְהוָֹה לַאדֹנִי שֵׁב לִימִינִי עַד אָשִׁית אֹיְבֵיךְ הֲדֹם לְרַגְלֵיךְ ³ (אֲמַר יְיָ לְמָרִי תִּיב מִן יַמִּינִי עַד דַּאֲשַׁוֵּי בַּעֲלֵי דְבָבָךְ כְּבִשָׁא לְרַגְלָךְ) אִין דָּוִד קָרֵא לֵיהּ אֲדֹנִי (מָרִי) ² אֵיכְדֵין הוּא בְרֵהּ.

At first the title מָרִי, מָרְנָא, used in speaking to and of Jesus, was no more than the respectful designation of the Teacher on the part of the disciples. As soon as Jesus had entered into His state of kingly majesty, it became among His followers an acknowledgment of sovereignty ; and when they addressed Him as the Son of God, then "our Lord," as applied to Jesus, was not widely separated from the same designation for God. But it must here be remembered that the Aramaic-speaking Jews did not, save exceptionally, designate God as "Lord";[4] so that in the "Hebraist" section of the Jewish Christians the expression "our Lord" was used in reference to Jesus only, and would be quite free from ambiguity.

Among the Hellenists the case was different; for they had, and frequently used, the term $\kappa \acute{v} \rho \iota o s$ as a designation

---

[1] Cf. "Der Gottesname Adonaj," 16 ff.   ² Galilean הֵיךְ.

³ In Onkelos also נְאֻם is reproduced by אֲמַר, see Gen. 22^{16}; cf. also Targ. Ps. 110^1.

[4] See above, p. 179.

for God. The reason for always attaching a possessive pronoun to κύριος when applied to Jesus would to them be unapparent. So in this case also they said ὁ κύριος only ; and it might thus often be difficult to determine whether Jesus or God were meant.

With regard to the sense attached by the primitive Church to κύριος when applied to Jesus, an influence of some importance was doubtless exercised by the fact that ὁ κύριος, "dominus," was also the title of the Roman emperor. Augustus and Tiberius had declined to accept this title. But afterwards it became common enough, and was, moreover associated with the divine honours paid even to living emperors. The simple ὁ κύριος is applied to Trajan, Äg. Urk. d. Kgl. Mus. z. Berl. 115, 562; to Hadrian, ibid. 121, 420; to Antoninus Pius, 111, 472; to Agrippa I., Waddingt. 2211. The form ὁ κύριος ἡμῶν also appears afterwards; see Äg. Urk. 12 (Commodus), 266 (Severus), 618 (Marc. Aurel.), Waddingt. 2070e (?), 2114 (Severus). And still more recent is ὁ δεσπότης ἡμῶν, ibid. 1916 (Justinian), 2187 (Julian). Severus is styled "Dominus noster sanctissimus," Corp. Inscr. Lat. viii. 7062. Suetonius (Dom. 13)[1] says that Domitian ordered the procurators to use the written formula: "Dominus et Deus noster hoc fieri jubet." Aurelius Victor (De Cæsar. xxxix. 4) relates of Diocletian: "Se primus omnium, Caligulam post Domitianumque, Dominum palam dici passus et adorari se appellarique uti Deum." Even the formula: "edictum Domini Deique nostri," was possible; see Martial, v. 8. In general, however, it was merely κύριος or else θεός[2] that was prefixed to the name of the emperor. In the Acts (25²⁶), Festus speaks of Nero as ὁ κύριος. When the Christians called Jesus ὁ κύριος, they will have meant that He is the true "divine Lord," in opposition to the "God and Lord" on the imperial throne of Rome. Luke's frequent use of ὁ κύριος is certainly intended in this sense. The phrase

---

[1] Cf. Aurel. Victor, De Cæsar. xi. 2.   [2] See above, p. 273.

$X\rho\iota\sigma\tau\grave{o}\varsigma$ $\kappa\acute{v}\rho\iota\sigma\varsigma$ used in his Gospel, 2^{11} (cf. Acts 2^{36}), defines the term $X\rho\iota\sigma\tau\acute{o}\varsigma$ in this sense for the reader.

On the Jewish side there could not be an altogether similar development of language in regard to the Messiah, because they did not venture to ascribe to the Messiah a position alongside of God. But there was something akin in their emphatic affirmation that every Israelite has daily to take upon himself the "sovereignty of heaven," while he acknowledges the one God.[1] This formed a conscious protest, continually repeated, against the claims to divinity advanced by the "government," which the Jews readily identified with the "sovereignty of arrogance" (מַלְכוּת הַזָּדוֹן) or of "godlessness" (מ׳ הָרִשְׁעָה).

XIV. "MASTER" AS A DESIGNATION OF JESUS.

1. THE JEWISH USE OF THE TERM.

It is unnecessary to give proofs that רַבִּי was the usual form of address with which the learned were greeted. For the time of Jesus its use is expressly attested in Matt. 23^7.

The official deliverance of the Gaonim, Sherira and Hai (c. 1000 A.D.), concerning rabbinic titles has been the source of much confusion. According to Aruch, *sub verbo* אבײ, their verdict was as follows: "The earliest generations, who were very exalted, required no rabbinic title, neither רַבָּן nor רִבִּי nor רַב, and there was no difference in respect of this usage between Babylon and Palestine. For, take Hillel, who came from Babylon: no rabbinic title was coupled with his name. These were esteemed like the prophets, of whom it was said, 'as Haggai the prophet has said,' 'Ezra came not from Babylon'; in their case no rabbinic title is given when the name is mentioned. And, so far as we know, this custom of adding a title began with the 'princes' (the presidents of

---

[1] See above, p. 97.

the Sanhedrin) from the time of Rabban Gamliel the elder, and of Rabban Shimeon his son, who perished at the destruction of the second temple, and of Rabban Yokhanan ben Zakkai, who were all 'princes'; and in the same period the title 'Rabbi' began to be used among those who were duly ordained—Rabbi Zadok and Rabbi Eliezer ben Yakob, and the custom extended itself through the scholars of Rabban Yokhanan ben Zakkai. And by general consent 'Rabbi' is reckoned to be higher than 'Rab,' and 'Rabban' higher than 'Rabbi'; and still higher than 'Rabban' is the simple name; and we find none called 'Rabban' except in the number of the 'princes.' At the close of the Talmud tractate Eduyyoth, in a Tosephta there is given also the following explanation: 'He who has scholars and his scholars have likewise scholars, is called "Rabbi"; if his own scholars are forgotten, he is called "Rabban"; if both the first and the second generation of scholars are forgotten, he is called merely by his own name.' Nevertheless we find that the title רַבָּן is given only to 'princes,' Rabban Gamliel, Rabban Shimeon, Rabban Yokhanan ben Zakkai, Rabbenu ha-kadosh (Juda I.)." But this rabbinic attempt[1] to arrange the various titles in an order of merit is made to depend upon the estimate formed by successors of the personages who receive the titles, and is consequently of no historical value.

The actual condition of the rabbinical literature itself requires a different explanation. Since only Gamliel I., Shimeon ben Gamliel I., Yokhanan ben Zakkai, Gamliel II., Shimeon ben Gamliel II. are called רַבָּן, while after their time the title נָשִׂיא appears to take the place of the former designation, it may be concluded that רַבָּן was the earlier Jewish name for the head of the Jews recognised by the Roman government. In Latin his title was "patriarcha," in Greek ἐθνάρχης. In this theory the only strange circumstance is

---

[1] This representation is still followed by *C. Taylor*, Sayings of the Jewish Fathers[2] (1897), 27 ; *H. L. Strack*, Pirke Aboth,[2] 23.

that Gamliel I. and his son, who lived before the destruction
of Jerusalem, should also receive the title רַבָּן, while apart
from their case the magnates of that age not only do not
receive this title, but no corresponding epithet at all.   To
meet this, however, the conjecture is allowable that in the
case of Gamliel I., and of Shimeon ben Gamliel I., the title
was subsequently transferred to them from their successors
who did bear the name.   This explanation is the more
plausible because on other grounds it is impossible to be
always certain whether the first or the second of the couples
who bore the same name is really meant.

The fact that after the destruction of Jerusalem the
actual teachers of the law other than those specified always
receive the title רִבִּי, is to be explained from the custom of
referring to one's own teacher literally as such,[1] and from
the consideration that in the earliest collection of traditional
materials in the first half of the second century, those
authorities who had not still an uninterrupted succession of
disciples could not possibly be spoken of as רַבִּי.   In actual
fact, of course, men spoke of and to the learned, using the
form רַבִּי even before 70 A.D., as the Gospels themselves prove.
But at that time the suffix in the form רַבִּי had not yet
become so otiose as presumably it did in the third and fourth
centuries.   In that period it was possible even to say חַד רַבִּי,
" a certain Rabbi " ; see j. Sot. 24ᵇ.   Examples of רַבִּי addressed
to a teacher of the law are seen in R. h. S. ii. 9 ; j. Peah 21ᵇ ;
j. Keth. 35ᵃ ; b. Ber. 3ᵃ ; b. Taan. 20ᵇ ; b. Bab. m. 85ᵃ ; b. Sanh.
98ᵃ ; b. Makk. 24ᵃ ; see also Targ. 2 Kings 2¹² 5¹³ 6²¹ 13¹⁴
(for אָבִי).

From the fact that the Gospels so frequently employ
διδάσκαλε as a form of address, presupposing רַבִּי as the
original, it must be inferred that even then רַב was a current

---

[1] Yokhanan (c. 250), according to b. Sanh. 100ᵃ, said that Gehazi was punished because, in presence of the king (2 Kings 8ᵇ), he had spoken of his teacher
Elisha simply by name.

designation of a teacher. Examples to this effect are seen in
Ed. i. 3 ; Bab. m. ii. 11 ; Ab. i. 6, 16 ; Aram. j. Kil. 32^b (רִבָּךְ,
" thy teacher "); j. Bab. m. 8^d (רַבֵּיהּ, " his teacher "); j. Sanh.
25^d (רַבָּן, " our teacher," of Moses); j. Erub. 19^b (רִבְּכוֹן, " your
teacher ").

It must not, however, be forgotten that רַב was also
capable of other applications in accordance with its literal
meaning, " great." In Hebraising style רַב means the " master,"
as distinguished from the " slave " (עֶבֶד), Ab. i. 1 ; b. Taan.
25^b ; Shir. R. 1^1. Any Aramaic instance of the same sort is
not known to me. But in Onkelos we find רַב, plural רַבְרְבִין,
substituted for נָשִׂיא, " prince," singular Gen. 3^{24}, Num. 3^{24},
Ex. 22^{27} ; plural Ex. 16^{22}, Num. 7^2 ; and for בַּעַל, taken in
the same sense, Lev. 21^4 ; for אַלּוּף (plur.), Ex. 15^{15} ; for סָרִים,
Gen. 37^{36} 39^1 ; for שַׂר, sing. Gen. 39^{21} 40$^{2. 3}$, plur. Gen. 12^{15},
Num. 21^{19} 22^{14} ; for אָב, Gen. 4$^{20. 21}$. A " prince of demons "
is called רַבְּחוֹן דְּרוּחַיָא, j. Shek. 49^b ; a " brigand chief " is referred to as רַבִּי, b. Bab. mez. 84^a. In Palmyra the leader of
a caravan is called רב שירתא, de Vogüé, 7. The proper style
of the king of Israel is אֲדוֹנֵינוּ וְרַבֵּינוּ, Tosephta Sanh. iv. 4, and
in this title רַבֵּינוּ is considered the equivalent of the royal
title. The Samaritans addressed God Himself as רַבִּי.[1] Hence
רַבִּי is a deeply-deferential form of address, the full force of
which is nowise expressed by the Greek διδάσκαλε. " My
commander " would be no more than sufficient to render the
term. He who was addressed as רַבִּי is thereby acknowledged
to be the superior of the speaker. To some extent the Latin
" magister " corresponds, as it denotes superiors of various
kinds, among others the teacher especially.

The form רַבָּן[2] is a derivative from רַב, and not as A.
Geiger[3] has erroneously considered it, the plural suffix added

---

[1] See the rendering of אדני by רבי in the Samaritan Targ. to Genesis, and in
Marka, *Heidenheim*, Bibl. Sam. iii. 5^a.

[2] A kindred form is רִבְרְבָן put by Onkelos, Gen. 40^2, for סָרִים.

[3] *A. Geiger*, Lehr- und Lesebuch zur Sprache der Mischna (1845), ii. 129 ;
also Siddur Yemen, MS. Chamizer, i., has רִבּן throughout Ab. i.

to רַב ("our teacher"). In the Targum of Onkelos this word
is sometimes used for the Hebr. שַׂר, Gen. 37⁶, Ex. 18²¹·²⁵, Deut.
20⁹,[1] especially for military commander. In Ab. i. 10, רְבָנוּת
means "mastery," "lordship." As already observed, רַבָּן was
the title of the Palestinian patriarchs in the second century.
Later, however, רַבָּן became in Palestine a very common
designation of "a teacher" generally; see j. Ter. 46ᵃ; j. Bab.
m. 8ᵈ חַד רַבָּן, "a teacher (sage)." As the plural of רַב was
used exclusively for the adjective "great," there was no other
word available for the plural of "teacher" than רַבָּנִין; see j.
Sanh. 27ᵈ אִלֵּין רַבָּנִין, "those teachers" (sages); j. Ber. 10ᵃ רַבָּנִין
רַבְרְבַיָּא, "the great teachers"; Targ. Cant. 4⁹ רַבְּנֵי סַנְהֶדְרִין, "the
doctors of the Sanhedrin"; cf. רַבָּנַיָּה, ibid. 6⁵. Pronominal
suffixes are not attached to רַבָּן, except in the common form
רַבָּנַן, literally, "our teachers," contracted from רַבָּנָנָא, in which,
however, the suffix has lost its force; see, e.g., j. Taan. 69ᵇ,
רַבָּנַן דִּטִיבַרְיָא, "the teachers (sages) of Tiberias."

The Aramaic of Palestine prefers ōn to ān as a termina-
tion for nouns. This explains how it was that רִבּוֹן (which
afterwards became רִבּוֹ) should be in use as a collateral form
with רַבָּן. This form, which the Targums employ for "lord"
in all its meanings, was afterwards reserved by the Jews for
God alone; and hence hardly any trace[2] remains in the
Jewish literature to show its former application to the teacher.

As a designation for "teacher" which would correspond
to the Greek καθηγητής, Matt. 23¹⁰, Wünsche[3] proposes מוֹרִי
in the sense of "my teacher, my guide." But there is no
immediate connection between מוֹרֶה and "guide." In b. Keth.
79ᵃ מוֹרֶה הוֹרָאָה means one who is authorised to give legal
decisions; and in j. Sabb. 11ᵇ, j. Shek. 47ᶜ מוֹרְיָנָא is the
"teacher of the law," just as מַתְנְיָנָא is the "teacher of the
Mishna," j. Kidd. 66ᵉ. The form of address, מוֹרִי, which
appears frequently in the text of the Talmud as now extant,

---

[1] See also Targ. 2 Kings 8²¹, Eccl. 5⁷.   [2] See, however, above, p. 325.
[3] *Wünsche*, Neue Beiträge, 279.

cannot be regarded as original. In b. Ber. 3ᵃ the ed. Pesaro and ed. Venice i. have רבי ומרי, and not רבי ומורי. In b. Taan. 20ᵇ there is found, even in ed. Pesaro, a doubled רבי and מורי; but the Munich MS. has only רבי. Similarly, this latter MS. has in b. Sanh. 98ᵃ רבי for the formula רבי ומורי of ed. Venice i. In b. Makk. 24ᵃ, b. Keth. 103ᵇ, the true reading is רבי רבי מרי מרי. The Hebrew מוֹרֶה was in no sense a general name for teacher in that period, any more than מַלְּפָן, its Aramaic equivalent, according to Ber. R. 68, or than מַלֵּף,[1] which might be substituted for it, as in Targ. Isa. 43²⁷, Ezek. 3¹⁷.

2. THE SYNOPTIC USE OF THE TERM "MASTER."

The Aramaic רַבִּי, transliterated into Greek ῥαββεί, is explicitly recognised as the common form of address to Jesus, Matt. 26²⁵ (cf., however, v.²² κύριε), 26⁴⁹ (Mark 14⁴⁵), Mark 9⁵ (but Matt. 17⁴ κύριε; Luke 9³³ ἐπιστάτα). The Greek διδάσκαλε is attested with special frequency by Mark as an address to Jesus (4³⁸ 9¹⁷. ³⁸ 10¹⁷. ²⁰. ³⁵ 12¹⁴. ¹⁹), while in his Gospel κύριε is only once used (7²⁸), by the Syro-Phœnician woman.[2] The form ἐπιστάτα, occurring six times in Luke (5⁵ 8²⁴. ⁴⁵ 9³³. ⁴⁹ 17¹³) alongside of the commoner διδάσκαλε, is merely a Greek synonym for the latter, and both are to be traced back to the Aramaic רַבִּי.

Jesus forbade His disciples to allow themselves to be called ῥαββεί, on the ground that He alone was their "Master," Matt. 23⁸. In so doing He recognised that in reference to Himself the designation was expressive of the real relation between them. The form of address, διδάσκαλε ἀγαθέ, He, however, refused to allow (Mark 10¹⁷ᶠ·, Luke

---

[1] *Levy*, Neuhebr.-Chald. Wörterbuch, has a special entry under מַלְּפָא, מַלְּפָה, "teacher." But this form, intrinsically improbable as a noun, is an infinitive in the passages cited; and the whole entry should therefore be struck out. *Jastrow* in his Dictionary recognises the infinitive, but gives it the incorrect pointing, מְלַף.

[2] See, however, ὁ κύριος, Mark 11³.

18[18f.]).[1] This address was at variance with actual usage, and, moreover, in the mouth of the speaker it was mere insolent flattery. It is related, b. Taan. 24[b], how Eleazar of Hagronya (c. 340) dreamt that a voice called out to him: שְׁלָם טָב לְרַב טָב מֵרִבּוֹן טָב דְּמִטוּבֵיהּ מֵטִיב לְעַמֵּיהּ, "Good greeting to the good Rabbi from the good Lord, who in His goodness does good to His people." Here, of course, the epithet "good master" bestowed on Eleazar is reckoned a high distinction, especially as it attributes to him the same quality as to God. The like designation was declined by Jesus, because He was unwilling that any one should thoughtlessly deal with such an epithet; and here, as always, the honour due to the Father was the first consideration with Jesus. Further, the address רַבִּי טָבָא would not lead any one to think of moral goodness. The proper translation is "kind master." The rejection of the epithet, therefore, does not mean, as is generally supposed, that God alone is morally perfect, but that in Him alone is the quality of kindness personified. When it is maintained that God is טוֹב, Ps. 25[8] 34[9] 135[3], it is His benevolent character that is emphasised. In this sense also Jewish literature uses טוֹב of God. The thanksgiving prescribed for use on the receipt of good news, Ber. ix. 2, is: בָּרוּךְ הַטּוֹב וְהַמֵּטִיב, "Praised be He who is kind and sends kindness!" From Shimeon ben Chalaphta (c. 200 A.D.) we have the saying,[2] which recalls Luke 18[1-8], הַצִּיפָא נְצַח לְבִישָׁא וְכָל שֶׁכֵּן לְטוֹבוֹ שֶׁלָּעוֹלָם, "the importunate man prevails over the wicked, how much more over the All-merciful!" wherefore, it is argued, it must be considered certain that the people of Nineveh must have cried *mightily* for the mercy of God, as is said in Jonah 3[8]. According to Vay. R. 6, Bar Telamyon took an oath in the synagogue "by the compassionate Lord

---

[1] In Matt. 19[16ff.] we have no mere error in translation, but an alteration of the original text, due to doctrinal preconception.

[2] Pesikta 161[a], j. Taan. 65[b] (here less apt: הַצִּיפָא נְצַח לְכַשִׁירָא כָּל שֶׁכֵּן לְטוֹבָתוֹ שֶׁלָּעוֹלָם, "the importunate man overpowers the honest man, how much more the generosity that is in the world") ; cf. *Bacher*, Ag. d. Tann. ii. 535.

22

of this house" (בְּרֵיה דְּהָדֵין בֵּיתָא טָבָא). In Palmyra also טָבָא
וְרַחְמָנָא, "the kind and merciful," was commonly predicated
of God; see de Vogüé, 75, 77. If the word should be so
understood in the case of Jesus, then there is no need to
inquire in what sense Jesus disclaims sinlessness, or to
imagine such a connection between the address and the
expectation of the scribe, as would imply that he looked
for instruction regarding "goodness" from Him who was
"good." [1]

A number of persons address Jesus as διδάσκαλε, Mark
4³⁸ 9³⁸ 10³⁵ 12¹⁴ (Matt. 22¹⁶, Luke 20²¹) 12¹⁹ (Matt. 22²⁴,
Luke 20²⁸). This would imply the use of רַבָּא (רַבָּן), though
for such cases it may be called the general rule that an
Aramaic author would certainly *write* this form, while on
the actual occasion the speaker representing himself and
others might, of course, have used the form רִבִּי. The Peshita,
and in general the Jerusalem Gospel also, translates διδάσκαλε by מַלְפָנָא, but uses רב for διδάσκαλος only where pronominal suffixes had to be added; for ἐπιστάτα in Luke,
however, it always put רב with suffix, namely רבי, "my
master," Luke 5⁵ 9³³, and רבן, "our master," Luke 8²⁴· ⁴⁵ 9⁴⁹
17¹³. This form רַבָּן (רַבָּא) is also to be assumed for the
simple ὁ διδάσκαλος in discourse about Jesus, Mark 5³⁵
(Luke 8⁴⁹), 14¹⁴ (Matt. 26¹⁸, Luke 22¹¹). And the original
of ὁ διδάσκαλος ὑμῶν would be רַבְּכוֹן, Matt. 9¹¹ 17²⁴ 23⁸.[2]

In the sentence: οὐκ ἔστιν μαθητὴς ὑπὲρ τὸν διδάσκαλον,
Matt. 10²⁴ (Luke 6⁴⁰), the term τὸν διδάσκαλον is to be
referred to רַבֵּהּ, as in the Peshita.

Jesus forbids His disciples (Matt. 23⁸⁻¹⁰) to have themselves called ῥαββεί, πατήρ, or καθηγητής. The first and third
can refer only to Himself, "Father" only to God. It is implied
that πάτερ and καθηγητά were in use as forms of address.

---

[1] Thus *A. Seeberg*, "Abhandlungen Alex. v. Oettingen zum siebenzigsten
Geburtstag" (1898), 159.

[2] In this passage the Jerusalem Gospel has מלפיכון, the Peshita רבכון.

In regard to πάτερ, its equivalent אַבָּא in the Jewish
literature is principally known as an epithet of certain
persons in such a way that it appears as an element in their
name.[1]   Abba Chilkiyya (c. 50 A.D.), Abba Sha'ul, Abba Yose
ben Dosithai (c. 150), Abba Eleazar ben Gamla (c. 200),
Abba Mari (c. 320), were Palestinians with this style of
designation.   We never find אַבָּא as an address to a teacher.
The Targum to the prophets has even set aside the reverent
address אָבִי, 2 Kings 2¹² 5¹³ 6²¹ 13¹⁴, used in reference to
Elijah and Elisha, and inserted, where Israelites are speaking,
רַבִּי, and, when a heathen speaks, מָרִי (this in 2 Kings 5¹³).
This strange procedure may be due to the fact that the
Targumist had no knowledge of אַבָּא as a form of address.
Perhaps, however, the passage in b. Ber. 16ᵇ has some bearing on the case.   The prescription of a Baraitha is there
understood in accordance with the context to imply that in
naming only Abraham, Isaac, and Jacob "fathers" (אָבוֹת), it
is forbidden to call any one else by the name אַבָּא.   What
this Baraitha really implies is that these three alone should
bear the honorary title of Patriarchs of Israel; and another
Baraitha, recorded in the same passage (both found again
together in Semach i. 12, 13), prescribes that slaves only
should not receive the title אַבָּא, although this was the
practice in the household of Gamliel II.[2]   From the second
Baraitha, however, it is evident that among the free the
attribute אַבָּא was permissible.   It would therefore be common enough.   It may have been, however, that it was not
so much a form of address as an honourable appellation
added to the individual name.   In Onkelos the word אַבְרֵךְ,
which the people shouted before Joseph, Gen. 41⁴³, is rendered
אַבָּא לְמַלְכָּא, "father of the king."   The wise men of primeval

---

[1] It is not interchangeable with the proper name Abba, which will have
originated from Abiyya ; see Gramm. d. jüd.-pal. Aram. 142.

[2] j. Nidd. 49ᵇ also relates that in the household of Gamliel the slaves were
addressed as אַבָּא טְבִי, "father Tabi." and the female slaves as אִמָּא טְבִיתָא, "mother
Tabitha."

times are called אֲבוֹת הָעוֹלָם, "the fathers of the world," Eduy.
i. 4; j. Shek. 47ᵇ; see also Sirach 44¹ (Hebr.).

For καθηγητής, Matt. 23¹⁰, Delitzsch and Salkinson have
מוֹרֶה, which, however, is inadmissible, as already indicated.
Neither is the literal rendering by מדברנא of the Syriac
versions admissible. As καθηγητής occurs here in the sense
of "teacher," it is simply a Greek variation of διδάσκαλος.
And in that case v.¹⁰ is merely another recension of v.⁸, and
there is no occasion to look for an independent Aramaic term
for καθηγητής.

The form ῥαββουνί (see p. 324), used in Mark 10⁵¹, also
found in John 20¹⁶, cannot have been materially distinguished
from the form of address, רִבִּי, as indicated on p. 335; and
therefore John is right in interpreting it as διδάσκαλε. In
addition to this, the context in John implies that by using
this form of address, Mary desires to resume the old attitude
towards the "Master" which is not permitted by Jesus;
whereas the appeal of Thomas, מָרִי וֵאלָהִי ¹ (20²⁸), is accepted.

In this narrative of the Johannine Gospel there may be
seen intimations of the important fact that the primitive
community never ventured to call Jesus "our Teacher" after
He had been exalted to the throne of God. The title רִבִּי,
רַבָּנָא, expressing the relation of the disciple to the teacher,
vanished from use; and there remained only the designation
מָרָנָא, מָרִי, the servant's appropriate acknowledgment ² of his
Lord.

---

¹ So also Jerus. Gospel; cf. above, p. 180.
² See Matt. 10²⁴· ²⁵, where δοῦλος and κύριος, μαθητής and διδάσκαλος, appear
as correlatives.

INDEX FOR GREEK TERMS.

CITATIONS OF THE SYNOPTIC GOSPELS.

MATTHEW.		MATTHEW—*continued.*	
CHAP.	PAGES	CHAP.	PAGES
1 ^{1}	292, 303, 319	6 ^{24}	197
16	292, 303	26	190
18	292, 303	32	167, 190
20	183	33	95, 122
24	183	7 ^{1}	224
1 and 2	39	2	225
3 ^{16}	203	7f.	122 ff., 224
17	204, 276 ff., 288	8	125, 224
4 ^{1}	203	11	190
3	275	13	116 f., 161
6	275	14	156, 160 f.
8	166	21	116, 190
17	102, 106	22f.	260
18	303	8 ^{3}	315
23	95	11	110
5 ^{3}	127	12	95, 115, 121, 190
4	126	20	253, 261
5	224	22	105, 315
7	224	25	327 f.
9	199, 224	26	315
11	259, 261	29	199, 275, 304
12	206	9 ^{6}	213, 253, 259, 261, 315
14	166, 176	8	254, 262
16	190	11	338
18	5	15	116, 263
19	113	27	319
20	116	35	95
21ff.	315	10 ^{2}	303
30	156, 158	7	104, 106
34	206	10	46
37	228	20	192, 203
45	190, 199	22	155
48	66, 190	23	260 f.
6 ^{1}	190, 206	24	338
4	192	24f.	340
6	192	28	233
8	192	29	192
9	190	32	259, 315
10	107	32f.	190, 197, 210
12	281	37	315
14	190	41	306
18	192	11 ^{2}	303
20	206	5	102

Fuller expositions are given of the following :—